AMERICA'S SOUL IN THE BALANCE

AMERICA'S SOUL IN THE BALANCE

The Holocaust, FDR's State Department, and
the Moral Disgrace of an American Aristocracy

GREGORY J. WALLANCE

GREENLEAF
BOOK GROUP PRESS

Published by Greenleaf Book Group Press
Austin, Texas
www.gbgpress.com

Copyright ©2012 Gregory J. Wallance

All rights reserved.

No part of this book may be reproduced, stored in a retrieval system, or transmitted by any means, electronic, mechanical, photocopying, recording, or otherwise, without written permission from the copyright holder.

Distributed by Greenleaf Book Group LLC

For ordering information or special discounts for bulk purchases, please contact Greenleaf Book Group LLC at PO Box 91869, Austin, TX 78709, 512.891.6100.

Design and composition by Greenleaf Book Group LLC
Cover design by Greenleaf Book Group LLC
Cover photo courtesy Library of Congress, Prints & Photographs Division, photograph by Harris & Ewing, LC-DIG-hec-13333

Publisher's Cataloging-In-Publication Data
(Prepared by The Donohue Group, Inc.)
Wallance, Gregory.
  America's soul in the balance : the Holocaust, FDR's State Department, and the moral disgrace of an American aristocracy / Gregory J. Wallance. — 1st ed.
    p. ; cm.
  Includes bibliographical references.
  ISBN: 978-1-60832-293-0

  1. Holocaust, Jewish (1939-1945)—Romania. 2. Holocaust, Jewish (1939-1945)—Ukraine. 3. Conspiracies—United States. 4. United States. Dept. of State—History—1933-1945. 5. United States. Dept. of the Treasury—History—1933-1945. 6. United States—Foreign relations—1933-1945. I. Title.
D804.3 .W25 2012
940.5318   2011945097

Part of the Tree Neutral® program, which offsets the number of trees consumed in the production and printing of this book by taking proactive steps, such as planting trees in direct proportion to the number of trees used: www.treeneutral.com

Printed in the United States of America on acid-free paper

12 13 14 15 16   10 9 8 7 6 5 4 3 2 1

First Edition

PREVIOUS BOOKS BY GREGORY J. WALLANCE

Papa's Game

(Non-fiction)

Two Men Before The Storm

Arba Crane's Recollection of Dred Scott and the Supreme Court Case That Started the Civil War

(Historical Fiction)

To the Orphans of Transnistria

CONTENTS

AUTHOR'S NOTE ★ xi

INTRODUCTION ★ 1

EIGHTEEN MONTHS LATER ★ 9

I
THE GOOD GERMAN ★ 17

II
THE TRIBUTARIES OF THE DNIESTER ★ 34

III
THE RIEGNER TELEGRAM ★ 38

IV
THE ARISTOCRATIC ARCHIPELAGO ★ 48

V
THE MAGICAL VILLAGE OF MILIE ★ 69

VI
THE CROQUET PLAYER AND THE THIRD FLOOR ★ 72

VII
THE RABBI AND THE DIPLOMAT ★ 85

VIII
A REASON TO LIVE ★ 110

IX
THE CHIEF ★ 114

X
JEWS FOR SALE ★ 143

XI
FROM FOSTER PARENTS TO THE ORPHANAGE ★ 161

XII
BRECK AND ELEANOR ★ 165

XIII
THE FARMER ★ 192

XIV
THE ORPHANS OF TRANSNISTRIA ★ 219

XV
CABLE 354 ★ 222

XVI
"THIS MOVEMENT TO LET THE JEWS BE KILLED" ★ 226

XVII
THE CEMETERY OF BERSHAD ★ 237

XVIII
THE MARCH OF THE RABBIS ★ 240

XIX
THE ACQUIESCENCE OF THIS GOVERNMENT IN THE MURDER OF THE JEWS ★ 250

America's Soul In the Balance

XX
"WHY DIDN'T YOU COME SOONER?" ★ 265

AFTERWORD ★ 271

ACKNOWLEDGMENTS ★ 280

NOTES ★ 282

INDEX ★ 320

Author's Note

In a number of places, quotation marks are used to indicate the words spoken in conversations between various persons. The conversations either came from verbatim meeting transcripts, such as those maintained by the secretary of the treasury (part of what are known as the Morgenthau Diaries) or were based on the recollections of the participants as recorded in meeting memoranda, diaries, memoirs, or oral histories that provide quite detailed accounts of meetings and conversations, including descriptions of explicit statements or comments by the different participants.

At the time of the events recounted in this book, Romania was spelled "Rumania." To avoid confusion I have used the modern spelling, including in quotations from 1940s' documents or news articles. In a number of places I have used current spellings for official titles, for example, "undersecretary" instead of "under secretary." I have not included a bibliography because virtually all of the sources relied on are cited in endnotes.

INTRODUCTION

They were an underground "movement to let the Jews be killed." They were "vicious men" who may have been "accomplices of Hitler." They were "war criminals in every sense of the term."

These charges were made at the height of World War II. The men who made them were senior officials of the United States Department of the Treasury. But they were not speaking of French collaborationists or the satellite allies of Nazi Germany. They were referring to other *Americans*—indeed, Americans who happened to be highly placed officials in another governmental department.

This book is about the response of the United States Department of State to the systematic murder of six million Jews by Nazi Germany during World War II. Holocaust historians have handed up broad, sweeping indictments of American leaders and institutions for abandoning Jews in occupied Europe and the Soviet Union to the Nazi extermination machinery. The indictments cover a lengthy period, from the initial persecution of Jews by the Nazis in the 1930s—before Hitler apparently had even conceived of a "Final Solution" in the form it eventually took—to the end of the war. To be sure, Holocaust historians have described and criticized the State Department's conduct, but in the same breath, and often with the same vehemence, they have criticized all conceivable organizational and individual governmental and private actors, including President Franklin Delano Roosevelt and his aides, other government agencies, Congress, American newspapers and journalists, church groups, and even American Jewish leaders. Especially in recent years, as much time and effort have been devoted to books, articles, and even a play (*The Accomplices* by Bernard Weinraub) to the wartime infighting among American Jewish organizations over the rescue of European Jews as to the conduct of the State Department. One influential book about the American response to the Holocaust, David Wyman's *The Abandonment of the Jews*, contains a chapter titled "Responsibility" ("America's response to the Holocaust was the result of action and inaction on the part of many people."). Less than a page of the chapter's twenty-nine pages is devoted to the State Department's conduct, while three full pages are spent on the action and inaction of American Jewish groups.

The drawback to universal blame is the risk that the most culpable find refuge by simply being part of a guilty crowd. But when everyone is guilty, no one individual or group of individuals is especially guilty. The failure to rescue Jews becomes a matter of collective responsibility, not of individual misconduct. The premise of this book is that, while very few of these institutions and their leaders are free of responsibility for America's failure to do more to save Jewish lives, not all were equally guilty, and one particular group—officials in the wartime State Department—behaved in such a manner as to stand out from all others.

Authoritative eyewitnesses—young Christian lawyers in the wartime Treasury Department—concluded that State Department officials indeed were especially reprehensible. These idealistic but tough-minded lawyers, New Dealers from middle-class backgrounds, fought with the diplomats in the State Department to rescue dying Romanian Jews in a place called Transnistria (now a disputed land claimed by the Republic of Moldova). Many thousands who could have been saved perished while this bureaucratic battle played out. The Treasury Department lawyers not only believed that State Department officials were guilty of a failure to act but also became convinced they deliberately suppressed reports of the vast slaughter in occupied Europe and blocked efforts to rescue Jews in the few places where rescue was possible.

This is an extraordinary accusation; indeed, it is one of the most startling and provocative ever to be leveled against a discrete group of senior officials of the American government. Given the evidence supporting these claims, which the Treasury Department lawyers obtained by essentially stealing diplomatic cables from the State Department, the conduct of the State Department deserves a historical condemnation far greater than that leveled against other players in the drama of America's response to the human and moral cataclysm that became known as the Holocaust.

What possessed them to act in such a manner? As a start, anti-Semitism played a significant role in the State Department's response to the Holocaust. While this may be self-evident to many, some historians' judgments of collective American guilt have tended to minimize or entirely overlook the virulence of the anti-Semitism that pervaded the State Department bureaucracy like no other cabinet department in wartime Washington, D.C.

But it would be a mistake to explain the State Department's conduct simply on this basis, because other factors were at work. The State Department's most influential personnel—particularly in the Foreign Service—came largely from America's Christian aristocracy. In fact, they were Christian America's "best and brightest." They had followed a path far outside the experience or even awareness of most of their fellow Americans: from wealthy upbringings to exclusive boarding schools—especially one school, Groton, in Massachusetts—to Ivy League and other elite undergraduate educations, to diplomatic postings. Very few Jews, blacks, or women served in the wartime Foreign Service, and the few who did were largely relegated to backwater posts.

In some respects, therefore, this was the last group of people one would expect to behave so inhumanely. Many State Department officials had been given the best formal education that America had to offer, a strong grounding in religion (with its attendant emphasis on the eternal struggle between good and evil), exposure to different cultures, and knowledge of history, literature, languages, and science. But their education and maturation within an aristocratic cloister walled them off from the rest of America, especially from other ethnic and religious groups. This patrician upbringing, with its constant emphasis on Anglo-Saxon exceptionalism, also accounts for the callous response of State Department officials to the sufferings of human beings from different ancestries, religions, or economic backgrounds.

Another factor was that the State Department may have been the most dysfunctional wartime government agency in the nation's capital. At the highest level, Secretary of State Cordell Hull, a former Tennessee senator from a hardscrabble mountain upbringing, and his undersecretary, Sumner Welles, a Groton-Harvard graduate with an impeccable lineage, sumptuous homes, and a close friendship with First Lady Eleanor Roosevelt, loathed each other. The mutual enmity between these diametrically opposite personalities, which was no secret in official Washington, poisoned the State Department. Ultimately only one of these men would survive their bitter feud, but before their rivalry reached its denouement in the form of a sex scandal, no less—they contributed to a calamity that neither wanted.

Neither of them was either inhumane or anti-Semitic. Cordell Hull was married to a woman of Jewish descent, and Sumner Welles was the one high-ranking State Department official who appeared sympathetic to the plight of Jews in Europe; after the war, in fact, he became a committed Zionist. But their management styles and personal animosity allowed the unfeeling, anti-Semitic assistant secretaries and careerists in the State Department to step into, and ruthlessly exploit, a bureaucratic vacuum on refugee issues and thereby doom an unbearable number of Jews who could have been saved.

An important backdrop to the State Department's conduct was that, after the United States entered the war on December 7, 1941, a genuine opportunity arose to save Jewish lives: at least seventy thousand Romanian Jews who had been deported by their government, an ally of Hitler, to the killing fields of Transnistria. There, these Jews were left to perish from cold, disease, and starvation. In fact, one of the most distinct groups of Transnistrian Jews were the thousands of newly created orphans, including one, eleven-year-old Ruth Glasberg, whose valiant struggle to survive in Transnistria forms a part of this narrative. Short of defeating Nazi Germany, the United States and its allies had no realistic means to rescue most of the Jews who ultimately perished in concentration camps such as Auschwitz. But that was not true of the Transnistrian Jews and, as a result, their plight became a morally defining moment for the U.S. government, especially the State Department.

Finally, the specific personalities caught up in the State Department's response to the Holocaust account in no small part for the tragic course of events. The Holocaust illuminated the very worst and the very best in people. In their use of both state apparatus and industrial infrastructure to carry out a scheme to eradicate European Jewry, Hitler and his henchmen appeared more like a mutant species than human beings. But a prominent German industrialist courageously risked his life to get word to the United States and Britain of Hitler's "Final Solution," and a Catholic member of the Polish Underground also risked his life—and his sanity as well—by reporting on conditions in the extermination camps (which he infiltrated in the guise of a camp guard) and in the Warsaw ghetto. In the United States, which has never given rise to anything like the Nazis, the range of human response to the Holocaust was nonetheless remarkable. Indeed, it seems impossible that, given their opposite reactions to the plight of the European Jews, the uncaring Christian State Department officials and the idealistic Christian Treasury Department lawyers worked in the same government within just a few hundred yards of each other.

And then, of course, there was Franklin Delano Roosevelt, a towering figure in American history with a sunny but commanding personality and a spider-like mastery of his cabinet secretaries. Roosevelt's complex relationships with the State Department's Hull and Welles, on the one hand, and the Jewish Secretary of the Treasury Henry Morgenthau Jr., on the other, simultaneously enabled the State Department's opposition to rescue and the Treasury's campaign to save Jewish lives. But for once Roosevelt miscalculated, and the titanic interdepartmental battle turned into a race by the Treasury Department not just to save the lives of the Transnistrian Jews but also to salvage the historical reputation of the president himself.

According to the twelfth-century physician and scholar, Maimonides, "If one person is able to save another and does not save him, he transgresses the commandment '*neither shalt thou stand idly by the blood of thy neighbor*'" (Leviticus 19:16). In our time, as the wretched place-names have piled up—Cambodia, Kosovo, Rwanda, Darfur, to name just a few—we often debate the meaning of that decree: that is, what are the obligations of the United States to rescue victims of genocide? Typically, such debates end with retrospective regret at the failure either to intervene at all or to have intervened sooner. The precursor to those debates took place in 1943 between the State Department and the Treasury Department over the rescue of the Transnistrian Jews.

Parallels between the Holocaust and the more recent genocidal tragedies can be overstated. In its objective of biological extermination through modern industrial means, the genocide perpetrated by Nazi Germany stands qualitatively and quantitatively apart from the horrors of our own times. Moreover, during World War II, hundreds of thousands of American soldiers died in the cause of defeating Nazi Germany and its allies. While these soldiers fought in order to remove a mortal threat to the United States, the defeat of Germany also unquestionably saved the lives of the remaining two million Jews of Europe. The sacrifice of so many Americans must never be forgotten in any assessment of American responsibility as a whole. By comparison, relatively few American lives have been sacrificed to destroy or remove contemporary genocidal dictators.

But there is at least one similarity between what happened to the Transnistrian Jews and the fate of genocide victims since World War II. In all of these events, countless lives essentially hung on the outcome of a battle in the halls of government thousands of miles away in Washington. To be sure, the State Department's obstruction of efforts to rescue the Transnistrian Jews, as witnessed by the Treasury Department lawyers, was far more inhuman than anything done by American officials in connection with the more recent acts of genocide. Nor is it possible for any nation, not even one as powerful as the United States, to stop every instance of genocidal madness. But as we weigh the costs of intervention to stop genocide against the consequences of not acting, the story of the State Department in World War II is a cautionary tale that should always remind us that, in the words of the Talmud, "To save one life is as if you have saved the world."

The Treasury's responsibility . . . gave us a front-row view of those eighteen terrible months of inefficiency, buck passing, bureaucratic delay and sometimes what appeared to be calculated obstructionism—all devouring precious time while innocent people perished miserably in concentration camps and gas chambers.

Former Secretary of the Treasury Henry Morgenthau Jr.

Collier's, *November 1, 1947*

EIGHTEEN MONTHS LATER

The date was December 18, 1943, and the United States was approaching its third wartime Christmas. Americans fervently hoped that this was the last one, but there would be yet another to go. That day, two men met in an office in the State Department to review two State Department cables. They could not have felt much Christmas spirit because the reason for their meeting was a tragedy that should never have happened (the two men did not then appreciate that, in fact, it had begun nearly eighteen months earlier).

"It was made clear to me," said one, an official of the State Department, "that cable 354 is none of Treasury's business and that in no event should it be shown to Treasury." He added, "If it were known that I have shown you this cable, I might well lose my job. And I am confident that my telephone has been tapped and that my conversations with Treasury are being listened to."

With the swinging doors firmly closed, the State Department official handed two State Department cables to the young Treasury Department lawyer who had just entered his office (both men will be formally introduced to the reader later in this narrative). The two men had known each other for several years, ever since the economic warfare activities of their respective departments had brought them together. They had worked well together despite their different personalities: The Treasury lawyer was intense and combative by nature, while the State Department official was patrician and self-assured.

Their respective departments' sartorial styles could not have been more different as well, despite the general uniformity of government worker apparel in wartime Washington. Under War Production Board Regulation L-85, wool supplies for civilian use had been cut by more than a third, which ended the manufacture of men's suit vests, pocket flaps, and trousers with multiple pleats and cuffs.

Many Foreign Service officers and ranking State Department officials, wealthy by virtue of birth or marriage, had acquired ample wardrobes before the war, most typically English-tailored, with double-breasted, pin-striped suits, vests, and the inevitable white handkerchiefs neatly tucked into suit jacket pockets. Few lawyers in the wartime Treasury Department, however, possessed such wardrobes. Like many workers in the other government departments, they were from middle-class backgrounds and had been drawn by idealism to work in the New Deal.[1] As a result, suit styles defined wartime class distinctions between the State Department and other personnel in the burgeoning U.S. government.

Notwithstanding these class distinctions, on that day, the man from the double-breasted State Department had lost his customary self-assurance. The lawyer from the cuffless Treasury Department was in his office to look at diplomatic cables, which he had no business ever seeing. His own attempts to obtain the cables through normal State Department channels had been met with brusque replies: *Your request is denied; very few State Department officials have seen these; certainly, this is none of Treasury's business!* So the Treasury lawyer had gone to his friend and asked him to risk his career in the State Department to obtain the cables. His friend had reported considerable difficulty in obtaining the cables and the Treasury lawyer had all but given up hope of ever seeing them. But that morning, the State Department official left a message for the Treasury lawyer to be at his office at 2:30 PM.

★ ★ ★

It had been a short walk. The lawyer had only to leave the Treasury Department, walk past the White House, and enter the State Department. In that brief passage, however, he left the culture of an emerging twentieth-century nation at war—machine guns with antiaircraft capacities had been installed on the roofs of many government buildings, khaki-colored army jeeps drove here and there, and men and women in uniforms of varying hues (the army officers in their "pinks and greens," the WACs in olive drab wool jackets and skirts) were about—and crossed back into a Victorian age that had largely retreated to this final diplomatic redoubt.

Preoccupied with the reasons for his visit, which were essentially those of a spy making a rendezvous with an agent, the Treasury lawyer was hardly in the mood to reflect on the contrast between the State Department's opulent French Second Empire design and the straightforward classical architecture of the Treasury Department. Although both buildings had been constructed on the same basic plan, their appearances suggested that, in fact, they belonged to different eras.

The Treasury Department, designed in the Greek Revival tradition, was completed four years after the end of the Civil War and was then one of the largest office buildings in the world. Its notable but unadorned features included a colonnade on the building's east side of thirty stolid granite columns, each thirty-six feet tall and carved from a single, massive block. Consistent with the ongoing massive transformation of American power without the sacrifice of American democracy, the building projected earnest governmental strength in the heartland of a free republic.

The State Department (today known as the Eisenhower Executive Office Building), built decades later of gray granite, had mansard roofs topped by sculptural groups in segmental pediments, a touch added by an aristocratic Austrian architect on the construction payroll. The sculptural detail and dynamic motifs of the façades (the individual façade units "project and recede dramatically from the building line," in the words of a current government publication) left the impression of a Baroque palace in *Mitteleuropa*, lacking but a few accessories, such as inlaid coats of arms on the entrance portico, a glass-enclosed carriage drawn by high-spirited, red-plumed horses, and a haughty butler.[2]

The Treasury lawyer entered the State Department through a lavish portico. Until just a few years earlier, there had been no guards at the entrance to the State Department and only an aging doorman named Charlie, who moonlighted as a waiter in Washington's grander mansions. His evening job enabled Charlie to greet visitors to the State Department with a knowledgeable "That was a nice dinner last night at [Mrs. X's or Mrs. Y's]."[3]

Wartime exigency had replaced Charlie with the elaborate security checkpoints stationed at the entrances of sensitive government agencies. The Treasury lawyer displayed his government credentials and was cleared to go inside. Now he faced nearly two miles of corridors that ran through the building's fifteen acres, which contained 553 permanent offices. Wartime expansion had cut up much of the spacious interior into hundreds more offices. One assistant secretary of state tartly observed of the congested interior that "it was regarded as a horror."[4]

Visitors had their choice of elevators or wide spiral stairways with gray granite steps. On each floor, the long corridors running through this bureaucratic hive were twelve feet wide and paved with one-foot-square tiles of alternating black slate and white marble, like a high-priced chessboard. Strung along both sides of the corridors were offices with two-inch-thick wooden-latticed doors, which swung open much like the doors to a Western saloon. In a symbolic but wholly redundant touch of the nineteenth century, some of the offices even had spittoons.

The lawyer made his way to one of the hive's offices, knocked, and the swinging doors opened. He might have cautiously glanced up and down the corridor before entering the office even though it was a Saturday afternoon and relatively few people were in the building. His dominating emotion, however, may not have been trepidation but anger.

★ ★ ★

In truth, on December 18, 1943, it was not easy for many Americans to feel the Christmas spirit. "There is no peace upon the earth," a professor at Union Theological Seminary had written for the next day's *New York Times*, "and in many places good-will is eclipsed in bitterness and hate."[5]

Many tens of thousands of American soldiers had died—an already agonizing number—but most Americans had no idea just how terrible it would actually get or when it would be over, and no one could really be sure how it would end. That same weekend the American Fifth Army fought a fierce battle at San Pietro, the last great natural obstacle in the mountain pass on the historic route of armies on the march to Rome, which was separated from Berlin by more than seven hundred miles and impassable mountains. In the Pacific, as far as the United States Marines were concerned, predictions that the war would end in 1945 were wildly optimistic: Their rhyme was "The Golden Gate in '48." Two years earlier the Constitution and the Declaration of Independence had been packed in acid-free manila paper, placed in a specially designed, padlocked bronze container, removed from Washington under armed escort, and taken to Fort Knox in Kentucky for storage. No one thought it yet safe enough for America's founding scriptures to return to the nation's capital.[6]

On that mid-December day in 1943, an America transformed beyond recognition from just a few years earlier went about its bustling wartime business. The Commerce Department announced that corporate profits had set all-time records, and little wonder. Besides equipping the ever-expanding United States Army and Navy, as historian Doris Kearns Goodwin wrote, "American factories were supplying the Soviet Union with fully two-thirds of their motor vehicles and one-half of their planes . . . and supplying thirteen million Soviet soldiers with their winter boots, their uniforms and their blankets."

In addition to guns, government documents were also a wartime boom product. The war probably produced more government letters, memoranda, cables, and other documents than had existed previously in all of American history. And that Saturday afternoon, the Treasury Department lawyer had gone to the State Department to read two of those documents, which in their own way were as explosive as the tons of deadly munitions loaded daily onto United States Merchant Marine ships headed for the war fronts from both coasts.[7]

★ ★ ★

The Treasury lawyer closely studied the two cables. Since he could not take them back to his own office, he took notes. One was cable 482, dated and sent on January 21, 1943, by the American legation in Switzerland to the State Department. The other, cable 354, had been sent by the State Department to the same legation less than three weeks later, on February 10 (the cables were in different series).

The State Department official watched the lawyer take notes, knowing perfectly well that showing diplomatic cables to a Treasury Department official was an act of treason in the State Department. The power of the State Department bureaucracy came from control of the enormous cable traffic with dozens of embassies and legations and hundreds of consulates. The

Division of Communication and Records, which operated twenty-four hours a day, every day of the week, was by far the largest division within the department. In 1941, the division employed more than a hundred clerks in the telegraph section alone and had spent $500,000 just on telegraph messages. Even when cables were officially shared with other government agencies, the State Department provided only paraphrases of the text. On that day, however, the State Department official's conscience had prevailed over his agency's ironclad cable-handling procedures and his own career considerations.

Cable 482, sent to the State Department by the most senior American diplomat in Switzerland, the minister of the legation, relayed a report from the World Jewish Congress in Geneva.* The World Jewish Congress had requested that the minister urgently send its report to the State Department for transmission to Jewish leaders in the United States. The minister had done so, and on February 9, 1943, State Department officials reluctantly had disclosed the contents of cable 482 to a leading spokesman for American Jews. (The last time they had tried to keep American Jews from receiving information in such a cable *after* the cable reached the State Department, Jewish leaders had gotten the information anyway.) All the State Department officials could do was disclaim any knowledge of the truth of the facts described in cable 482, which could only have been obtained at considerable risk.

To describe the contents of cable 482 as a simple report, however, is a misnomer. It was more like an anguished scream from men driven nearly insane by human slaughter on an unimaginable scale.

```
6000 [Jews] are killed daily [at a single loca-
tion in Poland] . . . required, before execution,
to strip themselves of all their clothing, which
is then sent to Germany . . . about 2000 in hid-
ing [in Berlin] and there have been many cases
of suicide . . . it is reported from Prague and
Berlin that no Jews will be left in either city
by the end of March . . . 130,000 [Romanian] Jews
were deported to Transnistria . . . approximately
60,000 [had already died] . . . 70,000 are starv-
ing . . . living conditions indescribable.
```

---

* By that time, the distinction between higher-ranking embassies (and ambassadors) and lower-ranking legations (and ministers) had been all but abolished, but the nomenclature persisted—to everyone's confusion. One assistant secretary of state wrote in his diary after a diplomatic event, "Dined with Benes at Czech Legation (or Embassy, I forget which)."

Knowing from experience that the dissemination of such a report would cause American-Jewish organizations to bring pressure on the U.S. government to stop the massacres, State Department officials did not waste any time in taking countermeasures. The next day, February 10, they dispatched a cable—numbered 354—to the minister in Switzerland. Except for a cryptic four-word phrase, cable 354 made no reference to the bloody contents of cable 482. Cable 354 had been cleverly drafted.

As he read that four-word phrase in cable 354, the Treasury lawyer certainly experienced a detective's frisson of satisfaction. Now that he had both cables in his hands, he well understood why he had been stonewalled by the State Department—and why his friend had wanted him to see both. But, even taking into account what he already knew about the State Department and its behind-the-scenes response to the murderous insanity that had gripped Nazi-occupied Europe, the Treasury lawyer was more profoundly shocked than he had expected. Indeed, when he returned to his office that afternoon, he was still in a rage.

Cable 354 was what is known in a courtroom as a "smoking gun" piece of evidence, the kind that brings trials to an abrupt halt, sends people to prison, and ruins careers and reputations. Sometimes such evidence crushes doubt simply by its sheer depth and breadth, such as a recorded conversation where the participants talk with such candor that nothing is left to the imagination. But other times it's a buried phrase in a letter or a cryptic diary entry that, by itself, means nothing but can connect key events with such revelatory clarity that the observer's breath is suddenly taken away. Such was the character of the innocuous four-word phrase in cable 354 in the space reserved for referencing a related cable:

```
Your 482, January 21
```

Without those four words, cable 354 was indistinguishable in moral content from the thousands of cables and other correspondence sent back and forth daily between the State Department and its embassies, legations, and consulates. Without those four words, nothing connected cable 354 with the earlier cable 482, which reported on both a step-up in the implementation of the German government's plan to murder all Jewish men, women, and children on the European continent, using every twentieth-century industrial and scientific means at its disposal, and the plight of the dying Romanian Jews who had been deported to the nightmarish land of Transnistria in the Nazi-conquered Ukraine.

Cable 482 reported a horrific nightmare that was actually occurring, while cable 354 was the polar opposite—antiseptic, bland, and bureaucratic. But the four words made all the difference because they were a fingerprint on a murder weapon; instead of death by bullets, however, cable 354 was death by bureaucratic maneuver.

In part, cable 354, which politely rebuked the American minister for even having *sent* cable 482 to the State Department, read:

```
Your 482, January 21

In the future we would suggest that you do not
accept reports submitted to you to be transmitted
to private persons in the United States. . . .⁸
```

The blood from cable 482 splashed across the desks and onto the black-and-white-tiled corridors.

The State Department had tried to cover up the murder of millions of European Jews.

I

THE GOOD GERMAN

On August 1, 1942, a little less than eighteen months before the Treasury Department lawyer went to the State Department, two Jewish men entered the Hotel du Château in Lausanne, Switzerland, where a major chess tournament was under way. The two men went to the hotel's terrace, where they sat down at a table and began a conversation. To a passerby, they were two well-dressed European Jews—one, thirty, the other, early forties—enjoying each other's company on a summer Saturday in one of the rare spots in Europe where Jews could still do such things.

From the intensity of their talk, our imaginary passerby might have assumed they were discussing weighty wartime matters, but the conversation is too one-sided, he decides: see how the slightly built younger man with the premature widow's peak only listens as the older man speaks at length. No, concludes the observer, they are chess player and teacher, here for the great tournament, which would explain how the younger one listens without moving or even seeming to breathe, a look of such furrowed concentration on his brow that a bold chess move must be the topic.

The topic was not chess, however. The younger man was Gerhart Riegner, a lawyer and a representative of the World Jewish Congress in Geneva. The older man was Benjamin Sagalowitz, a freelance journalist, who had arranged the meeting to deliver a message. Riegner could not have been a better choice to receive that particular message, because by background and education he was a worthy representative of the Jews of Europe and, in light of the message's import, one of the last of his kind: the cultivated, intellectual, middle-class European Jew.

The Riegner family stretched back generations in Germany, solidly anchored in Jewish traditions and always conscious of the precarious position of Jews in Europe.

As a five-year-old schoolboy in Berlin, Gerhart Riegner had been taunted by another child, who called him a "dirty little Jew." The taunt, Riegner later wrote, was "completely unexpected, [and] shook me deeply. I felt that I had to react. I insulted him in turn, stupidly saying, 'Dirty little Christian.' This was really idiotic. But you have to understand that it was only an expression of my rejection of the insult." Such was the beginning of what Riegner called "my gradual discovery of anti-Semitism."[1]

After graduating from secondary school in 1929, Riegner migrated through several universities, as was then the style in Europe, ultimately choosing to study law. At the renowned university in Heidelberg, he reveled in a "sort of permanent intellectual force field" that now serves principally as a reminder that a great intelligentsia is no guarantee against national madness. At the University of Berlin, he and other Jewish students escaped a brutal beating by leaping from the windows of an auditorium when Nazi Brownshirt commandos stormed the building.

The ascent of Adolf Hitler in 1933 and the Nazi reign of terror against the Jews were the great divide in Riegner's life, beginning with the boycotts of Jewish businesses, the laws that all but banned Jewish social and commercial dealings with non-Jews, and the creation of the first concentration camps. Riegner was dismissed from his position as assistant to a Berlin judge, his father was disbarred, his older sister lost her job as a secondary school teacher in Frankfurt, and his younger sister was expelled from elementary school. One evening Brownshirts gathered outside the Riegner home chanting, "*Juden 'raus!*" (Jews out!)

Riegner decided to leave Germany for good. One of his former professors, a conservative, non-Jewish German nationalist, argued with him in vain that "the situation could not go on forever, that it was all just an episode and would soon be a thing of the past." After an emotional, argumentative farewell to his friends ("But don't you see that this is the end of German Jewry?"), Gerhart Riegner broke the ancestral ties to his native country. In the summer of 1936, he was recruited by the newly organized World Jewish Congress to staff an office in Geneva, which never consisted of more than Riegner, a secretary, a telephone, and a typewriter.[2]

In the spring of 1939, Riegner met with Dr. Walter Gerson, a leader of the Jews in the Free City of Danzig that abutted the Polish Corridor, a strip of German territory given to Poland after World War I to assure that country access to the Baltic Sea. Danzig's independent status had been guaranteed by the League of Nations. But Hitler, who for years had proclaimed to the world that he was responsible for German-speaking people wherever they lived, had already occupied Austria and the Sudetenland (and the rest of Czechoslovakia). Inevitably, Gerson and Riegner spoke of a coming war.

"Do you know what the war will mean for us?" Gerson asked Riegner. "It will be a catastrophe the likes of which we have never known. The Nazis are going to kill millions of Jews and we do not have the means to stop them, because of their brutality and their determination."

Gerson was among the first to die in the massacres of Jews that followed the German invasion of Poland on September 1, 1939. And now, almost three years later, on the first of August 1942, on the terrace of the Hotel du Château, the dead man's prophecy was coming true.

"One of my friends has been in touch with a prominent German industrialist," Sagalowitz told Riegner, "the head of a combine employing tens of thousands of workers and actively contributing to the German war effort. This function gave him access to the highest military circles. He has learned that at Hitler's headquarters the Nazis were discussing a plan. . . ."[3]

★ ★ ★

The conversation on the terrace of the Hotel du Château concerned a vital message that had been passed from hand to hand with remarkable speed and at great peril to those involved. The message had begun its journey just three days earlier, on July 29, 1942, with a train trip from the town of Breslau in eastern Germany, destination Zurich. The train chugged through the Oder Valley, then passed by German towns with names like Böblingen, Ehningen, and Herrenberg, racing through forests and traveling alongside the river

Neckar. The train flew past covered wooden bridges, churches with onion-shaped domes, and old castles. For a time, it paralleled a highway, still intact but with only a few cars.

No one could have known from the landscape that Germany was fighting a two-front world war and, according to its leader, on the verge of total victory. The pastoral countryside was untouched because the thousand-plane British bombing attacks at that time could not reach this far into Germany and, in any event, there were better industrial targets elsewhere.

At Singen, the passengers left the train for a border control inspection. They were led into the station building, where the border police inspected their passports. Among the passengers in the first-class compartment was a tall German industrialist who had often made the trip from Breslau to Zurich. His fellow passengers might have noticed his cold, commanding air and an obvious limp when he disembarked from the train, but no other remarkable qualities. He had every reason not to draw attention to himself and no doubt was well-practiced in the art of appearing to be—as much as possible for a man of his physical presence—just one of a crowd. Perhaps he occupied himself in the train station by continuing to read his newspapers, which that day reported on the fighting at El Alamein in North Africa and the retreat of Russian units from the river Don.

The passenger, Dr. Eduard Reinhold Karl Schulte, was the managing director of one of Germany's largest mining concerns, Georg von Giesche's Heirs, known as Giesche. And he was no ordinary businessman. He was a freelance spy against his own country, and this was not the first time he had traveled to Zurich to deliver vital intelligence to Germany's enemies.

Born in 1891 to an old Westphalian family, Schulte had grown up in a large home in Düsseldorf, catered to by servants and even a private gymnastic instructor. As did other aristocratic families, the Schultes had a passion for hunting and owned a hunting lodge that resembled a small castle. After completing his preuniversity schooling at age eighteen, Schulte worked as an apprentice in a company that specialized in geologic drilling. One day he looked out his office window and noticed workmen struggling to push a railway car onto a siding. He went to help, slipped, and the railway car crushed his left leg. It had to be amputated.

A cripple in a society that stigmatized cripples, Schulte stoically accepted his handicap, adapting to an artificial leg that took a long time to fit. He became a trainee in a leading German bank and then, at age twenty-one, earned a juris doctor degree. Thereafter, he was always "Herr Doktor." On a trip to London, at Kensington Gardens, he met a young strawberry blonde German woman, Clara Ebert, who was studying Charlotte Brontë at the University of London. Eight years later they married, but Schulte was not an easy husband, to say the least, and it was not a happy marriage, especially after Clara terminated her third, and last, pregnancy by abortion, to Schulte's extreme anger.[4]

During World War I, Schulte held a senior position in the office of supply in the Prussian War Ministry. When the war ended, he applied to Giesche for the position of general manager and, having made a favorable impression in the interviews, was hired even though he knew nothing about the production of nonferrous metals. After the war, Giesche had been split into two parts, one in Germany and the other in Poland. Schulte worked in Giesche's German head office, in Breslau. Borders changed after World War II, and today Breslau is part of Poland and named Wroclaw. In 1942, however, Breslau was on the German side of the border, several hours' drive from a backwater Polish town called Oświęcim. The town's German name was Auschwitz.[5]

Schulte had been contemptuous of the Nazis since 1933. That year, leading industrialists and businessmen had been invited to the Berlin residence of a top Nazi leader, Hermann Göring, where they had been promised an audience with the new chancellor, Adolf Hitler. It was a measure of Schulte's meteoric success that he was among the select group to be invited.

On February 20, more than twenty well-tailored, swaggering bankers and industrialists, including the heads of the Krupp steelworks and the chemical giant I.G. Farben, arrived at Göring's small palace–like residence in a fleet of sleek limousines. After the gathering had waited fifteen minutes, Hitler and Göring appeared. Hitler shook hands with each of the guests, seated himself at the head of the table, and launched into a speech. With his evident passion and sincerity, he apparently made a positive impression on all those present—save Schulte. Hitler had an unhealthy complexion, but his flashing blue eyes mesmerized the gathering.

Hitler spoke about how Bolshevism, Liberalism, and Social Democracy were unacceptable and Marxism had to be smashed. How he preferred a peaceful, stable transition to the new order but implied that an armed takeover would be inevitable if the Nazi Party and its allies did not achieve absolute power. How he would first lay his hands on "all the means of power" through the coming elections and then commence a "second action" against Communism. Tomorrow belonged to the Nazis, went the subtext of his message, and no mercy would be shown to anyone who tried to stand in the way.[6]

Hitler abruptly left and Göring took over. He told the gathering that, especially because the bankers and industrialists were not directly involved in political struggle, they should make substantial financial contributions to support Nazi candidates in the elections. On this cue, a leading banker, who would later become the economic minister under Hitler, turned to the others. *"Meine Herren, zur Kasse."* (Gentlemen, take out your checkbooks.) The bankers and industrialists, some of whom would be prosecuted many years—and tens of millions of dead—later as war criminals, were operating under the soon-to-be-dashed illusion that Hitler and Göring were their instruments, not vice versa. They pledged generously.

But Schulte thought Hitler's speech delusional and left the meeting convinced that the Nazis would unhesitatingly use violence to achieve their goals and, in the process, lead Germany into an abyss.[7] None of the other prominent guests apparently reached the same conclusion. Indeed, according to one historian of the Third Reich, the German business community, more than any other group, "assisted the Nazis most in seizing power . . . there can be no gain-saying industry's role as chief grave-digger of the Weimar Republic."[8]

Schulte's biographers, Walter Laqueur and Richard Breitman, suggest that he disliked the Nazis because "Nazism made him do things he loathed." One was to allow the indoctrination of his young sons with the "brown poison" of the Hitler Youth, in which membership was mandatory for all but Jews and the physically handicapped. Another was the necessity of enrolling in, among other National Socialist organizations or fronts, the German Hunters Union and the German Labor Front. Without these memberships he could not hunt on his own property or hold a high position at Giesche. Schulte, his biographers write, resented "being given commands by leaders who had no claim to respect."[9]

But a sane, intelligent, independent-minded man did not need a personal motive to reach the only possible conclusion about Hitler (especially after meeting him) and his Nazi Party, and to act on it. Even as early as 1933, Schulte had grasped the fact that had eluded virtually all of his countrymen: The Nazis were essentially a gang of criminal thugs led by a messianic orator psychopathically bent on murderous conquest and revenge.

In a country where newspapers were daily filled with fantastic lies; where the average citizen, in historian Richard Grunberger's phrase, lived "in a state of delusion tinged with delirium," especially as the war began turning against Germany; where women in childbirth pains were known to reflexively cry out their leader's name; and where some who harbored doubts avoided surgery for fear they would betray themselves under anesthesia, Eduard Schulte was a sane, intelligent man.[10]

That and his willingness to act on his convictions about the Nazis made Schulte almost a freak of nature in his own country. Combining personal courage with a dose of aristocratic vanity ("Proud, vain, and rich," in the words of one historian), a Germanic romantic streak, and ideal cover as a businessman who had to travel regularly to neutral Switzerland, where he had a large network of foreign contacts, Eduard Schulte was, in John le Carré's phrase, "a perfect spy."[11]

For a time after the meeting with Hitler, on social occasions Schulte expressed scorn for the Nazis, to the point that friends cautioned him to be more careful. His first opportunity to do more than show contempt came in August 1939, when Schulte learned of Hitler's plans to invade Poland. He promptly informed a Swiss banking contact that the invasion would take place on September 1. His report ultimately reached Paris and London. As Schulte had predicted, Germany invaded Poland on September 1 and World War II began.[12]

In the spring of 1941, from his perch at Giesche, "Schulte was easily able to pick up the signs of a vast mobilization." In April, Schulte took the train to Zurich, this time to warn a Polish contact that Germany shortly planned to attack the Soviet Union. Preparations for the attack, later postponed to June, involved not just the German army but leading industrialists and had been under way in Germany for some time. The Polish contact relayed Schulte's information to London. Whether it reached the Soviet Union is unclear, although a number of sources were reporting to the Kremlin the likelihood of such an attack, including Stalin's own top spy in Tokyo. Stalin ignored all the invasion warnings that reached him.[13]

On June 22, more than three million German soldiers launched a surprise attack on the Soviet Union. Within a matter of weeks, millions of Jews in the Soviet Union came under Nazi control; within five months, half a million of them were murdered by the *Einsatzgruppen*, mobile killing squads who followed the invading German Army and killed Jews and Communist Party officials.[14]

★ ★ ★

On July 17, 1942, twelve days before Schulte's train trip from Breslau to Zurich, he had been in his office, notable for its high ceilings, tall windows, and drawings and photographs of mines and factories. The frosted glass door opened and Otto Fitzner, Schulte's deputy and the director of Giesche's production, entered. A fanatical Nazi, Fitzner had joined the party even before Hitler's rise to supreme power.

It was Fitzner's pleasure to announce to Herr Doktor Schulte that an important visitor was expected to arrive that day, although he had not come to visit Giesche; his business was elsewhere in the area.

"Who is it?" asked Schulte.

"Himmler."[15]

The Nazi leadership was filled with extravagant, plundering, and perverse Caligula-like ghouls. Himmler's rival, the corpulent and heavily rouged Hermann Göring, now the chief of the Luftwaffe, swaggered about in a white uniform (among other gaudy outfits) bedecked with jewels that only hinted at the enormous wealth he had amassed by looting the museums and art galleries of Europe. "[He] strongly resembles the hind end of an elephant" was how one American diplomat described Göring's appearance. The Hitler myth minder, the cadaverous-looking minister of propaganda, Joseph Goebbels, believed that Hitler was Christ and that the "greater and more towering I make God, the greater and more towering I am myself."[16]

Reichsführer SS Heinrich Himmler's ability to strike awe and terror at the mere utterance of his name was directly disproportionate to his ordinary, inscrutable appearance. Himmler was anything but extravagant. Although he owned a villa in Berlin-Dahlem and an estate in Bavaria, he did not parade around in ostentatious luxury, his speeches never roused the masses, and he did not engage in self-serving Hitler worship in the manner of Goebbels. Unlike his athletic deputy Reinhard Heydrich, who was an accomplished fencer, Himmler—short, balding, and wearing pince-nez—hardly fit the

Aryan-Nordic racial ideal. A Nazi Party official once joked (out of his hearing, of course), "If I looked like him, I would not speak of race at all."[17]

His personal life likewise was subdued by Nazi standards. His marriage to a woman seven years older produced a daughter, Gudrun, but was apparently lacking in love, even if otherwise cordial. In keeping with the sexual mores of most top Nazis—promiscuity in private, a family-man façade in public—Himmler also kept a mistress (his secretary) with whom he had two children. This arrangement may also have been intended to further Nazi eugenic policy, since just one child through his marriage could hardly propagate a master race.[18]

One senior SS officer recalled that Himmler behaved responsibly toward his mistress's children: "He did what he could for these children within the limits of his own income." For her part, Gudrun told Himmler's biographers that she still had "memories of him which remain affectionate."[19] At the close of the war, Himmler took only his own life, unlike Goebbels, who murdered his children before committing suicide. All of which illustrates, to quote Auschwitz survivor Primo Levi, "how readily evil can replace good, besieging it and finally submerging it—yet allowing it to persist in tiny, grotesque islets: an orderly family life, the love of nature, Victorian morality."[20]

But one aspect of Himmler's appearance revealed the man within. Himmler suffered from a variety of ailments, including severe stomach pains. Since 1940, he had been attended by a Finnish masseur named Felix Kersten, whose touch was "like balm" to Himmler. Kersten, who may have spent as much time in intimate attendance on Himmler as anyone, became his confessor as well. Kersten's first impression of Himmler was of a "narrow-chested, weak-chinned, spectacled man with an ingratiating smile."

But Himmler's eyes were different. Kersten recalled them as "extraordinarily small, and the distance between them narrow, rodent-like. If you spoke to him, these eyes would never leave your face; they would rove over your countenance, fix your eyes; and in them would be an expression of waiting, watching, stealth." If the eyes are a window to the soul, as the medieval proverb goes, Himmler's soul was that of a viper.[21]

Accordingly, if Göring's power was the most ostentatious and Goebbels's the most self-declared, "Himmler's power was the most secret." One of Himmler's secret powers had been especially entrusted to him by Hitler, a power of such a breathtaking magnitude as to make it unprecedented in human history. Hitler had ordered Himmler to destroy the Jewish race in Europe.[22]

Hitler had all but made his ultimate intentions clear in a speech at the Berlin Sportpalast on January 30, 1941, the eighth anniversary of the Nazis' seizure of the German government. The Sportpalast was a huge neo-Baroque sports and entertainment center where Hitler rallied the Nazi Party faithful into the frenzy of Führer worship. Typically, the thousands of assembled Nazis —"carnivorous sheep" in Winston Churchill's biting phrase—interrupted almost every sentence with shouts of *"Sieg Heil!"* and, at the end of the speech, chanted *"Führer befiehl, wir folgen!"* (Führer command, we will follow!). After listening by radio in 1938 to Hitler rage against the Czechoslovakian government for refusing to meet his territorial demands, a German-speaking foreigner described this speech at the Sportpalast as "the most horrible thing . . . more like the snarling of a wild animal than the utterance of a human being. There was something terrifying and obscenely sinister in this outpouring of sheer hatred."

At the eighth-anniversary celebration, Hitler recalled a prophecy he had given in a speech two years earlier: "If the rest of the world should be plunged into general war through Jewry, the whole of Jewry will have played out its role in Europe."

Hitler reached his crescendo. "They can still laugh today about it, just as they laughed at all my prophecies. The coming months and years will demonstrate that here, too, I have seen things correctly."[23]

★ ★ ★

In the summer of 1941, Himmler summoned Rudolf Höss, the commandant of the Auschwitz concentration camp, to Berlin. Contrary to the custom at such meetings, Himmler's aide was not present. Höss recounted the meeting in his autobiography, which he wrote in prison after his capture in 1946. Although his account contained inconsistencies, historians have accepted the basic narrative.

The two men were alone in Himmler's office.

"The Führer has ordered that the Jewish question be solved once and for all," said Himmler, "and that we, the SS, are to implement that order." He went on, reported Höss, to say: "The existing extermination centers in the east are not in a position to carry out the large actions which are anticipated. I have therefore earmarked Auschwitz for this purpose. I have now decided to entrust this task to you. It is difficult and onerous and calls for complete devotion." Höss was instructed to obtain more details from Sturmbannführer (Major) Adolf Eichmann in the Reich Security Main Office, where Eichmann's responsibilities included the planning and coordination of deportations to the extermination camps.

Himmler ended the meeting by reminding Höss that "the Jews are the sworn enemies of the German people and must be eradicated. Every Jew that we can lay our hands on is to be destroyed now during the war, without exception. If we cannot now obliterate the biological basis of Jewry, the Jews will one day destroy the German people."[24]

Now, in July 1942, Himmler had come to inspect progress at the Auschwitz concentration camp. He might have entered through the main gate that bore the Orwellian slogan, *Arbeit Macht Frei* (work makes you free). Himmler's entourage included Höss, Obergruppenführer (Lieutenant General) SS Ernst-Heinrich Schmauser, and Gauleiter (regional Nazi party boss) Fritz Bracht, who had a close relationship with the Giesche firm. The inspection lasted two days.

The first stop was the SS officers' mess, where Höss explained the camp layout with the aid of maps. The party then adjourned to the architects' office to review construction designs and models. Afterwards, Himmler toured the camp and "made a most thorough inspection of everything, noting the overcrowded barrack-huts, the unhygienic conditions, the crammed hospital building." On an earlier visit, Himmler had been especially interested in the facilities for the tens of thousands of able-bodied prisoners whose lives would be spared—for the time being—so they could work as slaves, for, among others, I.G. Farben. In effect, Himmler had monetized genocide.[25]

Many of the cavernous gas chambers and the crematoria were still under construction, and the "actions," as they were known, were then relatively small. Even so, in the midsummer of 1942, Auschwitz was well on its way to becoming, in the words of historians Ray Brandon and Wendy Lower, the "nadir of Western civilization." By now, wrote Höss, it was a "collecting place for Jews, exceeding in scale anything previously known. Whereas the Jews who had been imprisoned in former years were able to count on being released one day and were thus far less affected psychologically by the hardships of captivity, the Jews in Auschwitz no longer had any such hope. They knew without exception that they were condemned to death, that they would live only so long as they could work."[26]

The condition of the women inmates was particularly horrible. Many women, no longer human beings but "stumbling corpses," had lost all will and wandered like ghosts, pushed by others until they expired. It was a "terrible sight," wrote Höss knowledgeably, since he had seen more than a few such sights.[27]

Himmler also inspected the children in the Roma (Gypsy) camp. They were sick with noma, a cancerous disease caused by starvation and weakness: "Their little bodies wasted away, with gaping holes in their cheeks big enough for a man to see through, a slow putrefaction of the living body." Of Himmler's reaction, Höss notes only that "he saw it all, in detail, and as it really was—and he ordered me to destroy them."[28]

Finally, Himmler and his group watched the "whole process of destruction of a transport of Jews, which had just arrived."[29] Höss wrote: "I cannot say on what date the extermination of the Jews began. Probably, it was in September 1941, but it may not have been until January 1942." Höss and Eichmann had invested much effort in perfecting a method for mass killing that would spare the Nazis the demoralizing task of shooting, machine-gunning, or throwing grenades among the Jews. Finishing off wounded women who attempted to crawl away from the heaps of machine-gunned dead had been particularly grueling for the *Einsatzgruppen* in the Soviet Union. Following the bloodiest killings, some members became alcoholics or otherwise unfit for duty; there were even suicides. In any event, these methods were regarded as hopelessly inadequate for the task at hand.[30]

After a period of trial-and-error experiments, Höss and his assistant developed a killing method using an insecticide called Zyklon-B. First tested on Russian prisoners of war, Zyklon-B was then applied to the transports of Jews arriving daily from across Europe. "I must even admit that this gassing set my mind at rest," wrote Höss, relieved that he could murder millions without spilling any blood.[31] Auschwitz survivor Primo Levi understood the irony better than anyone: "It's one thing machine-gunning a bunch of naked people on the edge of a pit that they themselves have dug; but inserting a container of poison gas through an air conduit is fundamentally different."[32]

As Himmler and his colleagues watched, a transport of Dutch Jews was sent into Bunker II. In his autobiography, Höss provided an account of a typical "action," such as witnessed by Himmler. "The Jews were made to undress near the bunker, after they had been told that they had to go into rooms (as they were also called) to be de-loused. All the rooms, there were five of them, were filled at the same time, the gas-proof doors were then screwed up and the contents of the gas containers discharged into the rooms through special vents."[33]

The previous September, hundreds of Russians, along with sick prisoners from the camp hospital, had been put in an underground detention cell. The windows were covered with dirt and SS men wearing gas masks opened the Zyklon-B canisters, which contained blue pellets the size of peas, and left, sealing the doors behind them. But even the next day, some of the Russians were still writhing, and the SS men had to open more canisters.[34]

By 1942, the actions had become more efficient. "After half an hour the doors were re-opened, the dead bodies were taken out, and brought to the pits in small trolleys which ran on rails."[35] As to the action he witnessed that summer, Himmler made "no remark regarding the process of extermination, but remained quite silent." However, always the good manager ferreting out weakness in subordinates, Himmler closely observed the demeanor of the "officers and junior officers engaged in the proceedings, including myself."[36]

Himmler had recognized the need to steel both himself and the SS to do their duty. Höss claimed that "we were all tormented by secret doubts. I had to watch coldly while the mothers with laughing or crying children went into the gas-chambers." He wrote about one occasion, "My pity was so great that I longed to vanish from the scene."

There were limits to his pity. On the occasion that he longed to be elsewhere, two small children, engaged in a game, refused to let their mother pull them toward the gas chambers. The mother, who knew what awaited her and her children, had an imploring look in her eyes. Even the "Jews of the Special Detachment were reluctant to pick the children up." But, the "people were already in the gas-chamber and becoming restive, and I had to act." Höss ordered a junior officer to pick up the struggling children and carry them into the gas chamber. Walking alongside was their mother, "who was weeping in the most heart-rending fashion."[37]

Himmler told Felix Kersten of the plan to destroy the Jews. The masseur was horrified, according to his memoir: "I emphatically begged him to give up this idea. The suffering and the counter-suffering were not to be contemplated." Himmler replied that he knew it would mean much suffering for the Jews. "Yet," he told Kersten, "we must create new life, we must cleanse the soil or it will never bear fruit. It will be a great burden for me to accept." An SS general later claimed that Himmler was "deeply oppressed by the decision that he was to be ultimately responsible for this crime, the greatest that any man has ever committed in recorded history against his fellows."[38]

Or so we read in their memoirs, in the Nuremberg war crimes trial transcripts, or, in the case of Himmler, in his masseur's memoir. Perhaps tiny, grotesque islets of humanity still persisted in July 1942, but they surely would not survive much longer because the Nazis' crime was without precedent on the face of the earth. As one German historian has written, "Never before had a state with the authority of its responsible leader decided and announced that a specific human group, including its aged, its women, its children and infants, would be killed as quickly as possible, and then carried through this resolution using every possible means of state power."[39]

Equally remarkably, the conspirators believed that the very monstrosity of their deeds would immunize them. "Our system is so terrible that no one in the world will believe it to be possible," Höss observed with more prophetic insight than he probably appreciated. "If someone should succeed in escaping from Auschwitz and in telling the world, the world will brand him as a fantastic liar."[40]

That evening, Himmler, Höss, and the others adjourned to Bracht's villa near Kattowitz, where Himmler was to spend the night. Giesche had built the villa for use by its then American directors during their visits to the firm in the 1920s. It was luxurious, with amenities that included a swimming pool and a golf course, unusual in Europe in that era. After the invasion of Poland in 1939 and the annexation by Germany of Polish Upper Silesia, Giesche faced the threat of losing its Polish holdings to the powerful German state conglomerates, especially the voracious Hermann Göring Werke. As insurance against this, Giesche secured the good will of Bracht by giving him the villa for his personal use.[41]

The evening was pleasant and filled with lively conversation and not a hint of self-doubt. Höss recalled that Himmler was "in the best of spirits, took a leading part in the conversation, and was extremely amiable, especially toward the ladies, the Gauleiter's wife and my own wife." Himmler even drank a few glasses of red wine. The gathering talked of books and architecture and the upbringing of children. Himmler regaled guests with tales of his front-line visits with the Führer. "Everyone was under the spell of his good humour and lively conversation. I had never known him like that before."[42]

No one mentioned the inspection. Himmler "deliberately avoided saying one word about day-to-day events or about service matters, and ignored the attempts of the Gauleiter to get him to do so." The next day, the inspection continued. In the women's camp, Himmler, who had previously ordered "intensified" beatings of undisciplined prisoners, witnessed the whipping of a prostitute who had been caught stealing. He then held a conference in Höss's office, where he dismissed Höss's complaints about unreasonable construction schedules and other obstacles to expansion of the camp.

"Eichmann's programme will continue to be carried out and will be intensified month by month. You must see to it that swift progress is made with the building of Birkenau. The gypsies are to be destroyed. The Jews who are unfit for work are to be destroyed with the same ruthlessness."[43]

Before leaving Auschwitz, Himmler stopped by Höss's home, with its unusually devoted staff of servant-prisoners. "The prisoners never missed an opportunity for doing some little act of kindness to my wife or children." Höss proudly showed Himmler his furniture. "He spent some time in animated conversation with my wife and children." Himmler also rewarded Höss for his accomplishments. "I have seen your work and the results you have achieved," he told Höss, "and I am satisfied and thank you for your services. I promote you to Obersturmbannführer [Lieutenant-Colonel]!"[44]

Himmler returned to Berlin. A week and a half later, Eduard Schulte, who had not been at the dinner party at Bracht's villa, boarded the train to Zurich. Although exactly how he did so has been lost in history's mists, Schulte had found out why Reichsführer SS Himmler had come to this obscure part of Poland.

★ ★ ★

Schulte's train pulled into Zurich's Hauptbahnhof. The Hotel Baur-au-Lac, alerted by Schulte's office, had a porter waiting for him on the platform. After carrying the luggage to a limousine, the porter drove Schulte along the Bahnhofstrasse, Zurich's main street, passing the offices of major Swiss banks, chocolate shops, luxury clothing stores, the Jelmoli department store with its decorative red Swiss flags emblazoned with white crosses, and the elegant jewelry stores that sold wares removed from the murdered Jews in Auschwitz.[45]

The German occupation of most of the rest of Europe had left Switzerland a neutral oasis; instead of water in a desert, however, Switzerland offered information in a world war. The country was an espionage mart whose currency was betrayal. Spy networks were operated by, among others, Swiss military and civilian intelligence, the remnants of the French Deuxième Bureau operating on behalf of de Gaulle's Free French, the British Secret Intelligence Service (SIS), the American Office of Strategic Services (OSS), Soviet Intelligence, known as Moscow Centre, and, not least, the German military intelligence, the Abwehr. During World War II, an estimated one thousand German-trained spies, most of them Swiss citizens who supported the Nazis, operated in Switzerland. "Directly or indirectly all the Intelligence services of the world were talking to each other and making deals with each other in the only country where such a communal meeting place could have existed at the time—Switzerland." In Zurich, informants and double agents were as common as bank accounts and bankers.[46]

One theory as to how Schulte found out about the Nazi plan to murder the Jews has been offered by his biographers. Schulte, they suggest, may have been told by "either Otto Fitzner, the number two man at Giesche, or Jakob Werlin, a high executive at Daimler-Benz—or both," although neither had accompanied Himmler on his inspection of Auschwitz. But certainly, if Fitzner knew, the impulse to flaunt his insider status before his imperious boss might have been irresistible. "Ach, Herr Doktor, if you only knew what the Gauleiter confided to me about the Jews. . . ."[47]

Schulte kept no diary and, even after the war, revealed his wartime activities to very few persons. We have no record of his feelings during the train trip to Zurich. But, contrary to Höss's contention that no one would believe "it to be possible," Schulte was obviously convinced that a few hours' drive from his office millions of human beings were about to be murdered. As one historian pointed out, "Schulte's latest information was not of mere military significance; he assigned to it the highest political and moral importance." So important was this information that he was willing to risk his life to convey this terrible secret to the Allied governments, even if it meant traveling into the country with the greatest concentration of spies in the world.[48]

II

THE TRIBUTARIES OF
THE DNIESTER

More than a dozen tributaries nourish the Dniester River, which flows south through a valley along Romania's eastern border. Between the Dniester and the Bug River to the east, the land was called Transnistria or, sometimes, Trans-Dniester. Transnistria was an area of fifteen thousand square miles carved out of the Nazi-occupied Ukraine, a geographic enclave that could not be found on any map. Along with other Soviet territory, Transnistria was a gift of Nazi Germany to its ally, the Romanian government of Marshal Ion Antonescu. "When it's a question of action against the Slavs, you can always count on Romania," Antonescu told the Nazis in 1941 when informed of the soon-to-be-launched German invasion of the Soviet Union.

Few native Jews remained in Transnistria after the invasion; most had either fled or been killed by the Einsatzgruppen. The units put their education and skills to efficient, lethal use (in one, half of the leaders had a doctor of laws degree). One unit developed a technique called Sardinenpackung, in which the "victims to be" were placed "face down on top of those who had just been executed."

Antonescu ordered the deportation of Romanian Jews from the border provinces of Bukovina and Bessarabia into what would become, geographically at least, the largest concentration camp in the world. He would thereby demonstrate that Romanians could be as bestial toward Jews as Germans, even though Romania lacked the modern infrastructure necessary for industrial genocide.

"As regards the Jews," Antonescu told officials of his government, "I have taken measures to remove them entirely once and for all from these regions. If I do not purify the Romanian nation, then I have achieved nothing, for it is not frontiers that consolidate a nation, but the homogeneity and purity of its race."[1]

To the water tributaries of the Dniester Antonescu added dozens of human ones, marching columns of stunned Jewish men, women, and children who had been forced out of their homes by the Romanian army and police. The columns were far thinner as they neared the Dniester than when they had left their various villages, towns, and cities inside Romania.[2]

This was a death march. In one town on the Dniester, devastated by battle, the exhausted Jews were ordered to enter the bombed-out buildings and sleep there before resuming the march in the morning. One group entered a synagogue with a red-tiled roof that somehow had managed to survive largely intact. By candlelight, the new arrivals read Hebrew messages written in blood on the synagogue's walls by those who had come before. "Here they slaughtered my wife and children, before my eyes . . . very soon I will lie beside them." "Here we were killed! No one has remained alive of our family." The arrivals stood silently for a long time, staring at the messages.[3]

This column of Jews was ordered to wait on the riverbank of the Dniester, where they remained for the next day and watched as bodies floated by. They were then ordered to camp for the night. After dark, a terrible rumor swept through the camp: "They are demanding ten women." It was no rumor. Soon shouts were heard throughout the camp as Romanian soldiers dashed here and there pulling off blankets. Screaming or pleading, regardless, women were dragged away. A young man clung to his fiancée while an officer beat him with a pistol butt. Bleeding badly, the young man refused to let go, and as the young woman was dragged away, he was dragged along with her, leaving a trail of blood on the frozen ground. Finally, he could hold on no longer and let go. The camp fell silent.

Later that night the woman returned, her clothes torn. She lay down next to her betrothed, still lying where he had lost his grip, and wrapped her arms around him, softly moaning as the two of them huddled under a coat. At dawn, the Romanian soldiers woke the encampment. These Jews would be allowed to cross the river into Transnistria.

The couple did not get up. A soldier beat them with his rifle butt, but they still refused to move. Finally, he lifted the coat and found them in a fierce embrace. Blood soaked their clothes. Their slit wrists eloquently testified to a love that now would last for eternity.[4]

As one marching column reached the Dniester, the Romanians issued orders to open fire on the marchers. But during the march, Moishe Katz, a natural leader, had made friends with the Romanian commanders. At the last minute, one of them offered Katz a deal: for enough money, the Jews could cross the Dniester and live. Katz collected money from the other Jews and handed it over. As the column began crossing the bridge, the commander ordered machine-gun squads to open fire. Katz was the first to be cut down, and like the rest soon to follow him, he fell into the river and floated south toward the Black Sea. The human and water tributaries of the Dniester had become one.

A human stream flowed through the city of Czernowitz, the predominantly German-speaking capital of Bukovina province that lay at the folds of the Carpathian Mountains. In the stream, which was not of sufficient size to be a tributary, was Katz's eleven-year-old niece, Ruth Glasberg. Had she known what would befall her uncle, it would scarcely have added to her state of shock. That had been her condition since Romanian soldiers, pounding on the door of her family's apartment, ordered the family into the street, where they joined a marching column.

For a lucky few who could pay the driver, horse-drawn carts carried their luggage. Otherwise, men pushed wheelbarrows with family heirlooms concealed in bedding. Women carried crying babies. The elderly bent under the weight of heavy sacks and bundles. Children supported the sick.

Ruth was fortunate. She rode on top of a luggage cart in a stream of two thousand bewildered Jews, some wailing, others chanting, "Shemah Israel" (Hear, O Israel), still others morose, and most in a state of near panic. The Jews were marched to a railroad, where thirty cattle cars awaited them.

Ruth, a golden-haired girl with two braids and bright blue eyes, loved train trips as much as any child. Trains were, for most children, a magic carpet—an effortless journey spent staring out a window at the wondrous landscape. For many years, Ruth thought the train was stationary and it was the scenery that moved alongside. How fast the trees rush by!

Now, as the train jerked forward with the shrill scream of iron on iron and then picked up speed, Ruth found herself taking a train trip into a world of pain, *madness, and death where no child should ever go. Her train car had only one small vent for air. In the daytime, some light penetrated. At night, the Jews of Czernowitz stood or, in the case of the lucky ones, sat on the floor, in the pitch black, their senses overwhelmed by the smell of feces and urine and the moans and cries of the weak, exhausted, or near mad.*

Ruth, like many children on the train and in the marching columns—indeed, throughout all the lands occupied by the Nazis and their allies—began a personal dialogue with God. Why the children? Why us? Why me?

God did not respond because He did not know the answer.

What will happen to us? Where are they taking us? How will we live?

God did not respond because the answers to these questions He knew all too well.[5]

III

THE RIEGNER TELEGRAM

A smiling concierge met Herr Doktor Schulte at the Hotel Baur-au-Lac. The hotel manager appeared "to express his profound appreciation at the arrival of such an old and esteemed friend of the house." Schulte was given his usual suite with a lake view. He first telephoned his mistress at her dress shop and then called a private banker in Basel at the *Internationale Kapital Anlage Gesellschaft*, which provided investment advice to wealthy clients. In the past, Schulte had communicated on military matters with contacts directly tied to Allied intelligence services. This time, however, a different approach was necessary. "Schulte did not expect intelligence agencies to respond to the kind of news that he had obtained." Schulte needed someone with diplomatic contacts—especially American diplomats—which he thought made the private banker a logical choice.[1]

His name was Isidor Koppelmann, a brilliant entrepreneurial banker. Koppelmann was Jewish, unusual in the Swiss banking community, and therefore more likely to believe what Schulte was about to tell him. Indeed, all that Schulte had to say was that he was in Zurich and needed to speak with Koppelmann urgently. Koppelmann simply replied that he would be on the first train in the morning to Zurich. He knew that Schulte's visits to Switzerland did not involve only business.

That evening, Schulte rang the doorbell at an apartment on the Alfred Escher Strasse, close by his hotel. Doris, then in her early thirties, opened the door.

The motives of any spy are complicated. The visit certainly served as cover in the event anyone had followed Schulte since his arrival in Zurich. But Schulte was in love with Doris, whom he had met before the war. And, to further complicate Schulte's motives, Doris was Jewish. As Schulte's biographers wrote, "It is difficult to fathom the human heart; all we know is that this was Schulte's only serious affair and that it was to become a lasting relationship. It is even more difficult to know to what extent his love for Doris had impelled him to engage in this rescue mission in the middle of the war."[2]

The next morning, Schulte and Koppelmann met at the Hotel Baur-au-Lac, whose private garden offered seclusion. The conversation was terse because this was not an occasion for small talk. The gist of what Schulte had to say was: *I am in possession of information that sounds incredible but is absolutely authentic. It concerns the fate of the Jews of Europe, not just some but all of them. This information must be transmitted immediately to the leading Jewish organizations in America.*

And then the dreadful disclosure: Hitler's headquarters is considering a plan to kill all remaining European Jews. Three or four million will be transported to the east and gassed. An enormous crematorium has been built. It is unclear whether the plan has yet to be implemented or whether they have already begun, but if not, then it is only a matter of days or weeks. Unless the Allies act, there will be few Jews, if any, left in Europe at the end of this year.

Schulte emphasized that there was no doubt as to the truth of what he was saying and that Koppelmann must communicate his information to others in a position to do something.

Koppelmann did not reply at first. He knew of Schulte's access to the highest level of Nazi business and military circles; that Schulte was a serious man not given to rash judgments; and that, in the past, Schulte had provided information that had proven deadly accurate. Koppelmann was also aware of reports of Jews dying in Eastern Europe in pogroms and from starvation.

But Koppelmann also had a personal consideration that doubtless affected his reaction. "Only a few weeks earlier Koppelmann had received terrible news from a lawyer in Bucharest, Romania. His beloved only sister had been deported to Transnistria, which meant almost certain death for her."

Koppelmann knew only that Transnistria was an area in the Nazi-conquered Soviet Ukraine to which Romanian Jews had been sent. Since their deportation, nothing had been heard from them. It was as though they had disappeared into a gaping hole in the face of the earth.

"Get me a visa to some foreign country" was the last word that Koppelmann had had from his sister. He had called the Jewish Palestine Office in Geneva, but they had no immigration permits to British-occupied Palestine; even if there had been available permits, they could not be obtained by Romanians, since Romania was a German ally.

Without asking a single question, Koppelmann accepted Schulte's information as authentic and of the utmost importance. But, Koppelmann explained to Schulte, in fact he did not know the Swiss Jewish leaders or the diplomats—these were not circles he moved in.

Schulte urged him to consider all his acquaintances who could act in this matter; he must know someone. Eventually Koppelmann suggested a man whom Schulte knew: Benjamin Sagalowitz, the press officer for the Federation of Jewish Communities of Switzerland, based in Zurich. Schulte wanted to know if Sagalowitz had the right connections and, above all, whether he could be trusted.

Koppelmann assured Schulte that Sagalowitz knew everyone of importance in Switzerland and that he was a leading expert on the Nazis. On the spur of the moment, Koppelmann called Sagalowitz at home, only to learn that the journalist was in Lausanne for a chess tournament. Koppelmann started calling hotels in Lausanne. The Hotel du Château confirmed that Sagalowitz was registered as a guest. As a competitor in the Swiss national chess championship, the hotel explained, under no circumstances could Herr Sagalowitz be disturbed. Koppelmann left a message that he had urgent need to speak with Sagalowitz. The call was returned within an hour.

A matter of the gravest nature has arisen, Koppelmann said to Sagalowitz. You must return to Zurich.

This was out of the question, replied Sagalowitz. It was the first major Swiss chess tournament since the start of the war. If Sagalowitz left for even a day, he would lose whatever hope he had of a good finish.

Koppelmann was firm. He would not be making this request if it were not a matter of life and death.

In that time and place, such statements were not made lightly. After more discussion, Sagalowitz agreed to come to Zurich the next day. Returning to Schulte, Koppelmann asked whether he would meet with Sagalowitz. Schulte declined, at least for present purposes; later, he said, there would be other opportunities.

The two men parted. Schulte checked out of the hotel and went back to Germany, having passed on his secret to the first in a series of men who involuntarily became the carriers of information so unbearable that each in turn was compelled to find another messenger, one who might finally get the information out of Switzerland and into the hands of those who could immediately do something to stop the Nazis' insane scheme. In their minds, above all, that meant the government of the United States of America.[3]

Before we follow those messengers, what of Eduard Schulte, who literally had carried the terrible secret from the gates of Hell? He returned to his job at Giesche and, in May 1943, became no. 643 in the records of the OSS, reporting directly to American spymaster Allen Dulles (later head of the CIA). His near undoing came neither through his own carelessness nor the diligence of the Gestapo (his tradecraft was always flawless) but from an inexcusable blunder by the OSS network. A non-American OSS agent carelessly mentioned Schulte by name in a message that was intercepted by the Gestapo. OSS Bern barely got a message to Schulte, then attending a business meeting, that critical negotiations required his immediate presence in Switzerland. And so, "Schulte left the Third Reich on December 2, 1943, never to return."[4] He plays no further role in this narrative.

After a bad night's sleep, Sagalowitz boarded the first train to Zurich. Born in Russia, Sagalowitz "was a pleasant and friendly person, a truly good man with probably not an enemy in the world." Well educated and tactful, "he had the gift of inspiring confidence and making friends without trying very hard." His father, a wealthy Jewish merchant in Russia, had fled after the pogroms of 1905, finally settling in Switzerland. Sagalowitz had completed law school in Zurich but was blocked from pursuing a legal career by lack of Swiss citizenship, which the Swiss authorities had denied because, in their prudish eyes, Sagalowitz was a womanizer. Even worse, "the ladies concerned were not of the demimonde but, on the contrary, came from good families; some were even married women." Sagalowitz then embarked on a career in freelance journalism.

From the train station, Sagalowitz went directly to his apartment in the Nüschelerstrasse, adjacent to the Zurich central synagogue. Koppelmann arrived early. In effect, he told Sagalowitz: *A German industrialist known to you was in Zurich. He has an urgent message for you.*

Each time the message was relayed, first to Koppelmann and now to Sagalowitz, the recipient first had to absorb the stunning information and then gather his thoughts. Unlike Koppelmann, Sagalowitz, a skeptic by virtue of his journalistic training, did not as readily accept what he was hearing.

Did he give his source?

He would not tell me.

May I quote him when I pass it on?

Under no circumstances; in fact, he wanted your word of honor that his name will be kept out.

Sagalowitz emphasized that, while the Nazis were capable of anything, people he might contact would want proof. Their conversation did not progress beyond this exchange, and Koppelmann left to catch a late train to Basel.

Another frequent reaction of those who were given Schulte's information was to go for a walk, often a long one. Walking was a tonic to hearing perhaps the worst news ever delivered. The recipients found it impossible to simply stay in an apartment or sit in a garden.

Sagalowitz went for a walk. July had started out unseasonably cold, but now it was warm. "Sagalowitz walked toward the Limmat, crossed a bridge over the river and found an empty seat in the corner of his favorite coffeehouse, the Odeon." A group of chess players spotted him in the coffeehouse. He had had to leave the tournament in Lausanne unexpectedly, he explained, but it was a wonderful competition. He asked to be left alone and the chess players, perhaps sensing that he was unusually preoccupied, withdrew.

Another response of the men who received Schulte's message was to reflect on recent events, both confirmed and rumored. Suddenly developments in wartime Europe, especially the roundup of Jews, which had been noted with alarm but not comprehension, took on a new meaning, as though pieces of a giant puzzle had begun to fall into place. Sagalowitz, an avid reader of newspapers, kept coming back to a story that somehow had passed the Swiss censors, about a message from Winston Churchill to a rally of American Jews in Madison Square Garden: "Hitler apparently will not be satisfied until the cities of Europe in which Jews live are turned into giant cemeteries. But the Jewish people will not bow to the decision of its extermination."[5]

All who came into possession of Nazi Germany's greatest secret also asked themselves, to whom should I give this information? It was no easy matter to find a person who could understand the implications of the Nazis' scheme, had contacts in the right places, and was, above all, someone who could be trusted. Sagalowitz considered and rejected a number of options. His superiors at the Federation of Jewish Communities? No, they were timid businessmen, influential in the Swiss Jewish community, but they would have no idea how to reach Allied leaders. Foreign journalists? No, for them this would just be another story.

What about the representatives of Jewish organizations, such as the Jewish Agency for Palestine or the World Jewish Congress? These avenues appeared more promising. Sagalowitz considered several agencies and their representatives, but one name stood out. He was Gerhart Riegner, the Geneva representative of the World Jewish Congress. The congress was more a name than an organization; as one historian has written, "Its real center was whichever hotel room Nahum Goldmann, its peripatetic general secretary, happened to be in at the time." Nonetheless, the World Jewish Congress had a key link to the United States. Its president, and the president of its American affiliate, the American Jewish Congress, was Rabbi Stephen Wise, a friend of President Franklin D. Roosevelt and a prominent figure.[6]

Apologizing to his fellow chess enthusiasts, Sagalowitz left the Odeon, went home, and immediately telephoned Riegner and asked if they could meet the next day in Lausanne to discuss an urgent matter. The answer was yes and they agreed to meet at the Beau Rivage.[7]

★ ★ ★

On Saturday, August 1, Sagalowitz returned to Lausanne. His train arrived early enough for a visit to the chess tournament in the great hall of the Beau Rivage Hotel. The tournament was in the final rounds, but Sagalowitz could not watch for long. A bellhop informed him that he had a visitor at the reception desk. Riegner and Sagalowitz left the Beau Rivage and went to the Hotel du Château and found a table on the terrace.

Over lunch, Sagalowitz delivered Schulte's message. Then the two men walked for a long time. The spectacular setting for their grim stroll was the shore of Lake Geneva, with the crystalline Alps in the distance, behind which—out of sight, but never far from anyone's mind—a war raged. But the beautiful scenery was lost on Sagalowitz and Riegner, preoccupied with too many questions for which they had no answers.

Can we take this seriously?
Can the Nazis be planning to murder millions of human beings?
Could this be a ruse, some kind of provocation?[8]

They relived the unhappy past, which now appeared more like a prologue to a nightmare. The ruthless, violent history of the Nazis had included the torching of the Reichstag, which Hitler used as an excuse to tighten his grip on power; Hitler's remilitarization of the Rhineland, in violation of the Treaty of Versailles that had ended World War I; the annexation of Austria; *Kristallnacht* (night of broken glass), when thousands of Jewish shops and synagogues were destroyed or damaged (and ninety-one Jews were killed in the first twenty-four hours) in a national anti-Semitic rampage like nothing seen since the Middle Ages—that had begun on cue following the assassination of a German diplomat in Paris (by a teenage Polish Jew whose family had just been forcibly expelled into Poland by the Nazis from their home in Hanover); Hitler's occupation of all of Czechoslovakia in violation of his Munich agreement with the British Prime Minister Neville Chamberlain, in which Hitler solemnly promised that, if he was given one-third of that country, he would make no further demands for Czech territory; and the German invasion of first Poland, then Denmark, Norway, the Low Countries and France, and, finally, the Soviet Union.

For both men, the fact of the virulent, demonic Nazi hatred of the Jews loomed the largest: the Jews as a pestilence; as the source of all evil on the face of the earth; and, in an insanely contradictory accusation, as responsible for Communism, capitalism, and all other political systems that were the enemies of the Third Reich. Hitler's speeches had predicted the demise of the Jews in the event of another European war. And, just two weeks earlier, Riegner had received reports of massive roundups of tens of thousands of Jews from across occupied Europe.[9]

Gerhart Riegner almost confirmed Höss's theory that, apart from the Nazis themselves, the rest of the human race could not believe that people were capable of such unimaginably monstrous acts. Under Höss's reasoning, while there was no limit to the Nazis' twisted imagination, other mortals lacked such faculties of imagination; even if they possessed them, the very exercise of such faculties was too painful to ever put into practice. That has been an enduring, shattering legacy of Nazi Germany: the unendurable knowledge that there are no limits on humanity's capacity for state-organized mass murder and bestial conduct, certainly not the limits of normal imagination. "In spite of all the information in my possession, in spite of the discussions we pursued in ever greater depth, in spite of what I had already experienced myself, I still needed another two days to convince myself that these events really were possible and, finally, to believe in them."[10]

Riegner knew he had to act on Schulte's message, but he told Sagalowitz that the involvement of so many emissaries created a risk of error. He insisted on meeting with Isidor Koppelmann "and hearing from his mouth the exact message that had been communicated."

Two days later, on August 3, Riegner met with Koppelmann in Zurich, who confirmed in detail everything described by Sagalowitz. However, Riegner could not bring himself to believe that the Nazis were constructing giant crematoria in which the Jews of Europe would "go up in flames," and later wrote, "I must admit that I could not succeed in picturing it to myself and did not mention it in the course of the steps I subsequently took."[11]

The meeting with Koppelmann convinced Riegner that the American and British governments had to be informed. Equally important, the information had to be given to the American Jewish community. Riegner drafted a cautiously worded telegram (a Western Union "cablegram") to Rabbi Wise.

```
RECEIVED ALARMING REPORT THAT IN FUHRERS HEAD-
QUARTERS PLAN DISCUSSED AND UNDER CONSIDERATION
ALL JEWS IN COUNTRIES OCCUPIED CONTROLLED GERMANY
NUMBER 3½ TO FOUR MILLION SHOULD AFTER DEPORTA-
TION AND CONCENTRATION IN EAST AT ONE BLOW EXTER-
MINATED TO RESOLVE ONCE FOR ALL JEWISH QUESTION
IN EUROPE STOP ACTION IS REPORTED PLANNED FOR
AUTUMN METHODS UNDER DISCUSSION INCLUDING PRUS-
SIC ACID STOP WE TRANSMIT INFORMATION WITH ALL
NECESSARY RESERVATION AS EXACTITUDE CANNOT BE
CONFIRMED STOP INFORMANT STATED TO HAVE CLOSE
CONNECTIONS WITH HIGHEST GERMAN AUTHORITIES AND
HIS REPORTS GENERALLY RELIABLE STOP.
```

Sending the telegram to Rabbi Wise through a Swiss telegraph service was out of the question. German intelligence intercepted every telegram or letter sent to Allied countries from Switzerland. In any event, the Swiss, who employed strict military censorship to avoid antagonizing Germany, would simply have refused to transmit it.[12]

On August 8, 1942, Gerhart Riegner went to the American Consulate in Geneva with the telegram. Consul Paul Squire was away for the holidays. Riegner met with Vice Consul Howard Elting Jr. and talked for a long time. Riegner struck Elting as deeply distraught.[13]

"The number involved is said to be between three and a half and four million and the object is to permanently settle the Jewish question in Europe," Riegner said. "Mass execution will allegedly take place this fall."

"This report seems fantastic to me," said Elting.

"It had struck me in the same way. But mass deportations have been taking place since July 16. We have reports from Paris, Holland, Berlin, Vienna and Prague so it is conceivable that Hitler is considering such a diabolical plan as a corollary."

As Elting listened to Riegner, whom he regarded as serious and balanced, he was struck by Riegner's confidence in the German businessman (whom Riegner had described without providing identification). Slowly, Elting himself was becoming upset.

Riegner had three requests of Elting.

First, I am asking you to inform your government.

Second, you have a secret service; I do not. Have your secret service verify the accuracy of these allegations.

Third, send this telegram to Stephen Wise, the president of the World Jewish Congress in the United States. He is a well known public figure and a personal friend of President Roosevelt.[14]

After consulting with Consul Squire upon his return, Elting transmitted Riegner's information to the American legation in Bern. He recommended that the report be sent to Rabbi Wise. The legation in Bern cabled the State Department, explaining that "Gerhardt [sic] M. Riegner Secretary World

Jewish Congress Geneva called on Vice Consul Elting Geneva Saturday eighth greatly agitated and requested following message be transmitted for information American and other Allied Governments and be notified in Department's discretion to Dr. Stephen Wise New York City."

The Riegner telegram was then quoted from, but a "confidential Legation note" was also appended to the cable by Minister Leland Harrison. "Legation has no information which would tend to confirm this report which is however forwarded in accordance with Riegner's wishes. The report has earmarks of war rumor inspired by fear." In his own correspondence with the State Department, attaching the memorandum of his meeting with Riegner, however, Vice Consul Elting stated, "I desire to reiterate my belief in the utter seriousness of my informant."[15]

Eduard Schulte had left Germany just eleven days earlier, on July 29, to undertake, at great personal risk, a mission to warn the world that millions of innocent persons were about to be murdered. In little over a week, three men—Isidor Koppelmann, Benjamin Sagalowitz, and Gerhart Riegner—had considered, evaluated, and successfully passed along Schulte's secret under wartime conditions in a spy-ridden country. Schulte's information fit and explained the pattern of Nazi deportations of Jews from every major city in occupied Europe. It was fully consistent with, and corroborated by, longstanding Nazi doctrine that the Jews were the mortal enemies of the Third Reich; Hitler's own writings and speeches, which left no doubt that, one way or the other, there would be no Jews left in Europe by the end of the war; and the dire warnings of no less a figure than Winston Churchill.

Two weeks after his meeting with Elting, Riegner still had received no word from the consulate. Then, on August 24, Consul Squire contacted Riegner, informing him of the instructions he had received from the State Department in Washington—specifically, from the career professionals in the Division of European Affairs on the third floor.

The State Department, without conducting an investigation, had refused to even give Riegner's message to Rabbi Stephen Wise (which left the American Jewish community ignorant of the Nazi extermination plan) because of "the fantastic nature of the allegation and the impossibility of our being of any assistance if such action were taken."[16]

IV

THE ARISTOCRATIC ARCHIPELAGO

The wall covering in Mrs. E. Livingston Ludlow's drawing room on the second floor of 8 East 76th Street in New York City was a pale amber yellow satin brocade. On this special occasion, Mrs. Ludlow's drawing room had been opened to create a large salon extending into the drawing room of the adjoining residence of her daughter, Mrs. Henry Parish. The drawing rooms, which glowed in candlelight, were decorated with ferns, palms, and pink roses. The wedding presents totaled 340 separate gifts, including flatware and china, several silver tea sets, four inkstands, thirteen silver trays, and thirteen clocks.

The bride, preceded by six bridesmaids, descended the wide flight of stairs from the third floor of the Parish home (where she had been living) on the arm of her uncle, the president of the United States. The bridesmaids were dressed in white faille silk frocks. Each wore tulle veils attached to white Prince of Wales ostrich feathers and carried large bouquets of pink roses.

The bridal procession crossed the large foyer at the rear of the Parish drawing room, passed between the retracted sliding doors, and entered the Ludlow drawing room. There, ushers, all holding white satin ribbons, had formed an aisle leading to an altar set up in front of a fireplace.

The buoyant, charming bridegroom waited at the altar for his shy bride, who wore a white satin princess gown, flounced and draped with old rose-point Brussels lace and trailing a white satin court train. Her lace veil was caught with orange blossoms and a diamond crescent; her bouquet was of lilies of the valley. The bride's wedding train was carried by her younger brother's twelve-year-old friend, who would later become an undersecretary of state.

The bridegroom had given the bride a gold watch decorated with her initials in diamonds. Reverend Endicott Peabody, the headmaster of the Groton School, which the bridegroom had attended, performed the ceremony at an altar set under a bower made of bouquets of pink roses and palms.[1]

The wedding of Franklin and Eleanor Roosevelt on March 17, 1905, was described in the next day's edition of the *New York Times* as "one of the most notable weddings of the year." In light of what was to come—a "partnership that would help change the face of the country," in the words of one historian—it can more accurately be called the wedding of the century. The *Times'* lengthy account of the wedding mentioned that "The bride is an orphan, her parents, Mr. and Mrs. Elliott Roosevelt, having died a dozen or more years ago." The poignant comment prudently did not call attention to the diphtheria that killed the bride's mother (it would have been her birthday that day), who might have lost the will to live because of her husband's womanizing and alcohol abuse (which eventually killed him as well).[2]

Eleanor Roosevelt's closest remaining relative was her uncle, President Theodore Roosevelt. Before the ceremony, he told the bridegroom, "Well, Franklin, there's nothing like keeping the name in the family." When the Reverend Peabody brought the ceremony to a close, the guests flocked to the president, who had gone into the dining room to enjoy the refreshments. As one of the bridesmaids, the president's daughter Alice, later recalled, "My father lived up to his reputation of being the bride at every wedding and the corpse at every funeral and hogged the limelight unashamedly."

In a short time, as Eleanor Roosevelt wrote in her autobiography many, many years later, "This young couple were standing alone!" None of the guests, of course, or the bride and groom for that matter, had the slightest notion that Franklin Roosevelt's role in American history would overshadow even that of his boisterous distant cousin Teddy from the Oyster Bay, Long Island, side of the Roosevelt clan.[3]

An extraordinary American transformation can be traced to the wedding of Franklin and Eleanor Roosevelt. But the wedding was also a prism of the incubating cultural, social, and political forces that would determine the response of the State Department to the greatest human and moral catastrophe in civilization's history. Four of those present—then President Theodore Roosevelt, the Reverend Endicott Peabody, the future President Franklin Roosevelt, and the future undersecretary of state Sumner Welles (the young wedding trainbearer)—would do as much as any individuals to create the culture of the State Department that shaped that response.

★ ★ ★

Until the first decade of the twentieth century, the American diplomatic corps had a low reputation at home and abroad. Training was almost nonexistent, salaries were minimal, no system for promotion or inspection existed, and some overseas posts were even held by foreigners with greater allegiance to local interests than to the United States. Political cronyism was so rampant that a consular turnover of as much as 90 percent accompanied each change of presidential administration. An iconic image was an American consul "under the proverbial palm tree with his bottle beside him."

In 1904, Joseph Grew—a recent Harvard graduate later to serve as ambassador to Japan prior to the attack on Pearl Harbor and as undersecretary of state—tried to enter the Consular Service. All he initially could obtain was a largely clerical position in the Cairo consulate. His aspiration to fill an opening as an official secretary (assistant) to the ambassador to Austria-Hungary was blocked by politics. As he recalled in his memoirs, "I had high hopes which were sadly dashed when one day the press announced the appointment of the son of a prominent politician to the vacancy. That is what counted in those days—political pull."[4]

A Grew family friend who was the assistant attorney general complained to President Theodore Roosevelt, who replied: "Too much political pressure. I can't do it." The family friend persisted and finally found an approach that salvaged what would become a blazing diplomatic career. He described to the president how young Grew, while on a tour of the Far East several years earlier, had tracked a tiger into a small tunnel-like cave in the countryside near Amoy in China. The tiger declined to come out, so Grew went into the cave, whose passageway was sufficiently constricted that he had to drag his gun behind him. The only light came from long bamboo torches that Grew's companions had pushed into the cave. When Grew finally reached the tiger, the tunnel at that point was so narrow that the tiger, four feet away, could not charge and Grew had to fire from the hip. He missed, but the explosion blew out the torches, leaving both prey and hunter in the dark. Grew fired two shots in the pitch black and killed the tiger, which measured more than ten feet from nose to tip of tail.

Teddy Roosevelt, himself an enthusiastic big game hunter, listened to the story with interest, pulling out his notebook. "By Jove, I'll have to do something for that young man." The next day, newspapers announced the appointment of Joseph Grew as third secretary of the American Embassy in Mexico City. Twenty years later, Grew became chairman of the Board of Examiners of the Foreign Service. He relished telling the applicants: "You gentlemen have a very easy time entering the Service. All you have to do is to answer a few questions. I had to shoot a tiger."[5]

This president would not have needed much prodding to make tiger hunting a permanent qualification for consular or diplomatic appointment. He was America's first hyper-president, a protean personality with a walrus mustache, exploding with energy and intellect. Had camera shutter speed control not improved by the beginning of the twentieth century it is doubtful any photographs would have shown much more than a blurry image of the whirlwind president, gesticulating with his arms and shaking his head for emphasis while his pince-nez clung for dear life to the bridge of his nose.

Apart from a political career that culminated in the presidency at the age of forty-two, Theodore Roosevelt, the youngest man ever to hold the job, at one time or another, was a leader of the Rough Riders in the Spanish-American War, the president of the American Historical Association, a big game hunter in Africa, and a cattle rancher in the American West. His interests knew no geographic or intellectual boundaries, which made for some strange philosophical bedfellows. Tiger hunting qualified young Grew for a diplomatic appointment because America's future, in the vision of Roosevelt the Social Darwinist, depended on preserving "the iron qualities that must go with true manhood," now that the time was long gone when "the weakling died as the penalty of inability to hold his own in the rough warfare against his surroundings." But, with America emerging onto the world stage, Roosevelt the Progressive fully understood the need for a professional diplomatic corps.⁶

Between 1889 and 1895, Roosevelt had served on the National Civil Service Commission. Marshaling all his considerable combative energy (when Roosevelt died during the night in 1919, the vice president of the United States observed, "Death had to take him in his sleep. If Roosevelt had been awake, there would have been a fight."), he fought the institution of political patronage almost postmaster by postmaster, down even to the fourth-class appointments. He once wrote, "There is in American public life no one other cause so fruitful of harm to the body politic as the spoils system." By the time Theodore Roosevelt left the National Civil Service Commission, more than fifty thousand employees of the national government were under the protection of the Civil Service system, including the employees in the railway mails, free delivery post offices, the Indian schools, and the Internal Revenue Service. Even so, Roosevelt was frustrated by his inability to reform what he condemned as the "peculiarly gross manifestation of the spoils system which now obtains in the Consular Service, with its attendant discredit to the national honor abroad."⁷

That changed after Vice President Theodore Roosevelt became president following the assassination of President William McKinley in 1901. On November 10, 1905, Roosevelt issued an executive order that, among other reforms, required lower-ranking consular appointees either to possess a satisfactory record of prior service in the State Department or to perform satisfactorily on an examination. The next year, Roosevelt issued another executive order that further broadened these Civil Service–type reforms in the Consular Service. This proved so successful that, three years later, Roosevelt's successor issued an executive order doing much the same for the Diplomatic Service. (In 1924, the Diplomatic and Consular services were merged into the Foreign Service, albeit retaining their separate identities.)⁸

The man who gave the bride away at the wedding of the century created the foundations for a permanent, professional diplomatic and consular corps to serve the growing needs of a country now playing a larger role in world affairs than at any time in its history. The man who performed the wedding ceremony, Endicott Peabody, along with many of his fellow boarding school headmasters, issued a moral call to service that led young, wealthy East Coast Christians to fill the ranks of the new corps.

★ ★ ★

Groton was hardly the only private school in the United States by the end of the nineteenth century; in fact, if one counts parochial schools as private educational institutions, there may have been thousands. If such winnowing words as "Christian," "northeastern," "boarding," "aristocratic," and "wealthy" were applied to those thousands, however, only a dozen or so would have been left. These included, in addition to Groton, Phillips Exeter Academy, Choate School, Lawrenceville School, and St. Paul's School. One mid-twentieth-century historian of the American upper class, E. Digby Baltzell, maintained that these schools "serve[d] the sociological function of differentiating the upper classes in America from the rest of the population." To be sure, no one disputes that these were exclusive institutions. The average yearly tuition at Groton and St. Paul's in 1893 was $600, an amount greater than the annual wages of more than two-thirds of adult male workers in America. But the contrarian view of historian James McLachlan focuses less on the wealth and background of the students and their families and more on the middle-income headmasters who, he argues, "worked instead to *prevent* the development of aristocratic attitudes" and to foster classic middle-class values, especially that of public service. "How successful they have been in this," McLachlan added, "is another matter."[9]

Both Baltzell and McLachlan cite Groton as "Exhibit A" to support their views. Indeed, Groton was the emblematic private, New England, Christian, aristocratic boarding school. Founded in 1884, Groton was an American private school counterpart to Eton, the British boarding school which nineteen British prime ministers by now have attended. Groton's first brochure unhesitatingly stated that the school's purpose was to develop "manly, Christian character." Reverend Endicott Peabody, a founder and the headmaster for Groton's first fifty-six years, was the perfect embodiment of those virtues.

Peabody, known as the "Rector," had been educated in England at Cheltenham and at Trinity College, Cambridge, where he rowed and played cricket. Victorian to the marrow of his bones, striding purposefully across the Groton campus (shortly after the turn of the century it consisted of several main academic buildings and three football fields for 150 students in six forms), Peabody was tall, muscular, and intimidating. "Regarding his body as a temple," wrote the biographers of several prominent graduates of Groton and other elite private schools, "he always dressed in highly polished black shoes, blue suit, and white starched bow tie." As one thirteen-year-old Grotonian wrote to his parents, "You know he would be an awful bully if he wasn't such a terrible Christian." Endicott Peabody was America's last Puritan.[10]

The Rector was no academic, however. He taught in just two fields: Christian studies and football. At Groton, football was a metaphor for life, and a Groton education, like the game, was for men and men only. Even the faculty was entirely male (in an era when 70 percent of the teachers in American public schools were women). "The private schools," explained Peabody, "have the advantage of commanding the services of men teachers alone. There are indeed many women who are altogether efficient instructors—some certainly superior to the men, but it is the belief of many parents that their sons during the period of adolescence, beginning at twelve or thirteen and continuing until eighteen years of age, should be under the direction of the male mind and personality and they act accordingly."[11]

The parents were more than willing to subcontract their parental responsibilities to Peabody. Charles Francis Adams Jr., a prominent railroad executive whose grandfather and great-grandfather had been presidents of the United States, sent his sons to Groton. "I have been so much occupied of late years that I have been wholly unable to give that time and attention to my two boys which every boy ought to receive from his father," was how he explained his decision. By stepping into the void that the fathers, especially, had left in the lives of their sons, and filling it to overflow, Peabody had a lasting impact on his charges, whose daily lives he simply overwhelmed.[12]

As designed by Peabody, a boy's life at Groton at the dawn of the twentieth century, though certainly manly in the military sense, left little room for inner reflection. The students lived in six-by-nine-foot bare wooden cubicles. The only permitted decorations in the cubicles were family pictures. A loud, clanging bell woke students at 6:55 AM on weekdays and Saturday and half an hour later on Sundays. A cold shower was followed by breakfast and prayers and then psalm and hymn at chapel (attended twice on Sundays), all led by Peabody. The boys then assembled in the huge room of the Schoolhouse (with a desk for every boy in the school) where Peabody announced the day's academic schedule: "First Form—History. Second Form—Latin. . . ." Classes followed, interrupted by a break for calisthenics. Lunch was presided over by Peabody, who invoked the blessing. The afternoons were devoted to team sports (individual sports being disfavored,) with Peabody often participating. For dinner, the boys wore stiff white collars, dark suits, and patent leather pumps; Peabody joined them to ask the blessing before the meal.

According to a biography of Peabody, every night ended with the same ritual. As the boys filed out to go to their cubicles, each boy shook Peabody's gargantuan hand.

"Good night, sir."

"Good night, my boy."

They would always be the "boys." In 1934, President Franklin Roosevelt, then in his early fifties, visited the school for its fiftieth anniversary celebration. When he arrived, despite meticulous plans to address him as "Mr. President," Peabody's wife ran down the steps, kissing him and exclaiming: "Franklin, dear boy. I am *so* glad to see you."

It wasn't all hardship and discipline. The boys "did not have to make their beds or wait on tables, and their shoes were polished overnight by servants." Had Sparta been run by wealthy Episcopalians, this is what it might have looked like.[13]

The curriculum included Latin and Greek, ancient history, and European studies, with a special emphasis on England. One graduate recalled that the history faculty "made us learn all the names and dates of the French and English kings while neglecting to tell us that one hundred years before the Pilgrim fathers landed in Massachusetts, the Spaniards were in California."[14]

Grades were handed out weekly, and each month Peabody ranked the students according to performance. Parents lived in dread of receiving a bad report from Peabody on their son's performance, such as this one: "irresponsible, forgets books, doesn't remember lessons, makes excuses." Such reports were followed by a summons from Peabody—although in the case of this particular boy, Peabody may have regretted summoning the mother to Groton because she was the rare parent who was more than a match for the Rector.

"We have failed to make a Groton boy out of Dean," Peabody said in a simultaneous rebuke and confession.

"I want him educated, not made a Groton boy," retorted the mother.

"Oh, we can educate him," said Peabody confidently.

"Then," she said, "I suggest you do it."

The mother's wayward son, Dean Acheson, would graduate last in his class of twenty-four, chafing every minute under Peabody's rule, and then go on to be one of America's greatest secretaries of state.[15]

One difference from Eton was that the students were not whipped by their teachers. In spirit, however, Groton emulated Headmaster Dr. John Keate's warning to the Eton student body: "Boys, be pure in heart, for I'll flog you if you're not." (It was not an idle threat; one evening Keate flogged eighty boys.) When an alumnus suggested that chapel services need not be compulsory for the boys, Peabody rejected the idea. His sermons, not flogging, would make the boys spiritually pure of heart: "Create in me a clean heart, O! God, and renew a right spirit within me."[16]

Peabody saw in Groton an opportunity to train America's future leaders. Side by side with both Christian values and Groton's less than subtle theme of Anglo-Saxon superiority, Peabody preached to his young patricians the necessity of service. The school's motto was *Cui Servire Est Regnare*, "to serve Him is to rule," or, as loosely translated by Peabody, "whose service is perfect freedom." Service to God and service to country were the well-drilled themes of a Groton education. "If some Groton boys do not enter political life and do something for our land," Peabody declared, "it won't be because they have not been urged." Or, as President Theodore Roosevelt, a long-time friend of the Rector, bluntly told the school on its twentieth anniversary: "Much has been given you. Therefore, we have a right to expect much from you." He also urged "the boys not to take champagne or butlers with them on camping trips in the Adirondacks."[17]

Peabody had an uplifting message for his charges. Indeed, Franklin Roosevelt later cited Peabody as "the biggest influence on my life." Given the impact of that particular Groton graduate's public service, Peabody could be said to have succeeded in his ambition to shape America's leaders, perhaps even beyond his wildest dreams. Ironically, Peabody later recalled Roosevelt as "not brilliant" and athletically "rather too slight for success." Peabody didn't vote for Roosevelt in his first presidential race in 1932, and initially considered some of his New Deal policies "mistaken" and others of "doubtful value." Of course, many Groton graduates, especially those in businesses or industries then coming under the thumb of government regulation, expressed a great deal more than just disapproval; some were so apoplectic they could not even bring themselves to utter the name of the man who was a "traitor to his class."[18]

Other graduates, including Averell Harriman, a governor, cabinet secretary, and diplomat, and Acheson, also went on to inspiring careers in public service. But relatively few, Franklin Roosevelt being the most obvious exception, pursued political careers that required mixing with voters from varying ethnic backgrounds and appealing for their votes. Those who went into public service from Groton (and the other select boarding schools) invariably entered the upper-class branches of government, such as the Office of Strategic Services (and its later incarnation, the CIA) and the State Department; in effect, they looked for and joined the government institutions that most closely resembled Groton, or at least the ones that could most easily be molded into a close imitation. Overall, relatively few Grotonians pursued careers in the ministry; almost none became artists; and the largest career choice of Groton graduates up until World War II had been business, especially finance and the stock and bond markets.[19]

Peabody preached the duty of public service, especially service that promoted America's role in the world, even above the accumulation of wealth. But other than assuring that America would be led into the future by Christian gentlemen, exactly to what purpose should such public service be put? He never clearly answered that question, left it to his boys to decide for themselves, and only made modest attempts to expose them to the burning moral issues of the day. Peabody did express disapproval of the Ku Klux Klan and Hitler, but his consistently passionate moral interests were conventionally Christian: the virtues of temperance in the Prohibition era, helping the poor, and the sin of divorce at any time. Peabody organized the Groton School Camp for poor Boston boys, who were counseled by relays of Groton students. He once invited the black educator Booker T. Washington to speak, although it's not likely that either speaker or audience acknowledged the irony of the prominent representative of an oppressed racial minority speaking to a student body from which any minorities were rigidly excluded.

Peabody appeared never to have challenged his boys to think independently or creatively, to question their (or his) assumptions, or to appreciate that in some circumstances tradition and authority must be defied in the name of a higher morality. "I am not sure I like boys who think too much," he once said. "A lot of people think a lot of things we could do without. Manifestly the world is full of evil that we all encounter as we go along. Nobody denies that. But why emphasize it ahead of time?" Ultimately, the unconventional call to service was insufficient to overcome the privileged school's suffocating ethos of conformity to the tribe's self-image, which was offended by using dirty words, wearing a cap, or failing to make the requisite enthusiastic contribution to the regimented cheering at the football games (failing to attend the games was practically a capital offense).[20]

Repeated transgressions of that self-image were brutally punished, with Peabody's approval. First offenders were only "boot-boxed," a mild punishment in which the transgressor, typically a new boy, was forced by upper-form boys to "double up in the locker in which they kept their overshoes." But several times a year a more effective measure was employed to punish recidivist boys whose violations of the code were particularly unforgivable. The occasion resembled a cross between the Spanish Inquisition and *Lord of the Flies*. With the boys assembled in the School Room in the Hundred House (built before the Schoolhouse and so named because it was designed to accommodate one hundred boys), upper-form boys met in a study to discuss the offense and the offender. When a decision was reached, Peabody was informed, and he strode out with his Bible and prayer book.

A gong rang to keep the boys, including the offender, seated. Among others, a dozen of the larger boys, usually including several who played on the football team, left the room. The offender, typically a new boy who had not taken the code seriously enough, was called out. He rose from his seat and, with his fellow boys utterly silent, trudged out of the room like a condemned man. "If anyone took his eyes from the desk-lid, he did it covertly," remembered one boy years later.

Outside, the hapless boy was grabbed by the football players, lifted from the ground, and carried to the lavatory, where one boy sat with a stopwatch. The offender was hoisted over one of the black soapstone sinks, facing upward. He was then forced down under the faucet with his mouth held open. Recalled the same former student, "The water came from the open spigot with tremendous force and the stream could be concentrated in violence by thumb and forefinger." The offender was "forcibly drowned" for at least eight to ten seconds or until the boy holding the stopwatch called out. Then the offender was jerked to his feet, "coughing, choking and retching." Sometimes, he was put under again "if he hadn't had enough the first time."

Here was a strong deterrent against "bumptiousness and a powerful incentive to remain inconspicuous." The technique, a staple of the Spanish Inquisition and used in the early 1900s by American soldiers in fighting Philippine insurgents, was unquestionably a form of torture. The boys called it water pumping. Today, it goes by the name of water boarding.[21]

Sometimes boys were pumped simply because they were "fresh and swellheaded" (Teddy Roosevelt Jr.) or "cheeky" (Dean Acheson), even if they had not committed a specific breach of the unwritten code. "The Biddle boy is quite crazy, fresh and stupid," wrote young Franklin Roosevelt to his mother about one nonconformist. "He has been boot-boxed once and threatened to be pumped several times." The logic and necessity of tribal conformity meant that should water pumping sometimes be applied less than discriminatingly, so be it. But at least it was applied democratically. In one vivid illustration of the time-honored principle that "what goes around comes around," Peabody's own son, Malcolm, was pumped (for bad "tone"). "The Rector was splendid about it," wrote one observer. "He certainly could take it on the chin."[22]

The tactic instilled the unquestioning conventionalism and conformity that, when all was said and done, were the real hallmarks of a Groton education. "One could understand and accept rendering unto Caesar the things which were Caesar's, the control of one's external life," recalled Acheson of his unhappy experience at Groton. "The mind and spirit were not Caesar's; yet these were demanded too. And I, for one, found it necessary to erect defenses for the last citadel of spiritual freedom."

Then, as now, parents of boys on the brink always had a final, desperate card to play. One young mother, pleading with Peabody not to expel her son for failing to meet Groton standards, threw the card on the table. Her son, she beseeched the Rector, had merit because he was a "very unusual boy."

"Groton, madam," replied the Rector, "is no place for the unusual boy."

It might have been the school motto. Perhaps it was not a coincidence that Acheson (like Franklin Roosevelt) disliked Groton and achieved greatness. In fact, wrote one Roosevelt historian, "The boys who were the best 'Grotties' usually turned out to be non-entities later; boys who hated Groton did much better."[23]

But Peabody's philosophy contained a revealing contradiction that may well have done more to shape the outlook of his boys than his good works, such as inviting Booker T. Washington to the school. In a letter to an acquaintance in 1896, Peabody expressed frustration at the U.S. government's unwillingness to join England in "stopping the frightful massacres of the Armenians." But in the same paragraph, in expressing regret at tensions between the United States and England over this and other issues, he emphasized that "Believing as I do in Kidd's Theory that the Anglo-Saxon race should be the predominant one for the good of the world, I regret to see other nations trying to block her [England]."

Peabody's moral nearsightedness, however well-intentioned, made it impossible for him to see that a theory of world order based on racial hierarchies was more likely to cause rather than prevent ethnic massacres. He appears to have been equally insensitive to the impact on his students' self-perception (and their perception of non-Anglo-Saxons) of the message that Groton was designed to deliver from wake-up bell to lights out, and which his theory of Anglo-Saxon superiority only reinforced: We boys are the chosen, the select, the aristocrats by virtue of our breeding, our membership in the Anglo-Saxon race, and our very presence at this institution.

The cloister-like conditions at Groton that Peabody and the other headmasters thought would create the greatest opportunity to mold their charges for public service were actually at odds with Peabody's inspiring message. Peabody believed that the most thorough training was possible only if a boy was taken out of the home—away from parents with a "tendency to overindulge their children, to wish to make life easy for them, a natural result of which is that the children sometimes lack intellectual and moral and physical fibre"—and put into the hands of the "masters" morning, noon, and night. But his educational philosophy had another, barely hidden agenda: to create a wealthy Christian enclave, walled off from foreign immigrants. It was not by chance that Groton and many of the other leading boarding schools were located in bucolic country settings, far from metropolitan areas.

As America was emerging into the world, immigrants from many countries and backgrounds were flooding into American cities. Groton and the other schools formed an aristocratic archipelago for the self-regarded best and brightest, who were almost uniformly wealthy. "Ninety-five percent of these boys came from what they considered the aristocracy of America," wrote Grotonian George Biddle. "Their fathers belonged to the Somerset, the Knickerbocker, the Philadelphia or the Baltimore Clubs. Among them was a goodly slice of the wealth of the nation."[24]

The members of Somerset and Knickerbocker sat in their plush chairs in the card rooms, with servants, spittoons, and silver ice tongs always at the ready, and looked on with disgust and revulsion at the men in their bulky coats or matted sheepskins or white kilts; the women with long dresses and bonnets or handkerchiefs on their heads; and, worst of all, the babbling, dirty, foreign-tongued children in ragged pants and a sailor's shirt, or white blouses and blue caps.

Simply put, the wealthy class had no intention of exposing their sons to such rabble; Groton, St. Paul's, Phillips Andover, Phillips Exeter, Lawrenceville, and the others offered a sanctuary for wealthy men's sons from America itself. A 1903 survey of the top boarding schools politely concluded that they had been founded in part because of the parents' belief that "in certain localities the companions of the boy in all but the higher grades of day school are, from their nationality, objectionable personal habits, or what not, undesirable." The schools remained cloistered from American life for decades, both fearing and despising the lower classes—not least, the Jews. Fifty years after Groton's founding—partly because of the "rapid growth in the cities" as the founders explained in their mission statement—one student with an impeccable WASP family lineage was called "Rebecca for the Jewish appearance of his nose [and] kicked and shoved." But by then, America had passed them by.[25]

Peabody wrote of the school's mission circumspectly. "So long as people dwell in great cities where the atmosphere, physical and moral, is in large measure unwholesome, at least for young people, so long the boarding schools will continue to minister to the children of those who can afford to send them out of the towns."[26]

Theodore Roosevelt, whose sons attended Groton, was characteristically direct. "Two-thirds of our increase now comes from the immigrants and not from the babies born here, not from young Americans who are to perpetuate the blood and traditions of the old stock. If you do not believe in your own stock enough to wish to see the stock kept up, then you are not good Americans, you are not patriots."[27]

★ ★ ★

The aristocratic archipelago included not just the boarding schools but also the universities to whom the schools passed on their students, principally Harvard, Yale, and Princeton. From 1906 to 1932, of 405 Groton boys who applied to Harvard, only 3 were rejected.[28] Some found a way to expand their comfortable but narrow horizons. Acheson, after graduating from Groton in 1911, used family connections to find a summer job with a work crew of immigrants building the Grand Trunk Pacific Railway in northern Canada, which revived his "sense of freedom amidst uncoerced order." But he was one of the few who had resented the Rector's stifling hand. Most remained cloistered in the "national, inter-city metropolitan upper class" that had formed by the opening of the twentieth century.[29]

The State Department beckoned these graduates the way the Knickerbocker and the other clubs had lured their fathers. Educated in European history, fluent in foreign languages, especially French and German, and accustomed to foreign travel, many heeded the call to service by seeking a career in diplomacy just as an American empire was taking shape. Endicott Peabody and the other headmasters were not all-out imperialists, but they certainly believed that, if there was to be an American empire, it was of the utmost importance that Christian aristocrats run it. One historian of the State Department has written of these eager, well-educated, service-inspired young men: "Rejecting both the mundaneness of business and the crudities of the working class, these young Harvard graduates sought an overseas calling. Grander in aspiration than their parents, they entered diplomacy in high excitement." And, of course, these graduates found the perfect substitute for the Knickerbocker and Somerset clubs of their fathers in the gray granite, mansard-roofed building next to the White House.[30]

The World War II generation of diplomats, such as tiger hunter Joseph Grew, generally began service as secretaries in embassies or legations. As their careers took off, they gathered around them Groton and other boarding school graduates. For example, Grew became first secretary in the Berlin embassy in 1914 and chose a staff laden with fellow Groton-Harvard alumni. He was able to do so because of support from William Phillips, the third assistant secretary of state in Washington who had traveled the Groton-Harvard route two years ahead of him. As one historian of American boarding schools noted, "Groton alumni would be playing a significant role in shaping American foreign policy well into the second half of the twentieth century."[31]

During the four decades preceding the Riegner telegram, hundreds of graduates of the fashionable boarding schools and universities became Foreign Service officers. In fact, even by 1942, just six universities (and a few European universities) furnished "roughly half the candidates who [won] their way into the Foreign Service and the policy-making offices of the State Department." These were Harvard, Yale, Princeton, the United States Naval Academy, the United States Military Academy, and a newcomer begun only in 1919, the Georgetown School of Foreign Service. Indeed, three-fourths of the embassy secretaries recruited between 1914 and 1922 to serve in Europe had attended prep schools, "particularly at St. Paul's and Groton."[32]

The young American diplomats relished their overseas postings and life among the international aristocracy. From pigeon shooting in Egypt to court functions in Berlin to dining at the Club des Chasseurs in Warsaw, diplomatic life offered exotic experience along with accustomed comforts and comradeship. Joseph Grew's biographer wrote:

> *Service spirit bound the secretaries together. In a sense they knew each other before they ever met. The career only deepened and circumscribed existing ties. They possessed a common background, common experience, and a common liking for old wines, proper English, and Savile Row clothing. Indeed, the Diplomatic Service most nearly resembled a club.*[33]

The "club" was closely modeled on those to which their fathers had belonged, especially the admittance criteria. "Style, grace, poise, and above all, birth were the key to the success." While there was an entrance examination for the Foreign Service, the only important question was the one never asked out loud: "Is he one of us?" In 1941, only 18 percent of applicants did well enough on the written examination to qualify for the oral part. But the crucial hurdle *was* the oral examination, of which less than half of those 18 percent passed. Its principal purpose was to permit "whatever personal prejudices the examiners may have to operate without the possibility of appeal." The oral examination began with biographical questions, which was not only a logical way to proceed but also immediately revealed the applicant's social background. The personal prejudices were unmistakable: "If a black slipped through the net, he was sent to Liberia until he resigned. Women were sent to the jungles of South America. Jews could not be handled as crassly, but they were made to feel unwelcome and shut out of the better assignments."[34]

Getting dismissed from the Foreign Service was even harder than getting in. Dismissal of one of its officers first required an unsatisfactory efficiency rating, which had to be confirmed by the secretary of state. At that point, the officer received notice of the rating but remained in the service on a form of probation. If he received further unsatisfactory ratings, he was entitled to a hearing before dismissal. By the 1940s, this procedure had been invoked just once. As one State Department official phrased it, "Even if you should turn out to be a radical your job is safe, although your fellow-clubmen will probably give you a wide berth and treat you as something of a freak."[35]

Despite a disproportionate representation in the Foreign Service and senior policy-level positions, graduates of Groton and the other boarding schools were nowhere near a majority, or even a sizable minority, of the overall State Department personnel at the time the Riegner telegram was received in Washington. For example, at that time, fifteen Foreign Service officers were assigned to the Division of European Affairs, where the decision was made to withhold from American Jews Riegner's report on the Nazi extermination plan. Of these, four were from East Coast boarding schools (one Groton, two St. Paul's, and one Lawrenceville).[36]

But these archipelago graduates were leavening agents in the manner that yeast ferments dough; they had a wholly disproportionate impact on the State Department's culture. The majority of department personnel did not come up through Groton and Harvard, or similar institutions, but many wished they had, and attempted to compensate for their handicap through imitation. As journalist I.F. Stone, a ferocious but incisive left-wing critic of the World War II State Department, told an interviewer: "If you look through the foreign service register, you will see that a majority of the FSOs [Foreign Service officers] do not come from east coast prep schools. But the guys from the Midwest schools soon come to conform to the east coast preppy patterns."[37]

While the boarding school graduates found that dinner parties and European court rituals were second nature to them, nothing in their background or education had prepared them for encounters with the European masses; indeed, that was the whole point of secluding them in the archipelago. Here, the Grotonians and their imitators successfully emulated their British counterparts. George Orwell, writing of middle- and upper-class Brits' disdain for the lower classes, noted the "four frightful words which people nowadays are chary of uttering but which were bandied about quite freely in my childhood. The words were: '*The lower classes smell.*'"[38] The young American diplomats agreed. Grotonian Joseph Grew, then the minister to Denmark, had to cut short trips to the beach in Denmark in 1921 because of the "dirty, smelly crowd of all the rabble of Copenhagen." Jay Pierrepont Moffat, another Groton graduate who would later head the Division of European Affairs until 1940, was stationed in Warsaw after the end of World War I when fighting broke out between Poland and the Soviet Union. As Soviet armies neared Warsaw, Moffat went to the train station to bid farewell to departing diplomats. He described the scene at the station to a fellow diplomat with these words:

On the next track stood a refugee train, and into this poured a swelter of humanity. They sounded like so many cackling geese. They stormed the compartments, climbed over the roof, struck each other, and generally behaved in a manner that made us pray like the pharisee, 'Lord, I thank Thee that I am not as other men.'[39]

And, of course, there was pervasive anti-Semitism at the State Department—contrary to the claim of leading Holocaust historian David Wyman in *The Abandonment of the Jews* (a work that has shaped the perception of the American response to the Holocaust for more than two decades) that "direct proof of anti-Semitism in the department is limited" and that he could find only "two documented examples," both involving mid-level officials. Anti-Semitism went hand in hand with revulsion for the lower class and, by the end of World War I, for Bolshevism.

The "regent and guiding spirit" of the Georgetown School of Foreign Service was Father Edmund A. Walsh (the school today is known as the Edmund A. Walsh School of Foreign Service at Georgetown). In a 1938 article for the *Atlantic Monthly* reflecting on the Russian Revolution, he wrote: "The Jew was not the cause of the Russian Revolution, but the *entrepreneur* who recognized his main chance and seized it shrewdly and successfully." He also pointed out in the same article that Christians could not be blamed for stigmatizing Jews as "the Old Moneybags of Society" because even while Christianity was a "political minority too weak and insignificant to persecute anybody," the Jewish "moneylender was steadily increasing his control of mobile capital and accumulating the resentment which occasioned much of the anti-Semitism of later ages."[40]

Joseph Grew met with Soviet diplomats at the Lausanne Conference in 1922–23. Grew wrote that Soviet Commissar of Foreign Affairs Georgy V. Chicherin looked like a "Bolshevik bird of prey, with malignant eyes and a beak nose." It did not matter to Grew that Chicherin came from a Russian family sufficiently aristocratic to qualify him for admission to Groton (had Groton been inclined to admit Russian aristocrats).[41]

Moffat, who would later marry Grew's daughter, wrote a friend after meeting the Soviet delegate to the League of Nations: "Then Litvinoff, with the malevolent look of an untidy Jew, rose to speak." And, after watching a Communist May Day parade in Warsaw, Moffat wrote in a letter: "You would have thought from seeing the streets that it was a Jewish holiday. The main focus of infection was in the square just in front of the legation." Hugh Gibson, later an American ambassador to Brazil and Belgium in the 1930s and three times on the cover of *Time* magazine, wrote to a friend while serving as a young diplomat in Warsaw, "On Christmas night, Mike found an orchestra of yids who were about the most disreputable specimens you ever saw."[42]

The diary of William Phillips (twice an undersecretary of state) contains derogatory references to Jews, such as the observation that Atlantic City was "infested with Jews" and that on weekends "slightly clothed Jews and Jewesses" were at the beach. The diary of Wilbur Carr, later to become an assistant secretary of state during Franklin Roosevelt's first term, characterized 1924 Detroit as filled with "dust, smoke, dirt, Jews." Loy Henderson, who worked on Eastern European and Soviet issues from the 1920s to the 1940s (and who later served as ambassador to India and then to Iran), in one cable to his superiors blamed "international Jewry" for being an "important supporter" of the Soviet Union and, following a visit to New York City, said of the people jostling him in the streets and restaurants that they "seemed to have little in common with me."

In a letter to a colleague in the State Department, William C. Bullitt, an ambassador to the Soviet Union and later to France, despite having Jewish ancestors, described an official in the Soviet Foreign Ministry (later the official became the Soviet ambassador to the United States) as "a wretched little kike. It is perhaps only natural that we should find the members of that race more difficult to deal with than the Russians themselves." And, after reading Hitler's ravings in *Mein Kampf*, Assistant Secretary of State Breckinridge Long, later to play a decisive role in erecting visa barriers to Jews fleeing the Nazis, wrote in his diary in 1938 that the book was "eloquent in opposition to Jewry and to Jews as exponents of Communism and chaos."[43]

The upper-class echelon in the State Department also had distinct leanings toward totalitarian governments. Princeton graduate Long initially praised Mussolini and his fascist government while serving as ambassador to Italy in the early 1930s.[44] The officials of the Division of European Affairs had been openly sympathetic to Spain's future dictator Franco during the Spanish Civil War and, even after the attack on Pearl Harbor and Germany's declaration of war against the United States, likewise sympathetic to the Vichy government that collaborated with the Nazis after the fall of France. One apocryphal story was that, following Pearl Harbor, FDR joked that "his State Department was neutral in this war and he hoped it would at least remain that way."[45]

But they were not fascists themselves so much as upper-class sympathizers. In 1943, Pulitzer Prize–winning foreign correspondent Edgar Ansel Mowrer, the first American journalist to be expelled from Germany by the Nazis, noted the large number of American diplomats and State Department officials who belonged to "what is called Society with a capital S all over the world." It was "natural for them to trust their own kind abroad. In any controversy involving, let us say, on the one side, labor agitators and workmen, unwashed peasants, suspicious intellectuals, New Dealers, and on the other side, diplomats, dukes, bankers, bishops, wealthy and pretty hostesses, our salonnards just naturally gravitate to the latter."[46]

Indoctrinated in their class's inherent superiority, intimidated (and brutalized, if necessary) into a "don't rock the boat" conformist's mentality, imbued with the notion that America needed them more than they needed America, and walled off from almost every ethnic, cultural, or religious group different from their own, the archipelago graduates, especially those who went into the mid-level ranks of the State Department, had emerged from their educational years with attitudes that far transcended the anti-Semitic norms of the era. They had a heartless indifference to the suffering of anyone without similar background and breeding, especially the dirty, smelly, cackling geese with their beaked noses. It was as though whatever nerves transmitted normal human compassion had been amputated.

But in many respects, it was the Grotty wannabes, eager to flatter their aristocratic colleagues through exaggerated imitation, who exhibited the most striking inability to empathize. The efforts to rescue the Jews of Romania had begun even before the United States entered the war. In 1941, the American minister in Romania reported to the State Department that his Turkish counterpart was promoting discussions among the Turkish, British, and French governments of a plan to evacuate 300,000 Jews from Romania to Syria or Palestine "for temporary cantonment, pending a radical solution of the Jewish problem." The Turkish minister requested American support for the evacuation plan.

The American minister's report landed on the desk of one Cavendish W. Cannon, a Foreign Service officer in his mid-forties then in the State Department's Division of European Affairs. Cannon was not a product of the East Coast boarding schools; in fact, he was a graduate of Salt Lake City High School and the University of Utah.

After reviewing the proposed evacuation plan Cannon wrote a memorandum to his superiors that identified certain "considerations" regarding the proposed evacuation of Jews: not enough shipping; the project would "at once reopen the Arab question"; the plan was likely to bring about new pressure for "an asylum in the western hemisphere"; and in view of the lack of progress on Jewish issues, the "cantonment" was likely to be less temporary and more permanent. Not one item on his list reflected humanitarian concerns.

One consideration mentioned by Cannon does deserve special mention, however. "By removing from Romania the remaining Jews," he wrote to his superiors in all apparent seriousness, "[the plan] in a backhand fashion would demonstrate that the brutal policy of the Romanian authorities had been effective and realistic."[47]

In other words, the Romanian government must not be rewarded with an international effort to evacuate the Romanian Jews it was trying to murder—better to let them die than concede a debating point to the Romanian government. What seemed to have eluded Cavendish Cannon was that the rescue effort was vital precisely because the Romanian government's Jewish policy *had* been brutally effective, that the Romanian government hardly needed a reminder of the effectiveness of its own policy, and, absent rescue, the Romanian Jews, especially those in Transnistria, *were* going to die.

V

THE MAGICAL VILLAGE OF MILIE

The train stopped in a field to let the Jews out. Sheer relief overcame inhibition or even embarrassment. After two days in the cattle cars, the Jews understood that privacy is a luxury unavailable at any price. The Jews gratefully gulped in fresh air while they relieved themselves, until the Romanian soldiers, who cursed the Jews as naturally as they breathed, ordered them back into the train.

Two days later the train stopped again. Soldiers unbolted doors, shouting, "Out, out, you dirty kikes." Jews, including Ruth Glasberg and her family, tumbled out of half of the cars and began to march toward the Dniester River. These cars were uncoupled from the train, which rumbled away into the night. From time to time on that train trip, bodies were tossed from the remaining cars: the elderly and the babies who had died en route.

It rained heavily on the marching column, which had to wade through ankle-deep mud. The rain saturated the Jews' clothes and bundles, making walking even more difficult. Suddenly, marchers at the front of the column cried out, but Ruth could not see what was happening. Later she learned that the lead marchers had come upon a ditch filled with bodies—more than a thousand Jews of all ages, men, women, and children—stacked one atop another.[1]

Children have powers of imagination denied to adults. Throughout the marching columns, boys and girls took refuge in fantasies, and Ruth was no exception.

A favorite sanctuary for her was her grandfather's farm in the magical village of Milie, which she and her family visited in the summers. As she marched along, she retreated there. The farm, which bordered the Teplitza Creek, came right from a child's storybook, with a field of colorful cornflowers, poppies, and daisies; pens of baby chicks; and a cow named Ruzena, who grazed peacefully with her calf in a verdant pasture. Each summer, a Roma caravan of canvas-covered wagons arrived to horse-trade, sell wares, and read palms. The Roma set up a camp by pitching tents in the village's main meadow. Ruth watched the colorfully dressed women as they carried their babies in giant slings fashioned from shawls, which left their hands free for chores. Sometimes, the Roma women would read her palm in return for a small amount of money. If the Roma palm readers saw the future in Ruth's palm, they never told the little girl.[2]

But under the harsh conditions of Ruth's reality, her imagination could bear up for only a limited period. Ruth returned from the fantasy of Milie to the marching column. Before reaching the Dniester, the column camped in a forest. The Jews' cries of "Water! Water! Water!" were ignored by the Romanian soldiers while they watered their horses. Some Jews used sheets and coats to fashion makeshift tents that, for a fleeting moment, reminded Ruth of a Roma encampment. She and her family huddled under the sweeping branches of a giant tree. Shots and screams punctuated the night. The next day, the column crossed the Dniester over a rickety wooden bridge into Transnistria. This stream of humanity, unlike Uncle Moishe's and others, did not merge with the river.

The winter that year was the coldest in a long while. By some accounts, the temperature plunged as low as 40 degrees below zero Fahrenheit. In Transnistria, along each side of the road, were strange objects that appeared to be felled, snow-covered tree trunks. Beyond, a landscape of snow-covered sugar beet fields stretched to the horizon. The fields were the result of the Soviet Union's collective farming, which promoted single-crop agriculture. The famished Jews, caring nothing about Communist agricultural theory, scraped the snow away to feast on the beets.[3]

But as Ruth neared what she thought were tree trunks, they turned into bloated human bodies, the corpses of those who had not kept up. That night, Ruth and her family shared a barn with other live Jews and many dead ones. After a few days' pause, the march resumed. Eighteen miles each day, sustained only by the raw sugar beets (which soon became the source of stomachaches and diarrhea), Ruth traveled a road lined on both sides by the dead.[4]

The Jews were infected with typhus by blood-sucking lice. Because of the lice, her mother cut Ruth's blonde, curly hair; a barber shaved her head to the scalp. Freedom from her hated braids made her happy for a time, but upon seeing how the other girls looked with bald heads, Ruth covered hers with a woolen hat.

She no longer even looked like a girl. Without her hair and half starved, she looked like a skeleton-boy.[5]

VI

THE CROQUET PLAYER AND THE THIRD FLOOR

On a typical weekday afternoon in 1940, Americans—at least those who had jobs—were at work in factories, farms, or offices. But several times each week in the nation's capital, a small group of aristocratic-looking men gathered at Woodley, the former summer home to four presidents, to play croquet in the afternoon. The large Southern Colonial house set on a hilltop had a breathtaking view of Washington, D.C.

An observer might have mistaken the croquet players for retired men of leisure, secure in their fortunes and social status, pursuing a centuries-old sport. In fact, they were some of the most powerful men in government: The owner of Woodley was the newly appointed secretary of war, Henry L. Stimson. Even though their responsibilities by 1940 included nothing less than dire threats to the United States from both Japan and Europe, they still found time for afternoon croquet. Croquet was especially fitting for senior government officials in Washington since, unlike golf, the game allows one player to attain a good position by knocking another player's ball into a bad one.[1]

One elderly player, a courtly white-haired man with a Southern accent, had a strange habit of muttering whenever he struck a ball with his mallet. One unverified account suggested that he was speaking the names of the foreign dictators then giving the United States the most difficulty and that the names changed as events progressed. Mussolini. Thwack! Hitler. Thwack! Konoe (and later Tojo). Thwack! It was just as possible, however, that the Southerner was muttering the name of a certain State Department official whom he would much rather have struck with his mallet than the dictators. And that name never changed.²

The muttering white-haired croquet player was Secretary of State Cordell Hull. At the time the Riegner telegram was sent, Hull was seventy-one years old. His birthplace was spiritually and physically as far from the homes of the intercity metropolitan upper class as was possible in America, and even though Cordell Hull ascended the heights of government, he never completely left his ancestral home.

He had been born in a log farmhouse in Tennessee's Pickett County, which straddled rich bottomland and poverty-ridden mountains, six years after the Civil War ended. In the lawless closing days of the war, a band of supposed Yankee guerrillas (loyalties by then were questionable), instigated by one Jim Stepp, shot Cordell Hull's father, known as "Uncle Billy," in the head. Uncle Billy Hull survived, although with one less eye. In the best tradition of the Tennessee mountains, he plotted his revenge. Uncle Billy patiently tracked his target, finally catching up with him in a town in Kentucky.

"Do you know me?" Uncle Billy asked Stepp.

"I believe not."

"Look me over now and see if there is anything you recognize," Uncle Billy said, pulling away the bandage over his empty eye socket. "I have come to do to you just what you tried to have done to me."

Uncle Billy then emptied his gun into Stepp, killing him instantly, and went home to Tennessee to greetings of approval. "He felt, and apparently the community at large agreed with him, that Stepp deserved to be killed and that [Uncle Billy] was the logical executioner," explained Cordell Hull's biographer.³

The young Cordell Hull, who would later display the same patience in seeking vengeance on his own enemies, attended Montvale Academy in Celina, the county seat; spent a year at the National Normal University in Ohio; and completed a one-year law course at Cumberland University back in Tennessee. He became a judge, was elected a U.S. congressman, and in

1930 was elected a U.S. senator. By the time of Franklin Roosevelt's election in 1932, Hull was an immensely popular and reassuring national figure, which was a principal reason the president elect offered him the premier cabinet post.

Hull reminded Americans struggling in a turbulent world of the bygone days of the seemingly more placid nineteenth century. One biographer wrote of Hull that he "was strongly religious, and regularly attended church services with his wife. He possessed a rigid sense of morality, was a devoted husband, preferred old friends to suave dilettantes, and had an abiding distaste for social engagements." Indeed, the tall, chivalrous Hull looked every inch the aristocratic statesman in the mold of a Daniel Webster or a Henry Clay, except for a sad face and a speech impediment like that of the *Looney Tunes* character Elmer Fudd, who started appearing in movie cartoons in the late 1930s. Hull's one great, burning policy concern, the elimination of tariffs as a means of economic disarmament, was enunciated in a slow drawl as "wecipwocal twade agweement pwogwam to weduce tawiffs."[4]

But a reassuring appearance and a firm view on free trade was about all that Hull brought to the position of secretary of state. He was an insecure man in poor health, with no diplomatic background and without management skills, who was also brooding and suspicious by nature and indecisive to the point of paralysis. Even Assistant Secretary of State Breckinridge Long, a wartime Hull loyalist, described him as a "sweet person and a fine character, but he lacks decision and executive ability and he lacks a great deal of knowledge of European politics and affairs." At the time of his appointment, Hull had never even set foot in the State Department, a fact not known to his adoring public. He had also hidden the fact that he suffered both from diabetes and tuberculosis, the latter then a highly stigmatized disease.

After he became secretary of state, Hull's health caused him to be repeatedly absent from the State Department in the middle of a world war. In a history-shaking year, from the 1941 German invasion of the Soviet Union to weeks before the 1942 Battle of Midway in the Pacific, Hull was absent from the State Department for nearly four months.

August 1, 1941: Hull is not yet returned. He was exhausted and has been away nearly two months.

April 20, 1942: Hull back from his long rest—away about two months.[5]

Hull's insecurity was aggravated by his being surrounded by men from far more impeccable lineages and elite educational institutions than were Uncle Billy and National Normal University. By the time the United States entered the war, a Groton-Harvard graduate was in the White House; another was undersecretary of state (Sumner Welles), and a third was assistant secretary of state for economic affairs (Dean Acheson). The other assistant secretaries, though not Groton graduates, all nonetheless had Ivy League backgrounds, wealth, and social status and connections.

An important figure in this narrative, Breckinridge Long, assistant secretary of state for legislation, visa issues, and special war problems, among others, was descended from the prominent Long family of North Carolina and the Breckinridge family of Kentucky. He had graduated from Princeton University and married the wealthy granddaughter of Francis Preston Blair Jr., a Union officer from Missouri and later a vice presidential candidate. Likewise, Adolf A. Berle, whose responsibilities included Latin America, finance, and aviation, by age twenty-one graduated from Harvard University *and* Harvard Law School and then married into a wealthy New York family listed in the Social Register. Gardiner Howland Shaw, responsible for administration and the Foreign Service, was independently wealthy and "equipped with the standard Boston-Harvard background."[6]

The offices of the secretary of state and the assistant secretaries were on the second floor of the State Department building. Although they worked on the same floor, these wealthy, well-educated officials and Secretary of State Cordell Hull were like aliens to one another. When Hull was present in the State Department, these officials (most chosen for their posts, not by Hull, but by the White House) entered his office with not a small touch of envy, pity, disdain, or condescension, depending on the official, except Undersecretary Sumner Welles, who likely had all of those attitudes. Hull's office was suitably sized and fitted for his position: a large fireplace, a giant mahogany desk, a telephone connected directly to the White House, and the best view in the building—across the Mall to the Washington Monument. But the office was always too warm for anyone but its occupant. Even in the winter (the fireplace supplemented the heating system), the office temperature was never less than 80 degrees, which left one assistant secretary "half-fainting" and feeling "detached" from his body by the time a meeting had ended.[7]

Hull's absences and lack of managerial ability meant that the far more decisive and experienced Welles effectively ran the State Department, which likely is what Roosevelt had in mind when he appointed Welles to the post of undersecretary of state in 1937. If it was a Rooseveltian maneuver to keep control of a government department by putting bitter rivals in charge, it backfired badly.

Roosevelt privately derided Hull, for example, in 1937 telling the future Assistant Secretary of State Berle that Hull was "magnificent in principle but timid." Even when Hull was in Washington, Roosevelt frequently met alone with Welles, the ultimate slap in the face. Before the war, Berle noted in his diary: "There is some strain between Hull and Welles. The real difficulty is that Welles goes frequently to the White House and is considered a thoroughly capable man. Hull tends to be silent, cautious and quiet."[8]

The strain Berle alluded to dated to at least 1936, when Hull and Welles, then only an assistant secretary, clashed over a diplomatic conference in Buenos Aires, which Welles had persuaded Roosevelt to convene despite Hull's objections. At the conference, Welles took the lead away from Hull, in part because of his knowledge of Latin America and fluency in Spanish. As the U.S. delegation sailed for home, one American saw Hull staring at Welles. "He looked at him with hatred in his eyes," she recalled. "I've never seen such loathing." If there was any name that Cordell Hull muttered as he smashed croquet balls around the Woodley lawns, it had to be that of Sumner Welles.[9]

That loathing festered for years and consumed Hull. In 1940, across the ocean, as the German army launched the Blitzkrieg against the Low Countries and France, the centuries-old borders of Europe began to melt and re-form into a shape posing an incalculable threat to the United States. One assistant secretary wrote of the challenge facing the State Department: "It takes a cool mind and a solid foundation to project the present happenings against the pattern of past developments. Not only is our immediate future involved but the long-range trend of our political existence depends upon the policies evolved out of the muddled scheme of affairs today."[10]

But in his oversized and overheated office, on the day of the Blitzkrieg, with the world in free fall, the secretary of state dwelt on more mundane, but intensely personal matters, brooding over subordinates with less-than-complete loyalty to him. Hull immersed himself in bouts of alternating self-pity and anger, never naming Welles but leaving no doubt as to the principal object of his disaffection. "From the very inception of my incumbency I have been saddled first with one and then with another person who tried to give the impression that I am an insignificant figure and that all the important phases of the Department were attended to by the persons who were foisted upon me."[11]

Hull's jealousy and hatred knew no boundaries, nor would his quest for revenge. The entry of the United States into the war only increased the friction. In the middle of 1942, Welles gave a series of visionary speeches on postwar American policy. Shortly after, Assistant Secretary of State Berle confided to his diary: "Things are going badly in the Department. The Secretary and Sumner are farther apart than ever—in this case I am afraid it is so definitely Sumner's fault as not to be arguable. Briefly, he committed the fatal mistake of speaking as though he were the Secretary of State when there is an alive and very active Secretary of State in the immediate vicinity. This bodes no good for anybody concerned." Six months later Berle wrote: "The antagonism between Secretary Hull and Mr. Welles makes a good deal of difficulty: the Secretary resents Sumner's going to the White House too much. . . ."[12]

Welles had brilliance, dash, and powerful backers—the president and the first lady. So, like Uncle Billy, Cordell Hull brooded and bided his time until he could do to Welles what he felt Welles had done to him. As recalled by Dean Acheson: "His brooding led, in accordance with Tennessee-mountain tradition, to feuds. His hatreds were implacable—not hot hatreds, but long cold ones. In no hurry to 'get' his enemy, 'get' him he usually did."[13]

In light of the need for a forceful response by the United States to the Nazi persecution of the Jews, Hull had another problem. His wife, the former Rosetta "Rose" Frances Witz Whitney, was the Virginia-born daughter of a Christian mother and a Jewish father, a banker and industrialist who had served in the Confederate Army. Rose, tall and brunette, had been raised as an Episcopalian. The couple had no honeymoon or children. After Cordell Hull's election to the House of Representatives, they lived comfortably, but not lavishly, in an apartment at the Carlton Hotel near the White House. Frances Hull devoted her life to advancing her husband's career, even working in his campaign headquarters.[14]

But in those days, having a wife of Jewish ancestry was a liability for a Tennessee politician with national ambitions. American anti-Semitism peaked in the Roosevelt era; by 1940, more than a hundred anti-Semitic organizations existed in the United States. As Roosevelt's Secretary of the Interior Harold Ickes noted of Hull's presidential aspirations, "Mrs. Hull is Jewish, which is not a political asset, even in free America, at this time." One historian of the Hull-Welles rivalry observed that "In his entire public life, Hull never commented on his wife's religious heritage." A hero-worshipping biography of Hull, written in 1942 by an "intimate" acquaintance, Harold B. Hinton, a longtime member of the editorial staff of the *New York Times*, despite devoting many pages to Hull's wife, never mentioned her Jewish ancestry. In the State Department, Hull generally shunned Jewish issues such as the plight of refugees from Nazi Germany. One Holocaust historian wrote, "It is striking that almost nothing about [Jewish] refugees appears in the voluminous Hull files in the Library of Congress."[15]

Involuntarily and with slow-burning resentment, Hull had surrendered much of the second floor's daily work to Welles. Voluntarily, if not with a feeling of relief, Hull left it to Welles, Assistant Secretary Long, and the geographic divisions on the third floor to fight over Jewish rescue policy. The lives of an intolerable number of human beings would depend on the outcome of a bureaucratic battle shaped by ambition, jealousy, and prejudice.

★ ★ ★

On that third floor, symbolically above the offices of the feuding secretary of state and his undersecretary, were the offices of the graduates of the exclusive private schools and universities and the Grotty imitators. After starting their careers as junior Foreign Service officers and ascending the ranks in the embassies or legations, they were now back in Washington either running the geographic divisions or highly placed within them, with their eyes on the ultimate prize of an ambassadorial or a ministerial appointment. The dysfunctional second floor had rank and prestige, but power—especially control of the diplomatic cables—lay on the third floor, which was the home of the traditional four geographic divisions—European, Latin American, Near Eastern, and Far Eastern.

The Division of European Affairs, the crown jewel of the geographic divisions, was run by skilled bureaucrats, government operators who had graduated from the Washington school of survival. Unlike the political appointees on the second floor, these bureaucrats were lifetime members in Washington's permanent, nearly invisible government. Presidents and secretaries of state came and went, but they endured, operating stealthily in the shadows and leaving very few footprints. Hull, Welles, and the important assistant secretaries (Long, Acheson, Berle) wrote memoirs or kept diaries. Very few of the bureaucrats left any account of their handiwork to history; when they did, they barely dwelt on their role in America's response to the Holocaust. Indeed, they rarely mentioned the oppression and murder of the Jews at all other than to complain that Hitler's policy toward the Jews was complicating foreign policy by arousing American public opinion.[16]

As one State Department chronicler said of them: "Everything is done by indirection. They always yield and fall back without conceding anything. Like all good bureaucrats they are masters of the negative, the gentle objection, the postponement, the misplaced paper, the need for further consideration."[17] In his memoir, former Secretary of State Dean Acheson ruefully recalled the third floor's bureaucratic infighting when he served as an assistant secretary: "The heads of all these divisions, like barons in a feudal system weakened at the top by mutual suspicion and jealousy between king and prince, were constantly at odds, if not war. Obscurity in lines of command of the assistant secretaries permitted the division chiefs to circumvent them at will and go directly to the Secretary or the Under Secretary."[18]

At the outbreak of World War II, Jay Pierrepont Moffat headed the Division of European Affairs. In June 1940, he became minister to Canada, and Ray Atherton succeeded him as acting division chief. Although not a Groton graduate himself, Atherton was nonetheless the "standard Boston-Harvard career man," according to one State Department historian.[19]

Atherton became a near-caricature of what the Reverend Endicott Peabody had tried to achieve when he modeled Groton after Eton. In the late 1920s to mid-1930s, Atherton served as counselor of the American Embassy in London, where he all but went native. Aside from a brief marriage to a woman who, at one point, was the mistress of British novelist H.G. Wells, his most notable achievement was to prompt a complaint by the king of England about Atherton's ludicrous English dress and airs. While Atherton's attire apparently was not described by the king, it might have resembled that of one Foreign Service officer from Atherton's generation: "Bond Street topper, cutaway, tailored in Savile Row, cream-colored gloves, and Malacca stick." The king told an American diplomat that he preferred to see "America represented in London by Americans, not imitation Englishmen."[20]

The diplomat relayed the king's complaint to Roosevelt, who was more than happy to comply. Atherton, who was anti–New Deal, later openly complained to journalists that the country had gone flabby because of its "ten years on the dole." Roosevelt instructed an assistant secretary of state to transfer Atherton out of London, making Atherton the only American diplomat ever removed from his post for "excessive foppery."[21]

Atherton was transferred, but, as he was a member of the club, the other members looked out for him. He actually was promoted to minister to Bulgaria, where he served before returning to Washington to succeed Moffat. Atherton was firmly ensconced on the third floor, in the most powerful career post the State Department had to offer, when the Riegner telegram first made its appearance.[22]

★ ★ ★

The remorseless principles of bureaucratic hydraulics triggered by Hull's inability to control his own department were nowhere better illustrated than in the Marcel Peyrouton affair. Following the Allied invasion of North Africa in November 1942, Hull requested the transfer of Paul Appleby, the undersecretary of agriculture, to the State Department. A Protestant minister's son from the Midwest, Appleby was one of the hordes of idealistic young men who had descended on Washington in the New Deal years. Distinguished by their admiration for Roosevelt and convinced that they could change the world, which in many respects they did, the young New Dealers came from "state agricultural colleges and university campuses, from law faculties and social work schools." After observing the Agriculture Department almost bursting with the enthusiasm and energy of New Dealers like Appleby, novelist Sherwood Anderson wrote: "There is certainly a curiously exhilarating feeling. You cannot be there now without a feeling of the entire sincerity of many of these men." In other words, these young New Dealers were evangelicals, long on earnestness but somewhat naive about how the world really worked.[23]

As an Agriculture Department official, Appleby had been poised to assume responsibilities in the Lend-Lease program that had supplied vast quantities of war supplies, including food, to American allies. Secretary of State Hull recruited Appleby to instead take a leave of absence from the Agriculture Department and become head of the State Department's Office of Foreign Territories, which then was responsible for organizing civilian services in the North African territory liberated by the Allied invasion. Having given Appleby a position of serious responsibility, Hull then abandoned him to the tender mercies of the third floor. It was like throwing a puppy to a pack of wolves.

Upon assuming his new position, Appleby discovered that eighteen people in his area of responsibility alone had authority to sign Secretary of State Hull's name to diplomatic cables. None of them was under his supervision or control. No cables were withheld from him, but neither were any outgoing cables that concerned civil organization in North Africa ever cleared with him in advance. One incoming cable that did reach his desk, as later described by Appleby, was addressed: "To Hull, for Appleby, from Robert Murphy, signed by Dwight D. Eisenhower, or vice versa." Robert Murphy, a State Department official, was Roosevelt's representative in North Africa. One American official there, after observing Murphy ally himself with French Nazi sympathizers, commented: "One trouble with Murphy is that although he is up from the ranks, he is like so many people who have not had the advantages of the so-called well-born, but wish they had them, more 'Grotty' than the men who actually went to Groton in the State Department."[24]

The text of Murphy's cable read, in part, "Will State Department expedite transportation of Peyrouton from Buenos Aires. . . ?" and then gave a location in North Africa. General Eisenhower, then the supreme commander of Allied forces in North Africa, had requested that Marcel Peyrouton, a Frenchman living in Argentina, assume a role in governing liberated areas of North Africa, including the French colony of Algeria, where he was to become the governor-general.[25]

Appleby had never heard of Peyrouton and began making inquiries. He first spoke with Atherton, who referred Appleby to "the greatest authority in the world on France and French politics," a man on Appleby's small staff (which had been picked for him in advance). Appleby asked the staffer to identify Peyrouton.

"Well, he was a member of the French cabinet."

"Oh, what cabinet?"

A pause. "The Vichy cabinet."

He added, "He married—let's see, who was that he married?" Pause. "A daughter of a very, very wealthy businessman." An even longer pause. "What was her maiden name?"

The man thought for quite a while but could not remember the name of Peyrouton's father-in-law. That was all the "greatest authority in the world" on French politics could tell Appleby about Marcel Peyrouton. By checking with serious people elsewhere in the State Department, Appleby found out who Peyrouton was.

Following the fall of France in 1940, Hitler decided not to occupy all of France and allowed a collaborationist French government, with its capital in Vichy, to govern the unoccupied zone. The Vichy government was enthusiastically anti-Semitic. Marcel Peyrouton, a former colonial governor-general in French North Africa, had joined the Vichy government in September 1940. As its interior minister, he abrogated the Crémieux Law of 1870, by which Jews born in Algeria were decreed to be citizens of France. As Vichy historians wrote, "Algerian Jews found themselves in the position of their German co-religionists after the Nuremberg laws; having previously been citizens, they were reduced to subjects."

The Interior Ministry enforced the Vichy regime's anti-Semitic laws, which laid the groundwork for the creation of French concentration camps (ultimately, seventy-six thousand Jews were deported from both the occupied and unoccupied zones to the death camps in the east; only 3 percent returned). Although Peyrouton had left the Interior Ministry by the end of 1940 and the Vichy government by April 1942 (he was then the Vichy ambassador to Argentina), he was loathed by the French people as a Nazi collaborator.[26]

Appleby was stunned upon learning of Peyrouton's role in the Vichy government. Late on a Saturday afternoon, he set up a meeting for Monday in his office at the State Department to discuss Eisenhower's request. "It looked like he might be a fellow we wouldn't want to elevate," he recalled in his oral history.

On Sunday morning, Atherton telephoned Appleby.

"The Secretary asked me to read this cable to you." The cable expedited Eisenhower's request to transport Peyrouton to North Africa.

"The cable has been approved by the White House. It's going out tomorrow."

"I understand the English language," said Appleby. "You are informing me. You aren't asking me. I think this is a very unwise move and one that you will regret. I set up a meeting for tomorrow. This is a matter that is certainly within my jurisdiction." Appleby hung up on Atherton.

On Monday, Appleby confronted Atherton at the State Department. "I'm going to guess how it happened, and you tell me if I don't guess right."

Atherton listened without comment as Appleby explained what Atherton already knew quite well.

I guess that you picked this message [the Murphy cable] up from a copy that came to you. That you went to Hull with it. You told Hull that we ought to comply with any request from Eisenhower. The secretary then said that was wise, but that you should clear it with the White House. You then went over to the White House and told [Roosevelt aide] Admiral Leahy that Secretary Hull wanted to comply with the request and did Admiral Leahy have any objections, and Admiral Leahy said, no, if the Secretary wanted to send it, he didn't have any objections. You then came back and told Hull that it was cleared with the White House, and he suggested that you call me. Is that the way of it?[27]

Atherton made evasive noises but did not dispute Appleby's account. About two weeks later, Appleby told Cordell Hull that he was resigning from the State Department.

"I want to do this, of course, without creating any embarrassment. I will simply say that I had been called over here to organize this [civilian services in North Africa] and now that's done I'm going back."

Hull, much to Appleby's surprise, apologetically admitted that he had no control over what took place in his own State Department.

"I can see now why it probably couldn't work," said Hull. "I'd be one of the first to sin. I'd call a meeting in my office that would involve business that I'd assigned to you, and I wouldn't call you. I'd call in the people that have been around here that I've been in the habit of calling in to these meetings. This new office wouldn't work unless I would make it my business to police the function of that office. I know myself too well to know that I wouldn't do that. It's not the kind of thing I do."

Appleby, who was personally fond of Hull, had no idea until then that the secretary of state so well understood his own powerlessness in the State Department. Appleby only said, "I agree with your description of the situation and I don't have any complaints to make about you or anyone else."

Afterward, Appleby had an encounter with General Eisenhower's brother, Milton, who served as associate director of the Office of War Information. Appleby described the Peyrouton affair and how it began with the request from General Eisenhower to bring the Frenchman to North Africa. Milton Eisenhower checked with his brother and then reported to Appleby.

"He [Dwight Eisenhower] hadn't seen that message," Appleby told an interviewer many years later, "just like Hull hadn't seen a lot of the messages that went out from the State Department. This was a request that originated from Bob Murphy. [Dwight] Eisenhower said he didn't know anything about it."

Following the Allied landings in North Africa, the newly installed French administration, which included Peyrouton, repealed the Vichy decrees that the French Nazi collaborationists had imposed on the French colonies in North Africa, but the Crémieux Law of 1870 was not reinstated. More than 100,000 Algerian Jews, who had been French citizens before the war, remained without French citizenship. Governor-general Peyrouton justified the continuing disenfranchisement to Jewish leaders in Algiers by explaining that the Jews "have been declared responsible for the defeat [of France]" and the racial laws were "one of the essential conditions of the armistice" by which France had capitulated to Germany. Years later, in his memoir, *Crusade in Europe*, Eisenhower (who, in fact, may have had more familiarity with the implications of the Murphy cable than his brother suggested) admitted that "bringing Peyrouton to Algeria as governor was a mistake."[28]

The Peyrouton affair illustrated the State Department's disastrous mix of dysfunctionality and moral bankruptcy. With the exception of the overburdened Sumner Welles, who only intermittently engaged on Jewish issues, the archipelago graduates and their imitators decided American policy on the lives of countless Jews in Europe.

And so it was one of fate's cruel jokes that the terrible message—carried from Europe under perilous conditions in the desperate hope that the Nazi plan could be stopped if the U.S. government knew the secret—first fell into the hands of the bureaucrats on the third floor of the State Department.

VII

THE RABBI AND THE DIPLOMAT

When the Riegner telegram reached the Division of European Affairs' offices, a debate broke out. The debate was not over the authenticity of the information. On that point, there was a consensus: The Riegner telegram was simply a far-fetched war rumor. Jews were not being exterminated; they were only being deported to labor camps, just as many non-Jews were.

Ray Atherton and the third-floor Europeanists did not devote any time to whether Riegner's report should at least be investigated. Indeed, they were annoyed, in one official's words, at the Bern legation for having "put this thing in a telegram." They did briefly debate, however, whether or not to withhold the Riegner telegram from Rabbi Stephen Wise.[1]

Paul Culbertson was the head of the French desk. His main qualification for that position apparently was four months' service as a clerk in the American consulate in Paris twenty years earlier and an interest in aristocratic lineage. He was the only official to express concern about Rabbi Wise. "I don't like the idea of sending this on to Wise but if the Rabbi hears later we had the message and didn't let him in on it he might put up a kick. Why not send it on and add that the Legation has no information to confirm the story?"[2]

Culbertson had specific reasons for concern over repercussions from withholding the contents of the telegram. In 1941, he had received a report of the massacres of stateless Jews deported from Hungary. The report, which came from a "trustworthy Hungarian officer," placed the number killed "as high as 15,000 . . . Corpses are reported floating down the Dniester River." Culbertson had passed this report on to the American Jewish Joint Distribution Committee, an international Jewish aid group. In light of this experience, the Riegner telegram might have stirred doubts on his part about Atherton's dismissive treatment of it.[3]

The more senior Elbridge Durbrow, whose expertise was Russia and Eastern Europe, silenced Culbertson's timid suggestion. Durbrow ultimately prevailed in keeping the Riegner telegram from Wise because of what he termed, as previously described, "the fantastic nature of the allegation, and the impossibility of our being of assistance if such action were taken." Durbrow further proposed to instruct the Bern legation to refuse in the future to transmit similar messages intended for third parties, "unless after thorough investigation, there is reason to believe that such a fantastic report has in the opinion of the Legation some foundation or unless the report involves definite American interests." This proposal was not immediately implemented, but it was only a matter of time.[4]

Culbertson was right that Rabbi Wise would "put up a kick." What he and the other officials of the Division of European Affairs did not know was that Wise was about to receive the Riegner telegram anyway. In early August, Gerhart Riegner had given the contents of the telegram to the British consulate in Geneva and requested that the consulate transmit the information to the British Foreign Office for delivery to Samuel Sidney Silverman, a Jewish member of Parliament and chairman of the World Jewish Congress's British section. The Foreign Office received the report on August 10, hesitated for a week, and then concluded it could not withhold the report from a member of Parliament. The Foreign Office gave the report to Silverman, but with the disclaimer that "we have no information bearing on or confirming this story." This report from Riegner contained a line missing from the telegram he had given to the American consulate in Geneva: "Inform and consult New York."[5]

On August 28, Silverman cabled the report to the United States, where it reached Rabbi Wise. Riegner, waiting for word from either the American or

British diplomats in Switzerland, had no way of knowing that his report had found its way to the intended recipient, perhaps the most politically powerful rabbi in American history.

★ ★ ★

Then sixty-eight years old, with a square face, slicked-back hair parted in the middle, and a jutting jaw that resembled the prow of an icebreaker, Reform Rabbi Stephen Wise was the descendant of a line of distinguished Hungarian rabbis. He had been born in Budapest, but his parents emigrated to the United States when Stephen was little over a year old. Despite his rabbinical lineage and his own aspiration since childhood to follow in his father's and grandfather's footsteps, Rabbi Wise's autobiography begins with the Hancock-Garfield presidential election of 1880, where as a six-year-old he carried a torch in the Hancock parades. "Through many a weary street I bore my torch and had the smelly kerosene permeate my youthful clothes."[6]

Thus began an only-in-America saga of the Hungarian immigrant who combined devotion to the Jewish people with a passion since childhood for American politics in the raw and for winning. He did not accept defeat philosophically, either as a child or an adult. The six-year-old Wise read in the early edition newspapers that Hancock had lost the election. "I had begun to read, and I was overwhelmed with sorrow. I must have been, for my parents often told me that I came into the house weeping copiously and shouting before seven in the morning. What a shame! Hancock was defeated!" This was not the last time a Wise candidate would lose; indeed, he would go on to back the losers in mayoral, senatorial, and presidential contests over the next four decades. But he also picked enough winners and built a large enough following in the American Jewish community that he was invited to the White House by several presidents. Using his connection with an influential senator and contacts in the legal community, Wise helped persuade President Herbert Hoover to nominate a Jewish judge from New York, Benjamin Cardozo, to the Supreme Court.

The Reverend Endicott Peabody and Rabbi Stephen Wise could not have been more different in background, personality, and religious orientation. But they might have been surprised at the degree of their common ground had they met and talked over their respective spiritual philosophies—an event that, regrettably, apparently never took place. Peabody linked Christianity with public service, while Wise saw religion and politics as handmaidens: "To me neither religion nor politics was remote or sequestered from life. Religion is a vision or ideal of life. Politics is a method, or *modus vivendi*. To say that the minister should not go into politics is to imply that ideal and reality are twain and alien. Politics is what it is because religion keeps out of it."[7]

In serving his religion and his ideals, there was scarcely an important figure of his times that Wise did not come to know or a cause he did not find a way to support. He was an impresario of crusades. He met Theodor Herzl, who had founded the modern Zionist political movement for a Jewish homeland in Palestine, at the Second Zionist Congress in Switzerland in 1898 and became a committed Zionist himself; fought for the right to vote for women at the request of Harriot Stanton Blatch, daughter of famed suffragette Elizabeth Cady Stanton; organized a citizens' committee meeting at the Metropolitan Opera House in 1911 to protest the tragedy at the Triangle Waist Co., where nearly 150 workers, the majority young women, burned to death or leaped to their doom because some of the garment factory's doors could not be opened from the inside (and other exits were jammed from the press of the terrified workers) when a fire broke out; spoke against the racism of the movie *The Birth of a Nation*; like many others, urged clemency for the convicted anarchists Sacco and Vanzetti (who were executed anyway); and helped to drive one of the most corrupt mayors in New York City history, the high-living, song-writing Jimmy Walker, from office in 1932.

The last cause had led Wise to leak to the press a telegram he had sent to New York's then Governor Franklin Roosevelt, calling on Roosevelt to force Walker from office. After it became public, Roosevelt in turn had reproached Wise publicly, suggesting that he devote more attention to religion and less to politics. Privately, Roosevelt told Wise, "Rabbi Wise, it wasn't cricket of you to give to the press the telegram calling upon me to act." Nevertheless, in the end, Wise won, which increased his political clout. Referring to ex-Mayor Walker's abrupt departure on a boat to England following his resignation, a successor, Fiorello LaGuardia, joked, "When Rabbi Wise talks about mayors there is usually a run on Atlantic steamship accommodations." In his victory, however, lay the seeds of one of Rabbi Wise's greatest political miscalculations.[8]

The rabbi had first encountered Franklin Roosevelt in 1914, when he offered to support the New York Democrat in the Senate primary, which Roosevelt lost. In 1928, he supported Roosevelt for governor of New York over a Jewish candidate, "to the horror of a few of my Jewish friends who could never understand that I never voted as a Jew but always as an American." After Roosevelt won, Wise sent a note of congratulations that reminded the governor elect of the price Wise had paid in the Jewish community, some of whom claimed that Wise had released an "avalanche of Roosevelt sentiment. I hope I did. May this one merit plead for me on the Day of Judgment."[9]

But in the 1932 presidential election, Wise did not support Roosevelt, ostensibly because of Roosevelt's resistance to forcing Jimmy Walker out of the mayor's office. For once, Wise's political principles and political judgment parted ways. Wise had won the Walker affair and had no good reason to withhold support from Roosevelt, especially when the Republican candidate was the incumbent President Hoover and the country, in the depths of the Depression, was close to collapse. The only explanation was that Wise was still resentful of Roosevelt's comment about religion and politics. In other words, not surprisingly, Rabbi Stephen Wise had an enormous ego.

After Roosevelt won the election, Wise attempted to make amends with a congratulatory letter to the president-elect that he coauthored with a political ally: "We trust that, whatever have been the differences between us with regard to civic affairs, you may feel free to call upon us for whatever service it lies within the power of American citizens to render to their government and President." For his part, Roosevelt responded, "I am confident that your ultimate objectives and mine in the cause of better government are the same . . . though, as you know, I felt very strongly that you were using methods which would hurt rather than help the objective." But the two men had attacked each other too bitterly over the Walker affair. Several years passed before Wise was invited to the White House. When he finally went, it was with considerable misgivings. "It was not easy to go," he later wrote, because "no man of importance in public life had ever attacked" him as much as Roosevelt had over Mayor Jimmy Walker.[10]

When they met in early 1936, Wise and Roosevelt restored their political alliance. Wise discussed with Roosevelt the plight of Jews in Germany. "From then on I felt free to take to the President my knowledge and views on the Nazi situation—and from then on I found the President sympathetic and eager to be of help." Wise enthusiastically supported Roosevelt in the 1936 election and the ones that followed, swinging in the opposite direction by uncritically supporting Roosevelt even when criticism, if not opposition, was the right course. For example, Wise never directly criticized Roosevelt for the barriers to Jewish refugees erected by the State Department.[11]

Wise paid a heavy price for his access to Roosevelt. His unrelenting courtship of Roosevelt sometimes left him unsure whether he was the spokesman of the American Jewish community to the president or the other way around. "I don't know whether I'm getting to be a *Hofjude* [a "court Jew," installed at a royal court as a representative of his people]," he once complained to Jewish Supreme Court Justice Felix Frankfurter, "but I find that a good part of my work is to explain to my fellow Jews why our government cannot do all the things asked or expected of it."[12] Roosevelt's ability to bend people to his purposes was never more evident than in Wise's lament to Frankfurter.

But Wise's unqualified support for Roosevelt (about whom no misgivings were expressed even in his autobiography written after Roosevelt's death) certainly maintained and perhaps enhanced his role as the principal nongovernmental source of information for the president on the plight of Jews in Europe. This fact was well known to the officials in the Division of European Affairs. Their "debate" over disclosing the Riegner telegram to Rabbi Wise principally reflected a brief, reflexive calculation of bureaucratic self-interest and preservation.

As a result of the cable from MP Silverman, Wise was now the bearer of the devastating information that Eduard Schulte had brought out of Germany. Like the other bearers, he asked himself (and others) to whom should he pass the burden. Wise decided that the hideous information had to go to the only man in the world who, in fact, was in a position to act. But Wise wanted a highly placed administration official to deliver the message to the president. In early September, unaware that the Riegner telegram already had reached the third floor of the State Department, Wise sent a letter to Undersecretary of State Sumner Welles, attaching Silverman's cable. His letter requested that Welles, whom Wise regarded as "deeply understanding and sympathetic" to the plight of Jews in Europe, have the American minister in Switzerland, Leland Harrison, contact Gerhart Riegner to obtain corroboration. Wise further suggested that Welles bring the information in Silverman's cable to the attention of President Roosevelt.

★ ★ ★

Wise had valid reasons for starting with Welles, a brilliant diplomat, Roosevelt's chief foreign policy strategist, and a man willing to take risks like no one else. If a committee of foreign policy experts, fashion designers, and genealogists had been tasked with constructing the model for the ideal American diplomat, they would have come up with a prototype that looked very much like Sumner Welles. Tall, haughty, and impeccably dressed, from his tailored suits to his gold-headed Malacca cane to his 4711 eau de Cologne, which he liberally applied to handkerchiefs and shirts, Welles was a diplomat with dash and wit, a command of four languages, an encyclopedic knowledge of foreign affairs, and some of the best connections in Washington. He had an appropriate dose of gravitas, although one Roosevelt cabinet secretary caustically said of Welles, "He conducts himself with portentous gravity and as if he were charged with all the responsibilities of Atlas."[13]

His lineage was impeccable. A forebear, later to become third governor of Connecticut, had arrived in the American colonies in the 1600s. Welles apparently was named after another ancestor, Massachusetts Senator Charles Sumner, who had so eloquently spoken against slavery in 1856 that an enraged Southern congressman beat him nearly to death on the floor of the United States Senate. By the time of Sumner's birth in 1892, his family was part of the rigid, tradition-bound New York City upper class so devastatingly chronicled by Edith Wharton, who happened to be Welles's great-aunt. He grew up in a life of privilege, attended by nursery maids and governesses as a child, educated as a young boy at Miss Kearny's Day School for Boys at 42nd Street and Fifth Avenue, and doted on by his mother.

On the day she died, when Sumner Welles was a freshman at Harvard, he put on a black tie and thereafter wore one every day for the rest of his life. He was destined for stormy relationships with women, in part because he expected them to meet the impossible ideals of feminine beauty, poise, and sophistication set for him by his own mother. The relationships were stormy, as well, because Sumner Welles's sexual attractions were far outside the bounds of decency as defined by the Victorian morals of his social and professional circles, and, in some instances, even outside the elastic bounds of taste in our own times.[14]

His family circles were a key to his later success. At Miss Kearny's Day School for Boys, one of his classmates was Hall Roosevelt, brother of Eleanor Roosevelt. The Roosevelts lived just a block from the Welles family. Sumner Welles's biographer, who also happened to be his son from his first marriage, wrote that "the two families were close, and Eleanor, although eight years older, saw much of her younger brother's friend Sumner. It was then that their lifelong friendship began." That friendship was the reason that twelve-year-old Sumner Welles was a wedding trainbearer at the wedding of Eleanor and Franklin Roosevelt.[15]

Welles attended Groton but did not quite fit the school mold, principally because he was a poor athlete and apparently could not have cared less. While not a "water pumping" offense, lack of athletic interest and ability left a boy isolated at Groton, which in Welles's case was compounded by his tendency to ridicule his classmates. One boy, William Jay Schieffelin, beat up Welles for his taunts about the diplomatic ineptitude of Schieffelin's ancestor John Jay. The master who pulled them apart whispered, "Good work, Sheffie." Later, when asked if he had enjoyed Groton, Welles replied, "Oh, Lord no, I was a worm."[16]

After graduating from Groton in 1910 (ten years after Franklin Roosevelt) and Harvard (class of 1914), Welles spent time in Paris, where he bedded a succession of older women and, at a garden party, struck an older man who had propositioned him. His "omnivorous debauchery," as his biographer-son, Benjamin—a loving son but frank chronicler of his father's deeds and misdeeds—described it, "eventually took its toll, and he fainted one afternoon while walking Bobby [his dog] in the Luxembourg Gardens, awakening to find himself sprawled on the gravel path, the gentle animal licking his face." Welles left Paris for travel in Africa and, later, halfheartedly pursued an architectural career.[17]

With the outbreak of World War I, he decided to pursue a career in diplomacy and enlisted the help of family connections, including two Groton graduates: Assistant Secretary of State William Phillips and Assistant Secretary of the Navy Franklin Roosevelt. The latter wrote to Secretary of State William Jennings Bryan, "I have known [Sumner] since he was [a] small boy. He should give a very good account of himself in the [diplomatic] service."[18]

He did just that with a start in 1915 as third secretary in the American Embassy in Tokyo. Before setting out for Japan, he married Esther Slater, heir to one of the great family fortunes of Boston. The wedding was attended by the governor of Massachusetts and a thousand children from St. Joseph's parochial school, who lined the road to wave American flags at the wedding motorcade. There was one sour note: An anonymous letter to the bride's mother a few days before the wedding warned "on no account let your daughter marry Sumner Welles." The letter was traced to an unsuccessful Grotonian rival for Esther Slater's hand and ignored.[19]

Welles's tour in Japan was followed by a posting to the American Embassy in Buenos Aires. There, he pursued extramarital affairs that he scarcely concealed from his wife (driving by a cemetery, she said to a friend, "I wish I were there.") and, according to his biographer-son, may have finally surrendered to his latent bisexuality. One friend of Welles at the time suggested that in Argentina "respectable married men of high position, like himself, gave vent to deviation and he followed them. I am convinced that his preference for men was always there, only controlled by shame and a Puritan ethos. In Argentina, he found a different attitude and he let the reins slip."[20]

Welles became chargé d'affaires of the American embassy, a remarkable achievement for a diplomat in his mid-twenties. In 1920, he returned to Washington as the acting chief of the Latin America division of the State Department, where all were impressed with his brilliance, energy, and arrogance. And less than two years later, in an act that could have been dreamed up only by a Hollywood screenwriter or a supremely self-destructive personality, this rising star of the State Department, his horizons without limit, began an affair with the wife of a U.S. senator.

She was the wealthy Mathilde Townsend Gerry, then thirty-seven years old, and—it scarcely needs pointing out—eight years Welles's senior. Mathilde was unhappily married to a prominent senator from Rhode Island, and Sumner Welles stormed into her life like a hurricane. On the third anniversary of their meeting at a Washington dinner party, Mathilde wrote Welles, "Tonight at this very hour, I met you, and never have I loved anyone since, nor will I till I die."[21]

Welles resigned from the State Department to pursue both his and Mathilde's divorces and a banking career, but so formidable were his abilities that he was called back by the State Department for a special assignment in Latin America, which he performed brilliantly (while taking advantage of whatever local opportunity existed for an affair). In this period of shuttling back and forth between public and private sectors, Welles used a $100,000 loan from Esther, which he told her would enable him to join a New York banking syndicate, to buy jewelry for Mathilde, a gesture his biographer-son termed "as senseless as it was indefensible," given Mathilde's own wealth. Eventually, both divorces were granted by French courts.[22]

Sumner Welles's marriage to Mathilde on June 27, 1925, made the *New York Times* and led President Calvin Coolidge to scrawl a note on a list of appointees to a Central American mediation tribunal, where Welles's name appeared at the top: "All O.K. except Sumner Welles. If he is in the government, let him be dismissed at once. C." Welles's diplomatic career was over.[23]

Or so it only seemed. Eight years later, he was back in the State Department. (In the interim, Welles wrote, drank with shady characters, and was disinherited by his father after they fought over the father's affair with a French actress.) In 1933, FDR appointed him assistant secretary of state for Latin America; in 1937, Roosevelt promoted him to undersecretary of state, nominally the number-two position in the department. By virtue of his brilliance and his ties to the Roosevelts, however, Welles had more influence on American foreign policy than anyone other than the president.

Dean Acheson, who had been a year behind Welles at Groton, wrote in his memoirs that the undersecretary had an "incisive mind and decisive nature. He grasped ideas quickly and got things done. More and more he took over liaison with the White House on international political matters." As a consequence, by the time Rabbi Wise wrote him about the Riegner telegram, Welles was a man with as many powerful enemies—above all his boss, Cordell Hull—as anyone in Washington. Of the Hull-Welles rivalry, Acheson observed starkly, "It poisoned the Department."[24]

Welles's social status and wealth certainly would not have endeared him to a secretary of state born in a log farmhouse. In the early 1930s, Welles, then an assistant secretary of state, and his wife lived in her mansion on Massachusetts Avenue in Washington. The mansion had a huge library and a ballroom that comfortably hosted hundreds of stylishly dressed dancing men and women. On weekends and in the summer, he could retreat to one of two vacation homes. The closer place was a 255-acre Maryland estate that was a reproduction of a colonial plantation, with a long winding driveway, elegant gardens and terraces, a swimming pool, a kennel, and a tennis court. The estate's mansion had Louis XV chandeliers in the first-floor foyer, a ballroom that ran the length of the house, and an expansive servants' wing. The other summer estate was a thirty-eight-room "summer cottage" in Bar Harbor, Maine.[25]

Despite the availability of such lavish retreats, by the late 1930s Welles's position as de facto secretary of state meant that he functioned in a perpetual state of near exhaustion from overwork. In mid-August 1939, as a European war loomed, both Roosevelt and Hull were on vacation (one assistant secretary noted in his diary that "crises always happen when everybody is on vacation"). Welles canceled his own vacation to review a defense plan for the Western Hemisphere and convene a meeting of senior War, Navy, Justice, and Treasury officials to prepare all the paraphernalia needed in the event of war: "proclamations, supervision of neutrality, communications, prohibitions of loans and credit, cancellation of licenses, etc." Then, the State Department received official confirmation of a stunning development: Hitler and Stalin had agreed to a nonaggression pact, which left Hitler positioned to attack Poland. On August 25, Welles met Roosevelt at Union Station upon the president's return from vacation, and the undersecretary spent the next week sending peace appeals to European governments.[26]

The American appeals went unheeded. At 2:50 in the morning on September 1, President Roosevelt was awakened by a call from William Bullitt, the American ambassador to France. World War II had begun just a few hours earlier.

"Boss, the German Army has just marched into Poland."

"Then it has happened." ("God help us all," he added, according to some accounts.) Roosevelt telephoned Hull and Welles, who went immediately to the State Department, along with other officials. A few hours later Welles was at the White House, conferring with the president in his bedroom.[27]

The next day, Welles sent out telegrams calling for a Pan-American consultation on the outbreak of the European war. The meeting of Latin American foreign ministers was to take place in Panama and address such issues as barring the warring navies from seas adjoining the American shores. On Sunday, September 3, Assistant Secretary of State Adolf Berle was at the State Department without "much to do except consider the state of a world slowly smashing itself into fragments." He and Welles discussed which of the two of them should attend the Panama meeting.

"You can't be spared," said Berle bluntly.

Welles was equally blunt. "I have not been getting any sleep. I propose that I go. I can get three or four days rest on the boat each way."

Berle, realizing that Welles was near the edge, dropped his objection. Even so, Welles was close to collapse in Panama and drank heavily at the end of the conference's three weeks of nonstop negotiations. At a ball given by the Panamanian government for the delegates at the conference's closing, Welles passed his assistant, Louise Clarkson, on the dance floor. "I could see that his eyes were glazed."[28]

In early 1940, Welles reached the apogee of his diplomatic career when Roosevelt sent him on a mission to Berlin, Paris, Rome, and London without consulting Hull. Although it was ostensibly a fact-finding trip, one purpose of the mission was to explore the remote possibility (Welles later called it a "forlorn hope") of a peaceful resolution of the conflict before a widely anticipated German offensive in the spring against France and the Low Countries. Secretary of State Hull found out about the mission only after it was announced, but he managed, in his Tennessee mountain manner, to conceal his anger and issue a statement of support. Ambassador Bullitt, who thought of himself as Roosevelt's premier envoy in Europe, was pathologically jealous and openly swore revenge. In time, the patient Cordell Hull and the erratic William Bullitt would find common cause in trying to bring down Sumner Welles.[29]

Accompanied by great fanfare throughout Europe, Welles was received more or less cordially in the capital cities of the countries at war. In Berlin, Welles met with Herman Göring, whose girth impressed Welles as "monstrous." Welles also noted that Göring's hands were "shaped like the digging paws of a badger. On his right hand he wore an enormous ring set with six huge diamonds. On his left he wore an emerald at least an inch square." In the course of their conversation, which took place with both men seated in front of an open fireplace as snow fell in thick gusts outside the windows, Welles spoke bluntly about the Nazis' treatment of the Jews.

"The American people, as a whole, are profoundly moved by what they regard as inhumanity or cruelty to human beings. The measures taken by the German government against the Jewish people, and the hideous cruelties perpetrated upon them, have created a revulsion of feeling on the part of all the American people. The Field Marshal would be wise," Welles added, "not to minimize the importance of this issue."

"You are complaining of an intense racial feeling which exists not only in Germany," replied Göring, "but in many other parts of the world as well. I wonder if the American people are consistent. We question whether the same kind of discrimination against which the American people [are] now protesting is not in fact practiced by themselves."

Welles acknowledged the instances of white cruelties to blacks in America. But, he went on, "it is ludicrous for the Field Marshal to compare such incidents with an official policy initiated and persisted in by a government itself, which was carried on with the utmost barbarity and which aimed at the actual extirpation of hundreds of thousands of decent law-abiding citizens."

Göring did not pursue the subject.[30]

While he was in Paris, Welles paid a courtesy call on the Jewish ex-premier Léon Blum. Welles then was bombarded with three thousand letters from French citizens angry that an emissary from President Roosevelt had met with a Jew. In London, after a round of official appointments, Welles, Jay Pierrepont Moffat (then the head of the Division of European Affairs), and Ambassador Joseph P. Kennedy (father of the future president) were given a small "stag dinner" by Prime Minister Neville Chamberlain at No. 10 Downing Street. Conversation kept "rigorously off the war." Chamberlain was intrigued that both Welles and Moffat had attended Groton, and Moffat recorded in his diary that Chamberlain warmly "spoke of his old friend 'Coty' (Reverend Endicott Peabody)."[31]

The mission made Welles a world figure but failed to have any appreciable impact on events in Europe. Two months later in Washington, on the evening of May 9, the American ambassador to Belgium, John Cudahy, telephoned Roosevelt to advise him that the Belgian cabinet believed that German troops would attack at dawn. Just before midnight, Ambassador Cudahy reported to Secretary of State Hull, meeting in his office with several assistant secretaries, that German paratroopers had landed in Belgium and the country's airfields were under bombardment. More dispatches arrived: the Netherlands, under fierce attack, declared war on Germany (but shortly thereafter, the royal family fled the country); Belgium appealed to England and France for military assistance; and the government of Luxembourg fled its country.

Assistant Secretary of State Berle's diary entry reads: "We could merely watch the progress of affairs and let it go at that. It was a sort of murk of general destruction, with reports coming in on the radio and occasional cables indicating the long-promised Blitzkrieg, which lived up to the anticipated horror." In the course of the next six weeks, Germany defeated and occupied first the Low Countries and then France.

Two weeks before the French surrender, the deeply shaken chargé d' affaires of the American Embassy in Berlin returned to the United States and reported to the State Department that "nothing on earth will stop Hitler in the prosecution of his intentions in the United States in case he is successful in Europe." The Nazis, he went on, were "arrogant, drunk with power, intense in their hatreds, determined to achieve their objectives and in control of an inconceivably strong [war] machine."[32]

★ ★ ★

In the year that Sumner Welles became an international celebrity, he characteristically sowed the seeds of his own destruction. On a hot, oppressive evening in mid-September, the president, Welles, and other officials boarded a presidential train in Union Station in Washington. The destination was Alabama for the funeral of the late speaker of the House of Representatives. Secretary of State Hull was ill and Welles was there in his place, which meant that Welles had his own sleeping car next to the president's.

The following afternoon the train arrived in Alabama for the funeral, which was attended by tens of thousands. That evening, on the trip back to Washington, Welles began drinking in the dining car with companions, most of whom left at 2:00 AM to go to sleep. By 4:00 AM Welles was alone and drunk. He staggered back to his sleeping compartment and rang for coffee.

A Pullman porter named John Stone answered the bell. He wore the midnight blue Pullman uniform, buttoned to the neck, and was wearing a visored cap with a well-shined silver plate bearing the words "Pullman Porter." Pullman porters were all black men (the company preferred to hire those with "jet-black" skin). Despite the strict racial hierarchies that the Pullman cars represented—the porters were given strict instructions to avoid touching white passengers as they walked through the narrow sleeping cars—the job of porter was coveted by many blacks. It was akin to working in a luxury hotel, and many held their positions for decades.[33]

Stone entered the compartment. Despite the fact that Welles's sleeping car was immediately adjacent to the president's sleeper, Welles propositioned

Stone to engage in paid sex. Stone politely but firmly declined and returned to the dining car. Other porters who answered Welles's bell reported less direct but unmistakable advances. The porters reported what had happened to Pullman officials on the train, who alerted Dale Whiteside, the chief of the president's Secret Service contingent. Whiteside ordered a porter to bring coffee to Welles's compartment and leave the compartment door open, and then waited in the passageway. Welles came out of his compartment and exclaimed, "What is Whiteside doing in this car?" He went back into the compartment and slammed the door. The rest of the trip passed uneventfully.

Welles apparently assumed that knowledge of his behavior was confined to a few porters, whom no one would find credible. As his biographer-son wrote, "Possibly no one would believe that a senior government official in his right mind—least of all the patrician Undersecretary of State—would solicit Pullman porters on a train carrying the President, the cabinet, the Secret Service and railway officials." Indeed, as the years went by without apparent repercussions, that assumption must have appeared to Welles as an increasingly safe bet. Once again, Sumner Welles, a diplomatic alley cat with nine lives, had escaped disaster despite extraordinary imprudence.[34]

★ ★ ★

In part, Welles may have acted recklessly in the confidence that his patrons, Franklin and Eleanor Roosevelt, would always back him. Rabbi Wise, for one, grasped the importance of that sponsorship to Welles. In late 1941, nearly eight hundred Romanian Jews, preferring a desperate sea voyage to the horrors of Transnistria, had chartered a broken-down Danube cattle barge, the *Struma*, and sailed for Palestine. The *Struma*'s engines stopped working when the ship was off Istanbul, but Turkey would not allow the refugees to come ashore unless Great Britain granted them permission to enter Palestine. A British journalist's wife saw the *Struma* from the deck of a Royal Navy cruiser on an evening pleasure cruise around Istanbul harbor for diplomats and officials. The dancing on the cruiser "stopped abruptly when the searchlight paused on what appeared to be a derelict ship, illuminating rows of faces, white and unsmiling, as they stared back at the partygoers."

Britain refused to allow the *Struma* to go to Palestine. Turkey ordered the *Struma* to return to the Black Sea. By now, it was February 1942 and, despite the captain's insistence that the ship was unseaworthy, Turkish authorities towed it out of port, through the winding Bosporus, and set it adrift in the Black Sea with no working engines. At dawn the next day, in calm seas under a cloudy sky, with the crew still desperately trying to get the engines running, the *Struma* exploded, probably from a torpedo fired by a Soviet submarine, and in minutes sank into the frigid depths. All died in the explosion, drowned, or succumbed to hypothermia (including about one hundred children) but one, a dazed nineteen-year-old Romanian Jew who, in the refugee equivalent of a thousand-to-one shot, was later granted permission to enter Palestine.[35]

Rabbi Wise never missed an opportunity to advance the Zionist agenda. At his urging, his daughter, Justine Wise Polier, a judge in New York City, wrote Eleanor Roosevelt that Palestine must be opened to immigration, and she attached a memorandum about the fruitless attempts of Jewish refugees to enter Palestine (which included the *Struma* sinking). The first lady passed the letter to Sumner Welles. "Sumner's mother and mine were great friends and he went to school with my brother," she recalled years later. "Franklin never knew him as well as I did but appointed him because of his abilities." For Eleanor Roosevelt, like Stephen Wise, Sumner Welles was the one ranking official in the State Department who appeared sympathetic to humanitarian concerns. At the very least, Welles did not respond to her compassionate appeals with letters written in stiff and formal bureaucratese.[36]

In her letter to Welles, Eleanor wrote of Justine Wise's plea: "This memo seems perfectly shocking to me. We have taken British children [as war refugees] and I think [the British government] ought to pay some attention to us in return." Welles replied that the *Struma* sinking was one of the "most shocking tragedies . . . in a tragic year" but explained that the British were adamant about not allowing Jewish refugees into Palestine.

Welles then wrote to Ray Atherton in the Division of European Affairs that "If the British government did not wish this shipload of refugees to go to Palestine, some arrangement should have been made, purely from humanitarian considerations, to have found shelter for them during the war among the East African colonies."[37] He sent a copy to the first lady, who forwarded it to Stephen Wise. In turn, Wise responded, "It is very good of you to have intervened in this way with Mr. Welles." But he again pressed the Zionist cause, adding, "If Palestine is to be ruled out, the situation of the unhappy refugees indeed becomes hopeless."[38]

Both Wise and Welles were somewhat disingenuous in their approach to the *Struma* tragedy. Wise saw an opportunity to advance the Zionist cause and used the genuine humanitarian instincts of Eleanor Roosevelt to, in effect, put the creation of the state of Israel on the desk of the second-ranking official in the State Department. In turn, Welles was not about to ignore one of his most powerful supporters in Washington, but neither was he about to take on a close ally like the British, who like much of the State Department opposed finding a home for Jewish refugees in Palestine, let alone creating a Jewish state. So, Welles's "letter to the file" in the *Struma* affair—and his suggestion of East Africa as a temporary refuge—was a deft move by the undersecretary to placate Eleanor Roosevelt and Stephen Wise and deflect the issue of a Jewish homeland in the Middle East.

★ ★ ★

But Welles's overall record suggests that his concern over the fate of European Jews was genuine. Within a day of receiving Wise's letter and the Silverman cable with the Riegner report, Welles passed the cable to Atherton. His response was self-assured and dismissive despite the fact that a year earlier Atherton had received a report (never acted on) that German authorities in occupied Poland planned to "ruthlessly and entirely exterminate the Jewish element from the life of Aryan communities."

Referring to the Riegner report, Atherton advised Welles that "they are to be put to labor on behalf of the German war machine as is the case with Polish and Soviet and other prisoners-of-war who are now working for their daily sustenance in Germany." Atherton offered no source for his unqualified claim. Nor did he address the issue of why, after years of spectacular mistreatment of Jews compared to other religious or ethnic groups, the German government would have decided to treat Jews in the same way as non-Jews. Atherton did not recommend an investigation of the Riegner report's allegations. Rather, to allay Wise, Atherton suggested, "You should inform him by telephone that the American chargé d'affaires in Vichy has been instructed to protest in most emphatic terms against this inhuman act of deporting from France refugees capable of performing labor in Germany." Of course, weeks earlier the third floor had received the Riegner telegram and had decided not only to withhold it from Wise but also to not inform Welles or anyone else on the second floor.[39]

Welles then telephoned Wise. As the rabbi recalled that conversation: "Welles tried to be reassuring. He seems to think that the real purpose of the Nazi government is to use Jews in connection with war work in Nazi Germany and in Nazi Poland and Russia." Despite repeating the third-floor line, however, Welles did not fully accept the opinion of the European experts. He decided to investigate Riegner's report and asked Wise "not to release the information until an attempt had been made to confirm it."[40]

On faith, Wise complied with Welles's request, even though he had no way of knowing if it was a ploy to silence him or whether Welles really intended to investigate. But he knew that the third floor's explanation was wrong, if not misleading. And, by virtue of his promise to Welles, month after month went by and Wise did not disclose to his coreligionists that the greatest crisis in modern Jewish history was unfolding in Nazi-occupied Europe. He fully understood that Jewish blood might be on his hands. "Have you noted that I have kept the thing out of the press up to this time," he wrote to Justice Frankfurter in mid-September 1942, "thus accepting a great responsibility if the threat should be executed?"[41] (Wise apparently did not fully appreciate at that point that the mass murders were already under way.)

No less a figure than Elie Wiesel has said: "How could he pledge secrecy when millions of lives were involved? How was he not driven mad by this secret?" On the other hand, no less a figure than Gerhart Riegner rejected the charge that Wise had sacrificed Jewish interests for the sake of his relationship with Roosevelt. "This is not true," Riegner wrote in his memoir. "Wise worked his entire life in the political world. He was certainly not naïve. And, in fact, he changed his attitude towards Roosevelt several times."[42]

In fact, Wise felt he was close to madness, whether from guilt at his self-imposed silence or from the knowledge of the terrible contents of the Riegner telegram, or both. Since receiving the Riegner report the rabbi, already overstretched by too many commitments to Jewish and non-Jewish committees and in failing health, had been having trouble sleeping. Shortly after Wise's conversation with Welles, Jewish leaders in the United States received a telegram from the Bern representative of Agudath Israel, an Orthodox Jewish group: "According to numerous authentical informations from Poland, German authorities have recently evacuated Warsaw ghetto and bestially murdered about one hundred thousand Jews. These mass murders are continuing." Wise wrote to a prominent clergyman, "I am almost demented over my people's grief."⁴³

Certainly, of all his causes over many years, none had even remotely involved a humanitarian and moral challenge of this scope or urgency with such profound existential implications for the Jewish people. Wise was accustomed to unleashing his formidable organizing talent on behalf of the helpless, whether the cause was Zionism or unseating the mayor of New York. Even from his cage of self-imposed public silence, the American bearer of Riegner's report could not help but privately seek out his powerful friends, if only to ease the burden and perhaps have someone lined up to approach Roosevelt if Welles failed him.

In a somewhat aimless way, he wrote, called, or met with Vice President Henry Wallace, cabinet members, and other prominent Washington officials, but never pressed them very hard to take the matter to the president. In a letter to Justice Frankfurter, Wise wrote that he was "tempted to call up [Treasury Secretary] Henry [Morgenthau], Jr., and ask him to put it before the Chief, just that he might know about it, even though, alas, he prove to be unable to avert the horror." Wise then suggested that Frankfurter seek out FDR, although his hesitant tone was strikingly at odds with the number of lives at stake. Apparently referring to the Agudath Israel report, the rabbi wrote,

> *perhaps you will feel that in the face of this circumstantially confirming message from Bern, coming two or three days after the earlier message from Silverman [conveying Riegner's report], the Chief ought to know about it. Perhaps he will not be able to avert the thing, but one somehow feels that the foremost and finest figure in the political world today should not be without knowledge of this unutterable disaster which threatens and may now be in [the] process of execution.*

Wise and his son, James, the Washington representative of the World Jewish Congress for Latin American Affairs, did go to Treasury Secretary Henry Morgenthau Jr., although there is no indication that the rabbi asked Morgenthau to go to the president—or that Morgenthau offered to go. Morgenthau later said: "I will never forget the day in '42 as long as I live when Dr. Wise and his son James came to call on me in the Treasury and read me the unbelievable cable. I think that day changed my life. I will never recover from it."[44]

★ ★ ★

The most tangible result of Rabbi Wise's rounds occurred not in Washington but in Berlin. A memorandum written by Wise in September (since lost) fell into the hands of German intelligence agents, who forwarded it to Reichsführer SS Heinrich Himmler. The memorandum appears to have recounted the substance of the Riegner report. Upon learning that the Nazis' mass murder plan was known to American Jews, Himmler wrote to a senior official in the Reich Security Main Office: "You must guarantee me that everywhere the bodies of deceased Jews will either be burned or buried, and that nowhere will any other disposition of these bodies be made."[45]

★ ★ ★

Why didn't Rabbi Stephen Wise fight harder to get the Riegner report on President Roosevelt's desk sooner rather than later, or go directly to the press? One imagines that his tortured soul has been doomed to ask that question for all eternity. But, in fairness, at some level, Wise must have recognized that he first needed evidence that would silence the skeptics, especially on the third floor of the State Department. He also knew that Roosevelt would just refer the matter to the State Department anyway. And—at another, albeit less flattering level—as Wise had learned in the Jimmy Walker affair, his stature and influence as a Jewish American leader depended on his access to high officials. He was not prepared to burn his bridges to any of them, especially Sumner Welles.

After promising Rabbi Wise he would investigate the Riegner report, however, Welles did not move with alacrity, to say the least. He waited three weeks and then, on September 23, sent a triple-priority cable to the American ambassador to the Vatican: "Please ascertain whether the Vatican has any information which would tend to confirm the reports" of massacres of Jews in Europe, including more than 100,000 Jews in Warsaw. The Vatican replied that it had received reports of "severe measures" against Jews, but had been unable to confirm them.[46]

On October 5, Rabbi Wise met with Welles. The former pointed to more reports of Jewish massacres in Eastern Europe; some of these had begun appearing in the Jewish press. Welles cabled Minister Harrison in Switzerland, directing him to contact Riegner and obtain corroboration of Riegner's information.[47]

★ ★ ★

In Geneva, Gerhart Riegner had been profoundly shocked by the failure of the Allies to react to his information. "I felt they doubted the truthfulness of our reports," he later recalled. "This pushed me to redouble my efforts to obtain additional testimony confirming the plan for total annihilation."[48]

The first "testimony" obtained by Riegner was in the form of two coded letters written by a Warsaw Jew living illegally outside the ghetto to the Swiss representative of Agudath Israel, which in turn gave the letters to Riegner. The letters reported on the daily deportations of Jews from Warsaw "and left no doubt about the fact that these people were being exterminated." The first coded letter described how the "Germans are driving the Jews out of Warsaw in order to annihilate them." Under the code, *Uncle Akhinu* (our brethren) meant the Jewish people. The second letter closed: "I too was in sorrow, for I am now so lonely. '*Uncle Akhinu ist verstorben.*' [Our people are dead.]."

A young Latvian Jew brought news to Riegner of the extermination of the entire Jewish population of the capital, Riga, who were rounded up and brought to ravines outside the city. In less than two nights, the Latvian told Riegner, German machine gunners from specially trained units killed tens of thousands of Jews. An understated but no less harrowing report came when a Jewish doctor urgently requested that Riegner come to a hospital and speak with a Jewish patient from Brussels, who was suffering from badly swollen feet. When Riegner arrived, the patient recounted his arrest in Brussels and deportation to the front at the battle of Stalingrad, where he worked on German fortifications. With his driving and mechanical skills, he became a driver for a Wehrmacht officer who had lost two brothers in the war. Disillusioned and weary, the Wehrmacht officer decided to help his driver escape. Before they parted, he asked the officer about the fate of the Jews. His matter-of-fact reply: "Those who were fit to work with were taken for all kinds of forced labor, especially on military fortifications on the eastern front. The others were done away with. Those who were no longer fit for work were done away with too."

Riegner obtained more corroborative information from a law professor at the Swiss Graduate Institute of International Studies, who had spoken with a senior official of the International Committee of the Red Cross with contacts in Berlin. Later, Consul Paul Squire interviewed the Red Cross official, who described communications from German officials—one in the Ministry of Foreign Affairs, the other in the War Ministry—which revealed a Nazi plan to make Germany (and the occupied countries) "free of Jews." But, the Red Cross official indicated in so many words, "since there existed no country to receive the Jews, there could be no doubt about the significance of the term."

On October 22, Minister Leland Harrison met with Riegner and Richard Lichtheim, the Geneva representative of the Jewish Agency for Palestine. Harrison was "the very image of a dandified diplomat." He quite enjoyed the life of a minister in Switzerland, down to the governess for his children, the splendid mountain views, fine wines, and golf outings. He and his wealthy wife were both strong supporters of Franklin Roosevelt: In 1940, Nancy Harrison anonymously contributed to the Democratic National Committee to support Roosevelt's run for a third term. They were also close personal friends of Sumner Welles and his wife.

The Welleses' relationship was important to both husband and wife for reasons other than the personal. In Nancy Harrison's case, Welles afforded an opportunity for a diplomat's wife to play diplomacy. She wrote him long letters that mixed foreign policy advice, such as which side to take in the Free French infighting ("French unity is a vital necessity *right now* and it cannot be achieved by de Gaulle"), with the flattery that lower-ranking diplomatic wives shower on their husbands' superiors like confetti. In her case, it bordered on the flirtatious: "This little note is written dear Sumner with warmest friendship which is better perhaps than great wisdom." In Leland Harrison's case, Welles was an important superior, a key to advancement in the State Department. The cable from Welles required a prompt response, no matter that its subject was one that, as Harrison must have known, the Division of European Affairs strongly preferred to avoid altogether.[49]

In the meeting, Riegner and Lichtheim handed Harrison a lengthy memorandum summarizing country-by-country reports of the Nazi plan to exterminate the Jews of Europe. For twenty minutes, no one spoke while Harrison read the memorandum. (Riegner recalled that it was a "profound silence.") After finishing, he went through it one page at a time, asking for clarification. He showed neither skepticism nor sympathy.[50]

But the cascade of facts in the memorandum left no doubt that something monstrous—"four million Jews are on the verge of complete annihilation"—was taking place behind the shroud with which the Nazis had covered the occupied countries of Europe. The information in each country report so reinforced the other reports, and especially Schulte's message, that even the most skeptical had no grounds for dissent. Auschwitz Commandant Rudolf Höss's claim—"no one in the world will believe it to be possible"—was breaking down under the weight of the accumulated, shattering evidence.

> *Expulsions, deportations and mass executions are continuing thus decimating Polish Jewry to the point of complete annihilation . . . Of the 100,000 Jews living in Latvia in 1939 there are now only 4000 left . . . one-third of the 180,000 Jews of the Netherlands have already been deported; the whole of Dutch Jewry is to be deported [by] June 1943 . . . the Romanian government itself admitted that since October 1941, about 185,000 Jews have been deported to Transnistria where there are by now only 112,000 left; the remainder have probably perished . . . Thus the deliberate policy of extermination of European Jewry is systematically carried out quite in accordance with the announcements made in the last speeches of the Head of the German Government.[51]*

Without naming Schulte, the report described the German source for the information in the Riegner telegram ("he is a prominent German industrialist"). Harrison asked Riegner and Lichtheim to disclose his identity. Riegner and Lichtheim (who had by then been given Schulte's name by Sagalowitz) first obtained a firm understanding that if they provided a name Harrison would use it only to satisfy himself that Riegner's source was reliable and would under no circumstances disclose the source's identity to anyone, including in the State Department in Washington. After Harrison agreed to their condition, they provided Schulte's name, albeit reluctantly, on a slip of paper in a sealed envelope: "Managing director Dr. Schulte, mining industry. In close or closest contact with dominant figures in war economy." Harrison kept his word to Riegner and never disclosed Schulte's name.

Following the meeting, the American legation obtained corroboration from the Red Cross official, as described above, and from the law professor. In a cable on November 23, 1942, Harrison advised the State Department that the legation had been informed by "reliable sources independently that Hitler at beginning 1941 signed order" demanding the extermination of the Jews.[52]

The next day, a Tuesday, Welles urgently requested that Rabbi Wise come to the State Department that afternoon. Wise knew that he was about to receive the most dire news: *Uncle Akhinu ist verstorben*. He asked his son to accompany him. Their heels echoing on the black-and-white slate and marble floor, they went to Welles's corner suite adjoining the secretary of state's suite.

Ordinarily, Welles and Wise might have had reasons to comment on the positive war developments. A Soviet counteroffensive was prying loose the German grip on Stalingrad, and the Japanese had all but lost the ability to reinforce their garrison on Guadalcanal. The most prescient might have suggested that perhaps the war was near a turning point, which indeed was the case, as events on these two battlefields were to prove.

But as Rabbi Wise and his son seated themselves in Welles's office, their minds were not on the battles fought by armies but on a war against the Jewish people of Europe, which was nowhere near a turning point. The mood in the office was grim, but the moment was something of a symbolic high-water mark in the efforts of Jews and Gentiles to stop a terrible slaughter. Eduard Schulte's message, which had begun its journey from the vicinity of Auschwitz, traveled from hand to hand in Switzerland, and then crossed an ocean, had finally been delivered. And the recipient—the government of the United States of America—was about to officially acknowledge its awful truth. It was also a moral divide, a true before and after for those in the American government, especially the State Department, dealing with the plight of Jews in Europe. Henceforth, the existence of the extermination plan—not the now-exploded claim that Jews were only "being put to labor on behalf of the German war machine"—would be the backdrop against which the conduct of the State Department officials would be judged.

The patrician diplomatic scion of the eastern establishment and the rough-and-tumble Budapest-born rabbi both understood the historic nature of their meeting. Arrayed on Welles's desk were documents from the Bern legation adorned with bright red seals. Wise could not avert his eyes from the seals. They were his people's blood, "pouring forth in rivers."

Sumner Welles was suitably dignified and solemn. He held up the documents. He spoke quietly and movingly, as Wise later wrote, "every word etching itself into my heart."

"Gentlemen," said Welles, "I hold in my hands documents which have come to me from our legation in Bern."

The cries of millions had at last penetrated the State Department.

"I regret to tell you, Dr. Wise, that these confirm and justify your deepest fears."[53]

VIII

A REASON TO LIVE

Ruth, her family, and other surviving Jews finally reached the town of Bershad, the largest and most infamous of the more than one hundred dispersed ghettos in Transnistria. In Bershad, twenty thousand deported Jews were living in a town with two main roads, twelve narrow, unpaved streets, and—instead of the barracks of a concentration camp—just a few hundred small houses made of clay, many in ruins from bombing and shelling.

All over Transnistria the deported Jews were in a state of shock. They might have had some faint hope that their pain and suffering would ease once they reached their destination on the other side of the Dniester. But that illusion, like the memory of their existence before the Romanian government forced them out of their homes, faded fast in the face of the sight and stench of death everywhere.

In Bershad, Ruth and her family found temporary shelter in the rear room of a partly destroyed house with a leaking roof and no doors, windows, electricity, running water, or sanitary facilities of any kind, other than the back alleys. They shared the room with twenty other Jews. Meager amounts of food could be obtained by bartering with Ukrainian peasants on the fringe of the ghetto with the principal commodity of value possessed by the Jews—their clothing.[1]

Under these conditions, the room's poorly clothed and inadequately fed inhabitants steadily became corpses, often dying in their sleep. The living existed in such *close intimacy with the dead, the line between them so finely drawn, that the living often did not even know who the dead were until the corpses were roughly removed by undertakers.*

The undertakers in Bershad traveled from house to house on a horse-drawn sleigh in the winter. They stopped by the ruined hovel where Ruth lived and rang the sleigh bells to announce their arrival. "A meth?" (corpse) one shouted. If the answer was affirmative (it usually was), the undertakers came into the room, identified the corpse, and roughly dragged the body out of the room by the hands and feet. Then the wooden sleigh, piled high with corpses, went on its way to the next stop.

All across Nazi-occupied Europe and the Soviet Union most Jewish children not otherwise sent immediately to their death helplessly withered and died, except for a fortunate few. Ruth certainly had inner strength and physical stamina—she would not have made it this far otherwise—but she needed a reason to live, and nothing in the bleak and brutal landscape of her existence offered one. She and her family had endured the suffering of the march only to arrive in a charnel house; Ruth had only her imagination to keep her sanity.

The sound of the undertakers' sleigh stirred Ruth's protective imagination. In Czernowitz, horse-drawn sleighs provided transportation during the winter. Ruth clambered onto such a sleigh, reached up and handed a small coin to the driver, and glided off through the streets of Czernowitz. She was a child again, enjoying the simplest of childhood pleasures—a sleigh ride. But, as with her visit to Milie, her imagination could shield her only for so long. The death sleigh pulled away from the house in which she lived, the sound of its bells faded, and Ruth was back in Bershad, where she was no longer a child and where her family was dying around her. The first to die was her father, whether from the subzero cold, typhus, starvation, exhaustion, or sheer despair, it hardly mattered. One morning Ruth's brother shouted and her mother bent over her father.

As a little girl, Ruth had been badly spoiled by her father. Her mother had been hard on her, it seemed to the child, chastising Ruth for not eating enough and smothering her with concern for her health. Her father compensated with total adoration. Once, her father had left the house briefly without giving Ruth a hug and a kiss. She burst into sobs and ran to her mother to complain that her father had left without saying good-bye. When he returned, she curled up in his lap. She decided that someone else's father, not hers, had left without giving her a kiss good-bye.

And now, her father, her deity, was really gone. At the sight of her mother's stricken face, Ruth's heart seemed to stop and she began to choke. Then she cried for a long time until finally a cold numbness spread through her body.[2]

Even though people in the room were dying, no space was freed up for the living. The undertaker's sleigh came less frequently and so the corpses from all over the house were piled up against one wall of Ruth's room. Now, there were only a few left alive in the room: Ruth, her brother and mother, and the Sattinger couple, acquaintances from Czernowitz, and their two-year-old daughter.

"Frau Sattinger, remember what I am telling you," said Ruth's mother. "Everybody in the room will die except Ruthi and the two of you." Frau Sattinger was horrified and angry at such a prediction. When the Sattinger's child died, Ruth's mother, who had her wits about her, made Frau Sattinger swear over her dead child's corpse that she would take care of Ruth. The bereaved mother, who held her dead child through the night, could not refuse such a request from a dying one, which Ruth's mother fully understood. Ruth could not have known it then, but her mother had given her a gift.

All that Ruth knew was terror at the prospect of losing her mother and brother. She prayed that her mother's prophecies were wrong. "How can I survive?"

Then Ruth's brother, Bubi, stopped talking. And Ruth's mother, sitting opposite Bubi, announced that she could no longer see or move. She declined to drink their only nourishment—salty water in which potatoes had been boiled, the gift of a doctor who lived in a different room. (The doctor had bartered with Ukrainian peasants; he gave them medical assistance and they gave him potatoes.)

Ruth's mother asked her to check if her brother was breathing. Ruth did this regularly for a few days until her brother suddenly called out the name of the cow in Milie—"Ruzena-a-a-a!!!"—and then he was gone too. Ruth removed the fur hat that had slipped down over her brother's head as he had wasted away. His scalp swarmed with lice.[3]

"Ruthika," her mother explained, "you are the only one who will survive. People are kind and will take care of you. Be good, obedient, honest, and well-behaved and everything will be fine."

For the next two weeks, Ruth begged her mother not to die. "Please don't leave me alone." She stayed awake almost the entire time, shaking her mother and calling "Mama, Mama." Her mother only murmured faintly, "Hmm, hmm." By now, the Sattingers had left the room for another abode. Ruth and her dying mother were alone with the corpses. Ruth dreamed of Milie, where she planted onion and radish seeds in the little vegetable garden behind her grandfather's house. She watched them grow each day, life springing forth from the soil. It rained, and she stood face up, feeling the cool, fresh raindrops splash on her face, and she ran through the puddles in her bare feet. Then she was back in the hovel, where she put a hand to her mother's face. It was as cold as ice. Her reality was a child's worst nightmare—worse, even, because Ruth had not just lost her family. She was an orphan in a land of death.

"How could you leave me alone in this crazy place?" Ruth screamed as she clung to her mother's cold body. She hoped that her screaming somehow would bring her mother back to life.[4]

Her mother's prediction had come true. Ruth was the only survivor of the family. Three days after her mother's death, the Sattingers came to the room where Ruth dwelt alone with corpses only. They took Ruth to two sisters from Czernowitz who seemed willing to care for her. The sisters lived in a room in another house, which had no corpses. They fed Ruth a piece of potato now and then. The room was cold, but she gained warmth by nestling between the sisters while they knitted clothes to barter for food. Above all, she was grateful for the absence of dead bodies.

Every day, Ruth visited her dead mother. Standing on tiptoes, she stared for hours at her mother's corpse through the hole in the wall that used to be a window. Each day, her mother's body was in a different place in the room. She could not quite get her mind around it, and asked the sisters. They explained that hungry dogs often fed on the corpses. Ruth chased after the gravedigger's sleigh, begging the driver to take her mother. The sleigh now made fifty fully loaded trips each day to the cemetery. Finally, on the day of her fourteenth visit, her mother's corpse was gone.[5]

Tears frozen to her face, Ruth walked back to the sisters' room. She remembered her dead mother's words: "Ruthika, you are the only one who will survive." With a sudden insight, Ruth realized it was not a prophecy. It was her mother's command. And now, she had to fulfill it.

She had a reason to live.

IX

THE CHIEF

Nazi music could be heard in the distance. A rabbi solemnly intoned: "We are not here to weep for them. We are here to honor them and to proclaim the victory of their dying. For in our Testament are written the words of Habakkuk, prophet of Israel, 'They shall never die.'"

The children's faces were grey as corpses. Their white rags gleamed in the bright light. Standing over the children, fifty elderly rabbis intoned the Kaddish.

The children quietly murmured:

"Remember us who were in the Ukraine."

"Remember us who were put in the freight trains."

"Remember us who were not killed by the Germans but who killed themselves."

The Nazi music faded away. The sweet, mournful—and ultimately hopeful—sound of the Hatikvah miraculously replaced it.

"It is a problem," said a man, "that belongs to humanity. It is a challenge to the soul of man."

The curtain came down and the packed audience at Madison Square Garden (forty thousand witnessed back-to-back performances in a single night) rose at once, clapping, shouting hurrahs, and crying. The curtains parted and the cast—four hundred actors, including the children in their grey makeup, the rabbis in their black skull caps and alpaca frock coats (recruited at a meeting at Schwartz's Kosher Restaurant), and two hundred cantors ("each able to sing louder and higher than Caruso," said the show's writer)—came on stage and bowed as thunderous applause poured down on them from around the dark hall. Behind the bowing cast were two forty-foot tablets of the Ten Commandments crowned by a bright Star of David. The Hollywood actors Edward G. Robinson and Paul Muni received an especially loud ovation.

The performance of *We Will Never Die* on March 9, 1943, was the culmination of the publicity campaign in the United States mounted by Jewish organizations after the revelation of the Nazi plan to murder the Jewish population of Europe.[1]

★ ★ ★

At the end of their meeting on November 24, 1942, Undersecretary of State Sumner Welles, referring to the documents and affidavits bearing bright red seals, said to Rabbi Wise: "For reasons you will understand, I cannot give these to the press, but there is no reason you should not. It might even help if you did."[2]

Welles had finally removed the oath of silence to which Rabbi Wise had bound himself. In Washington that evening, Wise held a press conference. He told reporters that the State Department had confirmed reports of a Nazi "extermination plan" to annihilate the entire Jewish population of Europe.[3]

The next day, Wise was back in New York, where he convened a meeting of Jewish leaders to plan a campaign to send telegrams to five hundred newspapers requesting editorials on the Nazi scheme; to invite hundreds of prominent non-Jews to issue statements of condemnation; to hold a national day of mourning; and to seek a meeting with President Roosevelt. That afternoon, Wise held another press conference. He explained that his purpose in disclosing the reports from Europe was "to win the support of a Christian world so that its leaders may intervene and protest the horrible treatment of Jews in Hitler Europe."

One week later, on December 2, a national Day of Mourning and Prayer was held in the United States and twenty-nine foreign countries. In New York City, half a million Jewish union members, accompanied by non-Jews in their workplaces, stopped work for ten minutes. Religious and memorial services and moments of silence were held in other cities. A reporter for the *Dallas Morning News* was especially moved by the sobbing at the ceremony in Dallas.[4]

On the Day of Mourning and Prayer, Rabbi Wise wrote a letter to the man he sometimes called "the Chief":

> *I do not wish to add an atom to the awful burden which you are bearing with magic and, as I believe, heaven-inspired strength at this time. But do you know that the most overwhelming disaster of Jewish history has befallen Jews in the form of Hitler mass-massacres? Hitler's decision was to exterminate the Jewish people in all Hitler-ruled lands, and it is indisputable that as many as two million civilian Jews have been slain.*

In his letter, Wise asked Roosevelt to meet with a delegation of Jewish leaders. Roosevelt agreed, and the meeting took place at the White House on December 8, 1942, one year and a day since the attack on Pearl Harbor.

The Jewish leaders assembled outside the White House in the morning. In addition to Wise, they included representatives of B'nai B'rith, the Union of Orthodox Rabbis, the American Jewish Committee, and the Jewish Labor Committee. They were cleared at the security check point, entered the White House, and waited to be summoned to meet the president.[5]

★ ★ ★

Even today it is difficult to come to terms with the most famous Groton graduate's response to the Holocaust. One obstacle is the difficulty of assessing the moral legacy of a leader whose achievements still moisten the eyes in gratitude. On the day that Franklin Delano Roosevelt took office, March 4, 1933, the United States of America was collapsing. A friend said to Roosevelt that if he succeeded he would be remembered as America's greatest president, but if he failed then he would be recalled as the worst. "If I fail," replied Roosevelt, "I shall be the last one."

By Inauguration Day, with the Depression's talon-like grip now deeper in the country than ever, every state had shut its banks or restricted their operation; there was not enough money in the Treasury to meet the federal payroll; and the New York Stock Exchange had shut down with no date set to reopen. Just before the inauguration, the world's largest private savings bank, the Bowery Savings Bank, failed in New York City, turning away crowds of desperate depositors lined up opposite Grand Central Station.

Since the 1929 stock market crash, stock prices had plummeted 85 percent, and manufacturing in the United States had all but ceased: the automobile industry was operating at 20 percent of normal capacity and the steel industry at only 12 percent. The year before, 273,000 families had been *evicted* from their homes (one-fourth of the state of Mississippi had been auctioned off, according to some estimates).

A writer touring Chicago witnessed a hundred starving people clambering through a garbage dump, "falling on the heap of refuse as soon as the [garbage] truck had pulled out and digging in it with sticks and hands." One-fifth of the students in the New York City school system suffered from malnutrition. Nationally, a third of a million children were no longer being educated because their schools had closed for lack of funds. Two million Americans were wandering the nation's roads, one quarter of them between the ages of sixteen and twenty-one. Before the 1929 crash, there were almost no shoeshine boys in New York City; now there were thousands (nineteen on one block alone). And, among the more than fifteen million persons looking for jobs that were nowhere to be found, were nearly twenty-two thousand graduates of Ivy League universities.

But shortly after noon on March 4, it all changed.

Let me first assert my firm belief that the only thing we have to fear is fear itself—nameless, unreasoning, unjustified terror which paralyzes needed efforts to convert retreat into advance.

Throughout the stricken country people listened to the buoyant, confident voice on their radios. As historian William Manchester wrote, "In the three-decker tenements with radios, the hungry children looked up . . ."

I shall ask the Congress for the one remaining instrument to meet the crisis—broad Executive power to wage a war against the emergency, as great as the power that would be given me if we were in fact invaded by a foreign foe.

"in county courthouses the embattled farmers looked up . . ."

> *The people of the United States have not failed. In their need they have registered a mandate that they want direct, vigorous action. They have asked for discipline and direction under leadership. They have made me the present instrument of their wishes. In the spirit of the gift I take it.*

"housewives patching threadbare clothes looked up; there was a kind of magic in the air."

Listening to her husband speak and looking at the anxious faces of the 100,000 people assembled in front of the inaugural stand, Eleanor Roosevelt found the occasion "very, very solemn and a little terrifying." But for the rest of the country, Roosevelt was a beacon of hope and his speech was the best thing any of them had heard in a long, long time. And that week, "450,000 wrote Roosevelt to tell him so." With that one speech—by a crippled man, no less—the country had its confidence back.

The letters came in so fast that the White House Chief of Mails could not even count them. And the letters did not simply congratulate Roosevelt. The letter writers already thought of him as someone they could talk to directly.

"Dear Mr. President, I am worried about how we are going to . . ."

"Dear Mr. Roosevelt, the children have no shoes to wear to school . . ."

"Dear Frank, I have been driving a hack for ten years but now . . ."[6]

And later, after fifteen major laws had been passed in the hundred days (it was said that Congressmen did not so much debate them "as salute them as they went sailing by"); after all the agencies—CWA, CCC, TVA, NRA, and more—had been set up; and after "a presidential barrage of ideas and programs unlike anything known to American history," according to historian Arthur M. Schlesinger Jr., the letters themselves resembled nothing ever seen in the correspondence between Americans and their presidents.

> *Dear Mr. President:*
>
> *This is just to tell you that everything is all right now. The man you sent found our house all right, and we went down to the bank with him and the mortgage can go on for a while longer. You remember I wrote you about losing the furniture too. Well, your man got it back for us. I never heard of a President like you.*[7]

And the American people loved the theatricality of it all, from the nearly one thousand press conferences, where Roosevelt would make flourishing announcements ("I have some rather grand news for you.") to the radio broadcasts that came to be known as fireside chats ("My friends, I want to tell you what has been done in the last few days, why it was done, and what the next steps are going to be.") to the long cigarette holder and his great navy blue-black cape. "You know, Orson," Roosevelt once said to Orson Welles, "you and I are the two best actors in America." (Welles, perplexed since Roosevelt seemed serious, simply bowed.)[8]

Twelve years later, in mourning the news of his death, the *New York Times* editors wrote, "Men will thank God on their knees a hundred years from now that Franklin Roosevelt was in the White House in that dark hour when a powerful and ruthless barbarism threatened to overrun the civilization of the Western World." Fifty years after Roosevelt's death, former Secretary of State Henry Kissinger, hardly a sentimentalist, wrote, "No president, with the possible exception of Abraham Lincoln, has made a more decisive difference in American history." Now, two-thirds of the way to the centenary, the *New York Times* editors' prediction is likely to be fulfilled.[9]

An inseparable part of Roosevelt's leadership narrative is his personal triumph over the polio that paralyzed his legs. He was the cripple who, after being knocked flat on his back, rose and revived an America that had been knocked flat on its back and then led it to wartime triumph and global destiny. Shortly after the onset of FDR's polio in 1921, the tendons behind his right knee began to "jackknife and lock." As Eleanor Roosevelt's biographer Joseph Lash wrote, "His legs had to be placed in plaster casts into which *wedges* were driven deeper and deeper, to stretch the muscles." It was akin, suggested Lash, to being placed on a medieval rack.[10]

In 1923, Sumner Welles visited Roosevelt for the first time after his polio attack. "It was exactly as if all trivialities in life had been burned [out] in him," Welles recalled years later for an interviewer. "A steel had entered his soul; he never made any reference to his tragedy." In 1933, shortly after assuming the presidency, Roosevelt had lunch at the White House with the German minister of economics, Dr. Hjalmer Schacht. (Schacht was the banker who had been present, along with Eduard Schulte, at Hermann Göring's home for a Nazi fundraising meeting of German businessmen, and Schacht was the one who told them, "Gentlemen, take out your checkbooks.")

A State Department official was present at the White House luncheon for Schacht, which was just a routine event on the presidential calendar. That evening, the official wrote in his diary how FDR, leaning on the arm of an aide, had walked into the room "and seated himself in a dining room chair, unhitching in some way his braces so as to give him greater comfort." At the end of the luncheon, the president rose from the table. "The physical effort was enormous. He turned to one side and raised his weight entirely with his arms, while every vein in his forehead stood out from the strain." Roosevelt did this day in and day out, while carrying the woeful burdens of his country and the world. Here was the sheer grit, courage, and willpower that would be needed to free the country from the Depression and half the globe from two fanatic militarized tyrannies.[11]

Roosevelt's captivating, effervescent—and dominating—personality played no small role in his accomplishments. Groton graduate George Biddle recalled the young Franklin Roosevelt, who was several forms ahead of him: "He was gray-eyed, cool, self-possessed, intelligent, and had the warmest, most friendly and understanding smile." Winston Churchill said that to meet Franklin Roosevelt was like "opening a bottle of champagne." Unlike the stiff and unfeeling residents of the third floor of the State Department, Roosevelt could empathize with people of all backgrounds. "Gone is the fresh and spontaneous interest which this man took, as naturally as he breathed air, in the troubles and the hardships and the disappointments and the hopes of little men and humble people," wrote the grieving editors of the *New York Times*.[12]

And, unlike many second- and third-floor residents of the State Department, it is not possible to characterize Roosevelt as anti-Semitic. He appointed so many Jews to positions in his administration that both American anti-Semites (and isolationists and reactionaries) and the Nazis viciously attacked him. In the United States, a prewar anti-Semitic propaganda cartoon depicted Roosevelt as the Jewish leader of a "Jewish conspiracy." In Germany, a pre–Pearl Harbor propaganda tract by Joseph Goebbels, "The Jews are Guilty!" reminded Germans that a "war-monger named Baruch or Morgenthau or Untermayer [sic] [a prominent New York Jewish lawyer and outspoken critic of Nazi Germany] stands behind Roosevelt, driving him to war." Hitler once described Roosevelt as a "petty-fogging Jew," tastefully adding that the "completely negroid appearance of his wife" showed that she was "half-caste."[13]

Some of Roosevelt's defenders, in attempting to defuse the issue, concede that Roosevelt was not free of mild anti-Semitism in his earlier years. Even if that were true, it approached nothing like the callous anti-Semitic feeling in the State Department. More than anti-Semitism, however, Reverend Endicott Peabody's sense of Anglo-Saxon exceptionalism was clearly present in Roosevelt's outlook.

"Leo, you know that this is a Protestant country," the president said for no apparent reason during a meeting in early 1942 with Leo Crowley, a Catholic appointee who was then chairman of the Federal Deposit Insurance Corporation (among other positions). "The Catholics and Jews are here on sufferance. It is up to both of you to go along with anything I want at this time."

Shocked, Crowley reported this conversation to Treasury Secretary Henry Morgenthau Jr. Roosevelt so dominated his government that it was said of his aides and even his cabinet members that they were not much more than his "messenger boys." In reflecting years later on his tenure as Treasury Secretary, Morgenthau observed that Roosevelt "never let anybody around him have complete assurance that he would have the job tomorrow." So these two powerful men, like little boys who had discovered that their father had returned home drunk and passed out, swore never to reveal Roosevelt's comment.

"Leo, what are we fighting for?" asked Morgenthau. "Why am I killing myself at this desk if we are just here by sufferance?"

"That's what I want to know," replied Crowley, who added, "I have not discussed this with another living soul. I don't feel that I can dare do that."[14]

Probing a complex figure like Roosevelt for moral failings, especially as regards the Holocaust, has evoked passionately conflicting responses. Some historians have found fault with almost every action of Franklin Roosevelt and his government. If such a man were truly great, goes their subtext, then why didn't he do more to help the Jews, such as admit or rescue more Jews or bomb the railroads leading to Auschwitz? Others argue that Roosevelt, in successfully prosecuting the war, did more to save Jewish lives than any other man. He was a great man, goes their subtext, who did the most important thing there was to do to save Jews: he destroyed Hitler and Nazi Germany.[15]

Both themes are at least partly true. Roosevelt was as much a hard-nosed politician as he was an inspirational leader; his political calculations were as cold-blooded as his personality was sparkling. The psychiatrist Dr. Carl

Gustav Jung, after an audience with Roosevelt, commented, "Make no mistake, he is a force—a man of superior but impenetrable mind, but perfectly ruthless, a highly versatile mind which you cannot foresee." In Herman Wouk's historical novel *The Winds of War*, the fictional naval officer Pug Henry, after spending time in Roosevelt's presence, despite his sincere admiration for the president, comes to realize that "behind the warm, jolly aristocratic surface there loomed a grim ill-defined personality of distant visions and hard purpose, a tough son of a bitch to whom nobody meant very much, except perhaps his family, and maybe not they, either." The final judgment may be that Roosevelt won the war—and it took a "tough son of a bitch" to do that—and that was the single greatest contribution to saving Jewish lives. But in the process of doing so, his cold-blooded calculations gave short shrift to transcendent moral issues.[16]

In particular, Roosevelt feared fifth columnists and saboteurs. At a cabinet meeting shortly after the German invasion of Poland in September 1939, Roosevelt described a conversation between German Minister of Propaganda Joseph Goebbels and someone (not identified by Roosevelt) acquainted with Goebbels. The acquaintance had reported the conversation to Roosevelt as offering insight into the German government's thinking. In the conversation, which apparently made a lasting impression on Roosevelt, Goebbels had boasted that Germany expected to defeat Poland within a few days and then quickly defeat France and England.

"What next?" Goebbels's acquaintance asked.

"You know what is next," replied Goebbels. "The United States."

"You can hardly expect to conquer the United States from a distance of 3,500 miles of ocean."

"It will come from inside."[17]

That same month, Roosevelt received a telegram from the American ambassador to France, William Bullitt, reporting on a meeting in March of that year between Hitler and a small group of representatives from the German army, economic circles, and the Nazi Party. Hitler first described his plans for Europe, starting with an occupation of all of Czechoslovakia, to occur within days, followed by the conquest of Poland. Hitler continued: "In 1940 and 1941 Germany will settle accounts once and for all with her hereditary enemy: France. That country will be obliterated from the map of Europe. With France vanquished Germany will dominate England easily. Thus having for the first time unified the continent of Europe according to a new conception, Germany will undertake the greatest operation in all history."

That "operation" was the conquest of the United States.

"With British and French possessions in America as a base we will settle accounts with the 'Jews of the dollar' (dollar *Juden*) in the United States. We will exterminate this Jewish democracy and Jewish blood will mix itself with the dollars. Even today Americans can insult our people, but the day will come when, too late, they will bitterly regret every word they said against us."[18]

Hitler's prediction had unfolded on schedule. Shortly after the meeting, Germany occupied all of Czechoslovakia in violation of the Munich Pact; six months after that, in September 1939, the German army invaded and occupied Poland. Following the German invasions in April and May 1940 of Denmark, Norway, the Low Countries, and France (Hitler indeed "settled accounts" with Germany's longtime foe), Roosevelt addressed a Joint Session of Congress. The president had received reports that German agents disguised as tourists had infiltrated Norway six weeks in advance of the invasion of that country, and that German agents sent into the Netherlands in one guise or another had aided the German army by signaling German planes where to drop paratroopers. In his speech, Roosevelt warned of "the treacherous use of the fifth column by which persons supposed to be peaceful visitors were actually part of an enemy unit of occupation."

Based on his fear of fifth columnists, following the Japanese attack on Pearl Harbor and the German declaration of war on the United States, Roosevelt ordered the forced transfer from the Pacific Coast states of more than 100,000 persons of Japanese descent, of whom two-thirds were American citizens, to internment camps in remote and inhospitable areas in the western plains and deserts. When Eleanor tried to discuss the relocation issue with her husband, "He gave her a frigid reception and said he did not want her to mention it again." His order was enthusiastically supported by the American political establishment and, especially on the West Coast, by the American public.[19]

Only a "tough son of a bitch" could have given the transfer order, which produced some of the more morally hideous scenes in American history. More than a thousand military-aged sons from imprisoned Japanese-American families had volunteered to join, along with Nisei (American-born children of Japanese immigrants) troops from Hawaii, a Japanese-American unit, the 442nd Regimental Combat Team. The 442nd fought in Europe, where it suffered horrific casualties and became one of the most highly decorated units in the history of the American army. But in the internment camps, inside compounds surrounded by barbed wire and crammed with tar paper–covered barracks, and watched over by armed guards, Japanese-American fathers and mothers grieved for the sons who died defending the country that, for no reason other than ancestry, had deprived their families of their homes, most of their worldly goods, and their freedom. Even an admiring Roosevelt biographer like Doris Kearns Goodwin can only justify his actions by citing his overriding objective: "Totally focused on winning the war, Roosevelt mistakenly accepted the specious argument that incarceration of the Japanese Americans was a military necessity."[20]

After the war began, the Roosevelt administration's European immigration policy likewise sacrificed humanitarianism at the altar of perceived national security. Until then, Roosevelt had expressed considerable sympathy for the plight of Jews in Germany and elsewhere in Europe. In 1938, Roosevelt launched an effort to find refuge for German and Austrian Jews in other countries, which he called "my refugee proposal," and loosened American immigration quotas (even then the quotas for immigrants from the affected countries was under forty thousand per year).

In November of that year, after *Kristallnacht,* Germany's nationwide rampage against Jews, Roosevelt stated at a press conference, "I myself could scarcely believe that such things could occur in a twentieth-century civilization," and directed Secretary of State Hull to order the American ambassador to Germany to return to Washington for "report and consultation." (Hitler may have had these "insults" in mind when he addressed the elite gathering in March 1939.)

At another press conference a few days later, Roosevelt, while reiterating that he would not further relax existing immigration restrictions, discussed the approximately twelve thousand to fifteen thousand Austrian and German refugees, the majority of them Jews, in the United States on temporary visitor's permits. Roosevelt told reporters that he supported multiple six-month extensions, if necessary:

If the Congress takes no action, these unfortunate people will be allowed to stay in this country.

Will you repeat that, Mr. President?

They will be allowed to stay in this country under the six month extension law because I cannot, in any decent humanity, throw them out.

But that relatively benign approach changed after the outbreak of war in Europe. Roosevelt allowed, if not encouraged, the State Department to erect "paper walls" restricting Jewish and other refugees from entering the United States and to figuratively top them with barbed wire. By mid-1941, the new restrictions had reduced admissions to one-quarter of the applicable quotas. After Pearl Harbor, visa procedures were increasingly tightened to the point that "enemy aliens"—refugees either born or long resident in enemy countries—had to clear three separate "security-screening levels" and then provide proof that their admission would bring a "positive benefit" to the United States.[21]

The result was that the country that prided itself, in the words of the Emma Lazarus poem about the Statue of Liberty, as the beacon for the "huddled masses yearning to breathe free," doomed tens of thousands of refugees, most of them Jews.

- An American citizen in Vichy France tried to take her twelve-year-old daughter to the United States. *Visa Denied for the daughter*—the father was an Austrian, which made the daughter an enemy alien (never mind that her father was then in Cairo with the Allied forces).

- A German refugee in France, with a visa approved in 1941 in Washington, had to reapply in 1942 because, due to the entry of the United States into the war, she was now deemed to be an "enemy alien." Her niece in Washington applied for the new visa. *Visa Denied, Case May Not Be Re-opened for Six Months*—before that time elapsed, the refugee was deported to Auschwitz.

- A father in Amsterdam, after trying to navigate the State Department's visa labyrinth, decided not to wait for *Visa Denied* and, in the summer of 1942, took his family into hiding in a building on the Prinsengracht. His daughter, Anne, kept a diary, until the family was discovered and arrested by the Gestapo and sent to concentration camps where all, save the father, Otto Frank, perished.

"The strain of the past month has been something," wrote the Vienna representative of the American Friends Service Committee in 1940. "Day after day men and women just sat at my desk and sobbed. They are caught and crushed, and they know it."[22]

★ ★ ★

At precisely noon on December 8, 1942, the president's military aide, General Edwin "Pa" Watson, escorted the Jewish leaders to their meeting with the president. Roosevelt was behind his desk, smoking a cigarette in his jaunty, long cigarette holder, the Roosevelt trademark. The mood of the Jewish leaders was anything but jaunty.

Five empty chairs were arranged in front of the president's desk. Adolph Held of the Jewish Labor Committee, who took detailed notes during the meeting, noticed that Roosevelt's desk was piled with trinkets: "ash trays, brass rings, porcelain figures. There was not an empty spot on his desk. The figures were of all shapes and sizes."

"How have you been, Stephen?" Roosevelt greeted Rabbi Wise buoyantly. "You are looking well. Glad to see you looking well."

Wise introduced each of the Jewish leaders. Roosevelt responded to each by repeating the person's name, "How do you do, Mr. Monsky," and so on. After they were seated, Roosevelt opened the meeting.

"I am a sadist, a man of extreme sadistic tendencies. When I appointed Governor Lehman as head of the new Office of [Foreign] Relief and Rehabilitation [Operations], I had some very sadistic thoughts in my head. I had hopes that, when God spares my life and the war is over, to be able to go to Germany, stand behind a curtain and have the sadistic satisfaction of seeing some 'Junkers' on their knees, asking Lehman for bread. And, by God, I'll urge him to give it to them."[23]

The Jewish leaders apparently did not know what to make of Roosevelt's relish at the prospect of watching the Jewish Herbert Lehman, who ran the agency that would feed and shelter civilians in postwar Europe, toss crumbs to the defeated Germans, and none responded. Instead, Stephen Wise said, "Mr. President, we have an Orthodox rabbi in our midst. It is customary for an Orthodox rabbi to deliver a benediction upon the head of his country, when he comes in his presence. Will you, therefore, permit Rabbi Rosenberg to say the prayer of benediction?"

"Certainly."

Everyone but the president rose. Roosevelt bowed his head.

"O, God Lord of Kings, Blessed be Thy Name that Thou bestowest a share of Thy Glory upon the son of men."

"Thank you very much," said the president, visibly moved, as were the Jewish leaders.

The delegation took their seats again and Rabbi Wise read a two-page declaration, which stressed, "Unless action is taken immediately, the Jews of Hitler Europe are doomed."

"Mr. President," he continued, "we also beg to submit details and proofs of the horrible facts. We appeal to you, as head of our government, to do all in your power to bring this to the attention of the world and to do all in your power to make an effort to stop it."

Roosevelt spoke in a lordly manner, in his familiar rich aristocratic voice.

The government of the United States is very well acquainted with most of the facts you are now bringing to our attention. Unfortunately we have received confirmation from many sources. Representatives of the United States government in Switzerland and other neutral countries have given us proof that confirm the horrors discussed by you. We are dealing with an insane man—Hitler, and the group that surrounds him represent an example of a national psychopathic case. We cannot act toward them by normal means. At the same time it is not in the best interest of the Allied cause to make it appear that the entire German people are murderers or are in agreement with what Hitler is doing. There must be in Germany elements, now thoroughly subdued, but who at the proper time will, I am sure, rise, and protest against the atrocities, against the whole Hitler system.

Roosevelt promised to issue a statement and then invited suggestions by the Jewish leaders. Roosevelt listened but made no direct comments on the proposals. The meeting continued past the scheduled fifteen minutes until General Watson entered. As the Jewish leaders rose at this signal to end the meeting, Roosevelt said, "Gentlemen, you can prepare the statement. I am sure you will put words into it that express my thoughts. We shall do all in our power to be of service to your people in this tragic moment." He shook hands with each of the Jewish leaders. He had talked for 80 percent of the time.[24]

Historians have criticized the American press for doing a "mediocre job of informing their readers of Rabbi Wise's disclosures." To the thinking of the Division of European Affairs, however, Wise's press conferences and publicity campaign had been too effective. And now, after the meeting between the Jewish leaders and Roosevelt, the European Division faced a declaration by the U.S. government that confirmed Rabbi Wise's press statements that the Nazi regime was in the process of methodically murdering millions of innocent persons.[25]

★ ★ ★

The day before the meeting between the Jewish leaders and Roosevelt, the acting head of the Division of European Affairs, Ray Atherton, met with a division functionary named R. Borden Reams to discuss Rabbi Wise's publicity campaign. In every organization, there is a hapless employee at the bottom of the organizational hierarchy who is given the task that no one else wants because it offers little in the way of career advancement. In this case, the task was stopping Rabbi Wise and blocking efforts to rescue Jews. The employee assigned to do it was Reams, apparently because he had no means to fend off a directive from a superior to take responsibility for Jewish matters. His inability to shirk the Jewish assignment, combined with an apparent incapacity to empathize with suffering human beings, may have been his principal qualifications for the job.

Rarely has a historical non-entity like Borden Reams done so much damage to this country's moral stature or contributed to the loss of so many innocent lives. This is not to suggest that Reams was acting on his own initiative. To the contrary, he was zealously carrying out the wishes of his superiors, especially Atherton. But more than any other European Division official, Reams left a written trail of documents that illuminate the State Department's role in the American response to the Holocaust. While there was turnover among the high-level officials, Reams was present throughout as the department's point person in responding to the Holocaust. In effect, Reams had day-to-day responsibility for millions of lives about which he appears not to have cared very much, if at all.

Reams was born in Luthersburg, Pennsylvania, in 1904. After college and law school, he held jobs as a salesman and hotel manager until, at the age of twenty-five, he passed the Foreign Service examination. He served in several consulates before becoming second secretary at the American Legation in Copenhagen in 1940. In late 1941, he returned to Washington, where, in 1942, he was assigned to the Division of European Affairs and given the refugee portfolio. "The day to day activity is not very extensive," wrote Gardiner Howland Shaw, assistant secretary of state for administration, in recommending that Reams assume certain refugee responsibilities handled until then by other officials. He added— somewhat ominously, however—"recently the work has increased."[26]

Reams was very much up from the ranks and, in his emulation of his superiors, was "more 'Grotty' than the men who actually went to Groton in the State Department." Certainly Reams correctly perceived, and enthusiastically supported, the desire of his superiors to block efforts to officially acknowledge the Nazi extermination program.

At their meeting, Reams suggested that Atherton have "someone speak to Dr. Wise directly in an effort to call off, or at least to tone down, the present world-wide publicity campaign concerning 'mass murders,' and particularly to ask Dr. Wise to avoid any implications that the State Department furnished him with official documentary proof of these stories." Wise's autobiography makes no mention of any pressure put on him by the State Department. In all likelihood, he would have ignored it, confident in the backing of Roosevelt and Welles. When Wise continued to assert that the State Department had verified the existence of the Nazi plan, Atherton and Reams pursued a different strategy.[27]

One tactic authorized by Atherton was to deny that the State Department had confirmed the reports of mass murders, despite statements to the contrary by the undersecretary of state and the president of the United States. In effect, the Division of European Affairs would suggest that Rabbi Wise was disseminating unconfirmed and therefore unreliable reports. Following Wise's press conferences, the State Department's press spokesperson would not publicly confirm Wise's information or answer any questions. Off the record, he stated that the State Department had merely sought "to facilitate the efforts of [Wise's] Committee in getting at the truth," without indicating what the truth was.

On December 9, *The Christian Century*, a Protestant weekly, published an editorial questioning Wise's claims: "Although Rabbi Wise went out of his way to place the responsibility for the charges on the State Department, that branch of government has conspicuously refrained from issuing any confirmation." Wise wrote a letter to *The Christian Century* stating that the State Department had "not only authorized publication of the statement I made but for months had been seeking with our help to make sure of the accuracy of the statements with respect to Jewish mass slaughter." *The Christian Century* published Wise's letter but also appended its own statement that an "accredited officer" (apparently referring to the State Department press spokesman) had provided a response that, "unfortunately," was not for publication. "We have that reply in our files; it does not support Dr. Wise's contentions." (Neither did it deny Wise's contentions, a point that went unmentioned by *The Christian Century*.[28])

On December 10, a New York Republican congressman, Hamilton Fish, a prewar isolationist and ferocious Roosevelt opponent, telephoned Reams to ask whether, in fact, the State Department had confirmed the reports. Fish was disturbed by the reports of the Jewish extermination. "Does the State Department have any ideas as to the possibility of putting an end to these mass murders in the event that the reports are accurate?"

> *The whole matter is under consideration, [replied Reams] and it is difficult for me to provide any exact information. These reports, to the best of my knowledge, are as yet unconfirmed.*
>
> *Well, do you have any concrete ideas as to exactly what could be done about this situation?*
>
> *I do not.*[29]

But the State Department's tactics failed to stop issuance of a war crimes statement. The statement was an initiative of the British government, under pressure from its Jewish public and the World Jewish Congress's British section. The British draft statement cited "reports from Europe which leave no room for doubt" that the German government was carrying out Hitler's "oft repeated intention to exterminate the Jewish people in Europe.... None of those taken away are ever heard of again.... The infirm are left to die of exposure and starvation or are deliberately massacred in mass executions." The draft statement denounced "in the strongest possible terms this bestial policy of cold-blooded extermination."[30]

The draft statement reached Reams, who advised Atherton in a memorandum that he had "grave doubts in regard to the desirability or advisability of issuing a statement of this nature. In the first place, these reports are unconfirmed and emanate to a great extent from the Riegner letter to Rabbi Wise." Further, he wrote, "the statement will be taken as additional confirmation of these stories and will support Rabbi Wise's contention of official confirmation from State Department sources. The way will then be open for further pressure from interested groups for action which might affect the war effort. The plight of the unhappy peoples of Europe, including the Jews, can be alleviated only by winning the war."[31]

On the same day Reams spoke with Congressman Fish, he met with the first secretary of the British Embassy in Washington, W. G. Hayter, to discuss the draft statement.

"The Embassy agrees that the statement will do little good but feels that it could do no harm," said Hayter. "My government is anxious to release the statement. Extreme pressure is being encountered from various groups."

"The issuance of this statement," Reams replied, "would be accepted by the Jewish communities of the world as complete proof of the stories which are now being spread about. The various governments of the United Nations would expose themselves to increased pressure from all sides to do something more specific to aid these people."[32]

While Hayter apparently shared Reams's desire to avoid acknowledging the Nazi exterminations, he had his orders and held firm. Reams and his superiors did succeed, however, in persuading the British to soften the wording: for example, the crucial phrase "which leave no room for doubt" was deleted. Even so, David Wyman, a harsh critic of the American government's response to the Holocaust, observed that "despite the State Department's weakening modification, it remained a forceful statement, the strongest concerning atrocities against Jews to be issued by the Allied powers during World War II."[33]

The joint U.S.-British declaration, which vowed war crimes prosecutions against the responsible German officials after the war, was reported on the front pages of many papers in the United States, including the *New York Times*. Its editorial page pointed out what State Department officials had worked hard to deny—the declaration was "based on officially established facts; it is an official indictment."[34]

The official British reaction was more emotional than official reactions in the United States. British Foreign Secretary Anthony Eden read the declaration in the House of Commons, which had been bombed by the Luftwaffe. A Liberal MP spoke for five minutes, with tears in his eyes. A Conservative MP "feared that [the Liberal MP] might break down; the House caught his spirit and was deeply moved. Somebody suggested that we stand in silence to pay our respects to those suffering peoples, and the House as a whole rose and stood for a few frozen seconds. It was a fine moment, and my back tingled." Previously in all its storied centuries, Jewish leaders reported from Britain, the House of Commons had stood silently only to commemorate the death of a sovereign.[35]

★ ★ ★

To borrow Sumner Welles's phrase, the joint declaration confirmed the worst fears of the diplomats on the third floor of the State Department, namely, that publicizing the murder of millions would only increase pressure for rescue. Indeed, the public relations campaign by American Jews intensified in early 1943, led by a rival of the American Jewish Congress and Rabbi Wise. The rival was a handsome, charismatic, and militant twenty-seven-year old Palestinian Jew who called himself Peter H. Bergson, but whose real name was Hillel Kook. Bergson was decades ahead of his time in using public relations and lobbying techniques. Certainly, nothing like his publicity campaigns had ever been tried by Jews in America with such success.

Kook was born in 1915 in Lithuania to an eminent line of rabbis. (An uncle, Avraham Yitzak Kook, would serve as chief Ashkenazi rabbi of Palestine.) That year, the Russians expelled all Jews from Lithuania on the ground of their alleged "pro-German" sympathies in World War I. The Kook family fled to the Ukraine, where Hillel Kook's earliest memories were pogroms carried out by Ukrainian nationalists with axes and swords that left the streets in Jewish quarters covered in blood. In the mid-1920s, the Kook family emigrated to Palestine, where they settled in Jerusalem and where Hillel Kook acquired an identity as a Hebrew living in his peoples' ancient lands. After the Arab riots of 1929, in which more than five hundred Jews died, Hillel Kook first joined the Haganah defense force and then a more radical splinter group known as "Haganah Bet" (Haganah "B"), later called the *Irgun Zvai Leumi* (the National Military Organization).[36]

After the start of World War II, Hillel Kook went to the United States to campaign for a Jewish army to fight alongside the Allies in the Middle East. He adopted the name Peter Bergson to keep his activities in the United States from tarnishing his late uncle's reputation, and grew a mustache, which made him look older. He worked out of an apartment at 3 East 63rd Street in New York City, with the assistance of other young Palestinians ("Their eyes glinted with the mood of adventure," recalled one American supporter) and a young, dark-haired woman who lived down the hall and was intrigued by her mysterious, good-looking neighbor (they eventually married).

Peter Bergson was able to convert well-known politicians, public figures, and entertainers to the cause of a Jewish army. His intense, persistent plea was along these lines: "Imagine the kind of soldiers these Jews will make against the Germans. They will be like a suicide army. Given guns to fight Germans with, there is not a young Jew in the Middle East who would not gladly die on a battlefield."[37]

With his extraordinary talent at public relations, he was as much the young firebrand activist generating pressure from the outside as Rabbi Wise was the aging consummate insider who knew how to negotiate the corridors of power. Had they worked together, much might have been accomplished. Wise needed more leverage in dealing with Roosevelt and Bergson had no direct access to the president. But their generational divide, clashing stylistic approaches, and conflicting ideologies turned them into mutually contemptuous, bitter enemies. As Assistant Secretary of State Breckinridge Long observed in his diary, "The Jewish organizations are all divided and in controversies of their own. There is no adhesion nor any sympathetic collaboration—rather, rivalry, jealousy and antagonism."[38]

To the established Jewish leadership, Bergson led "front" organizations that presumed to speak for American Jewry "without having a mandate from any constituency"; that had created the "illusion of activity through press agentry"; and that had done a "disservice" to the cause "they have assumed to represent." So went a memorandum that the American Jewish Conference, an ad hoc organization of Jewish groups, publicly released to discredit Bergson. The cautious establishment leaders, largely middle-aged (or older) Jewish men, operated behind the scenes through ponderous committees, carefully written letters to the press or government officials or Eleanor Roosevelt, and the highly prized meetings (when they could get them) with the president, such as the one in December 1942. Rabbi Wise's press conferences and days of mourning were as confrontational as they were willing to be in a country where public opinion polls reported that between 30 percent and 50 percent of the public believed that Jews had "too much power in the United States." To them, Bergson and his Palestinian colleagues were young, brash, and irreverent self-promoting interlopers who cynically used the plight of Jews as a fund-raising device.[39]

To Bergson, the establishment Jews were self-important, wealthy businessmen and lawyers who devoted just a few hours a week to saving Jewish lives, which they were willing to sacrifice in favor of advancing the Zionist cause; he and his colleagues, on the other hand, were working sixteen hours a day, seven days a week. Above all, in Bergson's eyes, establishment Jews were unwilling to use creative but confrontational tactics and were working as hard to undermine Bergson in the Jewish community as they were to rescue Jews. By necessity, Bergson began approaching congressmen and senators in states without significant Jewish populations—and with considerable success. Over time, the establishment Jews claimed the executive branch, especially the president, as their turf to be zealously guarded from infringement, while the Bergson group burrowed deep into Congress.

Bergson and Wise barely concealed their mutual hatred—and fear. "*Mi samcha,*" Bergson recalled being asked by Rabbi Wise—in effect, "Who put you in charge?" In Bergson's telling, Wise had deliberately used a phrase from Exodus. (In the story, after Moses has killed an Egyptian for beating a Jewish slave, he tries to break up a quarrel between two Jews. "Who made you prince and judge over us?" one of the quarreling Jews asks Moses. "Do you intend to kill me, as you killed the Egyptian?") Indeed, Wise confided to one Treasury Department lawyer that he thought the Bergson group might try to kill him; a different Treasury lawyer commented that he thought Bergson would be the one to be murdered.[40]

What especially infuriated the establishment Jewish groups was Bergson's talent for using newspaper advertisements, then a relatively new form of publicity, and pageants to advance his cause and seemingly usurp their hard-won status as spokespersons for American Jews. On December 7, 1942, Bergson's Committee for a Jewish Army ran an ad in the *New York Times*—"A Proclamation on the Moral Rights of Stateless and Palestinian Jews"—which stated that "every footstep of the Jew in Europe is stained with his own blood." Twenty-seven senators, twenty governors, and hundreds of other prominent Americans had signed the ad. Among the names were Senator Harry Truman, former President Herbert Hoover, Cecil B. DeMille, Clare Boothe Luce, Katherine Anne Porter, Humphrey Bogart, Eugene O'Neill, Jimmy Durante, and Aaron Copland.[41]

As soon as the Riegner report became public in late 1942, Bergson began mapping out a crusade to save Jews in occupied Europe. A Bergson ally, playwright Ben Hecht—who had written or collaborated on the screenplays for *The Front Page, Scarface, Wuthering Heights, Gunga Din,* and *Gone With the Wind,* among others—wrote *We Will Never Die.* Kurt Weill, composer of *The Threepenny Opera,* contributed the music, based on *Kol Nidre,* the hymn traditionally sung during Yom Kippur, and other Jewish religious melodies. One of Bergson's supporters was the actress and method acting teacher Stella Adler. She later convinced one of her talented acting students to take a leading role in a subsequent Bergson pageant, *A Flag Is Born.* The acting student's name was Marlon Brando.[42]

After opening in New York on March 9, 1943, *We Will Never Die* was performed in other American cities and broadcast by radio. More than 100,000 Americans saw a performance. First Lady Eleanor Roosevelt, along with six Supreme Court justices, many cabinet members, three hundred senators and congressmen, diplomats from dozens of nations, and numerous military officers attended the performance in Washington. In her column, "My Day," Eleanor described the performance as one of the most "impressive and moving pageants I have ever seen. No one who heard each group come forward and give the story of what had happened to it at the hands of a ruthless German military, will ever forget those haunting words: 'Remember us.'"[43]

We Will Never Die was the single most effective attempt to bring the Nazi scheme to murder European Jewry to the attention of the American public. Even so, the American Jewish Congress (or its allies), already deeply antagonistic to Bergson's "circus show people," blocked performances in a number of cities. In Gary, Indiana, for example, preparations by the local committee organizing the pageant's staging were well under way. When the committee was advised that several mainstream Jewish organizations, including B'nai B'rith, the Jewish Welfare Board, and both the local Reform and Orthodox temples, had "unanimously agreed to present a demand to the American Legion that it be stopped," the preparations were abandoned and *We Will Never Die* was never performed in Gary.[44]

★ ★ ★

As pressure for rescue efforts increased, new reports from Europe reached England and America. One of the most harrowing was a report by Jan Karski (a code name; he had been born Jan Kozielewski), a young courier from the non-Jewish underground in Poland who had traveled all nine circles of Hell and returned to tell the tale. After the fall of Poland in 1939, Karski, a lanky Polish army artillery officer, had been taken prisoner by the Soviet army, which had crossed Poland's eastern border following the German invasion. The Soviets turned him over to the Germans. He escaped from a prisoner-of-war train by squeezing through a small window and leaping to the ground. He then walked, or rode on carts or wagons and on a train for the last leg, for six days until he reached Warsaw, where he joined the Polish underground.

While in the underground, Karski was captured by the Gestapo. He was beaten regularly but did not reveal any information. Between the beatings, the guards brought him to a lavatory so he could clean up the blood on his face. Lying on a windowsill above the sink was a used razor blade, which no one had noticed except for Karski, who hid it in a mattress until the beatings, which broke teeth and fractured several ribs, became unbearable. He slit his wrists with the razor blade and then waved his arms to keep the blood flowing, but the Gestapo found him before he had bled to death and put him into an SS-guarded hospital.

After a while, with so many white bandages wrapped around the splints on his wrists that it looked as though he wore white boxing gloves, Karski was removed for more interrogation. He pretended to collapse and was sent back for medical treatment. Finally, the Polish underground managed to rescue him from a local hospital. One of his rescuers said to him after they were safe, "Don't be too grateful to us. We had two orders about you. The first was to do everything in our power to help you escape. The second was to shoot you if we failed. You were lucky."[45]

After seven months spent recovering from his ordeal, and undergoing close scrutiny by the underground to eliminate their suspicion that he had become a German double agent while in the Gestapo's hands, Karski resumed work in the underground. In 1942, he was given a new mission. He was to travel to England and the United States to report on conditions in Poland. But first, to fulfill his job of witness, Karski had to experience the unimaginable. He was warned that he would have to risk his life and, if he lived, he would be haunted forever by what he was about to see.

Wearing a shabby suit and a cap pulled down over his eyes, Karski was taken to leaders of the Jewish underground, who would guide him through the Warsaw ghetto. His guides were doomed and desperate men, "their glances filled with a burden of despair, pain, and hopelessness they could never completely express." Even though they spoke in whispers, Karski had the sense that they were screaming. "Our entire people will be destroyed," they told him two days before entering the ghetto. "A few may be saved, perhaps, but three million Polish Jews are doomed. This cannot be prevented by any force in Poland nor the Jewish Underground. Place this responsibility on the shoulders of the Allies. Let not a single leader of the United Nations be able to say that they did not know we were being murdered."

"I will do my best to tell them and make them understand what you have told me."

"We demand still more," one leader insisted. "Let the Allied governments, wherever their hand can reach, in America, England and Africa, begin public executions of Germans, any they can get hold of. That is what we demand."

"But that is utterly fantastic." Karski was stunned. "A demand like that will only confuse and horrify all those who are sympathetic with you."

"Of course. Do you think I don't know it? We demand it so people will know how we feel about what is being done to us, how desperate our plight is, and how little we stand to gain from an Allied victory as things are now."

"One moment more," said one of his guides. "This we did not intend to tell you, but I want you to know it. The ghetto is going to go up in flames. We are not going to die in slow torment, but fighting."[46]

The ghetto was separated from the rest of the city by a high brick wall. As he approached the wall with his guides, Karski acquired the first of the memories that he would fight back for the rest of his life. Outside the wall were a few Jewish children who had escaped the ghetto. "They look less human than like monsters, dirty, ragged, with eyes that will haunt me forever—eyes of little beasts in the last anguish of death," he later recalled. "They trust no one and expect only the worst from human beings. They slide along the walls of houses looking about them in mortal fear. No one knows where they sleep. From time to time they knock at the door of a Pole and beg for something to eat." And that was *outside* the ghetto.[47]

Karski entered a building that, as he later termed it, was the river Styx of the city because it opened on the other side into the Hieronymus Bosch landscape that was the Warsaw ghetto. The building "connected the world of the living with the world of the dead."

Of those he encountered on the ghetto's streets, Karski later wrote: "These were still living people, if you could call them such. For apart from their skin, eyes and voice there was nothing human left in these palpitating figures." He entered a park with leafless trees. Mothers sat on benches nursing withered babies. "Children, every bone in their skeletons showing through their taut skins, played in heaps and swarms."

"They play before they die," commented one of his guides.

"But these children are not playing," said Karski. "They only make believe it is play."

Karski walked for hours. "As we picked our way across the mud and rubble, the shadows of what had once been men or women flitted by us in pursuit of someone or something, their eyes blazing with some insane hunger or greed." As he walked, Karski reeled from the stench of decaying bodies, the wails of the insane and the starving, and the catatonic stares of the near dead who had slipped to the ground and lay half-propped against a wall, their only sign of life the barely perceptible twitches beneath the dirty rags of their clothing. Here and there in the ghetto were well-fed German policemen, who appeared "abnormally bloated" in contrast to the ghetto's inhabitants. Two days later Karski forced himself to make a return visit to the ghetto so that he could report on conditions even more vividly to the Allied nations.[48]

Karski was then infiltrated into a death camp, near what he mistakenly believed was the town of Bełżec, in the uniform of a camp guard. As he neared the camp, he heard "a series of long screams or a particularly inhuman groan."

"What's happening?" he asked a guard. "What's the meaning of all that noise?"

"The Jews are hot," the guard replied, grinning at his witticism.

Inside the camp Karski came upon a long train of freight cars. Fighting nausea and an overwhelming impulse to "run and flee," and desperately clinging to his sanity, Karski watched as SS men forced 120 or more Jews into each car. "The [first] two cars were now crammed to bursting with tightly packed human flesh, completely, hermetically, filled. All this while the entire camp reverberated with a tremendous volume of sound in which hideous groans and screams mingled weirdly with shots, curses, and bellowed commands."

What he next witnessed compelled him to later write in his memoir, "I know that many people will not believe me, will not be able to believe me, will think I exaggerate or invent. But I saw it."

The floors of the freight cars had been covered with a thick, white powder—quicklime. When quicklime comes in contact with moisture—rain- or tap water or the bodily fluids of too many human bodies packed into too small a space—it bubbles and steams, releasing an enormous quantity of heat and chlorine gas. "From one end to the other, the train, with its quivering cargo of flesh, seemed to throb, vibrate, rock, and jump as if bewitched. There would be a strangely uniform momentary lull and then, again, the train would begin to moan and sob, wail and howl." Karski, losing control of his emotions, began weeping and nearly gave himself away.[49]

After a trip across occupied Europe worthy of a spy story in itself, Karski arrived in England in late November 1942. In London, Karski was given an audience with prominent English political leaders, including Foreign Secretary Eden, who listened to Karski's story.

"I would like to propose that the Allies drop leaflets in Germany describing the Nazi extermination policy. If the Nazis do not stop the killing, then there should be retaliatory bombing—"

Interrupting Karski, Eden raised his hand in a gesture that was a harbinger of things to come. "The Polish report on the atrocities has already reached us. The matter will take its proper course."

"Let's go to the window," said Eden. "I want to have a good look at you."

In the brighter light, the foreign secretary stared at Karski. "You seem to have been through everything in this war except one: the Germans did not shoot you."[50]

★ ★ ★

Rabbi Stephen Wise's press conferences, the Day of Mourning, the joint U.S.-British statement, the accounts of Karski's reports from Poland—State Department officials on the third floor watched all of this with growing concern as pressure mounted for rescue in the coming year. But "the greatest shock of early 1943 was another telegram from Gerhart Riegner in Switzerland," written in collaboration with Richard Lichtheim.[51]

The telegram was dated January 19, 1943. Like the earlier Riegner telegram, it was delivered to the American legation in Bern for transmittal via the State Department to Rabbi Wise. The telegram (excerpted earlier in "Eighteen Months Later") was precise in describing the acceleration of the Nazi plan: "6000 [Jews] are killed daily [at a single location in Poland] . . . required, before execution, to strip themselves of all their clothing, which is then sent to Germany . . . about 2000 in hiding [in Berlin] and there have been many cases of suicide . . . it is reported from Prague and Berlin that no Jews will be left in either city by the end of March."

The telegram emphasized the ongoing horror in Transnistria: "130,000 [Romanian] Jews were deported to Transnistria . . . approximately 60,000 [had already died] . . . 70,000 are starving." In a description that was accurate but still could not do justice to the suffering of Ruth Glasberg and the other Transnistrian Jews, the telegram reported: "The living conditions are indescribable. They are deprived of all money, foodstuffs and possessions, and are housed in deserted cellars, and occasionally twenty to thirty people sleep on the floor of one unheated room. Disease is rife."[52]

The Bern legation transmitted the telegram to the State Department in a cable sent on January 21. The cable was numbered 482. On February 9, the State Department sent a copy of the telegram to Stephen Wise. The transmittal letter had been drafted by the Division of European Affairs and sent under the signature of Sumner Welles. The letter stated: "The Department of State cannot assume any official responsibility for the information contained in these reports, since the data is not based on investigations conducted by any of its representatives abroad." The letter suggested that this disclaimer applied to the information provided by Welles to Wise the previous November, even though it had been the product of investigations by State Department diplomats.[53]

The release of yet another Riegner report coincided with the plans by Rabbi Wise and his allies and the Bergson group to hold a mass protest meeting and the premiere of the *We Will Never Die* pageant, respectively, at Madison Square Garden in early March. The last thing the third floor wanted was more mass rallies fueled by more reports of Jewish exterminations, especially any sent by American diplomats. The Division of European Affairs drafted a cable for transmission to the Bern legation. The cable instructed the legation to stop transmitting any more reports of the mass murders. The identity of the draftsman is unknown, but it likely was Borden Reams acting under Atherton's direction. The cable was also drafted for the signature of Sumner Welles. Four officials on the third floor approved the cable, which was dated February 10 and numbered 354.[54]

Two officials who initialed the cable were Ray Atherton, acting chief of the Division of European Affairs, and the State Department adviser on political relations, James Dunn. The other two responsible European Division officials were the assistant chief of the European Division, John D. Hickerson, and a Foreign Service officer, Elbridge Durbrow. The cable was then sent down to Sumner Welles on the second floor, who initialed it.

Historians agree that "almost certainly, [Welles] had simply initialed it in routine fashion. As the message crossed his desk, it would have attracted his attention only in the unlikely event that he had recalled what [cable] 482 from Bern actually was." That, of course, was the whole purpose of drafting cable 354 with only the barest of references to the earlier cable. In fact, several weeks later, at Rabbi Wise's request, Welles cabled the American legation in Switzerland to obtain more information.[55]

The authors of cable 354 had adopted the technique used during the Peyrouton affair of drafting cables with hidden agendas for the signatures of overburdened senior officials. As such, this was a conspiracy—and with a conspiratorial objective that defies belief. The Division of European Affairs was attempting to cover up reports of the murder of millions of human beings and make it appear that Sumner Welles, who had encouraged Rabbi Wise to publicize the Nazi extermination scheme, authorized the cover-up. It was done in defiance of the official policy of the U.S. government, which had both confirmed the existence of the Nazi extermination plan and vowed to try the responsible German officials as war criminals. Coming so soon after the reports by Jan Karski, who had risked both life and sanity to provide detailed accounts of the mass murders, it likely was the most shameful cable ever transmitted by the State Department.

```
To: American Legation, Bern

From: Secretary of State, No. 354

Date: February 10, 1943

Your 482, January 21


In the future we would suggest that you do not
accept reports submitted to you to be transmitted
to private persons in the United States unless
such action is advisable because of extraordi-
nary circumstances. Such private messages cir-
cumvent neutral countries' censorship and it is
felt that by sending them we risk the possibility
that steps would necessarily be taken by neutral
countries to curtail or forbid our means of com-
munication for confidential official matter.
HULL

(SW)[56]
```

X

JEWS FOR SALE

FOR SALE TO HUMANITY

70,000 JEWS

GUARANTEED HUMAN BEINGS AT $50 A PIECE

The advertisement by Peter Bergson's Committee for a Jewish Army ran on page 11 of the February 16, 1943, edition of the *New York Times*. Below the headline, the text stated: "Romania is tired of killing Jews. It has killed one hundred thousand of them in two years. Romania will now give Jews away practically for nothing."

★ ★ ★

The advertisement was no public relations stunt. On February 2, 1943, in a devastating defeat for Germany, the German Sixth Army finally had surrendered at Stalingrad. The Romanian army that had fought alongside the Germans in the Stalingrad campaign lost nearly 160,000 dead, wounded, or missing. The Romanian government, no longer confident that its ally Germany would win the war and seeking to ease otherwise harsh peace terms, had made approaches to Jewish organizations about relocating the 70,000 Jews still alive in Transnistria. A *New York Times* reporter in London, C. L. Sulzberger, had found out about the Romanian initiative and filed a story describing the terms of the offer. The Transnistrian Jews could be relocated to a location of the Allies' choosing, although the Romanian government suggested Palestine and even offered to provide Romanian ships to transport the Jews. In return, the Romanian government wanted its expenses paid, which was about 20,000 Romanian lei ($50) per refugee (according to the advertisement), not including shipping costs if Romanian ships were used.[1]

Three days after Sulzberger's story appeared, the "For Sale to Humanity" advertisement ran in the *Times*. In a message directed to the president (and less directly to the State Department), the advertisement—written by Ben Hecht—sarcastically stated: "Attention Four Freedoms!!! No spies were found among the 300,000 Jews who came to Palestine since Hitler assumed power in Germany. There will be no spies smuggled in among these Jews (If there are you can shoot them)."[2]

★ ★ ★

On February 22, 1943, two members of the British section of the World Jewish Congress, Noah Barou and Alex Easterman, telegraphed Rabbi Stephen Wise and others in New York. Their telegram stated: "Suggest we approach here Allied government occupied countries asking joint declaration similar that issued Polish government regarding maintenance repatriation refugees able escape. If you agree please approach Washington ambassadors accordingly cable instructions."

Three days later, a copy of the Barou-Easterman cable was on the desk of George Brandt, the executive assistant to Assistant Secretary of State Breckinridge Long. A legend had been added:

Special Notice—The attached information was taken from private communications, and its extremely confidential character must be preserved. The information must be confined only to those officials whose knowledge of it is necessary to prosecution of the war. In no case should it be widely distributed or copies made, or the information used in legal proceedings or in any other public way without express consent of the Director of Censorship. Byron Price, Director.

Brandt attached a note to the cable and sent it and one other to the State Department's Visa Division. "Here are copies of two intercepted telegraphic messages which crossed my desk and which Mr. Long thinks you should have to put with the presently developing file on the refugee question since they relate to that question."

Less than two weeks after the attack on Pearl Harbor, President Roosevelt had issued Executive Order 8985, which established the Office of Censorship, and appointed Byron Price, executive news editor of the Associated Press, as its director. The EO 8985 declared that the nation's security required that "military information that might be of aid to the enemy be scrupulously withheld at the source." As recounted by a historian of the Office of Censorship, Price established, among others, the Cable Division, which "censored cables, telegrams, radiograms, and telephone calls across the borders." The Office of Censorship began sharing intercepted communications with "the FBI, the State Department, and the Office of Strategic Services through an intelligence system established early in the war."

None of the intercepted cables given to the State Department concerning the plight of Jews in Europe contained military information. Rather, the cables reported—in anguished terms—what was happening to European Jewry: "terrible news . . . only a quarter of million Jews remain in Poland."

The Jewish leaders who sent or received these cables certainly knew that the Office of Censorship would intercept and review their communications. In fact, one cable, which concerned the availability of "neutral shipping" to transport refugees, included a paragraph intended to reassure the Office of Censorship that it contained no military information: "Note for censor explanation for censor the above is an answer to a cable we recd from Messrs Baron Easterman on March 9." Less clear is whether they suspected that the State Department would regularly receive copies of their cables, which described in detail the strategies of the Jewish organizations to pressure the governments of the United States and other countries to do more to rescue

Jews and stop "wholesale slaughter European Jewry." It was no secret that intercepts thought to be useful in detecting espionage were given to government agencies.

Perhaps if the Jewish groups had known that the State Department was reading their cables, they would have sent them anyway in the hope that the department officials might be moved if not by the plight of European Jews, at least by their fellow American citizens' torment. But nothing in the historical record suggests that the State Department officials with access to these cables, in fact, did anything other than continue unrelentingly to oppose efforts to rescue Jews or to otherwise stop the slaughter.[3]

★ ★ ★

The "For Sale to Humanity" advertisement provoked acrimony between Peter Bergson and Rabbi Wise, who accused the Bergson group of fraudulently soliciting donations in the guise of rescuing Romanian Jews at $50 per Jew (Bergson denied the accusations). Indeed, Wise initially dismissed the offer as a "swindle" by the Romanian government. But the Romanian government's offer also attracted attention at the highest levels of the Roosevelt administration. Secretary of the Treasury Henry Morgenthau Jr. brought the Sulzberger story to the attention of the president, who referred Morgenthau to Sumner Welles. On February 15, Morgenthau telephoned Welles and explained that he had called FDR:

> *[I brought to] his attention an article written by young Sulzberger from London in regard to Romanian Jews, in which it said that the Romanian Government was willing to help 70,000 Jews come out.*
>
> *I don't think I saw it, Henry.*
>
> *I sent it to you about five minutes ago.*
>
> *Oh, you have? Thanks.*
>
> *Now the President didn't know anything about it, and he said talk to you about it and the first time that you saw him, would you discuss it with him.*

Welles agreed to look into the Romanian offer and cabled the American ambassador in Turkey to investigate. The ambassador concluded that there was a basis for the Sulzberger story. A Dutch businessman living in Romania had conveyed the Romanian government's offer to the representative in Istanbul of the Jewish Agency for Palestine. Not only did the proposal appear "official," it had also been endorsed by the Catholic bishop of Bucharest, who was willing to permit "use of the Vatican flag on the ships" that would transport the Transnistrian Jews to Palestine or "another allied port." Welles sent the ambassador's report to Morgenthau, along with a note saying, "I am having a further investigation made and I shall keep you informed."[4]

The Sulzberger story and the Bergson advertisement prompted inquiries to the State Department, including from U.S. senators. On March 10 and 11, the State Department, which meant the Division of European Affairs, issued letters under Welles's signature:

> *This story is without foundation. It originated from an unofficial non-Romanian resident of Bucharest who was visiting Istanbul. The probable actual source is the German propaganda machine, which is always ready to use the miseries of the people of occupied Europe in order to attempt to create confusion and doubt within the United Nations.*[5]

Why did Welles sign these letters? The Romanian rescue plan had been brought to his attention by a cabinet member, who advised Welles that the president was aware of the rescue proposal; Welles had promptly cabled the American ambassador to Turkey, who replied that there was reason to believe that the Romanian government had, in fact, made the proposal; and Welles had personally promised Morgenthau he would continue investigating. Certainly, one explanation was that Welles routinely had signed the letters, as he had initialed cable 354, without appreciating their significance. At the least, however, Welles lacked consistent focus on Jewish rescue issues when they came across his desk (and, as explained in a subsequent chapter, by now, he may have been distracted by other concerns). Nonetheless, Welles, at Rabbi Wise's request, soon was actively soliciting information from Minister Leland Harrison about the Romanian rescue proposal.

By the end of March, Gerhart Riegner apparently had become concerned that the most recent information about the plight of European Jews, including the Romanian Jews in Transnistria, had not been given to Rabbi Wise. Riegner managed to get a message to Wise in New York City that he had urgent news. On March 31, Wise wrote to Welles:

> *We have received a cable from Dr. Riegner that he has some further information of considerable importance with regard to the Jewish situation in Nazi-occupied territories which he is anxious to convey to you and to us through your Minister in Switzerland. May I ask you to be good enough to ask your Minister to get this information from Dr. Riegner and to forward it to you.*[6]

On April 5, Welles, apparently unaware that the third floor had been blocking reports from Europe, sent a memorandum to Ray Atherton. "I feel we should at least instruct Leland Harrison to get in touch with Dr. Riegner and cable us a summary of the information which the latter has at his disposal. I have informed Rabbi Wise that we have taken this step." The Division of European Affairs could not ignore a direct request from the undersecretary. Five days later, the division sent a cable to Minister Harrison in Bern requesting that he contact Riegner and "cable summary of information at his disposal."[7]

Harrison, having received two contradictory cables in two months, responded on April 20 with cable 2460. In it, he expressed his frustration with cable 354, which had shut down the Bern legation as a conduit for Riegner's information.

```
While I have not transmitted R's messages as such
in compliance with the terms of your [cable] 354,
February 10, I have at the same time felt that
information which he is able to furnish and which
appears to be reasonably authentic should be in
your hands.
```

In a somewhat emphatic manner for an American diplomat communicating with his superiors, Harrison added: "May I suggest that messages of this character should not (repeat not) be subjected to the restriction imposed by your 354, February 10, and that I be permitted to transmit messages from

[Riegner] more particularly in view of the helpful information which they may frequently contain."[8]

Shortly thereafter, Harrison sent a report from Riegner to the State Department. But in doing so, Harrison displayed his ambivalence by demanding that Riegner promise to pay the costs of sending the lengthy cable. Considering the number of lives at stake and the insignificant cost of the cable to the U.S. government, it may have been one of the pettiest gestures by an American official in all of World War II. Riegner, perhaps no longer capable of astonishment when it came to the State Department, quickly agreed. "This was the most costly telegram of my life," wrote Riegner afterward. "The charge amounted to one month of my salary. But, considering the consequences that it later had, it was the most profitable telegram that I ever sent."[9]

Once assured that he could always defend his disagreement with the third floor over cable 354 by pointing out that at least the U.S. government had not been burdened by the cost of sending Riegner's reports, Harrison dispatched a multipart cable stating that "this message is sent by R[iegner] with a request that W[ise] be informed." The message reviewed the possibility of getting aid to, or even rescuing, Jews in several locations in the occupied countries, including the Jews in Transnistria and Jewish children in France. Echoing the Sulzberger dispatch and the Bergson advertisement, considerable space was devoted to a plan to rescue Transnistrian Jews, including orphaned children:

```
Wide rescue action equally possible for Roma-
nia especially Transnistria provided necessary
amounts available. . . . We received last few
days new urgent appeal for assistance Trans-
nistria and they need 100,000,000 lei of which
urgently 60,000,000 for clothing and most nec-
essary equipment for children and orphans who
should be transferred to Palestine. Transfer of
money to Romania not necessary if definite guaran-
tee be given that amount be put at disposal Swit-
zerland or America and paid after war.[10]
```

As it emerged in final form in the reports transmitted by Harrison, Riegner's proposal was that the funds demanded by the Romanian government would be paid in Romania, ostensibly by "well-to-do" Jewish businessmen who lived in the areas unaffected by the deportations to Transnistria.* These businessmen would be reimbursed at black market rates from private funds from American Jews that would be placed in a blocked Swiss bank account. The reimbursement, however, would take place only after the war had ended. The American legation in Bern, or else the consulate in Geneva, could have supervisory authority over the Swiss bank account. This arrangement, Wise stressed in a letter to Sumner Welles, "appears to be the only way to save thousands of Jews, who otherwise would be doomed to death in Transnistria and France."[11]

However, before Wise could approach the Treasury Department for a license to transfer the rescue funds to Switzerland, he went on to write, "We must know whether the State Department would be ready to recommend the granting of such a license to the Treasury," whose approval was required for these types of transactions. Ordinarily, the Special Division, under Assistant Secretary of State Long, would have dealt with such a proposal. But apparently because the rescue proposal involved economic issues or because he did not think the Special Division would be sympathetic, or both, Welles referred the rescue plan to Dr. Herbert Feis, the State Department's chief economic adviser.[12]

Feis, then fifty years old, was a Jew. Even though he was a Hoover administration holdover and never a New Dealer, the corridor gossip about Feis was unkind, inaccurate, and hinted of anti-Semitism: "He looks like Harpo and talks like Karl Marx." In fact, Feis was an intellectual, not an ideologue, and certainly not a Communist. A product of both the New York City school system and Harvard University, he strongly supported Cordell Hull's commitment to free trade. And, while he may or may not have had a sense of humor, he apparently did not think there was anything amusing about the plight of the Transnistrian Jews.[13]

---

* One mystery is why, if the rescue was to be initially financed by well-to-do Jewish businessmen in Romania, those businessmen did not simply go ahead and fund the rescue while waiting for the blocked Swiss bank accounts to be established. Nor is it entirely clear whether funding the rescue meant paying bribes to Romanian government officials or whether it meant only paying the costs of supporting and transporting the Transnistrian Jews, although it appeared common ground that, however earmarked, rescue monies would be received by Romanian officials. As well, some cables discussed only the rescue of children while other cables appeared to refer to the rescue of all of the surviving Transnistrian Jews. Part of the difficulty in understanding the proposal was that it had to pass through so many hands, from the sources in Romania to Riegner to Harrison, who would transmit the information to the State Department to give to Wise, who would then describe the proposal in his meetings and correspondence. The State Department, as will be seen, seized on these ambiguities as a basis for blocking the rescue.

Once Welles handed him the Romanian rescue proposal, Feis called in Bernard Meltzer, the acting chief of the Division of Foreign Funds Control. Then twenty-nine years old and the son of Russian immigrants, Meltzer was another rare Jew in the State Department. A graduate of the University of Chicago and of its Law School, where he had been first in his class, Meltzer had joined the State Department after serving on the staff of a national commission that identified the materials needed by U.S. military forces and America's allies for the war effort. Meltzer was also a serious person of real accomplishment.[14]

Feis and Meltzer conferred and quickly agreed that Assistant Secretary of State Long and his third-floor colleagues certainly would oppose the rescue proposal. As Jews in the State Department with responsibility only for economic issues, they would be encroaching on the turfs of both the Division of European Affairs and Long. The most that could be done, both men concluded, would be to buy time and hope that the Treasury Department could be persuaded to intercede.

Perhaps neither realized it then, but buying time meant engaging in an activity that resembled a bureaucratic delaying tactic. Meltzer persuaded Welles to send a cable to the Bern legation on May 25 that posed questions—"Is it contemplated that the official permission of the Romanian government for the departure of the refugees will be sought?" for example—and made comments—such as "There is no known plan for the evacuation of children from Romania to Palestine"—about the rescue proposal. Meltzer, like Paul Appleby, would later bitterly rue his fall into a bureaucratic black hole that defied the ordinary human physics of morality and compassion.[15]

On June 14, Minister Harrison in Bern responded with a detailed description from Riegner of the rescue plan for both the Romanians and the French children, even including the rates of foreign exchange for the blocked funds. On June 25, executing the second part of the strategy he had developed with Feis, Meltzer called John Pehle, the Treasury Department's director of the Division of Foreign Funds Control, and asked for a meeting. Meltzer also forwarded to Pehle paraphrases of his May 25 cable and the Bern legation's lengthy June 14 response. "I should appreciate discussing the problems involved as soon as you have had an opportunity to study these paraphrases."[16]

On July 15, State Department and Treasury Department officials met to discuss the issuance of a license. Bernard Meltzer was present, but so was

Borden Reams on behalf of the Division of European Affairs. Present from the Treasury Department was its general counsel, Randolph E. Paul, a fifty-three-year-old former New York tax attorney. A dapper man with a widow's peak, Paul was a tough, no-nonsense lawyer who had begun his legal career as a telephone switchboard operator in a New York City law firm and risen swiftly. In 1942, he had helped redraft the nation's tax code to meet wartime financial needs.[17]

From the start of the meeting, Reams fought the rescue approval, even though it did not involve admitting Jews to the United States, which so far had been the major flashpoint in the confrontation between Jewish refugee advocates in America and the State Department. Now, the Division of European Affairs sought to block Jews in *another* country from rescuing their fellow Jews and evacuating them to a country *other* than the United States.[18]

Reams ticked off his objections.

It would be probably impossible to work out satisfactory arrangements with the Romanian authorities. German consent would not be forthcoming. Under the British White Paper only about 30,000 Jews can be admitted to Palestine [and there are no] other areas to which the remaining Jews could be evacuated. The Turkish Government has refused entry to Jewish refugees.

"This is not a government-to-government arrangement with Romania," said Meltzer, openly disagreeing with his State Department colleague notwithstanding that they were in the presence of an official from another agency. "The proposal is based on underground methods. It's difficult to say that such methods might not be successful in at least getting some Jews out of Romania."

The one memorandum of the conversation makes no mention of the expression on Reams's face at this point. Paul, the most senior official present, apparently sat silently listening to Reams, who ended the conversation in bureaucratic fashion. "In a few days we expect a report from our Ambassador in Turkey which might throw some light on the problem. As soon as we receive the report, we can discuss the matter again."

Randolph Paul was no fool. As he later stated in a memorandum summarizing the meeting: "It is perfectly apparent to us from our dealings with the State Department on this issue that there is a very bitter fight going on in the State Department regarding the whole refugee question. While it is difficult to pierce the veil of secrecy surrounding the issue in State, there is reason to believe that the Foreign Service Officer group are the ones resisting proposals for assistance to the refugees."[19]

On July 16, the day after the meeting with Reams and Meltzer, Treasury lawyers advised the State Department that they were prepared to approve the license for the rescue of Romanian Jews and the French children. Two weeks later, despite having been admonished by Long's executive assistant that the Division of Foreign Funds Control "should confine itself to the question of whether this scheme would benefit the enemy and should make no proposal to the Department as to the proper means of dealing with refugee evacuations," Meltzer sent a strongly worded memorandum to Hull, Reams, Long, and Welles in support of the proposal. He emphasized that, as structured, the rescue plan would not involve payments to the Romanian government during the war; no improper action by American government officials would be required; and the Treasury could terminate the program whenever it desired. He ended with a plea that lives were at stake: "In view of the Department's humanitarian interest in rescuing refugees, it would appear that, unless there is some countervailing foreign policy objection, the Department should endorse, rather than veto the proposal."[20]

Meltzer's memorandum in turn galvanized the opponents of rescue in the State Department. Assistant Secretary of State Long, on vacation in Massachusetts for a "badly needed" rest, sent George Brandt, his executive assistant, to meet with Cordell Hull without Bernard Meltzer present. Brandt appeared in Hull's office on August 3. Meltzer's memorandum was on Hull's desk.[21]

"Mr. Secretary," said Brandt, referring to Meltzer's memorandum, "this concerns a proposal to make private funds available from the United States to guarantee clandestine payments in Romania for the relief and evacuation of Jews. As I understand it, it would make funds available to the enemy which would be in the nature of ransom payments. I therefore do not wish to associate myself with the proposal."

Since Meltzer's memorandum said just the opposite, Brandt must have assumed that Hull had not read the memorandum or, even if he had, did not understand it. Brandt then recommended to Hull that the State Department neither approve nor disapprove the rescue proposal but treat the issue as a Treasury responsibility.

It was a clever ploy. The Treasury Department had no authority over Minister Leland Harrison and the American legation in Switzerland. Without State Department direction, Harrison would not comply with a request from Treasury to transmit the license to Gerhart Riegner. State would seemingly shift responsibility to the Treasury but block the rescue plan by its own inaction. The State Department could even graciously agree to forward the Treasury Department's license to Harrison.

On returning to his office, Brandt sent a memorandum to Dr. Herbert Feis reporting on his meeting with Hull, which ended: "The Secretary then asked me to send the file to you with a memorandum saying that it was his opinion that the matter should be left to the Treasury Department to be handled."

Feis and Meltzer had been outmaneuvered. Hull was not about to disregard the advice of more senior officials, especially Brandt on behalf of Breckinridge Long, that, in effect, the State Department block the rescue plan without appearing to do so. Such discreet sabotage was all the more necessary now, since the president had become involved.[22]

★ ★ ★

A week and a half earlier, on July 22, Rabbi Stephen Wise—unaware of the Treasury Department's approval or the State Department's opposition, but frustrated with the delay nonetheless—was at the White House for a meeting with Roosevelt. The report from Riegner had convinced Wise that the Romanian government's offer was genuine, and he brought up the rescue plan during the meeting.

"I hesitate a little," Wise told Roosevelt," to bring the following to your attention. Even if you found that you could not comply with the extraordinary request I am about to make, you will understand and forgive." He then outlined the rescue plan in detail, explaining the need for Treasury Department approval. Making plain that in all likelihood the blocked funds in Switzerland would never be paid, even after the war ended, Wise suggested that he and the president double-cross the Romanian government (and effectively double-cross the businessmen in Romania), which might well have appealed to Roosevelt.

"These sums are not to be payable until after the declaration of peace," explained Wise. "Our armies will see to it that these Nazi mercenaries shall not live to reap the benefit of their hostage-holding, blackmailing plans."

"Stephen, why don't you go ahead and do it?" said Roosevelt without hesitation.

"Mr. President, I have not even felt free to broach this with [Treasury] Secretary Morgenthau until after I had consulted with you."

On the spot, Roosevelt called Morgenthau and explained Wise's idea. "Henry, this is a very fair proposal which Stephen makes about ransoming Jews." Wise, the president, and the secretary (at that point) apparently were unaware that the Treasury Department lawyers already had approved the Romanian rescue plan.[23]

The next day, July 23, Wise wrote Roosevelt to express his gratitude but also to confirm in writing the president's approval of the rescue plan.

> *It gave me deep satisfaction to find while with you yesterday that out of the depth of your understanding sympathy with Hitler's victims you welcome the proposal which is now before the State and Treasury Departments to permit funds to be forwarded to Switzerland by Jewish organizations of our country.*[24]

After receiving the letter from Wise, Roosevelt asked Morgenthau to prepare a reply for his signature. On August 5, Morgenthau sent a memorandum to Hull, attaching Wise's letter and informing Hull that "your Department was informally advised on July 16 that the Treasury was prepared to take the necessary action to implement this proposal." The memorandum stated, "The President has asked me to prepare a reply to the attached letter addressed to him by Stephen Wise." Morgenthau also attached a draft "Dear Stephen" letter for the president to send to Wise, which began, "I spoke to Secretary Morgenthau about your letter of July 23 concerning the proposal for the evacuation of Jewish refugees from Romania," and expressly endorsed the rescue proposal (the letter apparently went out on August 14 under the signature of "F.D.R."). In other words, there was no doubt that Roosevelt and the Treasury had approved the plan.[25]

At that point, Hull could have called Brandt back into his office and instructed him that, in light of the president's support of the rescue proposal, the State Department had to affirmatively support the Riegner plan, including instructing the Bern legation to issue the license to Riegner. Instead, as in the Peyrouton affair, Hull allowed his subordinates to dictate his actions.

On August 7, a memorandum initialed by Hull was sent to Morgenthau stating that the Romanian rescue proposal was now a Treasury Department responsibility and that the State Department would take no official action:

The Treasury itself is entirely free to act on this matter and to grant the necessary licenses if it should so decide. In the latter event the State Department would be pleased to send the appropriate notification through State Department channels to our Legation at Bern, informing them of the projected arrangement.[26]

In other words, while the State Department would *transmit* the license to the Bern legation, it would not instruct the legation to *do* anything with it; as events proved, the legation indeed refused to transmit the license to Riegner in the absence of clear instructions from the State Department. The rescue plan was blocked.

Bernard Meltzer was furious; shortly, he would resign and enlist in the armed forces. He called Josiah E. DuBois Jr., chief counsel for the Treasury Department's Division of Foreign Funds Control (and later an assistant to the secretary of the treasury), to vent his bitter resentment of the handling of the rescue proposal, but stopped short of disclosing what had taken place within the State Department. Meltzer promised DuBois that he would give him "more detail" but only "after he was in the Army." Several months later, Feis resigned from the State Department as well.[27]

At the time they left the department, both men believed that their defeat by Long and his allies had condemned tens of thousands of people to death. They had no way of knowing, however, that by getting the attention of DuBois, a first-rate investigator with a low tolerance for injustice, they had assured that the battle over the Romanian rescue proposal would continue.

★ ★ ★

The week after Roosevelt met with Stephen Wise, he met with Jan Karski, who had reached the United States in June 1943. In the weeks before meeting Roosevelt, Karski had audiences with a number of high officials of the American government. Several of the meetings were actually small informal dinners arranged by the Polish government in exile's ambassador to the United States, Jan Ciechanowski. To one dinner in particular he had invited three prominent Jewish officials of the Roosevelt administration: presidential adviser Ben Cohen, Assistant Solicitor General Oscar Cox, and Supreme Court Justice Felix Frankfurter. Their dinner lasted until nearly one o'clock in the morning.

The white-haired Frankfurter, the epitome of wisdom and reason, asked, "Mr. Karski, do you know that I am a Jew?"

Karski nodded.

"There are so many conflicting reports about what is happening to the Jews in your country. Please tell me exactly what you have seen."

Karski proceeded to do that. When Karski finished, Frankfurter rose from the dinner table and paced back and forth. The vivid firsthand accounts of the bestial side of human nature had simply overwhelmed his sensibilities.

"Mr. Karski," said Frankfurter, "a man like me talking to a man like you must be totally frank. So I must say: I am unable to believe you."

"Felix, you don't mean it!" Ambassador Ciechanowski was shocked by Frankfurter's comment. "How can you call him a liar to his face? The authority of my government is behind him."

In a sad, soft voice, Frankfurter said, "Mr. Ambassador, I did not say this young man is lying. I said I am unable to believe him. There is a difference."[28] He then waved his hands, as though he could make Karski and his dreadful story disappear, and left the room, muttering "no, no."[29]

Perhaps Frankfurter's reaction caused Karski to avoid mentioning the most terrible scenes he had witnessed when he met with State Department officials, also over dinner. Among those present were Assistant Secretary of State Adolf Berle and an official from the Division of European Affairs, Elbridge Durbrow (who had approved cable 354). The dinner again went past midnight, but based on Berle's account in his diary, the conversation principally concerned the recent death of General Wladyslaw Sikorski, the leader of the Polish government in exile. Berle did make a passing note of Karski's account of the concentration camps, but either he was not told about or could not grasp the magnitude of the slaughter beyond its impact on the ranks of the Polish leadership: "Possible replacements [for Sikorski] are dying by the hundreds in the German concentration camps. Unfortunately, we have pretty clear evidence of this; the eye witness account of Karski, an escaped member of the Polish underground."[30]

Finally, Karski was called to the White House for a meeting with President Roosevelt. "Be exact and brief," said Ambassador Ciechanowski, who accompanied him to the meeting. "Mr. Roosevelt is certainly the busiest man in the world."

To Karski, the White House reminded him only of a "country gentlemen's house on a large estate" in Poland. Where were the turrets, statues, and assorted decorations of the great residences of Polish leaders? Despite all he had been through, Jan Karski's heart was pounding.

He was immediately struck by the clutter of trinkets and memorabilia on the president's desk, and by Roosevelt's use of his cigarette holder like an orchestra conductor's baton to direct Ciechanowski and him to sit down. Karski began by expressing thanks for the meeting—"I cannot express my feelings. I cannot express the rights words"—when Roosevelt interrupted and began firing question after question about conditions in Poland, which Karski answered with detail and precision. The president struck Karski as remarkably well-informed and incapable of fatigue. Roosevelt projected, thought Karski, "majesty, power, greatness" and the "aura of a master of humanity."

"Tell me about the German methods of political terror."

"I am convinced, Mr. President, that there is no exaggeration in the accounts of the plight of the Jews. Our underground authorities are absolutely sure that the Germans are out to exterminate the entire Jewish population of Europe. Reliable reports from our own informers give the figure of 1,800,000 Jews already murdered in Poland up to the day I left the country." Karski described Auschwitz as the "most horrible concentration camp." He emphasized to Roosevelt that "the Germans want to devastate the biological substance of the Jewish nation. If there is no effort at Allied intervention, within a year and a half the Jewish people of Poland will cease to exist."

At the end of the meeting, Roosevelt held out his hand to Karski. "I thank you my friend, I thank you very much, but I am more than an hour late for my other appointments. What you told me is very important, and I wish you all luck in your work."

Karski, still in awe of Roosevelt, walked backwards toward the door, as though leaving the presence of an English monarch. He was exhausted, but Roosevelt appeared as fresh and energetic as at the start of the meeting. Afterward, Karski experienced a feeling of disappointment because, in reflecting on the meeting, for all his sympathy, Roosevelt had given no indication that he would do anything specific to try to stop the slaughter. In his report on the meeting, Karski acknowledged that he had not related the most horrific of his experiences, such as his death camp and Warsaw ghetto visits.[31]

Roosevelt administration officials later insisted that Karski's visit had made a difference and that Roosevelt had been deeply moved by their encounter. A few days after the visit, Secretary of State Hull told Ambassador Ciechanowski, "The President seems so thrilled by his talk with your young man that he can talk of nothing else." Recalled one official, an implacable foe of the State Department, "Overnight, [the Karski mission] changed U.S. government policy from indifference at best to affirmative action."[32]

★ ★ ★

Roosevelt had approved the Romanian rescue plan even before meeting Karski. Did he grant Wise's request out of humanitarian or political calculations, or both? From one perspective, the proposal offered a way for Roosevelt to reward a loyal supporter while remaining consistent with his policy not to risk admitting refugees who allegedly might be spies or saboteurs. Roosevelt's unqualified support for the plan suggests that as long as the issue did not involve breaking the domestic refugee barriers line he had allowed the State Department to erect, humanitarian considerations would prevail in his complex juggling act. Whatever his calculation, Roosevelt and the State Department were now on divergent paths on the issue of rescuing Jews, with Roosevelt supportive of rescuing the Transnistrian Jews if a home could be found for them elsewhere than in the United States, and the State Department opposed to rescuing Jews *even* if they were to go to other countries. Roosevelt almost certainly did not know of the State Department's efforts to block the rescue proposal. In view of those efforts, the last, reassuring line of Roosevelt's

August 14 letter to Stephen Wise (as drafted by Morgenthau), endorsing the Romanian rescue plan, rings with a terrible irony: "I am informed that the matter is now awaiting a further exchange of cables between the State Department and our mission in Bern regarding some of the details."

But Roosevelt had lost control of his bureaucracy. The State Department delayed forwarding the Treasury Department license to the Bern legation until September 28 and did not provide instructions to deliver the license to Riegner. On October 6, Leland Harrison cabled back that, "In the absence of specific instructions from the Department, the Legation is uncertain to exercise authority granted by the Treasury to issue licenses to implement the Riegner plan." The cable added that, pursuant to standing instructions, Harrison had discussed the license with British authorities, who do "not concur in the issuance of license [because] it would be most desirable that we should not be involved in any plans that might result in leakage of funds to the enemy."[33]

XI

FROM FOSTER PARENTS TO THE ORPHANAGE

For a time, Ruth had difficulty understanding the sisters when they spoke German, even though German was her native language. They used a code language, somewhat like pig Latin, in which the letter P was inserted between syllables. Ruth was annoyed and intrigued by the strange-sounding language. She listened carefully and soon figured out the trick, but she never let on that she could understand the sisters.

Ruth contracted typhus, which left her floating in and out of consciousness. From her "sick bed" on the cold, dirt floor, on one of her better days, she watched as a healthy-looking man (a rarity in Ruth's world) knelt next to her. As she later learned, he was a Feldsher (surgeon-barber). He examined Ruth by listening to her heart with his ear pressed against her chest and by checking her feverish body. He then spoke with the sisters and left. Ruth listened to the sisters talk in their code language.

"The doctor said her heart can't last much longer," one sister whispered to the other.[1]

A typhus epidemic had broken out across Transnistria. By now, the deported Jews were in a post-shock stage—a period marked by the organization of rudimentary government and social services in the towns, ghettos, and camps. The Jews established councils to fight disease, but the most that some could do was set up a few beds in a shed or stable, which was then declared to be a hospital. They had almost no medical equipment or medicines, and the doctors who had survived the march into Transnistria succumbed as quickly as the rest of the population.[2]

The sisters abandoned Ruth to die. "So this is it," Ruth thought. "Mama may not have been right after all. I'm going to join them in the other world." Exhausted and ill, she lay motionless on the floor, an emaciated eleven-year-old Jewish orphan.

Awareness of the world came and went in dreamlike waves. Shadowy figures, real and imagined, floated before her in a room that was never more than dimly lit because the sisters had only a candle or jury-rigged oil lamp. All of a sudden, the delirium lifted and Ruth focused on her surroundings for the first time in many days. The immediate thing she noticed was the disappointed expression on the faces of her foster parents.

Ruth had defeated death while lying on a cold floor, in a cold room, even though she had no nourishment, medical care, or the love of concerned parents. The sisters were indifferent to, even scornful of, Ruth's triumph because to them she was only a burden. They had already bartered many of her belongings while she was ill.

Another occupant of the room, a young boy, went to the Sattingers and told them about the sisters' thievery. Angry, Mr. Sattinger took Ruth away from the sisters and placed her with a Bershadian Jewish couple who had survived the Einsatzgruppen. They were Ruth's second set of foster parents.

The couple lived in a simple, clean two-room house with the wife's aging mother. It was Ruth's first real home since leaving Czernowitz. She concluded that she had gone to Heaven because she could sleep on her own sofa in a drawing room where the mother slept. Most of her remaining possessions were sold to pay for her space on the couch and for her food at the couple's home. That food consisted of a slice of sour bread with oil and garlic at breakfast. For lunch, she walked to the Sattingers; even though they were barely getting by, they gave Ruth the same delicacy.

But despite the luxury of the couch, the room was frigid. Ruth, in the early stages of a relapse, shivered all night from the cold and hunger.

"It hurts. It stabs!" she cried out.

"Stab back," shouted the old woman in Yiddish.

This weird exchange continued night after night until the couple took Ruth into their tiny bedroom and put her in a baby's crib, into which her emaciated frame fit comfortably. One blessing was that the room was modestly heated. But

Ruth had no choice but to listen in the dark to the couple's lovemaking in Yiddish. "Pameilech, pameilech, pameilech." (Gently, gently, gently.)

Huddled in her crib, pretending to be asleep, Ruth imagined that the woman was enduring an ordeal with groans and moans. Not wholly losing her concern for the woman, Ruth gradually grew intrigued and not a little excited. In some ways, this was Ruth's greatest triumph—the Romanian government, despite all that it had put Ruth through, hadn't killed the barely awakened but life-affirming spirit of a young girl.[3]

Despite the relatively warmer room to sleep in, Ruth's health did not improve. She suffered a relapse of typhus. The couple isolated her by moving her crib onto the unheated porch. Ruth was given very little to eat. She could have obtained more food by bartering the last of her family's belongings—a silver fork, knife, and spoon from their home in Czernowitz—but these were Ruth's last connection with her family, and she would rather starve to death than part with them.

Once more Ruth retreated to her guarded sanctuary, the memories of her beloved Milie, where the bonfires heated the giant copper vats filled with sugar and spices. She and the other children gathered plums from the trees, pitted them, carried them in baskets to the vats, and dumped them in. Her mother and an aunt stirred the aromatic mixture with oarlike spatulas. The smell of prune butter gently wafted on the summertime breezes through the entire village. Her mother handed her a piece of bread, made from wheat harvested in the fields of Milie and baked in a hot oven. Ruth inhaled the fresh aroma of the bread and then held it out in front of her with both hands. Her mother ladled the prune butter onto the bread. "Oh Milie!" she thought as she joyously ate the bread and prune butter.[4]

But the bread and prune butter were never there. She was in the initial stages of starvation, where the famished doubled over with hunger pains, as though knives had been plunged into their abdomens. Ruth may have also reached the point where the starving person hallucinates about attending fantastic feasts.[5]

The Sattingers, who appeared to be the only human beings on the face of the earth who cared about the sick girl, each day gave Ruth something to eat. They also brought a real doctor to their house to examine her. He diagnosed "paratyphus" and Ruth went back to the crib on the cold porch, where she lay as helpless as a baby until finally, like a small hibernating animal, she awoke as the air warmed.

But, lying in the crib, she had no strength left. She could barely hold her head up, and, like a baby, she first had to get out of her crib and then learn to walk. She *stretched first one leg, and then the other. With a great effort she sat up, then collapsed in exhaustion and shock at her condition. She reached again for the side of her crib, pulled herself up, fell back, and pulled herself up again, until she finally managed to climb out. Leaning against a wall, she gasped for breath. When her breathing and pounding heart slowed, the oversized "baby" Ruth now shuffled like an old woman to the door. She was greeted by the sight of green patches of grass and the sounds of children playing games in the dusty streets. Springtime had come to Transnistria, just in time to enable Ruth to begin a recovery.*

Ruth looked at her feet. They had swollen to twice their normal size; dreams of prune butter on home-baked bread do not stop hunger edema. She wondered, more out of curiosity than fear, What is in store for me next? That was how the Sattingers found Ruth, trying to play hopscotch with legs that would not allow her to jump like a child, when they came to give her the news. As kindly as one could under the circumstances, Frau Sattinger explained that they could no longer feed Ruth. The Sattingers did not even have enough for themselves.

Then Frau Sattinger told Ruth what awaited her. "Ruth," she said, "you must go to an orphanage."[6]

XII

BRECK AND ELEANOR

By the light of the moon, at a post near the corner of Nalewki and Gensia streets, Zivia Lubetkin and her comrades had watched the German forces gather outside the Warsaw ghetto's ten-foot-high walls, which the Germans had topped off with glass splinters embedded in plaster. Inside the walls, the windows had been blacked out; shadowy figures moved noiselessly through the streets, some disguised in German uniforms stolen from clothing factories.

Zivia, about thirty years old, was a commander in the ghetto's small underground army, made up mostly of boys and girls. At this post, twenty young Jewish fighters were stationed at windows, balconies, and around the corners of buildings. They were armed, like Zivia, mostly with pistols, grenades, or homemade bombs (they had to be lit with a match) because the Germans were preparing to destroy the remnants of the nearly four hundred thousand Jews who had lived in Warsaw before the start of the war.

At six o'clock in the morning of Passover, April 19, 1943, more than 850 heavily armed German soldiers, many from the Wehrmacht and the Waffen SS (the combat arm of the SS), goose-stepped into the Warsaw ghetto escorted by a tank and two armored cars. They sang in the manner of confident German soldiers, in cold, clear voices and at the top of their lungs. In their experience,

Jews were meek and docile; like sheep they lined up before machine-gun squads or marched into the gas chambers. What did a German soldier have to fear from this starving Jewish rabble locked up in the ghetto? The singing grew even louder.

Zivia's orders were to wait until the Germans had marched well inside the walls. At that moment, the Jewish fighters knew only one truth: they were going to die, regardless of whether they fought or not, and all that was left to them was to choose the manner of their death. But, having been able to choose the means—a gallant but doomed uprising against the Germans—their fear was tempered by an exaltation that approached ecstasy.[1]

Hundreds of the singing German soldiers, backed up by thousands more soldiers outside the walls, poured through the Nalewki Street gate "like ants out of a hole" and approached the post where Zivia and her fighters sat as still as death. A Jewish fighter near Zivia's position hurled a grenade into the sky. It arced down into the German ranks, where it exploded in an upward swirling geyser of metal fragments, smoke, and flesh. The singing turned to screams as more grenades fell on the Germans and Zivia and the other Jews opened fire. Under a bright blue sky, German soldiers were blown to pieces. "*Verflucht!*" (Damn!) shouted an SS officer. The Germans retreated, leaving behind their dead. German blood, for a change, had been shed in the streets of the Warsaw ghetto. Thus began the first uprising against the German occupation in any major European city since the start of the war.

While Zivia and the other Jewish fighters hugged each other and started stripping the dead Germans of weapons, American and British diplomats were about to mark Passover in an entirely different manner under the equally bright blue skies of Bermuda. As the sun reached midday in Warsaw, they opened the Bermuda Conference to Consider the Refugee Problem. At the Horizons resort, with its breathtaking views of the turquoise sea and pink sand beaches, three American delegates, supported by a secretary and five technical experts, conferred for twelve days with a British delegation. (The Horizons resort offered a special daily rate of 35 shillings per delegate, which included "food, lodging, transportation by carriage, and use of beach."[2])

Under guidelines from Assistant Secretary of State Breckinridge Long, the American delegates—the delegation head, Dr. Harold W. Dodds, president of Princeton University; Sol Bloom, a Jewish congressman from New York and chairman of the House Committee on Foreign Affairs; and Scott Lucas, a senator from Illinois (both Democrats)—were not permitted to place special emphasis on the plight of the Jews or propose any measure that would solely benefit Jews. It was as though a medical convention on curing infantile paralysis agreed never to discuss a cure that would only benefit children.[3]

The delegation staff had been carefully chosen. The secretary of the delegation was Borden Reams, who had waged the campaign to discredit Rabbi Stephen Wise and his reports of the Nazi murder campaign; had watered down the United Nations war crimes declaration of December 1942; and had fought the proposal to rescue the Transnistrian Jews. One technical expert from the State Department was Robert C. Alexander, assistant chief of the Visa Division. Alexander believed that the Nazis, for their own purposes, were "really behind the [Jewish] pressure groups."[4]

Since only military aircraft could fly to Bermuda, wrote one historian, Long "had the advantage of a perfectly controlled environment." Only selected wire service reporters were granted permission to travel to the conference. None of the major Jewish American groups was even allowed to attend as observers; Long blocked a British request to allow representatives of the Board of Deputies of British Jews, the central leadership of British Jewry, to attend the conference.[5]

In unusually strong tones, Rabbi Stephen Wise complained to Sumner Welles that, as structured by Long, the conference was a cynical exercise in futility. Non-Jewish American leaders, such as the president of the Congress of Industrial Organizations, expressed similar concerns. Long noted in his diary that "one Jewish faction under the leadership of Rabbi Stephen Wise" had been especially aggressive "in pushing their particular cause—in letters and telegrams to the President, the Secretary and Welles." None of the complaints had any impact on the events in Bermuda. Sumner Welles told one Jewish leader that the conference would be a success if just "50,000 people could be saved," but even that was a hopeless objective given that the Bermuda Conference was designed, not to save Jews, but to shield the State Department from pressure to rescue them.

After the Bermuda Conference opened, Long and his third-floor European Division colleagues, including Ray Atherton, collaborated on the instructions cabled from the State Department to the American delegation. "I worked late this evening with Dunn, Atherton, Murray and Brandt outlining our reply [to questions from the U.S. delegation] about the use of North African territory for an internment camp for German, Czech and stateless Jews now in Spain," wrote Long in his diary during the conference. "The whole Mohamedan world is tending to flare up at the indications that the Allied forces are trying to locate Jewish people under their protection in Moslem territory. Altogether it is a bad tendency."[6]

Throughout most of the conference, under this type of prodding, the American delegation maintained a unified position. But unity broke down, albeit briefly, over a suggestion by Congressman Bloom to approach Germany through a neutral country to negotiate the release of Jews. The ensuing debate revealed the underlying fear of both delegations that such an initiative might be all too successful. A British delegate, Richard Law, a Conservative politician then serving as parliamentary undersecretary of state for foreign affairs, had stressed in a public statement, "Every human life that can be saved is something to the good." In the confines of the conference, while debating Bloom's proposal, he and his delegation spoke differently.

"If Hitler accepted a proposal to release perhaps millions of unwanted persons, we might find ourselves in a very difficult position," warned Law. "For one thing, Hitler might send a large number of picked agents which we would be forced to take into our own countries. On the other hand, he might say, 'Alright, take a million or two million.' Then, because of the shipping problem, we should be made to look exceedingly foolish."

"We should at least negotiate and see what could be done," responded Congressman Bloom. "Perhaps we could propose that Hitler release each month the number of refugees that we find it possible to handle."

The American delegation chair, Harold Dodds, rebuked Bloom. "Your proposal is completely against the policy of our Government. We are on record against negotiating any terms with Nazi Germany."

Another British delegate joined in the general condemnation of Bloom's proposal. "It would be relieving Hitler of an obligation to take care of these useless people."

Bloom, now on the defensive, offered only tepid opposition. "All I wanted was to somehow not close the door." A cynic might have concluded that Bloom's principal objective was to establish a record for his Jewish constituency, many of whom would later angrily castigate him for his role at the Bermuda Conference.

Borden Reams ultimately cut him off. "There is no doubt whatsoever that the Department of State would oppose any negotiations with Germany."

Today, no historian disputes that the Bermuda Conference was solely a public relations vehicle for relieving the pressure on the American and British governments to help Jews escape the Nazis. Indeed, many years later, Law admitted that the conference was "a façade for inaction."[7]

But the Bermuda Conference also reflected the growing and increasingly powerful collaboration in the State Department between Breckinridge Long on the second floor and the Division of European Affairs on the third floor. By the summer of 1943, Long had effectively assumed the role played by the European Division's Ray Atherton, who had recently won the Holy Grail of a diplomatic career—appointment as American minister to Canada. The major difference between Atherton and Long was that the latter had no cloak of bureaucratic invisibility.[8]

★ ★ ★

Even in a government department filled with privileged and wealthy men who enjoyed elegant dining, fine wines, and stately homes, Breck Long stood out for his love of the good life. Long was a handsome diplomat in the Hollywood mold. With his hatchet jaw and hair conventionally parted arrow-straight along the side of his head, he resembled the jazz musician and actor Hoagy Carmichael. He dressed immaculately in double-breasted, three-piece suits adorned with a breast-pocket handkerchief. Very much to the manor born, Long came from a distinguished family and was married to a socially prominent woman, herself a descendant of the famous Blair family of the nineteenth century. After service in the State Department during World War I and unsuccessful attempts in 1920 and 1922 to win a Senate seat from Missouri, Long eventually turned to a diplomatic career. By the early 1930s, he was reveling in the pomp and luxury of his posting as ambassador to Italy. Finding the embassy quarters too shabby for his taste, he leased the sumptuous Villa Taverna, built in 1720 and famous for its ornate fountain and four statues representing the "four seasons" that greet visitors at the entranceway.[9]

"Your Ambassador to Italy has been part of a big Show," he wrote President Roosevelt, for whom he had raised campaign funds and was a floor manager at the 1932 Democratic Convention in Chicago; this meant that Long was in the "Roosevelt-Before-Chicago" club, whose members Roosevelt rewarded with important government posts. "The King [Victor Emmanuel III] received me yesterday and I was taken with my whole staff. A regular procession of coaches with footmen in gorgeous uniforms attended. There were four coaches, one empty carriage, like a spare tire, and one out-rider on horseback at the head of the procession."

Apparently taken in by the opulent parties on Rome's diplomatic circuit and by the city's newly clean streets and punctual trains, Breck Long became an ardent fan of Italy's Fascist dictator Benito Mussolini. "The Head of the Government [Mussolini] is one of the most remarkable persons," he wrote another State Department diplomat in 1933. "And he is surrounded by interesting men. And they are doing a unique work in an original manner, so I am enjoying it all." Essentially, Long's reports to his government were the product of an investigation of Italian politics conducted at Rome's dinner parties. "During his first year in Italy," wrote the editor of Long's papers, "Long accepted the views of his immediate social circle." Roosevelt adviser Louis Howe was more acerbic. "Long has been hypnotized by Mussolini," he told the president. "[He] is sending five or six cables a day little short of absolute Italian propaganda."[10]

It took two years—and Italy's invasion of Ethiopia—before it dawned on the American ambassador that Mussolini was a brutal, war-intent dictator. In 1936, suffering from severe stomach ulcers, Long left Italy and went into semiretirement. In 1939, Roosevelt called him back to the State Department following the German invasion of Poland. In 1940, Long became an assistant secretary of state, supervising twenty-three of the department's forty-two divisions, including the Visa Division. He commuted to the State Department from a Georgian-style mansion in Montpelier, Maryland, where he owned a renowned collection of silverware and bred thoroughbred racehorses in the surrounding pastures.[11]

As assistant secretary, Breckinridge Long enforced barriers to refugees with a zeal born from an unholy marriage of anti-Semitism, self-pity, and paranoia. His diaries became his father confessors where he poured out his anger at the refugee advocates. In one diary outburst in early 1942, for example, he wrote, "I have incurred the enmity of various powerful and vengeful elements: the Communists, extreme radicals, Jewish professional agitators, refugee enthusiasts who blindly seek the admission of persons under the guise of refugees. They all hate me." As Dean Acheson later archly observed of the many unguarded comments in Long's diary that would come back to haunt the reputations of Long and his colleagues, "Long was sworn to secrecy but his diary was not."[12]

Perhaps the most surprising aspect of Long's private fulminations was his own perpetual surprise at the anger he generated by doing more than perhaps any other single official in the American government to turn away desperate refugees from the nation's shores. A resourceful operator, intelligent and articulate; expert in working the levers of government; privy to the U.S. government's intelligence and its deepest secrets (in a clear breach of security, he knew about the American effort to develop an atomic bomb two years before the first one was tested in New Mexico); and confident of both Roosevelt's and Hull's support, he took on and handily defeated even cabinet members appalled by the refugee barriers—and then expressed astonishment at their fury.

In November 1940, the governor of the U.S. Virgin Islands, with the support of Secretary of the Interior Harold Ickes, issued a proclamation admitting refugees to the U.S. Virgin Islands (over which the Interior Department had jurisdiction) without passports or visas. The idea was that, after a short period of residence, the refugees could enter the United States (although the existing immigration law barred their entry under the quota system and therefore changes to the law likely would be needed). Alarmed that Ickes was trying to create a "pipeline to siphon refugees" out of neutral countries such as Portugal and into the United States, Long went to Roosevelt, who told him to speak to Ickes. That night, after talking with Ickes, Long wrote in his diary, "The inference was very plain that he was trying to take into the United States persons whom he thought the Department of State would not admit. He was rather obdurate and a little sarcastic."

Long went back to Roosevelt, who said, according to Long's diary, he "would send an order over there suspending the proclamation." Subsequently, Roosevelt sent Ickes a memorandum that, Ickes wrote in his own diary, "rather slapped my ears back by telling me that refugee matters were for him and the State Department to decide." But in a face-to-face meeting, Ickes and Roosevelt "discussed the subject in a friendly manner. It was clear that he had not quite understood our proposition. He thought that if certain conditions were met [including the approval of the Department of Justice], it might be all right to go ahead with the plan."

Long wrote in his diary, "The pressure that has been brought to bear on me has been astonishing. I antagonized Ickes irreparably by opposing his Virgin Islands scheme." Undeterred, however, a few months later Long sought to have the U.S. Navy declare the Virgin Islands a restricted area for naval purposes. "Lunched with Captain Kirk [chief of the Naval Intelligence Division] and I suggested to him that the Navy make a 'restricted area' of the Virgin Islands to prevent the raising of the political questions involved in this refugee and undesirable citizen traffic which is going on. Kirk took well to the idea and would see if he could put it through." Ultimately, Ickes could not obtain the Department of Justice's approval and, in the face of State Department opposition, the Virgin Islands plan died.[13]

In May 1940, with the German army pouring into France, Long noted in his diary: "There are many thousands of aliens, some of them known to be active German agents, and many of them illegally in this country." Long did not provide any basis for either this assertion or the many similar ones he made in the succeeding years. According to one historian who searched for corroboration of Long's claims, "The examples that appear in State Department and other sources are exceedingly few and not convincing."[14]

Nonetheless, in a memorandum dated June 26, 1940, to State Department Political Counselor James Dunn and Assistant Secretary of State Adolf Berle, Long outlined a plan that, recast as a work of fiction, might well have been coauthored by Franz Kafka and Samuel Beckett. Visas would not simply be denied outright; rather, they would be waved tantalizingly before the refugees, who were to be sent on fruitless errands to gather documentary evidence of good character, or that their admission would confer a "positive benefit" on the United States, that they could likely never obtain and, even if they did, would always be rejected, in Kafkaesque fashion, by American consular officials as inadequate. The result would send countless refugees to their doom, but only after they first suffered the fate of Estragon and Vladimir in *Waiting for Godot* ("We came here yesterday" . . . "And if he doesn't come?" . . . "We'll come back tomorrow."). Like Beckett's characters, the refugees desperately hoped for a salvation that would never come as they waited patiently with gloomy faces in long lines outside American consulates.

"We can delay and effectively stop for a temporary period of indefinite length the number of immigrants into the United States," wrote Long. "We could do this by simply advising our consuls to put every obstacle in the way and to require additional evidence and to resort to various administrative devices which would postpone and postpone and postpone the granting of the visas."

A little over three months later Long met with Roosevelt to discuss refugee issues. The meeting was at least in part an outgrowth of the angry criticism of Long's policies by James G. McDonald, the chairman of the President's Advisory Committee on Political Refugees. McDonald's criticism of Long led Eleanor Roosevelt to complain to the president, who "talked to Welles; and Welles suggested the President see me and talk it over." Long recorded in his diary that he had a "long satisfactory conversation" with the president "on the subject of immigration, visas, safety of the United States, procedures to be followed; and all that sort of thing was on the table. I found he was 100% in accord with my ideas."[15]

Subsequently, Albert Einstein wrote to Eleanor Roosevelt:

A policy is now being pursued in the State Department, which makes it all but impossible to give refuge in America to many worthy persons who are the victims of Fascist cruelty in Europe. Of course, this is not openly avowed by those responsible for it. The method which is being used, however, is to make immigration impossible by erecting a wall of bureaucratic measures alleged to be necessary to protect America against subversive, dangerous elements.

Einstein pleaded with her to bring the matter to the attention of her "heavily burdened husband," which she promised to do "at once," but with no tangible results.[16]

But Long's lack of humanitarian instincts transcended Jewish refugee issues. In June 1940, with Britain bracing for an invasion by Germany, sentiment mounted in both Britain and the United States to temporarily evacuate British children to America and Canada from English cities threatened by Luftwaffe bombs. Both Franklin and Eleanor Roosevelt publicly supported the evacuation proposal.[17]

Long was aghast at his countrymen's aberrational tendencies, as he confided in his diary: "There has developed in this country an enormous psychosis about British refugee children and wanting to get them over here. It is one of those peculiar phenomena that appear sometimes and I attribute it to a repressed emotion about this war."

Of course, he had a reason. One of the arts of Long and his colleagues in the State Department in the early 1940s was that they could supply a rationale for almost anything—and he confided it to his diary. "The very surest way to get America into this war would be to send an American ship to England and put 2000 babies on it and then have it sunk by a German torpedo." Just as with the argument that there was no place to put any Jews who might be rescued, Long's rigid outlook always assumed the worst and never considered whether a practical means existed to solve a problem.

The United States Congress was both more humanitarian and more practical than was Breckinridge Long, even though congressional sentiment was largely isolationist—only the attack on Pearl Harbor would really change it—and the last thing the majority of Americans then wanted was to fight in another European war. Even so, Americans were not prepared to turn away the British children. In a demonstration of just how extreme Long's views were, Congress passed an amendment to the Neutrality Act that permitted "unarmed, unescorted ships to sail to Britain to evacuate British children provided safe conduct was granted by all belligerents."[18]

In the face of an overwhelmingly receptive American sentiment, Long did not put up any overt resistance to the British evacuation effort. But when he fought efforts to admit Jewish refugees to the United States, he rarely lost. In fact, Long's one publicized loss on a Jewish refugee issue was at the hands of no less a figure than the wife of the president of the United States, who had become one of Long's most bitter opponents.

★ ★ ★

Franklin and Eleanor Roosevelt are a well-known study in contrasts. Franklin Roosevelt had been gay and charming since childhood; not even polio dampened his sunny personality. He was so supremely self-confident that an associate once remarked, "He must have been psychoanalyzed by God." But

Eleanor Roosevelt, left an orphan by the traumatic deaths of her parents, in the words of her biographer, Joseph Lash, "was a shy, solemn, insecure child, tall for her age, badly dressed, with blonde hair falling about her shoulders, and did not make friends easily." Even her mother told her: "Eleanor, I hardly know what's going to happen to you. You're so plain that you really have nothing to do except be good." Eleanor's marriage to Franklin was an upside-down version of the fairy tale about the princess and the frog. "I shall never be able to hold him. He is so attractive," wept Eleanor after she became engaged. And she was right.[19]

But as great a contrast as any between these historical figures themselves can be found in two of the most influential figures in their lives, the headmaster and headmistress of their respective private schools. At the age of fifteen, Eleanor Roosevelt was sent by her grandmother to Allenswood, a finishing school on the outskirts of London. The founder and headmistress was Marie Souvestre, a short, stout woman with milky white hair who had once been headmistress of a French boarding school outside of Paris.[20]

Allenswood and Groton had a superficial resemblance. Both educated the offspring of the elite families and both emulated, in their own ways, the austerity and discipline of the traditional British public school. At Allenswood, the girls wore long skirts, typically black, and white ruffled blouses. They made their own beds in the morning, following which, recalled Eleanor, "our rooms were inspected after breakfast and we were all marked on neatness and the way we made our beds." But discipline at Allenswood was a long way from water pumping: "Frequently our bureau drawers and closets were examined and any girl whose bureau drawers was out of order might return to her room to find the entire contents of her drawer dumped on her bed for re-arranging. I also saw beds completely stripped and left to be made over again."[21]

Mlle. Souvestre was the anti–Endicott Peabody. While he was a fervent Christian, she considered herself an atheist and believed, according to Lash, "that no area of human belief should be immune from critical inquiry and objective study." While Reverend Peabody preached Anglo-Saxon exceptionalism, she took up the cause of the underdog even to the point of expressing pro-Boer sympathies while England was fighting the Boer War in South Africa. Reverend Peabody distrusted the arts and promoted football, while Mlle. Souvestre's closest friends were artists (among them, Rodin) whose sculptures and paintings in her library struck the girls as "quite daring," and she did not appear to put any particular emphasis on athletics. The headmaster emphasized conformity, while the headmistress not only defied convention but also reveled in doing so. As Lash wrote, "In short, Peabody's values were those of order, discipline and power; Souvestre's were those of heart, vision and spirit."[22]

Mlle. Souvestre's passion for the downtrodden clearly had an impact on the sad young girl, who had no friends until she was fifteen. Neither did Franklin Roosevelt—"Much of his time, until he went to Groton, was spent with his father and me," wrote his mother—but it didn't matter in his case. His dominating but adoring mother created a calm, orderly world for her "darling boy" in their Hyde Park estate on the Hudson River. Once, during a North Atlantic crossing by the Roosevelt family, their ship encountered a terrible storm. When it appeared the ship might sink, with water flowing into their cabin, Sara Roosevelt took her baby son and wrapped him in her fur coat. "Poor little boy, if he must go down he's going down warm."[23]

By contrast, Eleanor Roosevelt was an unloved, hopelessly awkward orphan. Marriage to her distant cousin Franklin, which Franklin's mother had fought against, only deepened her sorrows. If she didn't know by the time of her marriage in 1905 that she was destined never to be happy, Eleanor surely learned that truth thirteen years and six children later, when she discovered the faintly scented, velvet-ribbon-bound letters that revealed her husband had been having an affair with Eleanor's part-time social secretary, twenty-seven-year-old Lucy Mercer. "The bottom dropped out of my particular world," she wrote later. Under the twin threats from Eleanor of divorce, which would end his political career, and from his mother of loss of his inheritance, which would end his aristocratic life, Franklin broke off the affair—or at least so he assured both women. But the barbed wound to Eleanor went deep and it never healed.[24]

Then it was his turn. Three years after Eleanor learned of the Mercer affair, Franklin Roosevelt contracted polio and lost the use of his legs. Eleanor was his nurse and, wrote a Roosevelt historian, "Partly because of careful handling by Eleanor and the doctors, partly because of some inner strength and stability, he became cheerful once the initial period of nervous collapse was over." The strain on Eleanor, who during part of the ordeal slept on a couch in her husband's bedroom, was crushing. She had to fight both her husband's illness and Franklin's mother, who wanted her son to retire from public life and live out his crippled days at Hyde Park as a Hudson River squire. Eleanor insisted that her husband remain active and reenter politics. She did not give any ground to either Franklin's polio or Sara Delano Roosevelt, but one day she broke down sobbing while reading a book to the two youngest children. The image of the emotionally wounded wife devoting every physical and emotional resource to the disabled husband who had so grievously hurt her is at once inspiring and chilling.[25]

Winning the presidency helped make up for Franklin Roosevelt's great blow and, in some ways, compensated Eleanor as well. Through him, she now had the ability to make a difference in the lives of those who, as Mlle. Souvestre had taught her girls, needed compassion. If she couldn't heal her own wounds, at least she could put salve on those of others. Coal miners, black Americans, the poor, refugees, children anywhere—there was scarcely a cause she did not take up. "For gosh sakes," said one underground coal miner to another in a famous *New Yorker* cartoon, "here comes Mrs. Roosevelt!"[26]

That was certainly how Breckinridge Long felt, although perhaps he would have used a more pungent phrase than "for gosh sakes." His diary, however, makes only careful but plainly annoyed references to her intrusions, as though to say, "Why can't her husband straighten her out on these issues?" Thus, "the Secretary asked me to handle the evacuation of children out of England to this country . . . Mrs. Roosevelt is much interested." Or, "He [the chairman of the President's Advisory Committee on Political Refugees] apparently approached Mrs. Roosevelt and she got a wrong impression."[27]

Her one clear victory over Breck Long arose when, in August 1940, a passenger ship named the *Quanza* left Portugal with several hundred, mostly Jewish refugees. "They were all Jewish. They all had money," Long sniffed to his diary. Two-thirds disembarked when the *Quanza* put in first at New York City and then at Veracruz, Mexico. One of the disembarkees was a French movie actress who would later appear in the movie *Casablanca*, in which many of the characters were desperate to get to Portugal, whence they could find passage to the United States. The rest were denied entry, and the ship sailed back up the coast to Norfolk, Virginia, to take on coal before returning to Europe. By now, the remaining passengers, who had been living on sardines since the ship sailed from Portugal, were in a state of despair.

With the ship anchored in the Norfolk harbor, a battle royal ensued over whether the *Quanza* refugees would be forced to return to Nazi-occupied Europe. No less an official than the solicitor general of the United States advised Long that it was legal for the *Quanza* passengers to land and undergo screening for entry into the United States. Long, who had had a small criminal and civil law practice in St. Louis before entering politics, disagreed with the solicitor general, who represented the United States government in cases before the Supreme Court. He was then "flooded with pressure groups and telegrams and telephones and personal visits to permit the landing of persons off of the boat."[28]

At this point, Eleanor Roosevelt intervened. On September 18, 1940, Long noted in his diary, the president's wife had "called me up and expressed her interest in the children and a few other categories." Apparently unimpressed by Long's response to a heartbreaking humanitarian issue—"I consistently declined to deviate from the procedure which we had adopted"—Eleanor Roosevelt then spoke to her husband. The president asked Long to telephone him but, understandably, did not want to get in the middle of a fight between his wife and the assistant secretary of state. "I called the next day, but it was apparent that he did not want to talk to me on the subject, and I inferred that he would leave the matter entirely in my hands."

In Breck Long's hands, that first meant a slight bow to political—or, more accurately, marital—realities. He made the gesture of allowing the President's Advisory Committee on Political Refugees, which included private citizens genuinely committed to the cause of refugees, to identify the *Quanza* passengers potentially eligible to enter the United States and those qualified for special visas, such as children. Long then fought tooth and nail to stop as many refugees from disembarking as he could.[29]

In the meanwhile, one passenger on the *Quanza* jumped overboard and tried to swim ashore but was captured and returned to the ship. A Newport News maritime attorney, Jacob Morewitz, began legal proceedings to keep the ship in Norfolk, but that maneuver could buy only limited time. The representatives of the President's Advisory Committee arrived and confirmed that thirty-five passengers had valid visas; certified forty-one passengers as eligible to enter the United States under existing immigration procedures (as political refugees); and certified another five as eligible under special visa procedures (three children under age sixteen and two mothers). In all, at least eighty-one Jewish passengers came ashore and then scattered in all directions. "Mrs. Roosevelt saved my life," said one passenger.[30]

Long, who had thought at most a handful would be allowed to leave the ship, was apoplectic in his conversation with the President's Advisory Committee. "I remonstrated violently; said that I thought it was a violation of law; that it was not in accord with my understanding with them; that it was not a proper interpretation of my agreement; that I would not be a party to it; that I would not give my consent; that I would have no responsibility for it." After the *Quanza* incident, Long confided to his diary that the chairman of the President's Advisory Committee somehow had "developed a very definite and violent antagonism to me." That it took a court proceeding and the intercession of the wife of the president of the United States just to admit several score Jewish refugees within swimming distance of American shores spoke volumes about the hopes for rescue of Jews in Nazi-occupied or satellite countries.[31]

At one point in her battles with Long, Eleanor Roosevelt had lunch with her husband. The topic of Breckinridge Long came up.

"Franklin," she said in frustration, "you *know* that man is a fascist."

"I've told you, Eleanor," said her husband with an annoyed tone, "you must not say that."

"Well, maybe I shouldn't say it," she responded. "But he is."

Eleanor Roosevelt had other, limited successes, including, along with the President's Advisory Committee and other refugee aid agencies, obtaining State Department approval in September 1942 for five thousand Jewish children to leave Vichy France and enter the United States (the Nazis did not permit them to leave). Long agreed to the plan with a noticeable lack of enthusiasm ("We can not receive into our own midst *all*—or even a large fraction of the oppressed . . . ").

But, beyond devoting attention in "My Day," to the pageant *We Will Never Die*, Eleanor did not spend significant time on Holocaust issues in the critical year of 1943. In one historian's judgment: "Eleanor Roosevelt cared deeply about the tragedy of Europe's Jews and took some limited steps to help. But she never urged vigorous government action. She saw almost no prospects for rescue and believed that winning the war as quickly as possible was the only answer." For the woman whose "glow warmed the world," it was a harsh judgment. Eleanor might have agreed. According to one of her sons, her failure to help more refugees was "her deepest regret at the end of her life."[32]

Long expressed no regrets to his diary, or anyone else for that matter, about sending Jewish and other refugees to their doom. What he did regret was how the constant pressure of refugee controversies interfered with his enjoyment of the finer things in life. His diary entries are remarkable for the pleasure he took in trips to the racetrack and the bouts of self-pity and anger at the Jewish organizations that were making his life difficult, if not miserable. On one day, Long would write, "Took the afternoon off yesterday and went to see Equipet run in the Aberdeen Stakes at Havre de Grace. She ran a good race and came in third."

On another day, he would write of Jewish leaders like Stephen Wise and non-Jewish advocates of admitting more refugees:

Each one of these men hates me. I am to them the embodiment of a nemesis. They each and all believe every person, everywhere has a right to come to the United States. I believe that nobody, anywhere has a right to enter the United States unless the United States desires. They would throw me to the wolves in their eagerness to destroy me.

Nowhere in Long's diary is there even the faintest hint of anger at his old friend, Franklin Roosevelt, who supported him in private but undermined him—or let others undermine him—when it was politically expedient. For all his bureaucratic savvy, Breckinridge Long could not bring himself to acknowledge that it was the president who had thrown him to the wolves.[33]

★ ★ ★

Two days after the opening of the Bermuda Conference to Consider the Refugee Problem, a clandestine Polish radio transmitter sent reports of the doomed Warsaw uprising. The radio managed only four sentences before transmission stopped. The last words were "Save us." As David Wyman aptly wrote: "Monitored in Stockholm, the appeal was radioed around the world. It reached London and Washington but was barely noticed. It certainly was not heard in Bermuda." By May 16, after nearly a month of resistance from the Jewish fighters, the German commander announced that the fighting was over and claimed that more than fifty-six thousand Jews had been killed or captured. The Germans leveled most of what was still standing in the Warsaw ghetto, as well as the great synagogue on Tlomacki Street, just outside the walls. Miraculously, Zivia Lubetkin survived although, as she later recalled, "Our hopes and dreams were buried here, all that was most precious to us."[34]

After twelve days of meetings, the Bermuda Conference adjourned. The joint conference report to the two governments was kept secret, possibly because so little had been accomplished. The one-page public statement mentioned merely that a "number of concrete recommendations" had been submitted to the American and British governments. These included a prohibition on approaching the German government to release Jews or other potential refugees; pursuing the mobilization of neutral shipping to transport refugees; suggestions for moving refugees out of Spain; and a suggestion that the British government allow refugees to enter Cyrenaica in eastern Libya.

Following the Bermuda Conference, in response to proposals to rescue Jews, the State Department would offer an incantation: "Bermuda, Bermuda, Bermuda." One standard reply was that "the Conference at Bermuda has examined in detail every possibility for the relief of the sufferings of the persecuted people of occupied Europe. Steps are now being taken to put into effect the recommendations made by the Conference." Borden Reams drafted a letter for a superior insisting that Bermuda "was not, as some sources have stated, a farce or cruel mockery. It was a sincere attempt on the part of the two Governments concerned to rescue as many people as possible from the torture house of Europe."[35]

★ ★ ★

On June 1, 1943, Rabbi Stephen Wise and four other Jewish leaders, acting as the Joint Emergency Committee for European Jewish Affairs, sent a letter to Sumner Welles conveying "our deepest distress and apprehension" over the Bermuda Conference. The letter stated that "Without retarding the military operations of the United Nations, the United States and Great Britain are still in a position to take some action which will succeed in saving a substantial remnant of European Jewry and other imprisoned populations." At the end, the letter urged four different forms of action by the American government, including establishing a war crimes commission to punish "those responsible for the crimes against Jews and other imprisoned populations"; implementing a program for "immediate rescue" of Jews in satellite countries; easing American visa regulations to allow the entry of more refugees; and vesting "the vital problem of rescue" in a "special authority in the United States." A week later, Welles referred the letter to, among others, Breckinridge Long: "In view of the importance of this letter, it seems to me a very carefully considered reply should be drafted for my signature."

On June 22, 1943, Long's executive assistant sent him a memorandum that attached the June 1 letter from the Joint Emergency Committee to Sumner Welles. The memorandum stated that the letter from Rabbi Wise to Welles should be "viewed in the light of the attached intercepts of communications" between a close associate of Wise in New York and Jewish members of the British section of the World Jewish Congress. The "intercepts" indicated a "considerable degree of acquiescence in the recommendations of the Bermuda Conference" by the World Jewish Congress, which had now decided to "concentrate on the establishment of the Commission on War crimes to bring the Axis criminals to justice." The memorandum further suggested that "in view of the intercepted correspondence, it may be considered that the remainder of the letter [from Wise to Welles], continuing to press for the adoption of other measures in behalf of refugee Jews, is now of less emphasis." Long sent his assistant's memorandum to Welles with a note: "Mr. Welles, you may care to read the intercept attached." Whether Welles read the intercepted correspondence is unknown.

The next day, June 23, Long noted in his diary, with evident relief, "The refugee question has calmed down. The pressure groups have temporarily withdrawn from the assertion of pressure." Apparently referring to the intercepted correspondence between American and British Jewish leaders that the State Department had been reading, he went on: "Information which we have received indicates plainly that they now see the correctness of the position which we have maintained from the beginning."

The following day, a letter signed by Welles but drafted by Long and Brandt with the benefit of the intercepted correspondence, went to Wise in response to the June 1 letter. Wise was advised that negotiations with satellite countries to rescue Jews had encountered "certain difficulties," which made "dubious that an extension of this movement will be possible in the near future," but an announcement on the organization of a "Commission on War Crimes" will be made "as soon as it is deemed feasible to do so."[36]

★ ★ ★

Jewish ability to obtain the help of the State Department was soon to be further weakened. Sumner Welles, the only man in the State Department with both the authority and the humanitarian instincts to help at least some Jews in occupied Europe, was fighting for his diplomatic life. Cordell Hull, with the ruthless assistance of the former American ambassador to France, William Bullitt, was about to get his man.

Hull had found out about Welles's sexual solicitation of the Pullman porters on the presidential train from the Alabama funeral of the Speaker of the House. Almost as soon as the president's train returned to Washington, rumors of the incident began circulating. Roosevelt could not afford to ignore the allegations and asked FBI director J. Edgar Hoover to investigate. FBI agents took unsworn statements from several of the Pullman porters, which Hoover gave to Roosevelt. When Attorney General Francis Biddle argued that Welles had to go, Roosevelt responded with the characteristic lightheartedness he often used to deflect difficult pressures. "Well, he's not doing it on government time, is he?" But Welles was a festering sore, and given the spreading rumors, it was hardly surprising that Hull found out about the statements in the FBI files. In effect, Sumner Welles had signed his own death warrant and handed it to Cordell Hull.[37]

That was in 1940. Like his father, Cordell Hull was a patient man. He waited years before using the FBI files to trap Welles. Hull, of course, was aware of Roosevelt's ties and loyalty to Sumner Welles—what one Roosevelt aide termed the "old Grotonian net"—and therefore had to proceed cautiously. At the same time, both Hull's wife and Bullitt were pushing him to act. Hull's wife shared her husband's bitterness at his perceived public humiliation by Welles; she was also affronted by what she called Welles's "physical idiosyncrasy." Bullitt was nearly pathological in his jealousy and hatred of Welles and embittered by the refusal of his old friend, Franklin Roosevelt, to give him a diplomatic post equal to the needs of his insatiable ego.[38]

The diplomat George F. Kennan, who served on Bullitt's staff in Moscow when Bullitt was the ambassador to the Soviet Union, reflected many years later on Bullitt's generation, which included Ernest Hemingway, Cole Porter, John Reed (the American Communist and author of *Ten Days That Shook the World*, about the Russian Revolution), and, of course, Sumner Welles. "They were a striking generation, full of talent and exuberance. But in most of them there seems to have been a touch of the fate, if not the person, of the Great Gatsby. They knew achievement more often than they knew fulfillment; and their ends, like those of Bullitt himself, tended to be frustrating, disappointing, and sometimes tragic."[39] Bill Bullitt also had more than a touch of Tom Buchanan.

Bullitt was the scion of a socially prominent Philadelphia family with Jewish ancestors, which did not hinder his later expression, as previously recounted, of anti-Semitic remarks (calling a Soviet diplomat a "wretched little kike"). A rebellious streak manifested itself on the day he was to leave home for Groton. "Every Groton fellow I know is a snob," he declared, and refused to go. Instead, he attended De Lancy, a private school in Philadelphia, Yale University (voted "most brilliant" in his class), and, briefly, Harvard Law School. Bullitt then pursued a career in journalism, which he soon left for an appointment by President Woodrow Wilson to the American delegation to the 1919 Paris Peace Conference that produced the Treaty of Versailles, which simultaneously ended one world war and laid the groundwork for another.

In September 1919, President Wilson began a cross-country speaking tour in support of ratification of the treaty and American membership in the League of Nations. Eight days later, Bullitt, who had resigned from the Versailles mission, brutally turned on Wilson by giving sensational testimony in the Senate against the League of Nations, even claiming that Wilson's own secretary of state was against the League. French Premier Georges Clemenceau, who had survived an assassination attempt during the Paris Peace Conference, commented: "I got my bullet at the conference. Wilson got his Bullitt when he returned home."

Bullitt's opposition to the treaty was genuine, and he had been subpoenaed to testify, but he cut up the treaty—and the League of Nations—like a knife fighter. "His testimony, more than any other single individual's," according to a *New Yorker* profile in 1938, "was considered to have brought the greatest weight against America's joining the League." Two weeks after Bullitt's testimony, his dream of American participation in a world peace organization in ruins, President Wilson collapsed and subsequently suffered a stroke that left him partly paralyzed, effectively ended his presidency, and may have shortened his life.[40]

Democrats were furious but had no opportunity to take it out on Bullitt because he had left the government; soon they would as well, losing the presidency in 1920. (Franklin Roosevelt was on the Democratic ticket in the vice presidential slot.) Bullitt spent the 1920s writing a novel; coauthoring with Sigmund Freud a book on Woodrow Wilson (not published for decades); and marrying and divorcing, or simply bedding, a succession of prominent but improbable women. Prematurely bald but fit and fair skinned, with mesmerizing blue eyes and always dressed in dashing style in London-tailored suits (he owned thirty), a fresh red carnation in the left lapel, Bullitt was immensely attractive to women. Among them, he married and divorced Louise Bryant, the widow of his close friend John Reed, and had an affair with Eleanor "Cissy" Patterson (while married to Bryant), later to become the right-wing owner of the *Washington-Times Herald*.[41]

By 1932, Bullitt had worked his way into the Roosevelt presidential campaign and managed to impress the president elect with his international acumen. Despite the bitterness of many Democrats over Bullitt's betrayal of Woodrow Wilson, Roosevelt appointed him the first American ambassador to the Soviet Union, where he threw dinner parties at Spaso House, the ambassador's palatial residence in Moscow, that featured pigeons in glass cages, baby bears and mountain goats in pens, and a "seal which served guests champagne from a glass balanced on its nose." A Russian woman acquaintance observed that Bullitt had not decided whether being an ambassador was a "job or a charade."[42]

Roosevelt next named Bullitt the ambassador to France, where he reveled in the "balls, entertainment and fine cuisine; he even employed his own chef." At embassy parties, Bullitt served vintage French wines, Beluga caviar flown in from Iran, and cigarettes imported from Virginia (the last as a patriotic gesture). "No one except ambassadors knows how or why ambassadors manage," observed the *New Yorker* writer. In addition to the embassy residence, Bullitt maintained an eighteenth-century chateau outside Paris and a tiny apartment in the city. "It was to this pied-à-terre where he took his lovers," according to the historian of the Welles-Hull rivalry.[43]

But by 1940, the Bullitt-Roosevelt relationship was waning and Sumner Welles's star was ascendant. The final rupture came when Roosevelt announced the Welles peace mission to Europe in the early spring of that year. Bullitt, then ambassador to France, exploded at FDR when Roosevelt discussed the mission. Bullitt tried to sabotage Welles by leaking a story to the *Chicago Tribune* that Secretary of State Hull and Bullitt were furious over Roosevelt's failure to consult them about the Welles mission. Roosevelt had been vaguely hinting at a cabinet appointment for Bullitt, but after the fall of France and the end of Bullitt's ambassadorship, no cabinet or other high-level appointment came his way. In effect, Roosevelt had chosen Welles over Bullitt. When Bullitt found out about the Pullman incident, possibly through his connections with the Southern Railway, he went after Welles with a near-demented thirst for revenge.[44]

In the spring of 1941, Bullitt, now out of office and with no worthwhile government posts in sight, went to see the president. Before he even finished making his charges against Welles, Roosevelt cut him off. "I know all about this already. I have had a full report on it. There is truth in the allegations."

"Mr. President, this could provoke a terrible public scandal that would undermine the confidence of the country in you." Bullitt spoke as though he had the upper hand on the president, which in fact he did.

"No newspaper will publish anything about this matter. It's too scandalous. Besides, I am having a bodyguard watch Welles to see to it that he does not repeat such a performance."

Bullitt then shifted tactics, apparently not realizing that he was in the process of destroying whatever slim hope he had of holding high office in the Roosevelt administration, or else not caring as long as he could destroy Sumner Welles. "Cordell Hull considers Welles to be worse than a murderer. The morale in the State Department and the Foreign Service is being ruined. You are thinking of asking Americans to die in a crusade for all that is decent in human life. You cannot have among the leaders of a crusade a criminal like Welles." He added audaciously, "Mr. President, I will not take any position in the State Department until you dismiss Sumner Welles."

Roosevelt rang the bell for General "Pa" Watson.

"Pa, I don't feel well. Please cancel all my appointments for the rest of the day." Watson wheeled him out and Bullitt left.[45]

By the fall of 1942, under the goading of his wife and Bullitt, Hull finally was ready to move on Welles. In September, he called Breckinridge Long to his office to discuss the widely circulated rumors. After his meeting with Hull, Long wrote in his diary, without mentioning Welles by name: "[Hull] is very much disturbed by a personal scandal. I shall not repeat it. I heard of it some months ago and dismissed it as malicious, impossible and incredible. I had little to offer—beyond my own expression of incredulity—except that the person in question be confronted with the charge and given an opportunity to disprove it."[46]

That may have been the last thing that Hull wanted to do. In October, Hull, who knew about the FBI files but had not seen them, summoned J. Edgar Hoover to his hotel apartment. Using an old Washington ploy, Hull explained to the FBI director that his wife had been hearing ugly rumors about Sumner Welles. He understood that Hoover had made an investigation and would the director be willing to give him the report? Hoover confirmed the existence of the report but prudently suggested that the secretary of state get it from the White House. Instead, in early 1943, Hull sent a State Department official to interview Secret Service agent Dale Whiteside and a Southern Railway official, both of whom had been on the train. The Southern Railway official disclosed all of the sordid details.[47]

Hull, as Welles's biographer-son wrote, began "moving in for the kill." He went to see Roosevelt, explained what he knew, and asked permission to read the Pullman porter statements in the FBI file. Roosevelt, about to leave for the Casablanca conference with Winston Churchill, certainly had other matters on his mind and "looked miserably at the ceiling." Hull could read the statements, Roosevelt said, but only at the White House after his return from Casablanca.

In late February 1943, Hull reviewed the file in the White House. Over the Easter holidays, Hull and Bullitt met at Hull's apartment to plot Welles's demise. Listening to the conversation between the secretary of state and a former diplomat with as much knowledge of European and Soviet affairs as anyone, an eavesdropper would never have guessed that a world war was raging with the stakes nothing less than the course of Western civilization.

Hull and Bullitt first vented their hatred of Sumner Welles, and then planned the final campaign to destroy him in which each would marshal their most readily available resources. Hull would solicit support from former colleagues in the Senate, especially the Roosevelt-haters, while Bullitt would mobilize his admiring network of powerful Washington women. Hull's wife overheard their conversation. "Mr. Bullitt," she asked, "won't you shoot that man for me?"[48]

Hull recruited the anti–New Deal senator from Maine, Owen Brewster, who immediately asked Hoover for the FBI file. When the file was not forthcoming, Brewster hinted to Hoover that he might demand that the Senate Special Committee to Investigate the National Defense Program, headed by Senator Harry S. Truman, open an inquiry. Bullitt's women also went into action. One was Cissy Patterson, the *Washington Times-Herald* publisher and a prewar isolationist. The *Times-Herald*, as well as other newspapers, began running stories about the feud between Hull and Welles that was allegedly damaging American diplomacy.

Another Bullitt woman, "onetime Bullitt flame" Alice Roosevelt Longworth, Theodore Roosevelt's tart-tongued daughter, "detested 'Cousin Franklin' and his entire New Deal." In 1940, she announced publicly, "I'd rather vote for Hitler than vote for Franklin for a third term." Alice Roosevelt was more than willing to spread salacious gossip in her well-patronized Washington salon where, in her elderly years ("The secret of eternal youth is arrested development," she liked to say), she held court on a sofa with a pillow embroidered with the words, "If you haven't got anything good to say about anybody, come sit next to me."[49]

On July 27, Bullitt went to the White House and again demanded that Welles resign. According to one unverified account of the conversation, he and Roosevelt had a "furious row."

"You are being un-Christian, Bill," shouted Roosevelt, now enraged. "You have been leaking to that bitch friend of yours at the *Times-Herald*. I need Welles, he's younger and more intelligent than that old fool, Hull."

"Mr. President," replied Bullitt angrily, "it is my duty as a friend and a supporter to point out to you that Welles can be blackmailed. And keeping him in office is a bad example to the Foreign Service."[50]

The coup de grâce was administered by Hull at a meeting with Roosevelt on August 10. With major newspapers championing Hull in his feud with Welles, a possible Senate investigation looming, and, quite simply, no basis to defend Welles's conduct on the train, Roosevelt was finally cornered. Hull gave Roosevelt an ultimatum: either Welles must resign from the State Department or he would.

The next day, Roosevelt called Welles to the Oval Office. Roosevelt could not bring himself to directly ask Welles for his resignation. Neither man directly mentioned the Pullman porters.

"Sumner, I have never been angrier in my life at the situation in the State Department. It has now reached an impossible climax. Cordell claims that he has been trying for a year and a half to make it clear to me that you must be replaced. You have been making admirable speeches, which he couldn't and wasn't prepared to make. And you have been taking the lead in post-war policy, which he should, but couldn't, do. This he resents bitterly. He complains about you to every Senator and newspaperman he talks to."

Welles understood instantly what had to be done. "Mr. President, if Mr. Hull had ever indicated to me that he wanted me to resign I would have done so in 24 hours. I will never embarrass you, especially in wartime. I will resign at once."

"I won't allow you to do that. I have known you since you were a little boy before you went to Groton," said Roosevelt in anguish. "I have seen you develop into what you are now. I need you for the country." Like Welles, he was also going through the motions. Both men knew the deed was done.

"Mr. President, I am deeply moved and touched. But I wish to resign. That is the best and wisest course."

Welles left without Roosevelt actually having accepted his resignation. That night, despite taking sleeping pills, Welles couldn't sleep. A day or two later, he went to Hull's office.

"The President told me that you have wanted to replace me for a year and a half. Why hadn't you told me so yourself?"

"Stop right there!" shouted Hull. "I didn't speak to you because you are an intimate friend of the President, much closer to him than I. I based my request on your personal habits. Your continuation in office would be, for the President and State Department, the greatest national scandal since the existence of the United States."

Welles rose, shook Hull's hand, and, without saying another word, walked out. That was the last time either man saw the other. That weekend, Welles had a mild heart attack. On Monday, he dictated his formal letter of resignation and a personal note to FDR. "I want you to know that so long as I live, I shall never forget the friendship and kindness you showed me in our last talk."[51]

In destroying Sumner Welles, William Bullitt also destroyed himself. Roosevelt later bitterly told Assistant Secretary of State Berle that when Bullitt came to see him, he appointed himself St. Peter. "'Two men will appear before me at the Pearly Gates,' Roosevelt claimed to have told Bullitt. The first was Welles. 'After chiding him for getting drunk, I will let Welles in.' The second was Bullitt. 'Bill, you've tried to destroy a fellow being. Go to Hell.'"

Ultimately, Roosevelt refused to appoint Bullitt to any other diplomatic post in his administration. At one point, Hull had asked Roosevelt to consider such a post for Bullitt. The president leaned back in his chair and contemplated the request. "That's right, Cordell," Roosevelt finally said, waving his cigarette holder. "What about Liberia? I hear that's available."[52]

Former Congresswoman Clare Boothe Luce later pronounced William Bullitt's epitaph. "So Sumner Welles was dropped. But they also dropped Bill. He couldn't get another job. The news went around that he was the kind of guy who brought up that kind of story." Bullitt's life was never the same again, and he lived the rest of it in resentful shadows.

Even a year later, Roosevelt had not gotten over the destruction of Sumner Welles. In August 1944, over lunch at Warm Springs, Georgia, with Vice President Henry Wallace, Roosevelt began talking about Bullitt and Welles.

"Bill Bullitt was perfectly terrible," said Roosevelt.

"Why was that, Mr. President?"

"Because of that awful story he spread all over town about Sumner Welles." Roosevelt added, "Bill ought to go to hell for that."[53]

Jewish leaders in the United States certainly shared Roosevelt's sense of loss. After the resignation of Sumner Welles became public, they had sent him accolades and sincere regrets. Rabbi Stephen Wise wrote, "My fellow Jews in all free lands will, when the story can be told, bless your name." Another advocate for refugees, Rabbi Morris Lazaron, in something of an understatement, wrote that even though he knew Breckinridge Long, "Somehow I don't feel the same warmth and understanding in my talks with him as I have always felt with you."[54]

Sumner Welles had not been consistently responsive to pleas to help the Jews of Europe, as shown by his delay in investigating the Riegner telegram; he had done little or nothing to alter the "façade for inaction" that was the Bermuda Conference; and Breckinridge Long and the Division of European Affairs often outmaneuvered him, aided by intercepts of Jewish leaders' communications. Yet, in the one government department with the responsibility, authority, and power to respond to the plight of the European Jews, Sumner Welles was the only senior official willing to acknowledge that a vast, continent-wide murder scheme was under way and to sympathize with, if not support, the efforts of those who tried to stop it.

And now he was gone. The Jewish leaders in America, demoralized by the Bermuda Conference and apparently unaware that the State Department was intercepting their overseas cables, and the doomed Jews in Europe, some of whom in the Nazi satellite countries still had the slimmest hope for survival, were alone.

XIII

THE FARMER

The township of East Fishkill, in Dutchess County in New York State, lies about eighteen miles south of the Roosevelt family's Hudson River estate at Hyde Park. In 1913, the tall, gangly twenty-two-year-old son of the former U.S. ambassador to Turkey purchased a thousand acres of farmland in East Fishkill. The farm was an escape for the young Jewish man: from a learning disability that had caused him to drop out of an elite boarding school (one of the few that accepted Jews in any number) after two years; from poor grades at Cornell University (despite the assistance of the private tutor hired by his family) that likewise led to his dropping out; from the pressure by the ambassador, now a prominent member of New York's German Jewish community, to join him in a construction business; and from a bout with typhus that required recuperation on a Texas ranch. It was there that the young man, a failure until then at everything he had tried, realized that his purpose in life was to be a farmer.[1]

The young man, Henry Morgenthau Jr., allowed the ambassador, Henry Morgenthau Sr., to choose his farming activities: dairy and apple growing. The son had little say in the matter since his father was paying for the farm and, in any event, his father dominated him. Denied by President Woodrow Wilson his cherished dream of appointment to the cabinet, Henry Sr. had vested all his ambitions in his only son. "I'll handle the boy," he told his wife, "you can take care of the girls." Despite his son's shortcomings, the ambassador never gave up.[2]

With Henry Sr.'s money, the dairy farm was up and running in short order, including a herd of fifty Holstein cattle (Henry Jr. sold some of the milk to the West Point Military Academy across the Hudson River). The apple orchard took longer and was constantly stressed by spring frosts and hailstorms, but it became Henry Jr.'s passion. Each spring, just around his birthday, the orchard exploded gloriously in fragrant pink and white, and throughout the year, Henry Jr. loved to ride his horse between the rows of apple trees. He even began publishing the *American Agriculturalist*, an influential agrarian periodical. He was his own man, free from his many failures and his father's smothering grip.

The apple trees were a beautiful feature of the farm, but in truth it was a hardscrabble place. The farm buildings were rarely painted, and repaired only on an as-desperately-needed basis. Still, few if any other farmers in the mid–Hudson River Valley could seek assistance from President Wilson's secretary of agriculture, who had loaned young Morgenthau a junior staff member to act as an adviser in buying the East Fishkill property.[3]

Even with the Department of Agriculture at Henry Jr.'s disposal, the farm lost staggering amounts of money. Sensitive to criticism, however, Henry Jr. convinced himself—and most of those around him—that it was a rousing financial success. Knowing the cold truth, Henry Sr. then desperately cast around for other avenues in which his son might yet succeed. Although the details are not known, Henry Sr. latched onto Dutchess County politics and a part-time gentleman farmer and up-and-coming Democratic politician named Franklin Delano Roosevelt.

The earliest record of the Morgenthau-Roosevelt relationship is a letter dated December 11, 1914, from then Assistant Secretary of the Navy Franklin Roosevelt to "My Dear Mr. Morgenthau," asking Henry Jr. for his assessment of a Democratic Party candidate for a local postmaster position. "I should much like to have your personal and confidential judgment on the matter." And, in classic Roosevelt consensus-building style, he added, "Of course, if possible I should like to have everybody united in the Township of East Fishkill."

Soon Morgenthau had joined the Roosevelt inner circle, the young men and women, mostly from New York State, who had hitched their wagons to that of the rising young political star with the famous last name. No surer sign of Morgenthau's ascent was the note about Morgenthau that Roosevelt sent a few years later to his closest political adviser, Louis Howe. "He is an awfully nice young fellow, and one who will be a tremendous asset to us in the county. Certainly, we ought to do everything possible to keep him interested [in Dutchess County politics]."[4]

The Roosevelt-Morgenthau relationship was strengthened by the friendship between Eleanor Roosevelt and Henry Jr.'s wife, Elinor, an athletic girl from New York City with stage ambitions. Defying convention among prosperous New York City families, whose daughters lived at home or, at most, commuted uptown to Barnard College, Elinor Fatman had insisted on going to Vassar College in Poughkeepsie. She graduated in the same year that Henry Jr. had purchased his farm, and their romance began shortly after that. (No one knows how they met, but it was inevitable, since both had been born on the same block, delivered by the same doctor, wheeled along the same Central Park walkways, and attended the same primary school.) Even before Henry, Jr. announced his plan to marry Elinor, the ambassador had sternly warned his son against an early marriage: "You are just now soaring onward and upward and no matter who you would have married, you would have developed your physical desires more than your intellectual and altruistic tendencies, and almost any smart girl would have cajoled and controlled you and dwarfed and stunted your growth."

If ever there was an Oedipal moment in the life of a Jewish scion, this was it for Henry Jr. Perhaps feeling independent of his father by virtue of his farm (never mind who paid for it), the son seized the moment. He proposed to Elinor during a stroll around the Central Park reservoir and they married in 1916. Finally, after the long struggle under the weight of Henry Sr.'s frustrated ambitions for him, Henry Jr. had burst his bonds.[5]

But the father had set the son on a political path and, if anything, Elinor kept him going down it. Henry Jr. brought his bride into the Roosevelt circle. Once, after he took her to the Roosevelt estate at Hyde Park to meet Franklin's mother, Sara Roosevelt wrote to her daughter-in-law, Eleanor: "Young Morgenthau and his wife called this pm. Young Morgenthau was easy and yet modest and serious and intelligent. The wife is very Jewish but appeared very well." Before long, Eleanor Roosevelt had pulled Elinor Morgenthau into her network, many of whom were single women by choice, widowhood, or divorce.

The Morgenthaus thus had a foot in each of the Roosevelt camps. This was a demanding and precarious balancing act, given the inherent tension between the two Roosevelts, which was exacerbated by Franklin's propensity to stimulate competition among his followers and Eleanor's need for affection, if not love. The Morgenthaus made financial contributions to Roosevelt political causes, supported Roosevelt-backed candidates, and rounded up audiences for Roosevelt events staged at Hyde Park. Henry Jr.'s son, Henry Morgenthau III, in a biography of his family, suggests that Roosevelt "in a fond, unpatronizing way always treated Henry Jr. like a younger brother."[6]

The affection was genuine and mutual. The Morgenthaus may have been the Roosevelts' closest Jewish friends. After Roosevelt was stricken with polio in 1921, Henry Jr. was often at his bedside, talking and playing marathon bouts of Parcheesi. In 1925, after Roosevelt's convalescence, he paid a visit to the Morgenthau farm, where he had to be carried from his car by a valet and Henry Jr. In a scene witnessed by then eight-year-old Henry III, the two men awkwardly maneuvered Roosevelt up the rickety front steps. Roosevelt, knowing that Henry Jr. was ticklish, began to poke him. "My father, scared beyond his wits that he would drop his precious burden, would cry for mercy while Roosevelt roared with laughter. I think the tickling was done partly to tease my father and partly to turn the embarrassment of displaying himself as a cripple into a joke on someone else."[7]

But the reality of the Roosevelt-Henry Jr. relationship was more complicated. Not to put too fine a point on it, each saw in the other a vehicle to further their respective ambitions or, more precisely in Henry Jr.'s case, Henry Sr.'s ambitions. To the father, Franklin Roosevelt, a former vice presidential candidate now making a political comeback, was his son's ticket to a cabinet post. To the Roosevelts, the Morgenthaus were among the many camp followers who could offer both some valued political assistance to Roosevelt's career—including assistance from Henry Sr. with Jewish voters and, somewhat improbably in Henry Jr.'s case, with New York farmers—and, above all, loyalty.

It was hardly a relationship of equals. Henry III, on the occasion of the tickling incident, had been sent to bed when the grown-ups sat down to dinner. He crept down to the stair landing and listened to the banter and cheery conversation. He could hear Roosevelt's rich voice dominating the conversation as he told story after cherished story. "It would invariably end with 'Don't you love it?' and a burst of his contagious laughter." The laughter was a cue, which no one missed, and all joined in. In the end, although the Roosevelt connection gave him a political base free of dependence on his father, Henry Jr. had traded only one form of dominance for another.[8]

To be a Jewish member of the Roosevelt retinue was to exist in a state of perpetual insecurity. One Jewish rival to Henry Jr. in the 1920s was Herbert Lehman, a wealthy New York Democratic politician who also happened to be Elinor Morgenthau's uncle. The Lehman and Morgenthau camps competed for the favor and attention of Franklin Roosevelt, but Lehman could far outdo Henry Jr. (and even Henry Sr.) in campaign contributions.

Elinor's longstanding resentment of the Lehman wealth only grew worse. Henry III wrote, "I think both my parents harbored the uneasy feeling that they might be outbid in their political ambitions, especially because of the unspoken fear that there was some kind of Jewish quota at the top." It was a political ménage à trois: for Henry Jr. *and* his wife, their most important relationship was with Franklin Roosevelt. As John Morton Blum, another Morgenthau biographer, wrote, Henry Jr.'s "first joy in life was to serve Roosevelt, whom he loved and trusted and admired."[9]

As they feared, the Morgenthaus were outbid. In 1928, Roosevelt was elected governor of New York and his Jewish running mate, Herbert Lehman, became lieutenant governor. Roosevelt tossed Henry Jr. a bone: an obscure post as the unsalaried chairman of the state Agricultural Advisory Commission, for which he had no apparent qualifications other than his money-losing farm venture and agricultural periodical. Swallowing his wounded pride and silently nursing the hurt feelings, Henry Jr. served diligently enough to merit a promotion. This came, however, only after Roosevelt's reelection as governor in 1930, when he appointed Henry Jr. to the far more important post of state conservation commissioner.

Thus Henry Jr. patiently and tenaciously fought his way back to the inner Rooseveltian circle. After FDR was elected president in 1932, he appointed Henry Jr. head of the newly created Farm Credit Administration, which provided financial assistance to struggling farmers. But the FCA was not a cabinet post. Henry Morgenthau Sr. took the appointment very hard. This was the moment for a Jew in the cabinet, and, by God, that was supposed to be his son.

Henry Sr.'s bitterness did not last long. In 1934, Roosevelt appointed Henry Jr., then forty-three years old, secretary of the treasury—only the second Jew in American history to be appointed to a cabinet position. Ironically, Henry Jr.'s questionable credentials as a farmer, which facilitated his elevation to the FCA (which in turn was the launching pad to the Treasury Department), may have proven decisive in overcoming the handicap of being Jewish. Certainly that was Henry Sr.'s view. Henry III wrote of his grandfather, "There was no question in his mind that his son's achievement was not because he was Jewish but in spite of it."[10]

Henry Jr. was now firmly entrenched as one of Roosevelt's closest and most influential advisers. The Treasury Department was involved, in one way or another, in virtually every New Deal program and the overall transformation of the American economy. When war in Europe loomed, in accordance with Roosevelt's wishes and his own convictions, Henry Jr. was among the government advocates of American preparedness.

But no one was a greater advocate than President Roosevelt himself. The turning point was the crisis over Czechoslovakia in September 1938. When war seemed inevitable, FDR had sent appeals to both British Prime Minister Neville Chamberlain and German Chancellor Adolf Hitler urging them to continue negotiations, which may have only added to the pressure for British concessions in response to Hitler's demands for Czech territory. At the Munich Conference on September 28–29, 1938, in a futile effort at avoiding war ("It was a replay of August 1914 with the film running in reverse," was how one historian described it), Great Britain and France handed over nearly one-third of Czechoslovakia's population and almost 30 percent of its territory to Hitler, which left it defenseless against Germany (which would soon occupy the rest of the country).

Chamberlain told the British people, "I believe it is peace for our time," while Winston Churchill saw it differently. "The Government had to choose between shame and war," he was reported as saying in some accounts. "They chose shame and will get war." But it was the Czech minister to Great Britain who pronounced history's verdict even before the conference, from which Czechoslovakia had been excluded. Trying to control his emotions, the minister told Chamberlain and his foreign minister: "If you have sacrificed my nation to preserve the peace of the world, I will be the first to applaud you. But, if not, gentlemen, God help your souls."

For Roosevelt's part, the Munich crisis left both a greater appreciation of Hitler's belligerent territorial objectives and doubts as to his own role in failing to stop them. "I am not sure now that I am proud of what I wrote to Hitler in urging that he sit down around the table and make peace," Roosevelt said to Morgenthau, army and navy representatives, and others at a key White House meeting in November 1938, following the Munich Conference (and just days after *Kristallnacht*). "That may have saved many, many lives now, but that may ultimately result in the loss of many times that number of lives later. When I write to foreign countries I must have something to back up my words."

Roosevelt then stated that the nation needed "10,000 planes a year" and the "capacity to produce twice that number." From that point on, Roosevelt's commitment to rearming the United States and stopping the dictators was unrelenting. "He had grasped the essence of [Hitler's and Mussolini's] challenge better than any European leader except Churchill," according to Henry Kissinger.[11]

In 1940, after the fall of France, Great Britain stood alone against the Nazi onslaught. In its evacuation of Dunkirk in late May–early June, the British Army had to abandon most of its military equipment. By the end of 1940, German U-boats and surface ships had sunk hundreds of British merchant vessels; Britain had to import forty-three million tons of goods each year, but only thirty-six million tons were getting through. Britain was slowly being strangled to death.

The three neutrality acts passed by an isolationist U.S. Congress between 1935 and 1937 forbade loans, financial assistance, and direct sales of arms and munitions to belligerents, regardless of which party was the aggressor. After the invasion of Poland in 1939, a fourth such act was passed, which effectively allowed Great Britain (but not Germany) to purchase arms and ammunition on a "cash and carry" basis—if it had the cash. But American public opinion was still largely isolationist, which meant that Roosevelt and Morgenthau increasingly resorted to various devices to funnel arms in particular, to Great Britain. Both men understood they were pushing, if not exceeding, the law and hardly leveling with the American public about it. At one point,

Roosevelt commented to his Treasury secretary that he had "used more weasel words in the last two weeks than in the last seven years." Today, he likely would face impeachment.[12]

Roosevelt's first priority after Dunkirk was to reequip the British Army. Over the War Department's opposition, Morgenthau's legal staff, in collaboration with the Justice Department and supported by Sumner Welles, advised Roosevelt that he could legally sell surplus military equipment to private manufacturers, who in turn could sell it to the British. Among the surplus shipped to Great Britain immediately after Dunkirk: nearly 22,000 machine guns of various types, 50,000 antiaircraft guns, 500,000 World War I–vintage rifles, 20,000 revolvers, 130 million rounds of ammunition, and 10 million pounds of TNT. "I am delighted to have that list of surplus material which is 'ready to roll,'" Roosevelt wrote to Morgenthau on June 6, 1940. "Give it an extra push every morning and every night until it is on board ship." Apart from tanks, the British Army was substantially reequipped within six weeks after the Dunkirk retreat.[13]

British spirits, at least publicly, never flagged. After the French capitulation, a London newsstand displayed a sign: "FRENCH SIGN PEACE TREATY: WE'RE IN THE FINALS!" But by the end of the year, Britain had run out of money to pay for military and other supplies. On December 7, Prime Minister Winston Churchill sent a letter to Roosevelt that one historian called "perhaps the most important letter of [Churchill's] life":

> *As you know, orders already placed or under negotiation many times exceed the total exchange resources remaining at the disposal of Great Britain. The moment approaches when we shall no longer be able to pay cash for shipping and other supplies. I do not believe the government and people of the United States would find it in accordance with the principles which guide them, to confine the help which they have so generously promised only to such munitions of war and commodities as could be immediately paid for. You may be assured that we shall prove ourselves ready to suffer and sacrifice to the utmost for the cause, and that we glory in being its champion. The rest we leave with confidence to you and your people.*

In effect, the British Empire had turned its future over to Franklin Roosevelt, whose countrymen, by and large, wanted nothing to do with another European war.[14]

The president received the letter while at sea on vacation aboard the USS *Tuscaloosa*. There had been "no staff studies, no diplomatic discussions, no touching of political bases," wrote historian Jean Edward Smith. Roosevelt just sat alone in his deck chair, reading and rereading the letter. He appeared lost in thought for two days. "I didn't know for quite a while what he was thinking about, if anything," recalled his close aide Harry Hopkins. "But then—I began to get the idea that he was refueling, the way he does so often when he seems to be resting and carefree. So I didn't ask him any questions. Then, one evening, he suddenly came out with it—the whole program. He didn't seem to have any clear idea how it could be done legally. But there wasn't a doubt in his mind that he'd find a way to do it."

Upon his return, Roosevelt told Morgenthau, "I have been thinking very hard on this trip about what we should do for England, and it seems to me that the first thing we should do is get away from the dollar sign." Roosevelt then described his idea for what became the Lend-Lease program. "We will say to England, we will give you the guns and ships that you need, provided that when the war is over you will return to us in kind the guns and ships we have loaned to you or you will return to us the ships repaired and pay us, always in kind, to make up the depreciation. What do you think of it?"

"I think it is the best idea yet," replied Morgenthau. "If I followed my own heart, I would say, let's give it to them; but I think it would be much better for you to be in the position that you are, insisting before Congress and the people of the United States to get ship for ship when the war is over, and have Congress say that you are tough, than to have the reverse true and have Congress say you are too easy."

Next to his "Nothing to Fear" inaugural speech, it may have been the finest moment in Roosevelt's presidency. At an almost unheard-of level of conceptual political artistry, with history at a crossroads, he had single-handedly created a strategy for extending crucial assistance to the one country in Europe still fighting Nazi Germany; preserved not just a strategic ally but what would become the vital staging area for the 1944 invasion of Europe; and then masterfully found a way to make the isolationist American public comfortable with what was essentially an overtly hostile act toward Germany that risked dragging the United States into the European conflict. It may have won a world war.

"I don't think there is any particular news," he said at a press conference on December 17, no doubt relishing one of the year's ranking understatements, "except possibly one thing." In a now classic discourse, he explained Lend-Lease in terms that the American public readily grasped:

Suppose my neighbor's home catches fire, and I have a length of garden hose four or five hundred feet away. If he can take my garden hose and connect it up with his hydrant, I may help him to put out the fire. Now what do I do? I don't say to him before that operation, 'Neighbor, my garden hose cost me fifteen dollars; you have to pay me fifteen dollars for it.' What is the transaction that goes on? No! I don't want fifteen dollars—I want my garden hose back after the fire is over.

On December 29, Roosevelt gave a fireside chat, best remembered for his call for the United States to become the "arsenal of democracy." Lend-Lease was necessary, he explained to the American people, because "No man can tame a tiger into a kitten by stroking it. There can be no appeasement with ruthlessness. There can be no reasoning with an incendiary bomb." If Britain fell, he said, "All of us in the Americas would be living at the point of a gun." At one point, he warned his listeners of fifth columnists: "There are also American citizens, many of them in high places, who, unwittingly in most cases, are aiding and abetting the work of these agents."

At 9:00 PM, the hour when Roosevelt began the fireside chat, attendance at movie theaters in New York City was noticeably lower. In London, wrote Doris Kearns Goodwin, German bombers carried out the "heaviest bombing of the war, hoping to counter the effect that Roosevelt's words might produce on British morale." The bombers destroyed or severely damaged the ancient Guildhall (seat of London's government since William the Conqueror), Dr. Samuel Johnson's historic house off Fleet Street, eight Christopher Wren churches, and the Old Bailey.

While German propaganda minister Joseph Goebbels wrote in his diary that "London has nothing to smile about at the moment," thousands of Londoners gathered by their radios in the early hours of the morning to listen to Roosevelt's talk, which kept British spirits high. Letters and telegrams to the

White House from Americans supported Roosevelt a hundred to one. Philosopher and historian Isaiah Berlin wrote of him:

> *[Roosevelt] looked upon the future with a calm eye, as if to say, "Let it come, whatever it may be, it will all be grist to our great mill. . . . In a despondent world which appeared divided between wicked and fatally efficient fanatics marching to destroy, and bewildered populations on the run, unenthusiastic martyrs in a cause they could not define, he believed in his own ability, so long as he was at the controls, to stem this terrible tide. He had all the character and energy and skill of the dictators, and he was on our side.*[15]

Morgenthau's Treasury Department was assigned initial responsibility for the legal and financial groundwork to implement the Lend-Lease program, which eventually was expanded to aid the Soviet Union after its invasion by Germany in 1941. He performed brilliantly, not least because of an outstanding Treasury Department staff and his own fierce conviction that the Nazis were a mortal peril to the United States. Later, Dean Acheson, reflecting on the Treasury Department's overall work in supplying Great Britain, commented that Morgenthau "was entirely responsible for the fact that between Dunkirk and [the beginning of 1941] . . . the English kept on fighting."[16]

★ ★ ★

Perhaps even more than his role in Lend-Lease, the ultimate measure of Henry Jr.'s ascent was his weekly lunch with the president at the White House. But there was no question who dominated the relationship and the price that Morgenthau had to pay to maintain it. In 1936, Roosevelt had decided to remove Adolph C. Miller, a distinguished economist, from the Federal Reserve Board. Miller, who had served on the board since its creation during the Wilson administration, was a friend of both Roosevelt and Morgenthau; in fact, they and their wives had regular dinners together during one period. Roosevelt brought Morgenthau and Miller to the White House and went over the reasons why Miller had to leave the board.

"Isn't that so, Henry?" Roosevelt kept saying, turning to Morgenthau. "Isn't that so, Henry?" Morgenthau later described it as "the most embarrassing thing of my life." Nonetheless, Morgenthau didn't disagree that "that was so," and Miller left the Federal Reserve Board.¹⁷

At that stratospheric level, the doubts and insecurity about his relationship with Roosevelt (it was said of Morgenthau that "the capacity for worry and suspicion of the burly, baldish man whose eyes glinted behind pince-nez was legendary") festered just below the surface. And, Roosevelt did not make it easy on him.

"Never let your left hand know what the right is doing," Roosevelt once told Morgenthau.

"Which hand am I, Mr. President?"

"My right hand," replied Roosevelt. But then he added, perhaps with a twinkle in his eye, "But I keep my left under the table."¹⁸

Indeed, he did, especially on Jewish issues. Morgenthau, crisp and knowledgeable on financial matters, became hesitant when he and Roosevelt discussed Jews. On one occasion in late 1942, Roosevelt mused offhandedly about moving the Arabs out of Palestine.

"Would you propose that the majority should be Jews in Palestine?" asked Morgenthau.

"Yes, 90 percent of them should be Jews," responded Roosevelt, who then seemingly did an about-face by adopting the British policy of limiting emigration. "But I don't want to bring in more than they can economically support, and I think that point has been reached." Morgenthau certainly knew this was not true, but he did not disagree with Roosevelt.¹⁹

On another occasion, Roosevelt had made a comment at a cabinet meeting to the effect that too many Jews were employed on a federal project in Oregon. Afterward, saying that he wanted to talk to the president "as one friend to another," Morgenthau expressed concern that Roosevelt's statement could leave the impression with the cabinet that he "didn't want so many Jews in the Government."

Roosevelt responded animatedly:

Well, you completely misunderstood the thing. I think it is much better to discuss this thing out in the open. Let me give you an example. Some years ago a third of the entering class at Harvard were Jews and the question came up as to how it should be handled. After discussing it with [the Harvard Board of Overseers] it was decided that over a period of years the number of Jews should be reduced one or two per cent a year until it was down to 15%. I treat the Catholic situation exactly the same as the Jews. You can't get a disproportionate amount of any one religion.

Morgenthau was speechless. At least, his memorandum to the file on the conversation did not report that he offered any objection to Roosevelt. All he wrote was "At least, that is the way the President feels on the issue. I don't know whether he is right or wrong that it is better discussed openly or not. While he talked excitedly about it, at no time did he make it personal." It could hardly have been much solace that a presidential desire to put a limit on the number of qualified Jews in universities and the government was nothing personal.[20]

Sometimes, the stress of the job and managing his relationship with Roosevelt became too much for Morgenthau, and he simply lost it. On one occasion, his secretary, Henrietta Klotz—so loyal that she named her daughter after Elinor Morgenthau—was asked by an assistant secretary to persuade Morgenthau to change his position on an issue about which he was going to testify in Congress. "He'll kill me," she replied, "but I've been killed before."

So Mrs. Klotz raised the issue with Morgenthau while they were having lunch together, and he nearly killed her. "He was infuriated. And without realizing quite what he was doing, he threw his fork directly at her face," wrote Henry III. (Why are biographer-sons so brutally honest about their fathers?) "It hit her forehead, which began to bleed profusely." There was a happy ending of sorts: Mrs. Klotz did not need any stitches and Morgenthau changed his position. He also sent her roses.[21]

★ ★ ★

One of the most remarkable aspects of Morgenthau's eleven and a half years as secretary of the treasury, longer than all but one other Treasury Department secretary in American history, is the written record of his day-to-day activities. The record, now known as the "Morgenthau Diaries," is an odd mix of documents that includes speeches and correspondence, press releases, newspaper clippings, and, most importantly, memoranda and transcripts of meetings and telephone calls. The Morgenthau Diaries are real-time history, and they offer a window on the Roosevelt-Morgenthau relationship—indeed, perhaps on the Roosevelt administration—like no other.

As the diaries reveal, FDR, who nicknamed Morgenthau "Henry the Morgue" apparently because of his conservative outlook, handled Morgenthau's insecurities with the deftness of a master conductor. In 1943, Morgenthau labored over a letter to Roosevelt in which he complained about the Treasury Department's apparent loss of authority over tax policy. In several single-spaced pages of well-crafted argument, he explained why the president should restore the Treasury's primacy. The letter implied that Morgenthau was no longer certain that he had the president's confidence regarding a core Treasury Department responsibility.

Roosevelt simply sent a teasing note to Morgenthau: "Aw HEN: The weather is hot and I am goin' off fishing. I decline to be serious even when you see 'gremlins' which ain't there! F.D.R." A week and a half later, Roosevelt asked Morgenthau, "Did you get my very snooty note?"

"Yes, I did and I didn't think it was snooty," replied Morgenthau. "I thought it was darling and I enjoyed it. I loved it." But, while Roosevelt told Morgenthau to proceed on tax policy as he always had done, he declined Morgenthau's request to instruct the other agencies to defer to the Treasury Department on tax issues. "This is all one big family and you don't do things that way in a family," he admonished Morgenthau, which meant that the Treasury had to continue jockeying with the other agencies over tax policy.[22]

The diaries also record occasions when both men were all business, terse and focused on a crisis, and leave no doubt as to who was in charge.

"Hello, Henry. Cabinet at 8:30."

"Yes, sir. I have some orders which we are getting out. I cleared all of them with Welles."

"Fine."

"We would like permission to put a detail of soldiers on the White House grounds."

"I don't think my idea is that. What you could do is this: Put up barricades between the White House and the Treasury and also on the [street] between the White House and State Department."

"We will do that tonight. All right, sir."

The conversation was at 6:40 on the evening of December 7, 1941. Some hours earlier the Japanese had attacked Pearl Harbor, killing twenty-four hundred Americans in a matter of minutes and heavily damaging the Pacific fleet.[23]

The Morgenthau Diaries also record Henry Jr.'s many meetings with the four Treasury Department lawyers who had begun to engage the State Department on the Romanian rescue plan. One of Morgenthau's signal achievements as Treasury Department secretary had been to build one of the best wartime legal divisions of any cabinet agency in Washington. Morgenthau's hiring policy consisted of asking two simple questions: "Does he want to lick this fellow Hitler, that is what I want to know. Does he hate Hitler's guts." He then put his legal division to work creating vital instruments with which to "lick" Hitler, including Lend-Lease. Even before the war, the Treasury Department lawyers had been the single greatest source of new ideas in the building; the outbreak of the war and Morgenthau's passion for defeating Hitler only stirred them up even more.[24]

So, when the Romanian rescue proposal landed in the Treasury Department, it received an entirely different reception from the one at the State Department. Four highly motivated, imaginative, and tough Treasury Department lawyers, selected on the basis of legal talent and hatred of Hitler, instantly threw their support behind the proposal. The senior lawyer was Randolph Paul, the Treasury's general counsel and former New York tax attorney. Paul was in his early fifties; the other three were in their early to mid-thirties. The second in seniority was John Pehle, then serving as director of Foreign Funds Control, who had grown up in Sioux Falls, South Dakota, graduated from Yale Law School and, after a year of graduate study, joined the Treasury Department. As Pehle later recalled with evident relish, "It was an organization that went into all sorts of things that weren't the Treasury's business primarily." Next was Josiah E. DuBois Jr., as described, at one point chief counsel to Foreign Funds Control and later assistant to the secretary of the treasury, and a dogged investigator. Finally, there was Ansel F. Luxford, a year younger than DuBois but with a cooler temperament and a keen eye for the weaknesses in the State Department's armor. The first three, by all accounts, were Christians, and Luxford probably was.[25]

By the beginning of October 1943, all four had experienced unaccustomed failure in advocating that Gerhart Riegner receive a Treasury Department license to save seventy thousand Romanian Jews in Transnistria and the French children. They had helped to keep Britain and the Soviet Union fighting through the Lend-Lease program; DuBois had narrowly escaped German bombs while on one overseas mission. They were not used to failure, yet:

July 16: *The Treasury Department advised the State Department that it was prepared to approve the license.*

September 28: *The State Department forwarded the Treasury Department's authorization to Minister Leland Harrison in Bern but gave Harrison no instruction to issue the license.*

October 6: *Harrison requested specific instructions from the State Department and advised that the license had been discussed with the British, who oppose it.*

October 20: *The Treasury Department, only after demanding to see Harrison's October 6 reply (which the Treasury lawyers had learned about informally), received a copy.*

October 23: *The Treasury Department delivered to the State Department a draft cable that instructed Harrison to deliver the license.*

Nearly three and a half months had elapsed since the Treasury Department had approved the license. Although they may not have known the details, the department's lawyers were aware that the Jews in Transnistria were dying. They were baffled—and growing angrier by the day.

On October 26, Pehle called Assistant Secretary of State Breckinridge Long and demanded to know why the cable requested by the Treasury Department had not been sent.

"I have been working on it for much of the day," said Long. "Our Minister in Bern acted properly in discussing the matter with his British colleague and in reporting his reaction to us before acting on Treasury's authorization to issue the license."

"I doubt that the British would have cleared a similar problem with us." Pehle spoke bluntly even though he was dealing with a more senior official in another department. "Our position can be explained to them, but we do not need British clearance before going ahead."

"I will try to get the matter cleared at State as soon as possible," replied Long.

In fact, the Division of European Affairs had already initialed the cable but only as a "transmitting agency" for the Treasury Department. Wrote the division functionary Borden Reams: "I do not believe we can or should accede to the desire of Treasury and send this message as a joint message from Treasury and from the Department. This proposal is objectionable from the Department's point of view. We are granting to a special group of enemy aliens relief measures which we have in the past denied to Allied peoples." In so many words, the Transnistrian Jews were being labeled enemies of the United States.[26]

Pehle called Long back two days later and told him, "We have received word that the British Ministry of Economic Warfare had approved, without prior clearance from us, a quite similar transaction involving [British] children in the Channel Islands [then occupied by German soldiers]." He added, "Obviously, this supports our contention that the British would not necessarily clear these matters with the State Department—"

"Well, as a matter of fact," said Long, cutting him off, "late on October 26, we instructed Bern to go ahead on Treasury's authorization to issue the license."[27]

A cable to Harrison had indeed been sent. But while the cable ostensibly directed the Bern legation to issue the license, the cable ended with the disguised but unmistakable implication that, in fact, this was a Treasury Department initiative and issuing the license was the last thing the State Department wanted to do. The cable simply restated the Treasury's request that the State Department issue the license, and then unenthusiastically offered, "You should, of course, comply with the Treasury Department's wishes."[28]

After receiving the cable in Bern, Harrison correctly read between the lines and concluded that he was not supposed to issue the license. An experienced bureaucrat, he recognized that he was in a triangular cross fire among his own department, the Treasury Department, and the British. Since his and his wife's close friend Sumner Welles was gone from the State Department, Harrison was now on his own. Ignoring the telegram, he simply disappeared from view into a bureaucratic foxhole while the bullets whistled overhead. Thereafter, he played almost no significant role in the ensuing events.[29]

The Treasury Department's battle had also partly shifted to the British, which may have been what Long, Reams, and Harrison intended. On November 13, Pehle received a cable sent by the British Ministry of Economic Warfare to the State Department and addressed, "For Personal Attention of Mr. Pehle." The cable asserted that the ministry was "unable to judge its [the rescue plan's] merits until they have received details." This message was followed by another from the Bern legation stating—just to emphasize the point in case the Treasury lawyers somehow missed it—that the British were withholding their consent to the rescue plan.[30]

Now alarmed at the prospect of further delay, Pehle took the issue to the secretary of the treasury. At a meeting on November 23 in Morgenthau's office, also attended by DuBois and Luxford, Pehle explained the State Department's opposition to the rescue plan and how, even though the Bern legation had been requested by the State Department to "comply with the Treasury Department's wishes," British objections now supposedly held up the license.

"What business is it of Harrison's to put this thing up to the British in Switzerland?" Morgenthau asked Pehle.

"There has been an attempt from the beginning in these commercial things to harmonize the British and American policy."

Pehle should have begun by citing the Channel Islands incident, but instead his answer had triggered Morgenthau's protective political instincts.

"Knowing that," asked Morgenthau, "should we have informed either the British Embassy here or our Embassy in London?"

"I don't think so, because this is not a commercial case, and besides, we wanted to get some action."

"It seems to me if we had forewarned them [the British] it would have been good."

"May I make a point?" Pehle did not back down in the face of the implied rebuke that he had left the Treasury Department vulnerable to a charge of not consulting with a close ally.

"If you please."

"This file is full of cables which we have originated and which State has sent, which are full of little remarks like the Treasury wants this, the Treasury desires you to do this, and the Treasury this, and the Treasury that. And Harrison, unless he is just a dumbbell, can see through that, that State is in effect saying this is what the Treasury wants you to do."

"Well, that doesn't influence me," said Morgenthau. "We are on new territory when we are taking up a matter of refugees." Recognizing that he might have been too harsh, he added: "Gentlemen, I can say on the record that I am delighted at your motives. No one would like to see this come out in the open more than I. Unfortunately, you are up against a successive generation of people like those in the State Department who don't like to do this kind of thing. I am all for you, not that I am a cynic or discouraged, but I don't think you are going to be able to nail anybody in the State Department—"

"I am not sure, Mr. Secretary," interjected Luxford.

"—to the cross."

"They will go too far."

Morgenthau agreed to send a note to Cordell Hull, although he was skeptical as to how the secretary of state would react. "If he says 'What is happening?' and begins to read through this thing, you have one [of] two reactions, 'God, the Treasury gives me a pain in the neck,' or 'I think this is outrageous, and I will send for so and so. Why have Harrison and everybody else made it difficult for the Treasury?' Neither I nor the President can make Mr. Hull see something different."[31]

The next day, Morgenthau sent the letter drafted by his aides to Secretary of State Cordell Hull. The letter reviewed the history of the Treasury Department's futile efforts to have the license issued to Gerhart Riegner. "I find the three and one-half months delay which has ensued since Treasury first indicated its approval, and you concurred, most difficult to understand." The letter closed with a sentence that less than subtly described the State Department's strategy. "Since programs of this character can be just as effectively vitiated by delay as they can by denial of the necessary licenses, your assistance is badly needed in order to expedite this matter."[32]

Nothing happened, and Morgenthau's aides had only frustration to show for their months of effort. That only worsened when, on December 6, Hull sent Morgenthau a letter disputing that the State Department had been responsible for the three-and-a-half-month delay. Rather, according to the Hull letter, *Gerhart Riegner* was to blame because he was unable to provide "an opinion on the feasibility of the plan until he had consulted with the Romanian Jewish organization. As far as the Department is aware, no further word has ever been received from Dr. Riegner in this connection." The letter, referring to the "unspeakable treatment which these poor people have received," then insisted that "it has always been the policy of the Department to deal expeditiously and sympathetically with proposals offering hope of their relief." In other words, the World Jewish Congress is dragging its feet on this matter while the State Department has been poised and ready to act.[33]

★ ★ ★

On the same day that Hull sent this letter, Randolph Paul and Secretary Morgenthau spoke about the State Department's delay in presenting to French liberation authorities in North Africa the views of the U.S. government that these authorities should take steps to undo the economic harm that the Nazis inflicted on "selected groups in Tunisia, particularly the Jews, through the impositions of fines, penalties and other levies." Paul advocated sending a strongly worded letter to Hull about the State Department's delay, but Morgenthau overruled him on the ground that "it would irritate Hull unnecessarily." Sensing Paul's frustration, Morgenthau awkwardly tried to assuage him.

"I admire you people for getting excited about it. God damn it! It makes me feel good."

"Well, I feel especially sore at all these Jewish episodes in the State Department and I'm convinced it's just a gang in there that are blocking everything and so I don't—when they won't—I get a little bit extra hot on that account." For a buttoned-down New York tax lawyer, this was nothing less than an explosive outburst.

"Well, I of all people," said Morgenthau, obviously aware that his Christian aides were (at least overtly) more upset than he was about the obstacles put up by the State Department to helping Jewish victims of the Nazis, "appreciate the sympathetic interest of you boys; on the other hand, I've got to be a balance wheel."

"Well, of course, you—" Paul caught himself, loyal to a boss who wanted to be thought of as *the* secretary of the treasury and not as *a* Jewish secretary of the treasury, "we all want to get results and it's a matter of technique."[34]

★ ★ ★

Randolph Paul initiated preparation of a lengthy memorandum to Morgenthau refuting Hull's December 6 letter point by point. Josiah DuBois Jr. was enlisted to draft the memorandum. Like many of his highly motivated, fiercely Nazi-hating colleagues in the Legal Division, DuBois had not joined the Treasury Department just to issue War Bonds.

He was an intense, round-faced young man with a thatch of dark hair combed straight up in the front, a favored style of the day. A graduate of the

University of Pennsylvania Law School, DuBois was a man not easily stopped from carrying out a mission. In his economic warfare job, DuBois had been part of a two-man, joint State–Treasury Department financial sapper team that traveled through Central America persuading governments to freeze funds in bank accounts used by the German government to pay for espionage and sabotage activities. DuBois was also sent to North Africa following the Allied invasion to dry up the Germany currency and manage the new currency issued by the Allies.

DuBois began by reviewing the paraphrases of certain cables between Minister Leland Harrison and the State Department about the Romanian rescue plan that had been given to the Treasury Department. One cable from Harrison caught his attention; in fact, DuBois may have become obsessed with it.

It was a cable dated April 20, but its significance was not in its contents as such but in its reference to another cable, which the Treasury Department had *not* been given: "While I have not transmitted R's [Riegner's] messages as such in compliance with the terms of your [cable] 354, February 10, I have at the same time felt that information which he is able to furnish and which appears to be reasonably authentic should be in your hands."

What was cable 354? What were its instructions? And why was Harrison so evidently uncomfortable with it? The Treasury Department file did not contain any such cable. DuBois called the State Department and asked for a copy of cable 354. The response was brusque, stating essentially: Cable 354 does not relate to any matters that concern the Treasury; it's political, not economic; it can be seen only by a few people in the State Department; and it cannot be furnished to the Treasury Department.

Now DuBois was fully engaged (this response may have reminded him of the stonewalling by banks in foreign countries that held German funds). He contacted a State Department official with whom he had worked on economic warfare projects. The acquaintance was Donald Hiss, an Assistant Secretary of State Dean Acheson's staff, with responsibility, like DuBois, for blocking the enemy's financial assets. The two men were friends and even drove to work together.

DuBois described cable 354 as best he could. "If possible, can you get me a copy?"

Several days went by with no word from Hiss. DuBois called him at home. The conversation was short and guarded.

"I am having considerable difficulty getting a copy of the cable—and the cable to which it refers," Hiss said. "I will let you know as soon as I have copies."[35]

Then in his late thirties, Hiss had a brilliant legal pedigree, including Harvard Law School and a coveted clerkship for the legendary Supreme Court justice Oliver Wendell Holmes. Hiss's brother Alger, also a State Department official, was better known. Later, both Hiss brothers would come under suspicion of being Communist spies, which Donald Hiss denied. (Alger Hiss would be convicted of perjury when, under oath, he denied engaging in subversive activities.) But that was in the future and now the issue was not Communism but Nazism and the greatest crime in human history. Donald Hiss in fact was prepared to betray the State Department because he was appalled at what it was doing. But he could not get his hands on cable 354.

DuBois went back to work on the memorandum requested by Paul. "After carefully reviewing again our file in this matter we feel that the conclusions arrived at by Secretary Hull are predicated upon his incomplete knowledge of the facts." He also prepared a draft letter from Morgenthau to Hull expressing concern "about the delay which has occurred."

The memorandum made no reference to cable 354. Donald Hiss had not called back.[36]

★ ★ ★

On December 9, while working on the memorandum to Morgenthau, Josiah DuBois Jr. took another step in what had become his unofficial investigation of the State Department. He went for lunch with Bernard Meltzer, the former acting chief of the Division of Foreign Funds Control for the State Department who had resigned in frustration over the failure of the Department to approve the Romanian rescue license and was now an ensign in the U.S. Navy. Meltzer bitterly poured out the story he had promised to tell DuBois after he was no longer with the State Department.

"He and I were the only two men in the Department who favored taking action to implement the proposal," said Meltzer, referring to Dr. Herbert Feis, the chief economic adviser in the State Department with whom he had been allied in fighting for the Romanian rescue proposal. "The rest of the State Department boys who had anything to do with the matter, particularly

Long, Brandt and Reams, all opposed taking any action. My tactic was to argue that the economic warfare aspects of this matter [were] for the Treasury to decide. I finally got agreement from the politicos to present the economic aspects to the Treasury but I was told to limit my memoranda purely to the financial aspects."

He added, "I didn't do that."

"What were their motives?" asked DuBois.

"I am in no position to accuse these men of opposing such proposals because of anti-Jewish sentiments," he responded. "I cannot support such an accusation with concrete evidence. And I prefer to be charitable in cases such as this." But he then pointedly added, "But it's striking that in a case like this such men should be arguing against a proposal on economic warfare grounds. Usually, it's my division which argues against a proposal on these grounds and usually it was the foreign service group that argued that economic warfare considerations were not important."

"Did Hull know that only you and Feis were in favor of the Romanian rescue and that the rest opposed it?"

"Yes."

"Why hadn't you attempted to clear the license with the British?"

"There were already enough obstacles in our way without adding that one."[37]

★ ★ ★

Four days later, on December 13, another meeting was convened in Morgenthau's office, this time to hear Josiah DuBois Jr.'s report of his lunch with Bernard Meltzer. John Pehle and Ansel Luxford were present. DuBois recounted what Meltzer had told him, concluding, "Well, that was the inside dope I got from him."

"I talked to [Donald] Hiss the other day regarding the Tunisian cable we were worried about," added Luxford. "He gave me exactly that same story as to exactly the same personalities being involved on that cable—just tying it up—Foreign Service Division, particularly Atherton, of the European, and Wallace Murray, of the Near East."

The reference to Hiss might have caused DuBois to start. Why hadn't Hiss called him back? DuBois had not told Morgenthau about cable 354 or his request to Hiss for a copy. He did not bring it up now, apparently because Hiss appeared to be getting nowhere.

Pehle underscored what was obvious to the non-Jews in the room. "In other words, there is no question as to what the underlying facts and motivations are." His barely disguised suggestion that anti-Semitism in the State Department was directly responsible for the deaths of many thousands of Jews failed to distract Morgenthau from Hull's preposterous claim that Gerhart Riegner was not supporting his own rescue plan.

"The direct implication is that even Riegner is holding back," said Morgenthau.

"In what sense, Mr. Secretary?" asked Pehle.

"Approving this transaction." Morgenthau's political instincts were engaged. If the State Department and Riegner had backed away from the Romanian rescue, then the Treasury Department was not about to take responsibility.

"Dr. Riegner," responded Pehle, "is the one who worked this out in Switzerland."

DuBois then explained that, according to one cable sent by the Bern legation, Riegner needed to check the feasibility of also providing for relief of the Transnistrian Jews *prior* to their evacuation, a separate issue from the rescue plan. But Riegner never expressed any doubts about the feasibility of the rescue plan itself. "That was one of the main things that troubled Riegner, and he wanted to check on it," DuBois added. "The implication, if there is any implication in their letter [of December 6] that Riegner was holding back, is entirely false. We can easily rebut that."

The discussion then focused on whether the Treasury Department on its own could issue the license. Pehle and the other aides argued that the Treasury only needed the Bern legation to supervise the blocked account, which could also be done by a private individual.

"Now let me put my two bits in," said Morgenthau. "Supposing the British say it is O.K. Then do we take full responsibility in issuing the license?"

"We propose to take full responsibility in the Treasury," replied Pehle, "yes, sir, full responsibility. If we were willing to tell [Minister Harrison] to issue it we should be willing to issue it ourselves."

"You know," said Morgenthau, "this is an awfully dangerous piece of business; and I have got to take the full responsibility for this thing."

His meaning was clear enough. Henry Morgenthau Jr. was not ready to act on his own authority to save the Transnistrian Jews. The meeting ended shortly afterward.[38]

★ ★ ★

Randolph Paul reviewed Josiah DuBois Jr.'s draft memorandum and the draft letter to Hull, which addressed the State Department's objections and reemphasized that "the benefits of a program such as this can be just as effectively lost through delay as through the failure to issue a license." On December 17, Paul sent the documents to Morgenthau, who summoned all four lawyers—Paul, Pehle, DuBois, and Luxford—to his office. Morgenthau's secretary, Henrietta Klotz, was present for part of the meeting.

"I have read this thing and I have certain objections."

Pehle asked Morgenthau if he had heard about the most recent letter from the British. "It was sent to you, Mr. Secretary, I think."

"What!"

"Three or four days ago," said DuBois.

"I never saw it," said Mrs. Klotz defensively.

The letter was finally located in Morgenthau's files. In it, the British Embassy in Washington reported that the Ministry of Economic Warfare, "from the purely financial angle," was prepared in principle to agree to the proposed license. However, the letter went on, "the Foreign Office sees grave disadvantages in general to the scheme and are telegraphing separately on the matter." The Treasury officials were left to guess at the Foreign Office's soon-to-be-telegraphed objections.[39]

The letter was a setback for Paul and the other lawyers; it instantly focused Morgenthau on the political risks of ignoring the forthcoming Foreign Office objections even before they had been received.

"It seems to me," said Morgenthau, "that Mr. Hull or anybody else in Congress could say, 'How could you, in light of that—you were put on notice that the British Foreign Office was going to object—go ahead and issue the license?'"

Morgenthau's aides were now on the defensive. All good advocates, they pointed out that Paul's draft letter to Hull said only that the Treasury Department was "prepared" to issue the license, not that the department would issue it. The arguments went on and on until finally Morgenthau—under strong pressure from lawyers he had hired precisely because they were fierce opponents of the Nazis, knowing that every day of delay meant more dead Jews in Transnistria, and obsessive in protecting his most important relationship—could not continue without unburdening himself.

"Look, gentlemen, let's call a spade a spade." It was an unusual outburst by a cabinet member in front of his staff. It reflected half a century of Morgenthau family history, in which first Henry Sr. and then the son achieved high public office in spite of their religion—indeed, by downplaying their Jewishness. But above all, it grew out of the uncertain relationship between Franklin Roosevelt and the most senior Jew in his administration, who precisely because of that fact was always in a precarious position when it came to Jewish issues. Morgenthau's single greatest fear was triggering an attack on Roosevelt by the president's enemies because his secretary of the treasury had been too far in front of the president—and the country—on Jewish issues.

"I am Secretary of the Treasury for one hundred and thirty-five million people, see? That is the way I think of myself; I represent all of them. But if Mr. Hamilton Fish [a virulently anti-Roosevelt Congressman] was to go after me, he goes after me because I am a Jew."

The lawyers arrayed before him could not dispute what he was saying because it was the truth. But that could not have made it any easier for the Christian lawyers to sit and listen to their Jewish boss resist their efforts to save Jewish lives because he might be attacked on the ground that he had done so only because he was a Jew.

"Let's use plain, simple language. He doesn't go after me because I am Secretary; he goes after me because he thinks I have done something for the Jews because I am a Jew."

"Mr. Secretary," offered Pehle, "that is what I certainly feel, and I think the rest of us feel."

Openly expressing his deepest fears, however, apparently was a cathartic process for Morgenthau. Grumbling about the letter to Hull—"but that is a badly drafted letter"—he then set about editing it with aides. Finally he said, "Somebody walk this last thing in to Mrs. Klotz and I will sign it."

While waiting for the final letter to be typed, Morgenthau's aides speculated about the British Foreign Office's political objections. "What can they be?" asked Pehle. One aide thought that concern about Palestine and the Arab reaction would be the basis for British objections. Another offered the opinion that any such argument would be "made with their tongue in their cheek and that is the real thing we have got to fight." This was shoptalk because the business of the meeting was essentially over. But then the shoptalk took a turn onto moral terrain that had not been trod by Breckinridge Long or by the residents of the third floor of the State Department.

"The British, by doing nothing," said Luxford, demonstrating clarity of insight into the British just as he had the State Department, "are condemning these people to death."

"I don't know how many of them have died so far," added Paul.

"That is right," said Luxford. "Inaction here is a positive action to that end."

"The British say condemn them to death," said DuBois, "and we say they should get out."

Paul had the last word.

"I don't know how we can blame the Germans for killing them when we are doing this."

It was a damning judgment, not just on the yet-to-be-articulated objections of the British but also on the State Department's months of delay and obstruction and, by implication at least, the government of the United States.

Like Paul, the other three lawyers were loyal, patriotic Americans. And not one of them disagreed.[40]

XIV

THE ORPHANS OF TRANSNISTRIA

The orphans crept out of the ghettos of Transnistria and scurried here and there like wild animals. They ravenously ate clumps of grass or scavenged through garbage piles. They foraged night after night even though many were shot by Ukrainian gendarmes or by bloody-minded, homeless Ukrainian youths for the crime of leaving the ghetto to search for food. Driven nearly mad by hunger pains, the orphans had no choice.[1]

In seven ghettos, Jewish councils established orphanages, but even at their best such places barely improved the lives of their wards. Orphans slept several to a bed and, when one of them died, the others in the bed did not tell the adults; that way, they could eat the dead child's share of the food. In one orphanage, a single room held between fifty and sixty children. In the winter, they did not leave their unheated room (and the windows were broken) for a month at a time. "Their food was served almost frozen," visitors were told, "and they relieved themselves there as well."[2]

The orphanages resembled homes for the elderly. Like old people, the orphans—whose faces had aged from their ordeals—compared their various pains, diseases, and miseries, and they reminisced about the past, when they had families. At night, they returned to a state of unloved childhood, discussing where to find food—"If you follow a funeral procession, they have at least a feast afterwards right in the cemetery. Anyone can come and eat. They don't chase anybody away"—and crying themselves to sleep.[3]

At one time, Ruth had been terrified of orphanages. When she was seven, aunts had taken her to one in Czernowitz to watch a performance staged by the children. The orphanage was a stunning villa set in a lush garden. The orphans were well cared for and relatively happy. Even so, the experience had left Ruth so shaken at the thought of losing her parents that she fell asleep that night dreaming that scientists had found the secret to eternal life.

Now, five years later, holding Frau Sattinger's hand, Ruth walked to Bershad's orphanage. In her free hand, she carried her family's silver fork, knife, and spoon. She wore her best outfit, which is to say, her only clothes: a ripped brown skirt, a plain blouse, and a dark-blue sailor coat with gold-colored buttons that somehow had not been torn off and sold to buy food. Otherwise, she had no belongings.

This orphanage was a shabby, three-room house on a small square. The orphans had been picked up from the alleys, rescued from ruined houses, and found among piles of corpses. They did not sleep in beds but simply lay on low platforms, jammed together like sardines. Most were ill with one disease or another, dirty, cold, and emaciated.[4]

"Consider yourself lucky, Ruth, to have a roof over your head," said Frau Sattinger. "The age limit is ten. They made an exception."[5]

Ruth was unceremoniously handed over to a woman volunteer. She took Ruth and looked for a place on the platforms. There was no room for Ruth, and so she was given a small space on the floor. Other volunteers cooked the meager rations for the orphans. But, by and large, orphans cared for other orphans. The older children looked after the smaller ones. Ruth took care of several children, including a one-year-old girl.[6]

She was a beautiful child, with sad, dark eyes. She had no name, never made a sound, and was very sick. Ruth, who loved the child like a mother, sang lullabies to her, told her fairy tales, and fed her a horrible cornmeal mush called mamaliga, which was all that anyone in the orphanage was given to eat. The nameless child was Ruth's life preserver in a wretched sea of death and disease. She would rebuild her family because, right now, more than anything on earth, Ruth wanted a family—any family.

Ruth prayed to God for the child's survival. But life slipped away from the child, who died cradled in Ruth's arms. Ruth lay down on her sailor coat, which *served as both mattress and blanket, in her little space in the corner of a room, and drew her knees up to her chin. She lost track of time; for all she knew, she had been lying in the corner for days.*

"Why do you take from me everyone I love?" she asked God.[7]

He did not answer Ruth's question. Perhaps He did not have an answer to this question any more than to Ruth's other questions.

Night after night Ruth remained in her near-catatonic state. She was haunted by kaleidoscopic images: Czernowitz, her mother and father, Bubi, Milie, Ruzena, the nameless baby, and God. She returned to a wakeful state only because something was gently nuzzling her hair. She brushed at whatever it was and the nuzzling stopped, but then it began again, except that this time it was not nuzzling but scratching and nibbling. She flailed at the intruder and her hand brushed fur. It was a large, hungry rat.[8]

XV

CABLE 354

```
We have now received the views of the [British]
Foreign Office. . . . The Foreign Office are con-
cerned with the difficulties of disposing of any
considerable number of Jews should they be res-
cued from enemy occupied territory. . . . They
foresee it is likely to prove almost, if not
quite, impossible to deal with anything like the
number of 70,000 refugees whose rescue is envis-
aged by the Riegner plan.¹
```

"Amazing cable," said Josiah DuBois Jr. in Secretary of the Treasury Henry Morgenthau's office. It was December 18, and the meeting had started at noon. "Their position is, 'What could we do with them if we got them out?' Amazing, most amazing position."

John Pehle and Randolph Paul likewise were dumbfounded at the cable from the American ambassador to Great Britain that transmitted a letter from the British Ministry of Economic Warfare stating the objections of the British Foreign Office to the rescue plan. While the Ministry of Economic Warfare had dropped its objections to the financial transaction aspects of the rescue plan, the British Foreign Office now claimed that the rescue plan was impractical because of the shortage of shipping and the difficulties of "finding accommodation in the countries of the Near East for any but a very small number of Jewish refugees."

"So we are away from all this smokescreen," said Paul. "Now, we are into the real issue."

Morgenthau had been largely silent. The British letter, perhaps more than any single event to date, had refocused his attention. Morgenthau suddenly offered: "I am seeing the President tomorrow at lunch, and after lunch I might have a chance to bring it up, although I have the Chinese thing which he asked me for, which will take precedent. I am quite sure I can work this in."

But in something of a role reversal, Pehle urged caution. "I think we ought to do some real thinking at this point, Mr. Secretary. The financial thing is out of the way, really, and the British are saying, in effect, that they don't propose to take any Jews out of these areas. Now that is the general broad, enormous issue that has been, to some extent, flushed out."

"Foreign policy," said Ansel Luxford tersely.

"Issue of foreign policy," Paul echoed Luxford. "Over which, unfortunately, the State Department has jurisdiction."

"When we had the conference with this man Reams, of the State Department, and Meltzer," said DuBois referring to the meeting in July where State Department officials Borden Reams and Bernard Meltzer openly disagreed with one another, "they pointed out that under the provisions of the British White Paper only about 30,000 Jews can be admitted to Palestine. They said they did not know of any other areas to which the remaining Jews could be evacuated. Now, even at that point, they raised with us the problem of what we are going to do with them."

"Then why don't I ask to see Mr. Hull about this thing?" asked Morgenthau.

"Mr. Secretary," said DuBois, "the only question we have in our mind, I think, is the bull has to be taken by the horns in dealing with this Jewish issue, and get this thing out of the State Department into some agency's hands that is willing to deal with it frontally.

"For instance," DuBois continued, "take the complaint, 'what are we going to do with the Jews?'" Answering his own question, DuBois bitterly mimicked, "We let them die because we don't know what to do with them."

The meeting ended with Morgenthau practicing what he would say to Secretary of State Cordell Hull.

"I would like to say to Mr. Hull, 'After all, if you were a member of the Cabinet in Germany today, you would be, most likely, in a prison camp, and your wife would be God knows where,' because Mrs. Hull is a Jewess, you know. Did you people know that?"

"Yes, sir," answered Luxford.

"Her name was Wirtz," said Morgenthau (misstating her name, which was Witz). "And if he was in Germany today, he couldn't hold the position he has, because he is married to a Jewess, even though she changed her name to Whitney."

Of course, Morgenthau had no intention of saying any of that to Hull. He telephoned Hull's office to set up an appointment.

"In fairness to Hull, I want to give him a chance, and then if he turns me down I will say, 'Well, Cordell, I am going to tell you now I want to see the President with you on this matter.'"[2]

★ ★ ★

A message was waiting for Josiah DuBois Jr. in his office. Donald Hiss at the State Department had called. DuBois should be at his office at 2:30 that afternoon.

★ ★ ★

"It was made clear to me," Donald Hiss began, "that cable 354 is none of Treasury's business and that in no event should it be shown to Treasury."

Hiss handed him both cable 354 and its predecessor, cable 482. As Josiah DuBois Jr. studied the cables, Hiss added, "If it were known that I have shown you cable 354, I might well lose my job. And I am confident that my telephone has been tapped and that my conversations with Treasury are being listened to."

As described in the scene that opens this book, DuBois took notes on cable 354, which was dated February 10, 1943, ten long months and an intolerable number of deaths earlier. Cable 354 referred to an earlier cable, cable 482, which reported the mass murders of European Jews, and the desperate plight of the seventy thousand ill and starving Romanian Jews then alive in Transnistria, whose living conditions, according to cable 482, were "indescribable."

But cable 354, signed by Sumner Welles and initialed by four senior State Department officials, including Ray Atherton, then the acting head of the Division of European Affairs, directed Minister Leland Harrison to stop transmitting any more reports about the plight of Jews in Europe:

```
Your 482, January 21

In the future we would suggest that you do not
accept reports submitted to you to be transmitted
to private persons in the United States. . . .
```

Most lawyers never find a piece of evidence that cracks a case wide open. The few who find such evidence generally experience a once-in-a-career feeling of elation and empowerment. This was no legal case. But, for the first time in the effort to save the Romanian Jews in Transnistria, DuBois had been empowered.

He returned to his office and wrote a confidential memorandum recounting what had just happened. "When I saw Hiss this afternoon, he gave me the signed copies of cable 354 and a previous cable to which 354 refers, a cable of January 21, 482. . . ." DuBois's immediate objective was to save Romanian Jews. But cable 354, DuBois realized, also offered an opportunity to take refugee and rescue issues away from the State Department.

His colleague, Ansel Luxford, had been right. The State Department had gone too far. And now, they were going to be nailed to a cross.[3]

XVI

"THIS MOVEMENT TO LET THE JEWS BE KILLED"

"**G**entlemen, this is some memorandum," Secretary Morgenthau had said when he finished reading the document. It was December 19, the day after DuBois's meeting with Hiss.

Now, the group was editing a memorandum to Secretary Hull that Henry Morgenthau Jr. would personally present. Morgenthau had even brought his wife, Elinor, to the editing session. The group haggled over paragraphs, phrases, and even single words. (For example, Morgenthau questioned: "Is that accurate? . . . I still think that is an awfully long sentence. . . . Now, why do you add that last thing?") The memorandum expressed the Treasury Department's astonishment with, and vehement objections to, the British position.

> *In simple terms, the British position is that they apparently are prepared to accept the possible—even probable—death of thousands of Jews in enemy territory because of the "difficulties of disposing of any considerable number of Jews should they be rescued." That is not our view and does not represent the views of your Department.*

And, after all the meetings and debate, the Treasury Department position on rescue was clear:

> *I propose for your consideration that we cut the Gordian Knot <u>now</u> by advising the British that we are going to take immediate action to facilitate the escape of Jews from Hitler and <u>then</u> discuss what can be done in the way of finding them a more permanent refuge. Even if we took these people and treated them as prisoners of war it would be better than letting them die.*[1]

The next morning, Morgenthau and his aides met to finalize the memorandum and plan tactics for the meeting with Hull, an hour and a half away. While Josiah DuBois Jr.'s discovery had energized everyone, the lawyers realized that it was essential to physically obtain the cables (or at least paraphrases). So, they had persuaded Morgenthau, in effect, to deceive the secretary of state by "casually" asking Hull for a copy of the infamous cable 354 without alerting Hull to its significance or letting on that the Treasury Department had already seen the cable. Although DuBois had taken notes, the Treasury lawyers wanted actual documents to use against the State Department. And their boss was to get them but he was unsure how to do it: "I want to ask you, where do I look, in what cable, to say casually to [Hull]—Where is cable 354?"[2]

John Pehle suggested that Morgenthau refer Hull to the April 20 cable from the Bern legation in which Minister Leland Harrison had stated, "While I have not transmitted R[iegner]'s messages as such in compliance with the terms of your [cable] 354, February 10, I have at the same time felt that information which he is able to furnish and which appears to be reasonably authentic should be in your hands." Because a paraphrase of the April 20 cable had been given to the Treasury Department, Morgenthau could legitimately bring it up.

Handing the Bern legation's April 20 cable to Morgenthau, Pehle said, "Here is the reference, Mr. Secretary, to that cable [354] underlined in blue."

"We asked for it?"

"We have asked for it several times and they say it is none of our business." Trying to bolster Morgenthau's confidence, Pehle added, "I think you can get it all right."

Morgenthau went back to the memorandum that he was to hand Hull. The memorandum had been reworked to emphasize that the issue was far broader than the Romanian rescue proposal. It pointedly stated that if the

British position prevailed, "It means we should give up trying to work out any proposal to rescue Jews in enemy country."

"Why do you say Jews? Is it just Jews?" asked Morgenthau.

"That is the real problem," responded Pehle.

"Look, boys, I am under awful pressure. Let me read this thing."

Finally Morgenthau said: "I think that is all right. I think that puts it on a better basis. Fix up that copy for me. Whose bright idea was that?"

"DuBois."

"It also gets us away from all technical arguments," said Randolph Paul, who added, "This is really our underground movement."

"How do you mean?" asked Morgenthau, speaking for everyone else in the room.

"This movement to let the Jews be killed is an underground movement here. Underground in the State [Department], and it is underground in the country."

"Surely," said Pehle.

Morgenthau, Paul, and Pehle left for the State Department to meet with the Secretary of State.[3]

★ ★ ★

Back from the State Department, Morgenthau reconvened a meeting with all four lawyers. The mood was gleeful, almost giddy.

"Have you heard the news?" asked Morgenthau.

"Don't you see us smiling?" said Luxford.

"This is one of the greatest victories." For the first time in weeks, Morgenthau was elated, and relieved.

"It is coming our way," agreed Luxford.

"You fellows don't know old man Hull. He has his teeth in this thing." Morgenthau was now the wise sage lecturing his young eager beavers. "I have told you fellows consistently not to say a fellow won't come through until the facts are in."

"Can I go ahead and dictate the meeting?" asked Pehle.

"Yes."

★ ★ ★

Cordell Hull and Breckinridge Long had greeted the Treasury Department delegation when it arrived. Before Henry Morgenthau Jr. could even present his memorandum, the white-haired secretary of state made a statement.

"I sent a cable to Ambassador [John Gilbert] Winant," said Hull, who appeared tired and worn out. He then read out loud the cable to the U.S. ambassador to Great Britain. The cable expressed Hull's astonishment at the British position, emphasized that it was not in accord with the American government's policy, and instructed Ambassador Winant to press the matter with the British government.

"A reply has been received from Winant. He is seeing [British Foreign Secretary Anthony] Eden."

Hull and Long had caved in the face of the Treasury Department's pressure even before Morgenthau entered Hull's office.

"Some of these matters don't always have my attention," added Hull, in effect pronouncing an epitaph on his stewardship of the State Department. "I have found it necessary to go into such matters from top to bottom and avoid people down the line raising technical points. In order to get any action, you have to rip through the objections."

"I drafted personally a license," Long jumped in, "and issued it and cabled it to Switzerland as of last Saturday." Long then reviewed what he claimed were efforts by the State Department to rescue Jews from occupied territories.[4]

"The German government succeeded in thwarting most of these rescue attempts," Long said regretfully. The apparent unsympathetic silence of the Treasury delegation caused Hull to say, "I am working with the British to get a revision of their attitude in the White Paper [limiting Jewish emigration to Palestine]."

Morgenthau handed over the memorandum, which Hull read without comment.

"By the way," said Morgenthau, "I have a cable in my hand from Harrison, number 2460, in which it mentions a cable, number 354. Would you mind getting that one for me?"

"Make a note of that," Hull directed Long. "And see that Morgenthau gets that."

★ ★ ★

"I mean it was a perfect opportunity, you see," said Morgenthau, pleased with his apparent success in wresting cable 354 out of the State Department.

"But the point," he continued, "is that from the time I called the State Department and said that I wanted to have an appointment with Hull—from that time on something must have happened damned fast. He must have gotten hold of Breckinridge Long. Long must have issued a license. It was that telephone call plus this fact that I was coming over, plus this outrageous cable from the British—"

"Yes," said Ansel Luxford, "they saw the record being built up against them."

"—it just dynamited this thing loose which has been hanging for five months."

Josiah DuBois Jr. was unimpressed with the backslapping going on before him in Morgenthau's office. "I think we all predicted that Long would have come through with some very prize statements as to how much he had been doing. My prediction still is, to the extent that this is left in the hands of Long that you are not going to have any substantial—"

"—it can't be said too often," said Randolph Paul, fully in support. DuBois had sobered them up. They had succeeded after months of effort only in getting the Romanian rescue license issued. At that rate, DuBois was pointing out, precious few lives would ever be saved.

"Mr. Secretary," asked John Pehle, "can we get something about your talk privately with Long?"

"This is really, if it weren't tragic, funny," said Morgenthau, and then he told them about his talk with the assistant secretary of state.

★ ★ ★

After the meeting with Cordell Hull ended, Breckinridge Long had said to Treasury Secretary Morgenthau, "I want to talk to you privately." He then led him into another room, where the two were alone.

"I just want to tell you," said Long, "that unfortunately the people lower down in your Department and lower down in the State Department are making trouble. There is a fellow by the name of Meltzer who used to be associated with Feis, and he has been spreading this stuff. Meltzer is one of the fellows who has been raising technical difficulties. I know that has been creating a lot of trouble. I think you ought to know it." Long then "spoke about everybody being anti-semitic."

Long was laying the blame for the delay in the rescue plan on one of the few men in the State Department who had tried to get the rescue plan approved. And, apparently not realizing or else forgetting that Meltzer was Jewish, Long was also bizarrely hinting to Morgenthau that Meltzer was anti-Semitic or at least had thrown in his lot with the anti-Semitic forces in the State Department.

"Well, Breck," said Morgenthau, looking Long straight in the eye, "as long as you raise the question, we might be a little frank. The impression is all around that you, particularly, are anti-Semitic!"

"I know that is so," said Long, somewhat fatalistically. "I hope you will use your good offices to correct that impression, because I am not."

"Well, since we are being so frank," said Morgenthau, in a polite but gloves-off way, "you might as well know that the impression has grown in the Treasury that the feeling in the State Department is just the same as expressed in that cable from London about the Foreign Office. That there is no difference."

Long protested. "I hope I can work with you."

"After all, Breck," continued Morgenthau, "the United States of America was created as a refuge for people who were persecuted the world over, starting with Plymouth." Morgenthau should have stopped there, but his insecurity over being Jewish in a largely Gentile government could not—even at this moment of moral and bureaucratic triumph—leave him alone. Morgenthau added, "And as Secretary of the Treasury for one hundred and thirty-five million people, I am carrying this out as Secretary of the Treasury, and not as a Jew."

"Well, my concept of America as a place of refuge for persecuted people is just the same," said Long.

"Delighted to hear it," said Morgenthau.

★ ★ ★

"Meltzer!" exclaimed Luxford in astonishment as Morgenthau recounted the conversation with Breckinridge Long. "That [was] our ally over there!"

DuBois added, "Meltzer is the one who gave me all this information, how he and Feis were in favor of it and all the rest opposed it, and how he tried to fight to put the thing through."

But Morgenthau by now seemed inured to the perfidy of State Department officials. "The tragic thing," he said, "is that—dammit!—this thing could have been done last February."

Morgenthau for the first time noticed that his aides were not entirely euphoric. "Don't you fellows feel a little good about this? Regular icicles over here."

"What do you want us to do?" asked Paul.

"Well, kick up your heels. I feel very, very happy inside, because I was taking an awful risk with the people over there, you know."

"Mr. Secretary," said Luxford, "I think that any solemnity that may have been evidenced here is at the next step."

"You see," said Pehle, "their issuing a license, Mr. Secretary, doesn't get anybody out of Romania."⁵

★ ★ ★

Four hours later, Morgenthau and his aides met to review a paraphrase of cable 354, which Pehle and Luxford had just received from Assistant Secretary of State Long. Long had not provided even a paraphrase of cable 482, the earlier cable of January 21, 1943 that, as previously described, reported the horrible plight of Jews in Europe.

Long had indeed complied with Hull's instructions and given the Treasury lawyers a paraphrase of cable 354. But the version of cable 354 given by Long to the Treasury Department was not the same cable 354 that DuBois had examined in Donald Hiss's office. This version of cable 354 contained the same text in the body, but the paraphrase had been edited by the State Department to *delete* the crucial four words—"Your 482, January 21"—that referred to cable 482.

"Mr. Secretary," said Luxford, "you did not get the cable of January [cable 482]." Then referring to cable 354, he added, "You didn't even get the reference to it."

"You mean 354 isn't there?" asked Morgenthau, mistakenly assuming that even a paraphrase of cable 354 had not been provided when Luxford meant that the paraphrase given to Treasury was incomplete in a crucial respect.

"They left out the reference [to cable 482]" Pehle repeated.

"Mr. Secretary," Luxford began to explain, because Morgenthau apparently had not grasped the implications, "[cable] 354 started in the true text: 'Your 482,' which was deleted in the copy we got."

The State Department, they all realized, was trying to conceal its cover-up of the murder of millions of Jews. Luxford was the first to see the opportunity that the State Department had handed the Treasury Department.

"You can easily fox them, Mr. Secretary."[6]

★ ★ ★

"We are having some trouble understanding cable 354," Randolph Paul told Breckinridge Long in a telephone conversation that afternoon. "Secretary Morgenthau feels that perhaps the paraphrase of cable 354 might have been garbled. He asked that I check the original cable to see if it might throw any light on the matter."

"I am very glad to get the cable."

At 5:20 that evening, Ansel Luxford entered Long's office. They had time to talk while an aide was looking for cable 354.

"I must advise you how shocked we were at the British attitude on this issue," said Long. "The tremendous amount of work that constantly flows over my desk makes it impossible to check in detail each of the many cables going out daily."

As Long talked, Luxford found himself in the role of Long's diary. "And there is so little reward for a man in this job. . . . The public misunderstands the State Department . . . Congress never gives us enough money to do the job."

After twenty minutes, Luxford apparently had had enough. "Mr. Long, I hate to be bothering you waiting for this cable and holding you from your work. Why don't I wait out in the other office until you get the cable?"

"Before you do that, I'll call in my secretary." Long told his secretary, "Will you again try to get that cable from Mr. Reinstein [the aide]?" She left and a few minutes later reappeared with a file.

"Well, Mr. Long, Mr. Reinstein says you have got that cable and you have had it all the time. It is in this file." She handed the file to Long and pointed at the cable.

"Well, no," said Long, "the Treasury wanted the original cable and this is only a copy of it."

"Well, if this is the text that is without paraphrase," said Luxford, "this will be all right. Let me take a look at this." He examined the cable. "I'd like to call your attention to the fact that the cable given to us earlier this morning had omitted any reference to cable 482 of January 21." Luxford pointed to the phrase in the cable he now held in his hand: 'Your 482, January 21.'"

Luxford went on. "This explains the difficulty we had in understanding cable 354, since it obviously can only be understood in terms of the cable referred to, that is, number 482."

"Well," Long replied, "I don't know what the contents of 482 are."

"If it's agreeable to you, I know that the Secretary would want to have the text of cable 482."

Long picked up the phone and called the file room. After a brief conversation, he hung up.

"They tell me that the file room is closed and that cable 482 cannot be obtained until the morning. I personally assure you that it will be delivered first thing in the morning."

Luxford thanked him and left, convinced that Long had doctored the paraphrase of cable 354 and then lied when he claimed that he had not known about cable 482. "The omission in cable 354 of any reference to the January 21 cable," the Treasury aides would later write in a memorandum to Morgenthau, "was not inadvertent. Breckinridge Long intentionally left this reference out when he paraphrased the cable."[7]

The assistant secretary of state had been foxed.

★ ★ ★

"No wonder they tried to hide the facts," said DuBois. It was the next afternoon and DuBois and his colleagues were examining the complete paraphrases of cables 482 and 354 in Morgenthau's office. The paraphrase of cable 482 had not been delivered as promptly as Breckinridge Long had promised; in fact, five clerks in the file room had spent the morning fruitlessly searching for the original cable. The reason they couldn't find it, ironically enough, was that Donald Hiss had removed it to show DuBois several days earlier and had not returned it. Finally, an aide to Long called Luxford to say that he had the cable but that the conditions it described were "pretty horrible." He then read the cable to Luxford on the phone. A secretary took notes, which were now under scrutiny by the Morgenthau aides and their boss.

"It describes conditions as being perfectly horrible in Poland, Germany, and Romania, as well as in other parts," said Luxford, referring to cable 482. "They are putting them in the ghetto, shooting the Jews four thousand [sic] a day, and taking their clothes from them and shipping them to Germany. Well, you can't read it without being horrified."

"You have got the full flavor of what they have done," said Pehle to Morgenthau.

"After they [got] that cable describing the horrible conditions," said DuBois, who had seen the originals, "in direct response they sent out a cable saying that private messages of this character shouldn't be transmitted. They are getting private messages by the hundreds from commercial firms in Switzerland, and yet they try to stop this on that ground."

"The thing that is significant," Luxford pointed out, "is the cable [354] that went out; by no way reading it could you determine what they were doing. It was very innocuous. It is a thing every one of us would initial, so the man who signed that cable [Sumner Welles] didn't have the slightest notion what he was signing. It just said '482.' And gave an innocuous statement saying no more cables for private persons. That cable [cable 354] was initialed by Atherton and Dunn."

"You fellows draft a letter for Hull, see?" Morgenthau had a plan in mind. "'I want to draw the following shocking facts to your attention.' See? And 'I am confident that you will agree with me that the kind of information contained in this cable certainly should come out. It not only should be expressed, but should be encouraged to come out so we can evaluate the situation, and certainly private corporations every day are allowed to send their stuff out. Matters affecting thousands or millions of human beings are as important as a cable from a trade concern.'"

"That doesn't hit it quite, though, Mr. Secretary," said Luxford. "The big point is that when we asked for that cable three times we didn't get it."

"Can we hit that?" asked Pehle.

"Try it," said Morgenthau. "You fellows write it."

"I think we ought to do whatever we can at any point to protect [Donald] Hiss in the situation," said Paul.

"That is why my inclination is to let it lie a week, so it doesn't come too close." Morgenthau was thinking of the risk to Donald Hiss's career if a prompt letter to Hull about the cables exposed Hiss's role in ferreting them to the Treasury Department. "What damage can we do to the Jews in Romania if we wait one week, as far as these cables are concerned?"

"Mr. Secretary," Luxford answered, "we have got them wobbling right now. Hit them again while they are wobbling. A week from now Hull may be thinking of something else."

"I think there is a possibility, Mr. Secretary," added DuBois, "that through this you may be able to get Long out of there. I think we can either get him out or divorce the issue from him."

"You fellows write a letter," said Morgenthau, capitulating. "Do the job. May I compliment all of you?"[8]

XVII

THE CEMETERY OF BERSHAD

Ruth now believed that she was immortal. How else to explain her many escapes from death? At one point, the Bershad orphans had been taken in horse-drawn wagons to a large regional orphanage from where, they had been told, they would board a train to Romania. When the convoy reached a hill, the older children got off the wagons to lighten the load on the horses. Marching uphill, in the middle of a column of children, Ruth collapsed and fell to the side of the road. Thinking of the forced march from Czernowitz, where those who fell by the wayside were simply left to freeze to death, Ruth assumed she would die. But she was put on a cart and taken to a makeshift hospital, where she was treated for malaria.

She somehow recovered and rejoined the other orphans. But the regional orphanage did not exist, and hundreds of orphans wandered around aimlessly until Romanian soldiers herded them into a walled-in yard. Afraid that they were to be shot, the orphans began screaming and wailing. The adult leaders calmed the children, who were then returned to their local orphanages; in Ruth's case, this meant an arduous return trip to Bershad and a new, larger orphanage, just as crowded as the first.[1]

There, she suffered a second bout of malaria. The convulsions from the attacks were so bad that she fainted, lapsing into yet another coma. She was thought to be dead but, just before the undertakers were called, faint breathing was detected. She again survived.[2]

Being immortal gave Ruth no comfort, however, only the vision of an eternity of suffering. She recovered her strength in a kind of Transnistrian Hades, a room known as the "sanatorium," where the most desperately sick and crippled girls were kept. Twenty shared a single-plank bed and two blankets, all sleeping in the same direction, lice- and sore-ridden bodies nestled against each other, all turning over whenever one girl turned. Left . . . Right . . . Left . . . Right.

Some of these girls suffered from a rare condition that affected their mobility. After their families had died, lack of space and the cold forced them to sit and sleep in a fetal position. Months of inactivity had caused their joints to stiffen and the muscles to atrophy. Unable to stretch their legs, these children moved around like ducks, squatting low to the ground and painfully shuffling their feet. That was their condition when they arrived at the orphanage.

But in the midst of this torment, human grace survived. The stronger children massaged the legs of the crippled ones, hoping to restore circulation that might make the duck-like movements less painful. Other children risked their lives to forage outside the camp for food to bring back to the other orphans. They shared their happier memories— above all, those of their parents.

★ ★ ★

A small band of shriveled wraiths, dirty and mostly bald, ventured out of Bershad. They wore potato sacks or tatters of clothing. The band of children, which included Ruth, trudged along the road, which was off-limits to the Jews and therefore a dangerous place. They had only recently heard of a Jewish cemetery a mile from Bershad. Ruth and the other orphans wanted to stand before the graves of their parents.

The orphans reached the cemetery and scattered among the gravestones, some ancient and others more recent, but none for Jews who died during the winter of 1941–42. Ruth saw bones and skulls lying here and there, like brittle seashells washed up on the shore.

She walked over to a skull, bent down and gently reached out a hand. At the touch, she spoke to the skull—"Is it you, mama?" She could barely see because tears had submerged her eyes; her body shook from the bottomless sobs that welled up in an eruption of grief and loss.

The tears cascaded down Ruth's face and her body convulsions grew worse. Ruth realized that one of her companions was forcibly shaking her to calm her down. Her grief seemed without light or rest, a state of violent mourning that smothered her in despair and sorrow. But even grief eventually exhausts itself, and so it was with Ruth. Finally, while her small group of orphan-pilgrims waited patiently, Ruth pulled herself together.

The children returned to the orphanage. Ruth's emotions had stormed back at her, but she could deal with that now. She had something else on her mind.

I will keep your names alive.[3]

XVIII

THE MARCH OF THE RABBIS

"Clear the way for those Rabbis!"

The main body of Orthodox rabbis, several hundred strong, had arrived in Union Station on a train that pulled in at 12:35 PM. Most were from New York, Philadelphia, and Baltimore. They were greeted by forty rabbis who had arrived earlier on trains from the south and the west. Accompanied by one hundred reporters and friends, the nearly four hundred rabbis (many of them bearded and dressed in long black coats and black hats) marched out of Union Station and solemnly headed for the United States Capitol. The marchers looked as though they'd been transported from a prewar Jewish *shtetl* in Poland, praying as they walked, a funeral procession for millions. They were a sight such as the streets of Washington had never witnessed before. It was October 6, 1943, days before Yom Kippur, the Day of Atonement.

★ ★ ★

Just before the march of the rabbis, Reichsführer SS Heinrich Himmler addressed SS officers in Poznan (in German, *Posen*), Poland. He used notes and was unusually candid. His talk, which lasted better than three hours and was recorded on a red oxide tape, mostly concerned the military situation and Germany's inevitable victory. Two hours into his speech, however, Himmler briefly addressed a different topic—one that he explained could never be discussed publicly.

"The evacuation of the Jews, the extermination of the Jewish people. We had the moral right, we had the duty with regard to our people, to kill this race that wanted to kill us."

Himmler continued: "And to have seen this through, and—with the exception of human weaknesses—to have remained decent, has made us hard and is a page of glory never mentioned and never to be mentioned. We have carried out this most difficult task for the love of our people. And we have taken on no defect within us, in our soul, or in our character."

Given the high moral purpose of the eradication of the Jews, Himmler explained, he did not want any blemishes on the murder of millions. On this point, his voice rose, filled with emotion. "We do *not* have the right to enrich ourselves even just with one fur or a watch or a mark or cigarette."[1]

★ ★ ★

It was sheer coincidence that, two days after Himmler's speech (the recording of it was found after the war and is now regarded as one of the most chilling documents of the Holocaust), Peter Bergson's recently organized Emergency Committee to Save the Jewish People of Europe led the march of the rabbis up Capitol Hill to demand the creation of a special U.S. government agency to rescue Jews in Europe; in other words, to take rescue away from the State Department.

The march may have had its genesis in an earlier conversation between Bergson and an aide to Vice President Henry Wallace.

"You should bring 500,000 people to the White House gates," suggested the aide, "and refuse to leave until this Administration acts to help the Jews."

For once Bergson was taken aback by what was essentially a publicity stunt. "Can that many people take up space on the trains in wartime given wartime travel restrictions?"

"That's the problem with you Jews. You always want to appear as gentlemen."

The procession marched to the steps of the Capitol. There—and this marked the awesome ability of Bergson to persuade leading non-Jewish political figures to support his cause—the rabbis were joined by the vice president, the majority and minority leaders of both legislative chambers, and Speaker of the House of Representatives Sam Rayburn, a tough Texan not known for his support of Jewish causes.

From the Capitol, the rabbis proceeded to the Lincoln Memorial, where a prayer was offered which, in that hallowed setting, joined the great domestic moral crisis of American history with a transcendent foreign one. Then the rabbis marched to the White House, where a delegation was received, but not by Roosevelt.

That morning the president had met with his aides to discuss the march. Likely out of deference to an old ally, Rabbi Stephen Wise, the implacable foe of Peter Bergson, Roosevelt declined to meet with the delegation. Instead, FDR's appointments secretary greeted the delegation. The appearance of such a low-level official in place of the president caused enormous pain, especially to those rabbis who had managed to escape from Europe after witnessing the horrors that had brought them to Washington. Some rabbis never got over the slight and remained bitter toward Roosevelt; some lashed out that day, telling the press that they regarded the president's failure to greet them as a "slap in the face not only to the delegation but to American Jewry."[2]

★ ★ ★

The purloining of cables 482 and 354 by the Treasury Department was part of a trap closing in on Breckinridge Long and the State Department—and on Franklin Roosevelt. The other part had begun as congressional pressure, fueled by Peter Bergson's lobbying and publicity campaign, built for an independent rescue agency. An advisory resolution urging the president to create such an agency had been introduced in the Senate by Democrat Guy Gillette of Iowa, who was joined by eleven other senators. Six of the twelve sat on the Senate Foreign Relations Committee. In the House, Democrat Will Rogers Jr. of California and Republican Joseph C. Baldwin of New York City cosponsored the rescue resolution. Editorials in major newspapers endorsed the resolution. And soon, Long, without intending to do so, would give it the biggest boost of all.[3]

Hearings in the House of Representatives on the rescue resolution began on November 19 and continued through early December, in parallel with the meetings at the Treasury where Secretary Henry Morgenthau Jr. and his aides plotted their strategy. On November 26, 1943, Assistant Secretary of State Long, accompanied by several State Department officials, including Borden Reams, testified at a closed meeting of the House Committee on Foreign Affairs. Long advised the committee that secrecy was essential because otherwise operations to aid Jews in Europe planned by the State Department "would not be possible to be carried forward, and it would react against the interests of the people that we are trying to help."[4]

He didn't directly oppose the resolution—that, he testified, "is more or less a matter for the decision of the committee"—but emphasized the efforts by the State Department to rescue Jews (which Long overstated to the point of deception). "Everybody that I know, everybody in the Department of State, and everybody that I have come in contact with is interested, and a lot of them have been active in endeavoring to save the Jewish people from the terrorism of the Nazis." He singled out the contributions of Borden Reams, praising his invaluable "understanding of the political situations developing in Europe and the benefit of his advice generally concerning the European theatre."[5]

The assistant secretary of state added, "Nobody can think of the United States except as being a government composed of the descendents of refugees and interested in saving those who are in danger of their lives or liberties because of religious, racial or political persecution." At one point, Long testified: "We have taken into this country since the beginning of the Hitler regime and the persecution of the Jews, until today, approximately 580,000 refugees."

A congressman posed a specific question. "Of the total of 580,000, how many have come in as permanent entries under quotas and how many have come in under temporary visas?"

"Most of them came in under the quota. We issued visitors' and transit visas, which would probably cover 85,000 [in one period]."

The congressmen took turns expressing their appreciation for the work of Breckinridge Long and his State Department colleagues. "Mr. Long," said one, "I want to compliment you on your statement. I think you have done a splendid job and I think you are doing everything that can be done." None of them yet realized that they had been badly misled.[6]

Long's testimony was a blow to the rescue resolution in the House Foreign Affairs Committee. Another setback for the resolution was the lukewarm response of American Zionists, including Rabbi Stephen Wise on behalf of the American Jewish Conference. Wise testified at the Foreign Affairs Committee hearings and, while saying that the American Jewish Conference favored the resolution, criticized it as "inadequate" because it did not provide concrete rescue plans or call for allowing Jewish refugees to emigrate to Palestine.

In advertisements, Peter Bergson's Emergency Committee called for passage of the resolution and accused Zionist leaders of trying to block it.

HOW WELL ARE YOU SLEEPING?

TIME RACES DEATH—WHAT ARE WE WAITING FOR?

FROM THE NAZI VALLEY OF DEATH OUR BROTHERS AND SISTERS CALL WITH THEIR LAST STRENGTH: AMERICAN JEWS, WHY DON'T YOU SAVE US?

The last line was particularly stinging–it was written in Yiddish.

Behind the scenes, the Zionists, according to one senator, "used every effort, every means at their disposal to block the resolution." Another exasperated senator said: "I wish these damned Jews would make up their minds what they want. I could not get inside the committee room without being buttonholed out here in the corridor by representatives who said that the Jewish people of America did not want passage of this resolution."[7]

Rabbi Wise's qualified support (at best) for the resolution may have partly resulted from his rivalry with Peter Bergson. The establishment Jewish organizations, David Wyman suggests, "recognized that success for the resolution would bring prestige, additional popular support and more strength to the Bergsonite faction." The Senate committee considering the rescue resolution seemed to understand best what was at stake. Their report to the full Senate could not have crystallized the issue any better:

> *The problem is essentially a humanitarian one. It is not a Jewish problem alone. It is a Christian problem and a problem for enlightened civilization. We have talked; we have sympathized; we have expressed our horror; the time to act is long past due.*

On December 10, 1943, as the Treasury Department lawyers were still piecing together the State Department's attempt to cover up the Nazi extermination plan, the House Committee on Foreign Affairs made Long's testimony public (with his support, despite his earlier professed need for secrecy). Notwithstanding the sympathy of the Senate committee and Bergson's newspaper campaign and lobbying, the rescue resolution was in serious trouble in the House; indeed, just one of the seven Jews in Congress had endorsed the resolution. Releasing the testimony, Long believed, would "prove even more effective in quieting Jewish pressure."[8]

Initially, Long's testimony was well received. The *New York Times* ran a story on the front page: "580,000 Refugees Admitted To United States In Decade." But several other newspapers raised questions about Long's figures, and the President's Advisory Committee on Political Refugees—Long's nemesis in the *Quanza* affair—asked Long for clarification. He replied that he had meant to say that 580,000 visas had been *authorized*, not that 580,000 refugees had actually entered the United States. The actual number did not exceed 250,000 (and not all were Jews).

But it was too late to undo the damage. On December 20, the same day that Treasury Secretary Morgenthau's aides finally pried loose from Long the undoctored cable 354, Democratic Congressman Emanuel Celler of Brooklyn made this statement about Assistant Secretary of State Long:

> *His statement drips with sympathy for the persecuted Jews, but the tears he sheds are crocodile. One gets the impression from Long's statement that the United States has gone out of its way to help refugees fleeing death at the hands of the Nazis. I deny this. On the contrary, the State Department has turned its back on the time-honored principle of granting havens to refugees.*[9]

A storm of outrage broke over the head of Breckinridge Long. To his diary, Long confided a long, woeful lament.

> *I made a statement to the Foreign Affairs Committee of the House. In the course of a long four-hour inquisition [I] made several statements which were not accurate—for I spoke without notes, from a memory of four years, without preparation and on one day's notice. It is remarkable I did*

not make more inaccurate statements. But the radical press, always prone to attack me, and the Jewish press have turned their barrage against me, and made life somewhat uncomfortable. The Jewish agitation depends on attacking some individual.[10]

In the Treasury Department, Morgenthau and his staff followed the uproar closely.

"They are scared," said one of those present. "Long is scared—no doubt about it in my mind. It has thoroughly frightened him. I don't think for one minute he is sincere, but it doesn't matter; he is frightened."[11]

★ ★ ★

On Christmas Eve 1943, President Franklin D. Roosevelt gave a fireside chat from the library of his home in Hyde Park, New York. He sat at a desk with several microphones in front of him. The library was filled with the broadcasting equipment needed so that sixty or seventy million people could listen on their radios. Typically, as the broadcast time approached, Roosevelt put out his cigarette, set out his reading copy, took a drink of water, waited for a nod from the chief radio engineer, and then began to speak. A cabinet member who had witnessed another such fireside chat recalled that Roosevelt's "voice and his facial expression were those of an intimate friend. His face would smile and light up as though he were actually sitting on the front porch or in the parlor with them. People felt this and it bound them to him in affection."

So it was that night. "My friends, I have recently returned from extensive journeyings in the region of the Mediterranean and as far as the borders of Russia."

The president discussed with the American people his meetings with Allied leaders, including his conference with Winston Churchill and Joseph Stalin at Tehran, where the "Big Three" agreed on "plans for stepping up our successful attack on our enemies as quickly as possible and from many different points of the compass." These plans included the opening of a second front in France in 1944, eventually to become D-Day and the Normandy landings.

Roosevelt asked his countrymen to reflect on how much they had accomplished in little over two years, but he emphasized above all how many of their sons were in harm's way. Ten million American men and women were in uniform: nearly four million of them were on duty overseas, with more than a million soon to ship out. FDR noted that in the parts of the world where it was already Christmas Day, Americans were fighting. He warned Americans that the war was now "reaching a stage where we shall all have to look forward to large casualty lists—dead, wounded and missing."

But he also sounded an optimistic note, the rich tenor tones of his voice seeming to draw the listeners even closer to their living room or kitchen radios:

But everywhere throughout the world—through this war that covers the world—there is a special spirit that has warmed our hearts since our earliest childhood—a spirit that brings us close to our homes, our families, our friends and neighbors—the Christmas spirit of "peace on earth, good will toward men." It is an unquenchable spirit. . . .[12]

★ ★ ★

Although it was Christmas Day, Josiah DuBois Jr. was in his office. DuBois was preoccupied with writing a document that was unlike any written by an official of the U.S. government in all of the war because it accused his government of complicity in mass murder. In doing so, he was deliberately defying the instructions Henry Morgenthau Jr. had given him two days earlier.

★ ★ ★

That day, Morgenthau's aides had handed the treasury secretary a memorandum, "For Secretary Morgenthau's Information Only," that summarized all that the Treasury lawyers had learned about cables 482 and 354 and the State Department's sabotage of attempts to rescue the Romanian Jews. The first sentence began, "We report to you herewith a story which is so shocking and so tragic that it is difficult to believe." The memorandum, to be sure, reflected the anger of the Treasury Department lawyers at the State Department's conduct. But that anger had a moral dimension. In the face of the State Department's obstruction, the Treasury lawyers were, to a degree, redeeming the good name of the United States of America.

> *To put it bluntly, Mr. Secretary, it appears that certain responsible officials of this Government were so fearful that this Government might act to save the Jews of Europe if the gruesome facts relating to Hitler's plans to exterminate them became known, that they not only attempted to suppress the facts but, in addition, they used the powers of their official position to secretly countermand the instructions of [Undersecretary of State Sumner Welles] ordering such facts to be reported.*

The memorandum reached its crescendo with a single, explosive line.

> *We leave it for your judgment whether this action made such officials the accomplices of Hitler in this program and whether or not these officials are not war criminals in every sense of the term.*

Morgenthau finished reading the memorandum. "What did you people think I was going to do with this?"

"I think there is only one thing to do," replied Randolph Paul. "I think that this is the ideal opportunity to get the most vicious men removed from their offices in the State Department that you will ever have."

"You still haven't answered my question."

"I think you have to talk to Hull about it."

"I mean, when you call these people accomplices of Hitler in this program, they are war criminals in every sense of the term, you are finding them guilty without trying them."

In the face of Morgenthau's discomfort, his aides again retreated, reassuring him that the memorandum was only internal to the Treasury Department.

"We all agree," said John Pehle, "that when you take this up with Hull you want a polished careful, cautious memorandum. Mr. Secretary, we agree on two points. One of them is that it must be presented to State in such a way that Hull will not rise to the defense of his Department, as such."

"That is the point," said Morgenthau.

"Secondly, we must not put him in a position so that this becomes a fight between Mr. Welles and people who are still in the Department."

★ ★ ★

DuBois, who had said little during the meeting, was now working on Christmas Day on another memorandum. He had been told that the next memorandum had to be less emotional, just give Cordell Hull the facts, don't try to anticipate Hull's reaction, let him draw his own conclusions. But DuBois, the angry young man of the Treasury Department, had decided to *broaden* the charges in "For Secretary Morgenthau's Information Only," not narrow them.[13]

★ ★ ★

". . . God bless us all," said the president to a nation at war. "Keep us strong in our faith that we fight for a better day for humankind—here and everywhere."

XIX

THE ACQUIESCENCE OF THIS GOVERNMENT IN THE MURDER OF THE JEWS

"I am not going to the President until I have exhausted Mr. Hull," Henry Morgenthau Jr. adamantly insisted to his aides at a meeting on January 10, 1944. In addition to the lawyers, another Morgenthau special assistant, Harry Dexter White, was present. A man of medium stature, White favored conservative gray suits and a rapid-fire conversational style. His high, balding forehead gave him an intellectual look that was somewhat counterbalanced by a trim Charlie Chaplin–like mustache. White was Jewish and about Morgenthau's age. After service in the U.S. Army in World War I, he had earned a doctorate in economics at Harvard University. But aspiring Jewish academics understood that there was not much of a future for them at this particular institution, and so White had taught at Lawrence College in Wisconsin before landing a job at the Treasury Department. He was destined to become an architect of the 1944 Bretton Woods agreements that established the International Monetary Fund and the World Bank—and then to be accused of collaborating with a Soviet spy ring, which he denied. Now, White, who had read "For Secretary Morgenthau's Information Only," listened as Morgenthau's aides pressed their boss to go over Hull's head to the president.[1]

"We would like to argue," said John Pehle. Over the Christmas holidays, Morgenthau's aides had come to the conclusion that, as one put it, "Hull isn't the right man to go to on this."

"When we get this report ready," suggested Josiah DuBois Jr., "which will be in a day or two, you could decide then whether to go directly to the President or not. I think most of us feel you should."

"I will wait until I see the report," said Morgenthau, "but I think we will have a hard time."

White, who had been largely silent, spoke up.

"With regard to the whole problem of the Jewish question in Europe," he said, "this Government has played a role that is little short of sickening."

Addressing Morgenthau directly, he went on:

There is only one man who can alter it, and one only, and that is the President. And there is only one man who can make the President alter it. And that is yourself. Roosevelt has the power to alter the complexion of this whole treatment in Europe if he feels keenly enough that he wishes to do so. He will never pay any attention to the problem, unless he is brought to the point where he has to make a decision. Now, I don't know whether you could be successful because it is a difficult job. But I know this—that if you can't do it nobody can and that nobody can have a chance to do it except you.

Ordinarily, the secretary and his four top lawyers were an argumentative group, interrupting, commenting, and interjecting. No one interrupted.

"I think the matter must be brought to the President's attention to just give him a survey and a picture of what the United States hasn't done and what he has permitted England to do on this whole question, and the consequences of that action in the last two years. Most of it is his own responsibility. Now how that can be brought to his attention without indicting him in his responsibility is a delicate task, but I think you have to have it out with him."

Morgenthau could not face it. Instead, he suggested that someone else, perhaps Chief Justice Harlan F. Stone, approach Roosevelt. "He feels this thing very deeply," offered Morgenthau by way of endorsement of the Chief Justice.

No one paid much attention, and Morgenthau dropped the idea. But he still wouldn't go to the president.²

★ ★ ★

"Do you know you have been on these memoranda about two weeks?" Morgenthau had complained to his staff.

"It is a very difficult memorandum to write," replied Randolph Paul.

DuBois had taken the "For Secretary Morgenthau's Information Only" and, while dropping the war crimes charge against specific State Department officials, provocatively retitled it "Report To The Secretary On The Acquiescence Of This Government In The Murder Of The Jews." Ignoring his boss's instructions, in effect, DuBois had expanded the report into an even broader indictment of the State Department and its policies toward Jews in Europe. While acknowledging the grave nature of his charge, he accused the State Department of "willful attempts to prevent action from being taken to rescue Jews from Hitler."

DuBois further asserted in the report that unless the U.S. government—meaning President Roosevelt, although that name was never mentioned—acted immediately, the blood of millions of human beings would be on its hands. Indeed, he all but said that Roosevelt's name would be blackened forever unless the president acted.

> *Unless remedial steps of a drastic nature are taken, and taken immediately, I am certain that no effective action will be taken by the Government to prevent the complete extermination of the Jews in German controlled Europe, and that this Government will have to share for all time the responsibility for this extermination.*

DuBois had to know that a report of this kind would make worldwide news if it were ever publicly disclosed, which may be one reason why he wrote it that way. Coming from the Treasury Department, in the midst of the uproar over Breckinridge Long's testimony and the rescue resolution, any newspaper handed this report would give it front-page, headline treatment. It was one thing for a newspaper to report on the "old" news of the massacre of Jews in Europe; it was something else altogether for that newspaper to get its hands on a secret, internal government document that accused the State Department of aiding the Nazi government in exterminating an entire people and suggested that the rest of the Roosevelt administration had looked the other way.

> *In their official capacity [they] have gone so far as to surreptitiously attempt to stop the obtaining of information concerning the murder of the Jewish population of Europe . . . the evidence supporting this conclusion is so shocking and so tragic that it is difficult to believe.*[3]

The "Report To The Secretary On The Acquiescence Of This Government In The Murder Of The Jews" was presented to Morgenthau at a meeting on January 13, 1944, that again included Harry White. It was not Morgenthau's only item of business. That same day, he had signed a letter asking Secretary of War Henry L. Stimson to reassign Captain Ronald W. Reagan, then attached to the army's 1st Motion Picture Unit in California, to duty at the Treasury Department to assist in the Fourth War Loan Drive. ("His services would be a great asset to the Treasury Department at this time."[4])

At the meeting with his staff, Morgenthau first told Mrs. Klotz to leave a block of time on his schedule for the coming Saturday, January 15, for a meeting at the Treasury Department with White House aides about Jewish refugee issues.

"Where is the report?" he then demanded, referring to the toned-down version of DuBois's fiery condemnation of the State Department that he was expecting from his aides. "I haven't received any."

Paul handed the new report to the Secretary. He had not changed DuBois's title. But Morgenthau's aides knew that the title, if not the content, was too inflammatory for their boss and assured him that, in effect, it was only an internal briefing paper. Morgenthau had been unwilling to accuse the State Department officials of being accomplices to Hitler; he was no more willing to accuse the Roosevelt administration of giving tacit assent to the murder of millions.

"This is just to the Secretary," said DuBois.

"This is in the Department, here. It is intended as a report to you," said Paul. "It is not an outside document."

"It has got a nice title, anyway," said Morgenthau with evident sarcasm.

"This is inside the Department–Intra-Treasury Report," Paul reassured him.

"Have you signed this thing?" Morgenthau asked.

"I initialed it," Paul acknowledged.

"Now, in the meantime, what do I do?"

Paul then explained that the lawyers would have a different version of "Report To The Secretary On The Acquiescence Of This Government In The Murder Of The Jews" for Morgenthau, which could go "to the President."

"If you could have it Saturday morning—"

"What we want, Mr. Secretary," said Paul, referring to the report he had just given Morgenthau, "is for you to master that stuff."

"You fellows better be ready Saturday morning," said Morgenthau. He and his aides then reviewed, with considerable frustration, several stalled rescue possibilities, including the rescue of several thousand French children.

"They require day-to-day decisions, impelled by the most forceful kind of desire," said White. "They require something which is not merely a statement of getting a specific paper, or a specific decision, but a whole host of little actions, little decisions, which depend upon the right kind of administration, and I think to seek—"

"Let me interrupt you, Harry, because I can't take too much pounding today. Supposing I go to the President with the most terrific document of condemnation of these people and he turns to me and says, 'Henry, I have never been so shocked in my life. What can I do?'"

"We have a specific proposal."

"An Executive Order, Mr. Secretary." The lawyers proposed that Morgenthau present to Roosevelt an order for his signature that would take refugee and rescue responsibility away from the State Department and vest it in a newly created agency.

"There have been hearings before both the House and the Senate on the ridiculous operations of State on the refugee problem," Ansel Luxford told Morgenthau. "To have this thing thrown out onto the floor of the House and debated on the basis that it will be debated, it will not be any pleasant thing."

"Therefore," said Paul, "[the] remedy is an Executive Order—let's do it without a statute."

"That's the point," agreed Luxford. "Let's do this thing and get credit for it."

Instead of confronting the president on *his* administration's deplorable lack of response to the murder of the Jews, Morgenthau could go to FDR with a political proposal. An executive order to create an independent refugee agency would keep Roosevelt from being tarred with the State Department's behavior while allowing him to wrest the initiative from Congress on the rescue agency proposal.

"When you get through with it," Morgenthau said at one point, "the attitude to date is no different from Hitler's attitude."

"Exactly," said Mrs. Klotz, perhaps sensing this was a turning point for her boss.

"You are unfair," said one cynic in the room, unable to resist. "We don't shoot them. We let other people shoot them, and let them starve."

"Starve and let them get all kinds of diseases," said another.[5]

After the meeting ended, Morgenthau called Judge Samuel Rosenman, a former New York Supreme Court justice and now a Roosevelt speechwriter, at the White House. *Time* magazine once described Rosenman as "a roly-poly who stands about 5 ft. 8 in. in his silk socks and weighs 205 pounds." Roosevelt had nicknamed him "Sammy the Rose."

"Now, look, Sam," Morgenthau said. "Saturday morning at 9:30, the Treasury is having a meeting here in regard to this whole question of refugees."

"Uh-huh."

"And I'm inviting you to come as Assistant to the President."

"Uh-huh." Rosenman's political antennae were on alert. "Well, now is that wise to have the President in it?"

"Oh, yes, because the chances are the thing will have to go to the President. Don't worry whether it is wise or not until you hear it."

"Well, there won't be any publicity about that?"

"There never is from Treasury."

"I don't suppose there will be any leak on the thing, will there?"

"There will be no leak."

Rosenman was focused on the fact that he and Morgenthau, and at least one other invitee to the meeting, were Jews. "The thing I am thinking about is whether when you talk about refugees you want to have three Jews. You're not only talking about Jewish refugees?"

"I'm talking about refugees."

"If there were to be publicity, I think the choice of the three people is terrible."

"Don't worry about the publicity," said Morgenthau, more than a little annoyed, but perhaps now appreciating how his aides must have felt in their meetings with him. "What I want is intelligence and courage—courage first and intelligence second."[6]

★ ★ ★

Judge Rosenman did not attend the Saturday morning meeting at the Treasury Department. The White House sent Ben Cohen, whom one magazine writer of the era mistook for one of "those minor state counselors in Shakespearian comedies who serve the Duke, make astute comments and are always perturbed at developments." In fact, Cohen, then in his late forties and counsel to the Office of War Mobilization, was a brilliant Jewish lawyer from Muncie, Indiana, who had drafted the New Deal legislation that transformed the financial markets in the United States. On occasion, he had served as a back channel for Rabbi Stephen Wise to communicate with President Roosevelt. Fittingly enough for a man of his intellect, Cohen had a high forehead, thin, dry hair, and owl-like eyes.[7]

Among those present were the four Treasury lawyers, Mrs. Klotz, and Harry White. Copies of what was now titled "Personal Report To The President" were distributed, and then John Pehle read aloud while the others followed on their copies. The report—first as the memorandum "For Secretary Morgenthau's Information Only" and then as the "Report To The Secretary On The Acquiescence Of This Government In The Murder Of The Jews"—finally had been toned down. What had been a war-crimes indictment was now an accusation that the State Department had engaged in "gross procrastination." Indeed, the report suggested that "whether one views this failure as being deliberate on the part of those officials handling the matter, or merely due to their incompetence, is not too important from my point of view."

But the new report made a less-than-veiled warning that Roosevelt could hardly ignore.

However, there is a growing number of responsible people and organizations today who have ceased to view our failure as the product of simple incompetence on the part of those officials in the State Department charged with handling this problem. They see plain Anti-Semitism motivating the actions of these State Department officials and, rightly or wrongly, it will require little more in the way of proof for this suspicion to explode into a nasty scandal.

The report ended by stating that "the matter of rescuing the Jews from extermination is a trust too great to remain in the hands of men who are indifferent, callous, and perhaps even hostile." The report attached a draft executive order establishing a War Refugee Board within the Executive Office of the President, to consist of the secretary of state, the secretary of the treasury, and the foreign economic administrator.[8]

Cohen asked a few lawyerly questions. When Pehle reached the part of the report dealing with Breckinridge Long's testimony in the House of Representatives, Cohen requested a copy of the testimony. Mainly, however, he listened. The meeting was orchestrated to convince Cohen that the Treasury Department had gathered damning evidence against the State Department. The stars of the meeting were cables 482 and 354. But this was also the first opportunity for the Treasury lawyers to describe to someone outside the Treasury Department how they had uncovered the State Department's conduct and, justly pleased with themselves, they got carried away. Although Cohen had argued cases before the Supreme Court, he was somewhat overwhelmed by the Treasury lawyers.

At one point, Cohen asked how the Treasury Department could have known about the reference in cable 354 to the earlier cable 482 before Morgenthau had even asked Hull for a copy.

"We have information termites over there," several of the Treasury lawyers said almost in unison.

"[Long] sent over a copy, Ben," explained Randolph Paul, "without that reference, and we knew it was wrong. I called up Long and said, 'This cable isn't clear to us the way it is paraphrased. I would like to send a man over to see the document.' He couldn't refuse that. That is the way we actually got to see it."

"That is the way we officially got to see it," Pehle added.

Cohen was intrigued with the cables. "I can see that there would be problems if things had gone through without the usual censorship as to whether the Department here should release or not release, but why the Department should want to debar itself from getting—"

"They were trying to stop Sumner Welles [from getting the cables]," Pehle interrupted, "because he was giving it to the Jewish organization[s], who [were] building up some pressure for action."

Cohen advocated a nonconfrontational approach. "It may be much more effective [to say to Hull] it undoubtedly is part of our basic policy to do what we can, but no group in the State Department regards itself as charged with the responsibility of actually doing what can be done to save these people."

He added, "I mean, we get so furious we can't believe it, and even if it isn't innocent, you won't be able to convince Hull that his most trusted Assistant Secretary simply doesn't care what happens."

"Mr. Secretary," said Ansel Luxford, "if that discussion that has just been made had been a year ago, we would all have agreed one hundred percent with it, but the time is rapidly running out. A year has gone by."

"That depends," shot back Cohen, "on whether the more effective thing you can do now is to change the minds of Long and Hull or whether the most effective thing you can do now is to get someone of outstanding rank put in the State Department who can't be pushed aside."

"What troubles me," said Josiah DuBois Jr., frustrated with Cohen's apparent resistance to confronting the State Department, "is you don't attempt to face the issue on its merits."

"I am," said Cohen coolly, "but I am not willing to write a memorandum that is more for the sake of making a record than for getting what you want."

The group then held the final debate on whether Morgenthau should go to Hull, or directly to the president.

White politely disagreed with Cohen. "Ben, I think, doesn't place sufficient stress on [the] State Department by virtue of being in a key position where they can sabotage surreptitiously and through a hundred different ways any effort which has taken place. When you are up against an organization whose technique has been perfected over years, and their job is to see that little is done, I don't think you will get very much done unless you scare them in the first place."

Until now, Morgenthau had been mainly listening. ("I would like to sit in the capacity of a judge," he had commented at the beginning.) Finally, he stopped the debate.

"If I go to Hull in the first instance—which I admit is a difficult thing to do—let's say I decide that is what we are going to do. Then he has a chance to get his case to the President before I do."

"That is the point," said Pehle.

"Wait a minute; I have an answer. My thought is to ask to see the President tomorrow and say, 'Look, Mr. President, here is the situation. I would like to discuss this and get your advice.' Chances are nine out of ten he will say, 'Make this easy for me. See Cordell.' I will go see Cordell, and then I go back, but I have gotten there first. I will have given [the President] all the dirt."

"It might be that the President will ask Hull to come over and talk it over with him and with you," Cohen suggested.

"I don't know, but I know the President well enough to go to him and say, 'I want to see you on a matter that is very, very close to my heart. I want your advice.'"

"That is wonderful!" exclaimed Mrs. Klotz, quite out of the blue (everyone ignored her).

"I personally hate to say this thing," Morgenthau continued, "but our strongest out is the imminence of Congress doing something. Really, when you get down to the point, this is a boiling pot on the Hill. You can't hold it; it is going to pop, and you have either got to move very fast, or the Congress of the United States will do it for you."

"Mr. Secretary," said Pehle, "there is one danger in using too much of that political thing, and that is what must be done here must be more than a symbol to satisfy and stop Congressional action."

Pehle's argument that rescue was, in fact, a moral issue that transcended politics had an impact.

"Look, if you don't mind," said Morgenthau, "I think I know him well enough to present a case to the President, and I can't get into all this legal thing, but I do think I know what will have weight with him. And to preface those remarks, I hate to say I have to use this at all. The arguments ought to be settled on the merits of the case we are talking about here in the Treasury family, and we are calling a spade a spade."

Morgenthau interrupted the meeting to make an appointment to see the president the next day.

"You can sit around and worry," said Morgenthau after the meeting resumed, "but you just don't know until you face the President what mood he is in. I have been up against him on so many tough propositions, and I never know how he is going to react."

He rehearsed for the others what he would say when he showed cables 482 and 354 to Roosevelt, and began echoing DuBois. "Here we find ourselves aiding and abetting Hitler. Now Mr. President, if they will do that kind of thing with millions of lives at stake instead of staying up nights to find out how they can help...."

Morgenthau then brought the meeting to a close. "I think we have covered it all, and DuBois will have the last worry that I am not going to be tough."

Paul said, "I told him to keep his mouth shut," to laughter.[9]

★ ★ ★

After the meeting, Cohen returned to the White House. Early that afternoon Morgenthau called Judge Rosenman, who said he had spoken with Cohen about the meeting; he knew that Morgenthau would not be dissuaded from seeing the president. Rosenman had also read the "Personal Report To The President."

"[It's] liable to give him the impression that this is purely Jewish," said Rosenman. "Of course, the Jewish problem is 99 percent of it."

"That's right."

"But from the public point of view, he might want to make clear that it is presented as a general issue. I think one paragraph would do it."

"I see. That would be easy to take care of. Well, I–I think it has gotten so now that I'd better go and see him."

Rosenman offered no resistance. His political unease had been overcome by the "Personal Report to the President."

"I think those examples of what happened across the street are damn good."

"Isn't that the most outrageous thing?"

"Yeah. Especially the one about the cables."

"Yeah."

"That's the God damndest thing."

"Are you going to give it to the President?" asked Morgenthau.

"Well, I'm not going to give him this document, but I am going to tell him what's in it."[10]

★ ★ ★

"Mr. Secretary, if it means anything, and if you want to, you can tell the president if he doesn't take any action on this report, I'm going to resign and release the report to the press."[11]

The Treasury Secretary must have been taken aback by Josiah DuBois Jr.'s statement just before his meeting with Roosevelt. Perhaps DuBois was just suggesting a talking point for the meeting, along the lines of "My aides are close to rebellion, Mr. President, I don't know if I can keep them from resigning." Or was he serious? DuBois certainly hadn't shown any hesitancy about expressing his anger at the State Department. And which report was he talking about? The "For Secretary Morgenthau's Information Only"? Or the "Report To The Secretary On The Acquiescence Of This Government In The Murder Of The Jews"? Or the "Personal Report To The President"?

★ ★ ★

On Sunday, January 16, 1944, Secretary of the Treasury Morgenthau arrived at the White House just before 1:00 PM. His worst fears did not come to pass. The meeting between President Roosevelt and Morgenthau was short—no longer than twenty minutes—and only symbolically historic, because the outcome had been determined once Rosenman told the president about the report that Morgenthau was bringing. Roosevelt was down with the flu, but not seriously ill. (Throughout that year, however, his health would worsen dramatically. The American public would learn of the president's failing health only after he died of a cerebral hemorrhage in April 1945.)

Morgenthau brought Randolph Paul and John Pehle with him. The meeting had a grim and fatalistic feel; it was devoid of Roosevelt's usual "Aw HEN" joshing. At the outset of the meeting, Morgenthau handed the "Personal Report To The President" to Roosevelt, who took the document but did not read it.

"Henry, I would prefer that the facts be summarized orally."

"Mr. President," said Morgenthau, "I am deeply disturbed about the failure of the State Department to take any effective action to save the remaining Jews in Europe. The Treasury Department has uncovered evidence indicating that the people in the State Department were not only inefficient, but they were actually taking action to prevent the rescue of the Jews." He then turned to Pehle.

With the president listening closely, and asking questions here and there, Pehle summarized the "Personal Report To The President," including the Treasury Department's discovery of cables 482 and 354.

Roosevelt resisted the conclusion that Breckinridge Long wanted to stop effective action. "Long has somewhat soured on the problem," said Roosevelt. "Rabbi Wise got Long to approve a long list of people to enter the country. Many of them turned out to be bad people."

"Mr. President," said Morgenthau, not giving ground, "at a cabinet meeting the Attorney General said that only three Jews of those entering the United States had turned out to be undesirables."

"I had been advised that the figure was considerably larger." Roosevelt did not explain why, since he had been at the same cabinet meeting, he had not said the same thing then to the attorney general. Both men then dropped the issue that was at the core of the State Department's rationale—and, by extension, the president's—for restricting entry into the United States of Jewish refugees fleeing the Nazis. Morgenthau was not about to confront FDR on his administration's Jewish visa policies since he already had enough on his hands.

Morgenthau and Pehle showed the president the proposed executive order. At no time did Roosevelt resist or disagree with Morgenthau's recommendation to set up the War Refugee Board. He merely dotted some I's and crossed some T's. One Roosevelt biographer has written that "Like a horse in quicksand, he had a highly developed sense of self-preservation and instinct for solid soil." The executive order was solid soil.[12]

"Well, I think the Secretary of War should be on the Board. Has Stettinius been consulted? He recently reorganized the State Department." (Roosevelt was referring to Sumner Welles's successor, the industrialist and former head of Lend-Lease, Edward Stettinius.) "I think he'll be sympathetic. And, I would like Judge Rosenman brought into this matter."

"I have already spoken to Judge Rosenman," Morgenthau answered. "I am convinced that effective action can be taken. My father had succeeded in getting the Armenians out of Turkey when he was the Ambassador and saving their lives."

"Henry, I agree with you about effective action. Some Jews are moving through Romania into Bulgaria and out through Turkey. At the present time, such channels are wide open, but they won't be if Turkey enters the war."

Roosevelt handed the "Personal Report To The President" back to Morgenthau. The three Treasury officials left and immediately set up a meeting with Stettinius at Morgenthau's home. Morgenthau was far blunter with Stettinius than he had been with the president.[13]

"People in the State Department," Morgenthau told the new undersecretary of state, "particularly Breckinridge Long, are deliberately obstructing the execution of any plan to save the Jews. Immediate action is necessary if this Government is not going to be placed in the same position as Hitler and share the responsibility for exterminating all the Jews of Europe."

Edward Stettinius was a white-haired man with blue eyes and a warm smile. In less than a year, he would succeed Cordell Hull as secretary of state. After succeeding Welles at the State Department, according to one account, he had attended a reception in his honor given by Foreign Service officers and was surprised that there were no Jews among them. Under the genial exterior, he was a tough manager who knew how to fire a subordinate and make it look like a resignation.[14]

"In my re-organization of the State Department," Stettinius told Morgenthau, "the only remaining function assigned to Long is 'Congressional Relations.'"

★ ★ ★

```
January 22, 1944

Caution: The following MUST BE HELD IN CONFIDENCE
until released.

Note: Release is for ALL REGULAR EDITIONS OF
MORNING NEWSPAPERS of Sunday, January twenty-
third, 1944.
```

Release by radio commentators, newscasters, etc. NOT EARLIER THAN 9:00 P.M., E.W.T., Saturday, January 22, 1944.

STEPHEN EARLY
Secretary to the President

The President today, by Executive Order, set up a War Refugee Board consisting of the Secretary of State, the Secretary of the Treasury and the Secretary of War to take action for the immediate rescue from the Nazis of the persecuted minorities of Europe—racial, religious, or political—all civilian victims of enemy savagery. The Executive Order declares that "it is the policy of this Government to take all measures within its power to rescue the victims of enemy oppression who are in imminent danger of death and otherwise to afford such victims all possible relief and assistance consistent with the successful prosecution of the war."[15]

XX

"WHY DIDN'T YOU COME SOONER?"

The representative of the International Red Cross in Turkey lived in a modest home on the outskirts of Ankara. On a bleak day in March 1944, a forty-three-year-old former vice president of New York City's Bloomingdale's entered the house. He had arrived an hour early and, to relieve the tension while waiting for the Romanian minister to Turkey, seated himself at the piano in the living room and played the stirring introductory chords of Beethoven's Piano Sonata in E Minor, op. 90. He was tense because he had come on a shopping expedition. Instead of purchasing flexible gooseneck lamps or Eames plywood chairs, however, the merchandise the Bloomingdale's man wanted to acquire were human beings.[1]

Ira Hirschmann played the piano beautifully. Music was his passion, the love of his life, and the mistress to his more prosaic pursuits, which included a successful advertising and business career and adviser to prominent New York Democratic politicians and senior Washington officials. A few weeks earlier, one of his Washington contacts, Assistant Solicitor General Oscar Cox, had called and asked if he would become a special envoy for the newly created War Refugee Board.

"To see that you do not work in a vacuum out there," Cox had said, "we are going to put teeth into this thing."[2]

Hirschmann then met with the War Refugee Board's executive director, John Pehle, who promised him unqualified backing; with Secretary of the Treasury Henry Morgenthau Jr. and Supreme Court Justice Felix Frankfurter; and with other prominent American Jews. Under Pehle, the War Refugee Board never had more than a staff of thirty. One observer characterized them as "young, dynamic, bold, clear and a bit brash."[3] Even though the senior staff was mostly non-Jewish, State Department officials could not refrain from calling the War Refugee Board's general counsel, Josiah DuBois Jr., "a Jew."

Nor did the existence of the War Refugee Board stop the State Department's opposition on Jewish issues. In addition to rescue, high on the agenda of Pehle and DuBois was the prosecution of the Nazi leaders for genocide, a word that was only then being invented for a crime still being committed. Pehle lobbied the new United Nations Commission for the Investigation of War Crimes to address the atrocities committed against the Jewish and other ethnic populations. At one meeting of a War Crimes Commission subcommittee, a State Department representative openly opposed the American delegate (who favored vigorous prosecution for these crimes), and later told the delegate's staff that he "would see to it that the War Crimes Commission did nothing for the Jews."[4]

Hirschmann was the War Refugee Board envoy to Turkey. Almost immediately after his briefings and rounds of meetings, he was on his way to the Middle East on a U.S. Army air transport plane filled with personnel ultimately headed to India to fly military cargo over the Himalayas (a route known as "the Hump"). It took him a week just to get to Cairo, where he was told that the Turkish government had not yet issued his entrance visa. Rather than spend time in Egypt, Hirschmann flew to Palestine on a Royal Air Force plane. There, standing on Mount Scopus, Hirschmann watched the setting sun turn the sky above the Judean Hills vivid shades of purple. He later met with David Ben-Gurion, the future prime minister of the State of Israel. Israel was then only a hazy mirage to most Jews, but not to Ben-Gurion. "We will *do* it," Ben-Gurion told Hirschmann.

A twenty-eight-hour train trip from Jerusalem finally brought Hirschmann to Ankara a full month after he had left the United States. He was under surveillance by German and Japanese agents, and even British intelligence shadowed him. One night in his hotel room, spinning the radio dial for good music, he stumbled on a Radio Berlin propaganda broadcast: "What is Jew Hirschmann doing in Ankara? Certainly, he can be up to no good." Any embarrassing mistakes, Hirschmann well knew, would cause the United States government to disavow him.

★ ★ ★

The Romanian minister to Turkey, Alexandre Cretzianu, finally arrived. Cretzianu was in his early forties, dapper and cosmopolitan, and seemingly just as nervous as Hirschmann. After Hirschmann explained that he was in Turkey by the authority of the president of the United States, the two men sat down and spoke in empty generalities for nearly an hour. Then Hirschmann mentioned the Russians, who were then driving the German army out of the occupied areas of the Soviet Union.

"It is the Russians we fear, not the Americans," said Cretzianu, a palpable shadow of terror in his face.

Hirschmann stared at him coldly. "Mr. Minister, you, Antonescu and your families are going to be killed." He added, although it was scarcely necessary, "The Russians will do it."

A long silence followed.

"I will offer you a visa for every member of your family in exchange for one simple act which will cost you nothing."

"And what is that?" asked the minister.

"Open the door of the camps in Transnistria. These are your citizens, but if you don't want them, we will take them."

"And why does the President of the United States send a personal representative to negotiate for some Jews?"

"That is why the United States is what it is," replied Hirschmann, "and why Romania is where it is today."

Over tea served by the International Red Cross representative, Hirschmann outlined the offer. In exchange for visas to the United States for Cretzianu and his family, the minister had to persuade his government to do three things. One was to cease persecution of the Romanian minorities; another, as Hirschmann had already explained, was to disband the Transnistrian concentration camps and ghettos and allow the survivors to return to their homes.

Hirschmann then outlined the final term of the deal. "Release five thousand children, facilitate their passage to Constanta [a Romanian port on the Black Sea], provide exit permits for them, and expedite the debarkation of ships which we will provide to take these children to Istanbul and from there to Haifa in Palestine."[5]

Cretzianu had been making notes and now he looked up. "It is not impossible." He promised to fly immediately to Romania. Unbeknownst to Hirschmann, however, Adolf Eichmann learned of the negotiations and urged German diplomats to see to it that "this planned emigration, if possible, be cancelled."

But Eichmann failed. A week later Hirschmann met Cretzianu again at the same location and the Romanian read a telegram from Marshal Ion Antonescu. Listening, Hirschmann felt as though an enormous weight had been taken away.[6]

★ ★ ★

Each morning, more frozen bodies were found hanging from telegraph poles. They were Jews executed by the Romanians, who draped signs around the hanging bodies to make the population of Bershad think the dead men were captured partisans: "This is the reward for collaborators."

Ruth, not entirely used to their swaying presence even though she had to walk underneath the bodies daily, pretended that they were just frightening stone statues. But they left her with nightmares. All that she and the other children could do now was to pray for a miracle because the success of the Soviet offensive had only intensified the executions of Jews.

But something had changed. A crate of clothing arrived at the orphanage from the American Jewish Joint Distribution Committee. The crate was opened to cries of wonder from the gathered orphans. Ruth was allowed to choose first. She selected a woolen baby-blue dress because it matched her eyes, a blue handkerchief to cover her bald head, and two more handkerchiefs to wrap around the sores on her hands.

And now, unbelievable rumors were everywhere. The camps will be closed— no, Antonescu will release all orphans under the age of eighteen—no, he will only release orphans under fifteen. Lists of orphans were compiled and then recompiled, bundles were packed and unpacked. Although no one had left Bershad, the orphans knew something was about to happen.

The orphans went to the cemetery and stood before a five-sided obelisk that the Transnistrian survivors had somehow managed to erect just a few months earlier. Plaques on four sides of the obelisk had been engraved with thousands of names. It cost money to have a name inscribed. Ruth paid for the engraving with money that an aunt in Czernowitz (who had escaped deportation) managed to get to her as conditions improved. Ruth went hungry in order to make good on the promise that she had made on her first visit to the cemetery. For those who could not afford an engraving, a plaque on the fifth side was dedicated to all the victims:

> *In eternal memory*
> *in commemoration of the destroyed world*
> *of the eternal people*
> *in the valley of destruction*
> *Do not keep silent*
> *At the sorrow of the myriads of Israel.*

The day finally arrived when the orphans, among those to be repatriated to Romania, left the orphanage for the last time. As their names were called one by one, they climbed into a caravan of horse-drawn carts. The caravan, a tiny tributary of children, slowly moved west and soon joined up with other such tributaries headed in the same direction. The orphans gathered in two transit orphanages, at Moghilev in the north and Balta in the south, where they washed and put on clean clothes. When they boarded trains for the final journey to the Dniester and the freedom beyond, they were frightened to find they were composed of cattle cars; this time, however, the trains stopped frequently, the children had adult escorts, and enough food and water was on board for all.

"For the first time in years we were extremely happy," wrote Ruth Glasberg a long time afterward. "The train soared westbound towards the Dniester as our tumultuous joy knew no limits."[7]

★ ★ ★

Before they parted, Romanian Minister Cretzianu had a question for the emissary from the War Refugee Board. The question caused Ira Hirschmann a "twinge of conscience," and he swore to himself that for the rest of his days he would never hesitate to act in a matter of humanitarian mercy.

"If this means so much to you in the United States," Cretzianu asked, "why didn't you come sooner? You could have saved more lives."[8]

AFTERWORD

War Refugee Board representatives were assigned to locations around Europe, including (in addition to Turkey) Switzerland, Sweden, Italy, and Spain, with diplomatic status as special attachés to American missions. The de facto War Refugee Board representative in Hungary was a Swedish diplomat named Raoul Wallenberg, who would later be personally credited with rescuing tens of thousands of Hungarian Jews. Working with the Joint Distribution Committee, the board arranged for the evacuation of between 5,000 and 6,000 Jewish children from France. Overall, the board directly or indirectly saved 200,000 lives; at no time did the board's work interfere with military operations against Germany and its allies.

The War Refugee Board (and American Jewish organizations) failed, however, to persuade the War Department to bomb the rail lines leading to Auschwitz. Its rationale was stated in an August 14, 1944, letter to the World Jewish Congress from Assistant Secretary of War John J. McCloy. While acknowledging the "humanitarian motives" behind the bombing request, McCloy wrote that the suggested air operation was impracticable. "It could be executed only by diversion of considerable air support essential to the success of our forces now engaged in decisive operations elsewhere. . . ." Nearly fifty years later, President Bill Clinton, in his remarks at the opening of the United States Holocaust Memorial Museum in Washington, acknowledged that "we must live forever" with the knowledge that "far too little" was done, including the failure to bomb "rail lines to the camps."

The U.S. government provided only about $1 million for War Refugee Board operations; American Jews raised nearly another $17 million. As Josiah DuBois Jr. bitterly commented, the War Refugee Board "did a fair amount [but] by that time it was too damned late to do too much."[1]

★ ★ ★

On April 30, 1945, as the Soviet Army closed in on the heart of Berlin, Adolf Hitler shot himself in his underground Berlin bunker, after which aides burned his body and that of his mistress, who had also died by suicide. Propaganda Minister Joseph Goebbels and his wife poisoned their six children—rather than permit them to live in a world without National Socialism—and then the parents committed a double suicide. Reichsführer SS Heinrich Himmler, accompanied by SS men, "moved around [Germany] in his Mercedes like some medieval warlord." Himmler delusionally believed he could negotiate peace terms on behalf of Germany, but was taken into custody at a British military checkpoint. At the interrogation center, his British captors ordered him to undress, searched him carefully, and then told him to open his mouth. A "small black knob" stuck out from a gap in his teeth. Himmler bit down on the poison capsule—and the fingers of a British army doctor trying to pry it out—and died within fifteen minutes.

Hermann Göring was captured and kept alive long enough to be tried and convicted by the Nuremberg International Military Tribunal of war crimes and crimes against humanity, for which he was sentenced to be hanged. While Göring was in the prison yard with other captured Nazis, the subject of surviving Hungarian Jews came up. "So, there are still some there?" Göring was reported to have said, "I thought we had knocked off all of them. Somebody slipped up again." Two hours before his scheduled execution, he swallowed a poison capsule that had somehow been smuggled into his jail cell. It could be said of Hitler and his other henchman, as it was of Göring, that they cheated the executioners by committing suicide. (The Auschwitz commandant, Rudolph Höss, was executed by the Polish government, who in 1947 hanged him—fittingly enough—in the former Auschwitz concentration camp.) The general consensus of experts is that the Nazi government murdered six million Jews (of the eight million who lived in Europe in 1939), including more than a million children, and many millions of non-Jewish civilians.[2]

Eduard Schulte eventually settled in Switzerland and married Doris. He died in 1966. He has been honored by Yad Vashem as one of "the righteous among the nations."

Gerhart Riegner worked for the World Jewish Congress for most of his life. He died in 2001 at the age of ninety after devoting his life to the cause of human rights. In his autobiography, he wrote: "I belong to the tragic generation that saw the catastrophe coming and tried to contain its effects, but who, given the lack of foresight, the moral indifference, and the political opportunism of the world that surrounded us, lacked the means to do so."[3]

Endicott Peabody retired as the headmaster of Groton in 1940 at the age of eighty-three. He continued to live in a house built for him by the trustees near the school grounds. He died on November 17, 1944, just days after his most famous student, Franklin Roosevelt, had been elected to a fourth term as president. His last words were, "You know, I think Roosevelt is an absolutely sincere man." The Groton School today is far different from the institution described in these pages. It is now a coeducational school that admits roughly equal numbers of young men and women and, as stated on its website, offers "exceptional opportunities to deserving students from diverse social, geographic, ethnic, and socio-economic backgrounds."[4]

Cordell Hull, the longest-serving secretary of state in American history, submitted his resignation on November 21, 1944, because of ill health. In December 1945, Hull was awarded the Nobel Peace Prize for his work in stabilizing international relations, but he was too ill to travel to Oslo to accept the honor. He died in 1955. As of the writing of this book, it has been more than fifteen years since the secretary of state has been a white man; since 1997, the holders of that office have been a woman with Jewish roots, an African-American man, an African-American woman, and a white woman.[5]

Sumner Welles never returned to government. After the war, he became an ardent and effective Zionist. Shortly after Israel declared its independence in 1948, its first president, Chaim Weizmann, telegraphed Welles: "I shall always remember your unfailing kindness, helpfulness and [the] unswerving support which you extended to our cause." Welles's heavy drinking contributed to his death in 1961 from pancreatic cancer. In an epitaph, his biographer-son quoted from the Persian *Rubaiyat of Omar Khayyam* to capture the inner demons that had smashed Welles's career to pieces just when Roosevelt, the country, and millions of Jews in Europe needed him most:

> *So when that Angel of the darker drink;*
> *At last shall find you by the river-brink,*
> *And, offering his cup, invite your soul*
> *Forth to your lips to quaff—*
> *You shall not shrink.*

But Sumner Welles had not quaffed from the Dark Angel's cup. Instead, as his son observed, he had drunk deeply from a cup offered by the Angel of Self-Destruction. "Casually, almost indifferently," wrote his son, "he had tossed his enemies—Hull, Bullitt and the others—the means to destroy him, and they had. His life had truly been one of light and shadows."[6]

The vendetta against Sumner Welles ruined William Bullitt. The rest of his life was a series of meandering, disconnected events. He unsuccessfully sought an appointment as a roving ambassador in the Truman administration, wrote a disparaging book about Franklin Roosevelt's last days, supported the Republican presidential ticket in 1952 in the hopes that it would lead to a government position (it did not), and experienced deteriorating health until his death from cancer in Paris in 1967. As one of his biographers wrote, "His death, as had much of his life, went largely unnoticed." But another student of Bullitt's life better captured the essence of the man: "[T]hose qualities . . . which enabled him to rise to a position of great influence also insured his ultimate downfall. He carried within him the seeds of his own destruction."[7]

The creation of the War Refugee Board, Breckinridge Long wrote in his diary in early 1944, "is good news to me. This insures me staying out. What they can do that I have not done I cannot imagine. In my opinion, the Board will not save any persecuted people I could not save under my recent and long suffering administration." By the end of the year, Long had retired from the State Department. "So, I am out of office—and a free man again—free to rest a little, readjust my life and plan for the future at age 63-1/2. My record in the Department speaks for itself. I am satisfied and happy." He never held another government position. He deposited his diaries with the Library of Congress where, in accordance with his wishes, they remained sealed until his death in 1958.[8]

Bernard Meltzer became a prosecutor at the Nuremberg War Crimes trials and then a distinguished professor of labor law at his alma mater, the University of Chicago Law School. He died in 2007 at the age of ninety-two. Dr. Herbert Feis pursued a successful career as a historian and was awarded the Pulitzer Prize in 1961. He died in 1972.[9]

The four officials who signed or approved cable 354 pursued successful diplomatic careers. Even before the creation of the War Refugee Board, as already described, Ray Atherton secured a coveted appointment as minister to Canada; James C. Dunn became an assistant secretary of state with responsibility for European, Far Eastern, Near Eastern and African affairs and an ambassador to France; John D. Hickerson became an assistant secretary of state, and then ambassador to Finland and later to the Philippines; and Elbridge Durbrow became an ambassador to South Vietnam at the outset of the Vietnam War.

R. Borden Reams, "one of the most highly regarded of the younger men in the State Department," according to an acquaintance, was appointed an assistant to the secretary of state during the Truman administration and later became chargé d'affaires in the American Embassy in Yugoslavia and ambassador to Niger. In *While Six Million Died*, first published in 1967, historian Arthur D. Morse, wrote: "In recent years the man once in charge of 'Jewish questions' has referred to his wartime role as that of 'master sergeant,' simply taking orders from higher authority."[10]

The State Department has yet to officially apologize for its conduct in response to the murder of European Jews.

The Polish government in exile refused to allow Jan Karski to return to Poland, possibly because they were afraid he might be captured by the Germans and forced to reveal political intelligence under torture—or perhaps because he might reveal to the Polish underground that the Allies were not prepared to confront the Soviet Union over such issues as Polish independence and the postwar Polish-Soviet border. In 1944, Karski wrote an autobiography, *Story of a Secret State,* which was reviewed in more than a hundred American newspapers and magazines. In April 1945, American and British armies overran the Bergen-Belsen and Dachau concentration camps. As Karski's biographers wrote, "A wave of revulsion swept through England and the United States, dampening the giddy air of impending victory. Newspapers and politicians expressed shock that such things could happen in the twentieth century. Jan was not shocked." Jan Karski eventually joined the faculty of Georgetown University, where he taught comparative government and theory of Communism. He became an American citizen in 1954. On May 12, 1994, in a ceremony at the Israeli Embassy in Washington, D.C., the State of Israel conferred honorary citizenship on Jan Karski. He died in 2000.[11]

After the war, Rabbi Stephen Wise fought for the creation of Israel. The United Nations Partition Plan for Palestine, approved by the UN General Assembly on November 29, 1947, led directly to the founding of Israel. Wise died less than two years later, on April 19, 1949, at the age of seventy-five.

Three thousand people attended his memorial service at Carnegie Hall, and outside fifteen thousand more listened to the memorial service on loudspeakers. Three days after the memorial service, Albert Einstein wrote a letter to Wise's children that included the following: "In times of great adversity, he helped the Jewish people to maintain dignity and win their independence, and to every individual he was an understanding friend."[12]

Peter Bergson left the United States in 1946 for Paris to establish a government in exile for Palestine. "Bergson Leaves, Vowing Revolution" was the headline in the *New York Post*. Still ready to take on all comers, he clashed with David Ben-Gurion, who called Bergson's government in exile "a group of self-appointed people who represent nobody but themselves." Bergson's return home in May 1948 coincided with Israel's declaration of statehood. Using his birth name, Hillel Kook, he was elected to the Constituent Assembly (shortly to become the First Knesset), "the first independent Jewish legislative body set up in two thousand years." He soon became disillusioned with Israeli politics and went into self-imposed exile in the United States and Cuba, where he amassed some wealth in commodity trading, oil, and finance. Later, he returned to Israel, where he died in 2001 at the age of eighty-six.[13]

Ruth Glasberg Gold clandestinely escaped Communist Romania in 1946, through Yugoslavia, and along with hundreds of other Jews, boarded a freighter bound for Palestine. The boat was shipwrecked in the Aegean Sea. Her British rescuers incarcerated her in the detention camps of Cyprus until the end of 1947. She was later allowed to go to Palestine, which she reached on New Year's Day 1948. There, she cofounded a new kibbutz in the Judean Hills near Jerusalem, where she served as the kibbutz medic; later, she graduated from the Hadassah Nursing School as a registered nurse.

In 1958 she married and left Israel for Bogotá, Colombia, where her son and daughter were born. In 1972 the family emigrated to Miami (her fifth country), where she still lives. She was widowed in 1982.

Ruth speaks frequently on the Holocaust and is a freelance interpreter in seven languages. She wrote a book, *Ruth's Journey: A Survivor's Memoir*, about her life before, during, and after the Holocaust.[14]

According to one source, of the 147,000 Romanian Jews who were forcibly sent to Transnistria, at least 90,000 died in the camps and ghettos, most from typhus and starvation.[15]

The Soviet-installed Romanian Communist government executed Romanian dictator Ion Antonescu and three of his senior officials in June 1946. Alexander Cretzianu, the Romanian minister to Turkey, escaped from the Russians with his family on American immigration visas arranged by Ira Hirschmann.[16]

Franklin Delano Roosevelt died on April 12, 1945, in Warm Springs, Georgia. The country was stricken. "Something which had filled all lives was gone," wrote Dean Acheson later. "The familiar had given way to an ominous unknown." An anonymous soldier said upon hearing the news, "America will seem a strange, empty place without his voice talking to the people whenever great events occur." Columnist Samuel Grafton reflected a year later:

One remembers him as a kind of smiling bus driver, with that cigarette holder pointed upward, listening to the uproar from behind as he took the sharp turns. They used to tell him he had not loaded his vehicle right for all eternity. But he knew he had stacked it well enough to round the next corner, and he knew when the yells were false, and when they were real, and he loved the passengers. He is dead now, and the bus is stalled, far from the gates of heaven, while the riders hold each other in deadlock over how to make the next curve.

These words could have been written today. At the very least, however, in failing to control his State Department and use his great powers of communication to personally condemn to the world the Nazis' extermination of European Jewry, Roosevelt missed a curve—the opportunity to save lives and leave not just a legacy of great crisis leadership but a great legacy of moral leadership, as well. (As Harry Dexter White said to Henry Morgenthau Jr., "Roosevelt has the power to alter the complexion of this whole treatment in Europe if he feels keenly enough that he wishes to do so.") But his vital role in preparing the country for the threat from Hitler and then stopping and ultimately defeating the Nazis must also be weighed on the historical scales. As a result, historians still passionately debate his response to the Holocaust—and, because the truth *is* somewhere in the elusive, unsatisfying middle of the debaters' polarized positions—the debate will never end.[17]

Henry Morgenthau Jr. last saw Franklin Roosevelt at a dinner at Warm Springs on April 11 (attended by, among others, Roosevelt's former mistress,

Lucy Mercer, now Lucy Mercer Rutherfurd). The next day, Eleanor Roosevelt called to tell him that the president had died. Morgenthau was devastated by Roosevelt's death. "I have lost my best friend," he told the press. He stayed on for a while as secretary of the treasury in the Truman administration but, as Henry III wrote, "On that final evening he spent with FDR my father's public career in government ended, except for the short, unhappy coda played out with Harry Truman, whom he found it difficult to address as 'Mr. President.'" After resigning from the Truman administration, Morgenthau devoted himself to Jewish causes—despite advice from Henry Sr. not to have "anything to do with the Jews. They'll stab you in the back"—and later to the new state of Israel. He died in 1967. Henry III made a career as a television producer; another son, Robert, became one of New York City's best-known district attorneys.[18]

Shortly after Roosevelt's death, Eleanor Roosevelt was told that Lucy Rutherfurd had been with her husband when he suffered the fatal stroke. According to her biographer, "She gave no outward sign of anger or hurt." Eleanor continued writing her column, authored many books, and represented the United States at the United Nations, where she played a crucial role in the drafting of the Universal Declaration of Human Rights. When she died in 1962, the United Nations held a moment of silence in her honor. She and her husband are buried side by side in the garden at the Roosevelt estate in Hyde Park.[19]

After the War Refugee Board was disbanded at the end of the war, John Pehle went into private practice. He died in 1999. Randolph Paul left the government in 1944 and cofounded a leading New York City law firm. He died in 1956, after collapsing while testifying before a congressional committee on tax and budget issues. Josiah DuBois Jr. served as lead prosecutor in the Nuremberg trials of the directors of I.G. Farben, after serving on U.S. delegations concerned with postwar reconstruction; he also went into private practice. He died in 1983. After leaving the Treasury Department, Ansel Luxford became general counsel of the World Bank; some accounts state that he died in 1971.

In 2007, the House of Representatives passed a resolution honoring Henry Morgenthau Jr., Josiah DuBois Jr., and John Pehle for helping rescue Jews and other persecuted minorities during the Holocaust. The sponsor of the resolution, Representative Lynn Woolsey, issued this statement:

After the horror of the concentration camps and extermination camps [was] revealed, the world said, "never again." And yet, we look around the world to see the hauntingly similar events occurring, particularly in Darfur. If we truly wish to honor the memory of the Holocaust victims, we must come together to stand up in the face of bigotry and hatred where "never again" means never again![20]

ACKNOWLEDGMENTS

The origin of this book traces to the newspaper reports of the discovery of the letters written by Anne Frank's father in his unsuccessful attempt to obtain visas for his family and himself to the United States (briefly described in these pages). Intrigued with the notion that American immigration policies might have doomed Anne Frank, but dissatisfied with the treatment in various works of the American response to the Holocaust, I decided to write a book that focused on the State Department. I was drawn in by the personalities: from heroic figures like Karski, Schulte, and the four Treasury lawyers; to American originals like Endicott Peabody; to Welles and Bullitt, talented but self-destructive personalities; and to Franklin Delano Roosevelt, whose like we almost certainly will never see again. I was also intrigued by the potential for a Washington political thriller built around a rescue. As well, my previous book had been a work of historical fiction about the infamous *Dred Scott* case (where the Supreme Court held that black Americans in bondage had no more rights than did horses) and the response by Americans to our country's great nineteenth-century moral crisis. This book was an opportunity to write about the great moral crisis that America (and the world) faced in the twentieth century.

I owe a special debt to my friend Ruth Glasberg Gold for her unstinting assistance, especially because she had to resurrect the details of searingly painful memories. She is a remarkable woman, and if this book serves no other purpose than to bring her story to the attention of anyone who may not have heard it, I will consider it a success. I am also indebted to the fine work of historians David Wyman (even though I did not always agree with his emphasis in assigning blame for America's failure to do more to rescue Jews) and Richard Breitman. I relied heavily on Wyman's compilation of historical documents in *America and the Holocaust* and on Professor Breitman, in particular, for his account of Eduard Schulte's heroism in *Breaking the Silence* (which he coauthored with Walter Laqueur). The staffs of, among other institutions, the FDR Library, the National Archives, the New York Public Library and its Dorot Jewish Division, the Jacob Rader Marcus Center of the American Jewish Archives, and the United States Holocaust Memorial Museum were invariably patient and helpful in answering my inquiries or in tracking down a particular document. Ed Stackler, as always, provided essential editorial guidance. My agent, Josh Getzler, was a constant source of support and guidance. Mary Lyons, my researcher, did a remarkable job of tracking down at the National Archives the intercepted cables between American and British Jewish leaders. Tom Crane provided invaluable help both in proofreading and fact-checking. The staff at Greenleaf Book Group Press once again turned out a first-rate product. And the encouragement and support of my wife, Elisabeth Van Veen, as much as anything, made this book possible.

NOTES

EIGHTEEN MONTHS LATER

1. Carol Nolan, "Men's Fashions of the 1940s" (The Costume Gallery), available at www.murrayontravel.com/carolnolan/fashionhistory1940smens.html.

2. The Executive Office of the President, Office of Administration, *The Old Executive Office Building: A Victorian Masterpiece* (U.S. Government Printing Office, 1984); Dean Acheson, *Present at the Creation: My Years in the State Department* (W. W. Norton & Co., 1969), 9. The wartime enlargement of the State Department required, in addition to the State Department building itself, seven additional buildings to house its activities. Graham H. Stuart, *The Department of State: A History of Its Organization, Procedure, and Personnel* (Macmillan Co, 1949), 363. See Shelby L. Stanton, *U.S. Army Uniforms of World War II* (Stackpole Books, 1991), 215.

3. Joseph W. Alsop (with Adam Platt), *"I've Seen the Best of It"* (W. W. Norton Co, 1992), 137.

4. Irwin F. Gellman, *Secret Affairs: FDR, Cordell Hull, and Sumner Welles* (Enigma Books, 1995), 31–32; Acheson, *Present at the Creation*, 9; T. H. Watkins, *Righteous Pilgrim: The Life and Times of Harold L. Ickes 1874–1952* (Henry Holt & Co, 1990), 730.

5. Walter Russell Bowle, "The Star That Gleams in the Blackness," *New York Times*, December 19, 1943, SM5.

6. "The Fort Knox Depository," available at http://www.globalsecurity.org/military/facility/fort-knox-depository.htm (GlobalSecurity.Org). In 1944, with the war turning in America's favor, the Constitution and the Declaration of Independence came back to Washington. See Herbert L. Matthews, "Italians Take Hill in San Pietro Area," *New York Times*, December 18, 1943, 4; Special to the NYT, "Back to Golden Gate in '48," *idem*, 17. (*Note*: Hereafter, all cited *New York Times* articles without an author's name are "Special to the NYT.")

7. Doris Kearns Goodwin, *No Ordinary Time: Franklin and Eleanor Roosevelt; The Home Front in World War II* (Simon & Schuster Paperbacks, 1994), 477; "Record Earnings Made by Business," *New York Times*, December 18, 1943, 24.

8. The Morgenthau Diaries, Book 688, Part II (DuBois memorandum to the files, December 18, 1943), 99–100; Rafael Medoff, *Blowing the Whistle on Genocide: Josiah E. DuBois, Jr. and the Struggle for a U.S. Response to the Holocaust* (Purdue University Press, 2009), 22; "He read the files, took notes and went back to his office. He was in a rage" [quoting from interview of wife of Josiah DuBois Jr.]), 22; Stuart, *The Department of State* ("One result of the critical international situation was the institution, beginning August 14, 1941, of an identification pass system to regulate the admission of employees and visitors to the Department of State Buildings."), 363–64 (describing the Division of Communications), 362–63.

CHAPTER I THE GOOD GERMAN

1. Gerhart M. Riegner, *Never Despair: Sixty Years in the Service of the Jewish People and the Cause of Human Rights* (Ivan R. Dee, 2006), 12. One of his relatives, the neo-Kantian philosopher Hermann Cohen, read an article by a distinguished German historian titled "Die Juden sind unser Unglück" ("The Jews are our misfortune"), a slogan later repeated with monotonous frequency by the Nazi weekly *Der Stürmer*. Cohen became the defender and spokesman for German Jewry. Riegner wrote in his autobiography (pp. 4–5), "From this branch of my family I inherited a very developed sense of Judaism." One of Riegner's ancestors, the choirmaster of the Oranienburgerstrasse Synagogue in Berlin, revolutionized modern Jewish liturgical music (3–4, 9).

2. Riegner, *Never Despair*, 12–13, 18–22, 27–34.

3. Ibid., 35, 38–39.

4. Walter Laqueur and Richard Breitman, *Breaking the Silence: The German Who Exposed the Final Solution* (Brandeis University Press, 1994), 11, 17–20, 25–26, 33–34, 115–16, 118.

5. Ibid., 26–28.

6. Ibid., 40–41; Hans Mommsen, trans. Elborg Forster & Larry Eugene Jones, *The Rise and Fall of Weimar Democracy* (University of North Carolina Press, 1996), 532; "Georg von Schnitzler, On Hitler's Appeal to Leading Industrialists on February 20, 1933" (November 10, 1945), reprinted at http://germanhistorydocs.ghi-dc.org/pdf/eng/English2.pdf; Ian Kershaw, *Hitler 1889–1936: Hubris* (W. W. Norton & Co., 1998), 447–48.

7. Laqueur and Breitman, *Breaking the Silence*, 41.

8. Richard Grunberger, *The Twelve-Year Reich: A Social History of Nazi Germany 1933–1945* (Holt, Rinehart & Winston, 1971), 167.

9. Laqueur and Breitman, *Breaking the Silence*, 51.

10. Grunberger, *The Twelve-Year Reich*, 27, 40, 85.

11. Peter Grose, *Gentleman Spy: The Life of Allen Dulles* (Houghton Mifflin, 1994), 159.

12. Laqueur and Breitman, *Breaking the Silence*, 67; Grose, *Gentleman Spy*, 159–60.
13. Grose, *Gentleman Spy*, 160; Laqueur and Breitman, *Breaking the Silence*, 101–2; Henry Sakaida, *Heroes of the Soviet Union 1941–45* (Osprey Publishing Ltd., 2004), 31.
14. Lucjan Dobroszycki and Jeffrey S. Gurock, eds., *The Holocaust in the Soviet Union: Studies and Sources on the Destruction of the Jews in the Nazi-Occupied Territories in the USSR 1941–1945* (M. E. Sharpe, 1993), 6; Walter Laqueur, ed., and Judith Tydor Baumel, asst. ed., *The Holocaust Encyclopedia* (Yale University Press, 2001), 610.
15. Laqueur and Breitman, *Breaking the Silence*, 12, 30; see Grunberger, *The Twelve-Year Reich*, 56.
16. Joachim C. Fest, *The Face of the Third Reich: Portraits of the Nazi Leadership* (Da Capo Press, 1999), 90; Will Brownell and Richard N. Billings, *So Close to Greatness: A Biography of William C. Bullitt* (Macmillan, 1987), 209.
17. Richard Breitman, *The Architect of Genocide: Himmler and the Final Solution* (Brandeis University Press, 1991), 4–5.
18. Grunberger, *The Twelve-Year Reich*, 62.
19. Roger Manvell and Heinrich Fraenkel, *Heinrich Himmler: The Sinister Life of the Head of the SS and Gestapo* (Greenhill Books, 2007), xiii (introduction), 17, 59, 95.
20. Primo Levi, introduction to *Commandant of Auschwitz: The Autobiography of Rudolf Hoess* (Phoenix Press, 2000), 19.
21. Manvell and Fraenkel, *Heinrich Himmler*, 100–101; Breitman, *The Architect of Genocide*, 4–5.
22. Manvell and Fraenkel, *Heinrich Himmler*, xiv.
23. Breitman, *The Architect of Genocide*, 155; Ian Kershaw, *Hitler: A Biography* (W. W. Norton & Co., 2008), 592–93; David Faber, *Munich, 1938: Appeasement and World War II* (Simon & Schuster, 2008), 369; Adam Gopnik, "Finest Hours: The Making of Winston Churchill," *The New Yorker*, August 30, 2010, 78.
24. Hoess, *Commandant of Auschwitz*, 183 (appendix one); Testimony of Rudolf Hoess at the Nuremberg Trials, April 15, 1946, reprinted at Famous World Trials, Nuremberg Trials 1945–49, available at http://www.law.umkc.edu/faculty/projects/ftrials/nuremberg/hoesstest.html; Laqueur and Baumel, *The Holocaust Encyclopedia*, 36 (noting that the pages in Himmler's appointment calendar for June 25–August 12, 1941, are missing), 609.
25. Hoess, *Commandant of Auschwitz*, 126, 205–7 (appendix two).
26. Ibid., 132; Ray Brandon and Wendy Lower, eds., *The Shoah in Ukraine: History, Testimony, Memorialization* (Indiana University Press, 2008), 6.
27. Hoess, *Commandant of Auschwitz*, 134–35.
28. Ibid., 126.

29. Ibid., 208 (appendix two).
30. Ibid., 147–48, 186 (appendix one).
31. Ibid., 147.
32. Ibid., 24 (introduction), 184–85 (appendix one).
33. Ibid., 186 (appendix one).
34. Breitman, *The Architect of Genocide*, 203.
35. Hoess, *Commandant of Auschwitz*, 186 (appendix one).
36. Ibid., 208 (appendix two).
37. Ibid., 149, 153–54.
38. Manvell and Fraenkel, *Heinrich Himmler*, 117 (paraphrase by authors), 184.
39. Breitman, *The Architect of Genocide*, 21, quoting from Eberhard Jäckel, September 12, 1986, article in *Die Zeit*.
40. Ibid., 4, quoting from Affidavit [September 14, 1945] of Isaak Egon Ochshorn, National Archives, Record Group 238, NO–1934.
41. Laqueur and Breitman, *Breaking the Silence*, 13–14.
42. Hoess, *Commandant of Auschwitz*, 210 (appendix two).
43. Ibid., 210–11; Manvell and Fraenkel, *Heinrich Himmler*, 147.
44. Hoess, *Commandant of Auschwitz*, 156, 212 (appendix two)
45. Ibid., 195 (appendix one) ("The entire Swiss jewelry market was dominated by these sales.").
46. Anthony Read and David Fisher, *Operation Lucy: Most Secret Spy Ring of the Second World War* (Coward, McCann & Geoghegan, Inc, 1981), 109, 114, 135.
47. Laqueur and Breitman, *Breaking the Silence*, 119, 265 (1994 epilogue).
48. Grose, *Gentleman Spy*, 160.

CHAPTER II THE TRIBUTARIES OF THE DNIESTER

1. Jordana Horn, "How Father Desbois Became a Holocaust Memory Keeper," *Wall Street Journal*, January 23, 2009, W11; Laqueur and Baumel, *The Holocaust Encyclopedia*, 610; Antony Beevor, *Stalingrad: The Fateful Siege 1942–1943* (Viking, 1998), 20; Brandon and Lower, *The Shoah in Ukraine*, 23, 57, 167.
2. Avigdor Shachan, *Burning Ice: The Ghettos of Transnistria*, trans. Shmuel Himelstein (Eastern European Monographs, 1996; distributed by Columbia University Press), 183.
3. Ibid., 173.
4. Ibid., 174–76.
5. Ruth Glasberg Gold, *Ruth's Journey: A Survivor's Memoir* (University Press of Florida, 1996), 18, 47–49, 54–55.

CHAPTER III   THE RIEGNER TELEGRAM

1. Laqueur and Breitman, *Breaking the Silence*, 119, 120.
2. Ibid., 121–22.
3. Ibid., 123–33.
4. Grose, *Gentleman Spy*, 161–62.
5. Laqueur and Breitman, *Breaking the Silence*, 125–27, 129–31.
6. Ibid., 132–33.
7. Ibid., 134.
8. Riegner, *Never Despair*, 35; Laqueur and Breitman, *Breaking the Silence*, 134.
9. Martin Gilbert, *The Holocaust: A History of the Jews of Europe During the Second World War* (Henry Holt, 1985), 32, 52–53, 57–58, 66, 68–70; see Robert C. Self, *Neville Chamberlain, A Biography* (Ashgate Publishing, 2006).
10. Riegner, *Never Despair*, 36.
11. Ibid., 39–40.
12. Ibid., 42–44.
13. Laqueur and Breitman, *Breaking the Silence*, 147; Riegner, *Never Despair*, 42–43.
14. Elting to Hull, August 10, 1942, SD 862.4016/2234, attaching memorandum re "Conversation with Dr. Gerhart M. Riegner," dated August 8, 1942 (providing details of Elting's conversation with Riegner), reprinted in *America and the Holocaust*, David S. Wyman, ed. (Garland Publishing, 1990), 1:190–92; Riegner, *Never Despair*, 42.
15. Harrison to Hull, August 11, 1942, SD 862.4016/2233, reprinted in Wyman, *America and the Holocaust*, 1:185–86; Elting to Hull, August 10, 1942, SD 862.4016/2234, 1:190–2.
16. Memorandum, Division of European Affairs, August 13, 1942, SD 862.4016/2235, reprinted in Wyman, *America and the Holocaust*, 1:194; see State Department to Bern Legation, August 17, 1942, SD 862.4016/2223, reprinted in Wyman, *America and the Holocaust*, 1:188; Riegner, *Never Despair*, 43.

CHAPTER IV   THE ARISTOCRATIC ARCHIPELAGO

1. "President Roosevelt Gives the Bride Away," *New York Times*, March 18, 1905, 2; Joseph P. Lash, *Eleanor and Franklin* (W. W. Norton, 1971), 204–5; Gellman, *Secret Affairs*, 59.
2. Goodwin, *No Ordinary Time*, 39.
3. Lash, *Eleanor and Franklin*, 204–5; *The Autobiography of Eleanor Roosevelt* (First Da Capo Press Edition, 1992), 49–50; Michael Teague, *Mrs. L.: Conversations with Alice Roosevelt Longworth* (Doubleday, 1981), 156.

4. Joseph C. Grew, *Turbulent Era: A Diplomatic Record of Forty Years*, vol. I (Houghton Mifflin, 1952), 12–13; Richard Hume Werking, *The Master Architects: Building the United States Foreign Service 1890–1913* (The University Press of Kentucky 1977), 4–5, 10 (describing turnover).

5. Ibid.

6. Hermann Hagedorn, ed., *The Works of Theodore Roosevelt: American Ideals, The Strenuous Life, Realizable Ideals*, (Charles Scribner's Sons, 1926), 13:456–57.

7. Ibid., 100, 115–16; Jean Edward Smith, *FDR* (Random House Trade Paperback, 2008), 166; Theodore Roosevelt, "The Present Status of Civil Service Reform," *The Atlantic Monthly* (February 1895), 239–46.

8. Grew, *Turbulent Era*, 13 n. 4; Waldo H. Heinrichs Jr., *American Ambassador: Joseph C. Grew and the Development of the United States Diplomatic Tradition* (Oxford University Press, 1986), 105; Werking, *The Master Architects*, 94, 100, 155.

9. James S. McLachlan, *American Boarding Schools: A Historical Study (Charles Scribner's Sons 1970)*, 8–12 (emphasis in original); E. Digby Baltzell, *Philadelphia Gentlemen: The Making of a National Upper Class* (The Free Press, 1958), 293.

10. Frank Freidel, *Franklin D. Roosevelt: The Apprenticeship* (Little, Brown & Co., 1952), 36; John Gunther, *Roosevelt in Retrospect* (Harper & Brothers, 1950), 171 (the number of students when Franklin D. Roosevelt attended); Walter Isaacson and Evan Thomas, *The Wise Men: Six Friends and The World They Made* (Simon & Schuster, 1986), 47. The young Grotonian was thirteen-year-old Averell Harriman. See Baltzell, *Philadelphia Gentlemen*, 313. I am indebted to Julius Walter Atwood, a long-time friend of Peabody's, who said that "Peabody is the last of the Puritans." Frank D. Ashburn, *Peabody of Groton: A Portrait* (Coward McCann, Inc., 1944), 88; see ibid., 89–97.

11. Endicott Peabody et al., *The Education of the Modern Boy* (Houghton Mifflin Co., 1928), 110–11; McLachlan, *American Boarding Schools*, 278.

12. McLachlan, *American Boarding Schools*, 269.

13. Ibid., 275–77; Isaacson and Thomas, *The Wise Men*, 47; Ashburn, *Peabody of Groton*, 96, 296; Benjamin Welles, *Sumner Welles: FDR's Global Strategist* (St. Martin's Press, 1997), 11 (describing how Peabody shook the hands of the first form boys, who came to his parlor in the evening for prayers).

14. Isaacson and Thomas, *The Wise Men*, 48.

15. Robert L. Beisner, *Dean Acheson: A Life in the Cold War* (Oxford University Press, 2006), 8; Isaacson and Thomas, *The Wise Men*, 55.

16. Ashburn, *Peabody of Groton*, 17, 244–45, 253. The author quotes Peabody, slightly inaccurately, as saying, "Make me a clean heart . . . "; McLachlan, *American Boarding Schools*, 152.

17. Ashburn, *Peabody of Groton*, 94, 113, 176–77, 220; McLachlan, *American Boarding Schools*, 277; Isaacson and Thomas, *The Wise Men*, 48.

18. Ashburn, *Peabody of Groton*, 322, 341, 345; Freidel, *Franklin D. Roosevelt*, 51; Jerome Karabel, *The Chosen: The Hidden History of Admission and Exclusion at Harvard, Yale, and Princeton* (Houghton Mifflin, 2005), 33–35.

19. Karabel, *The Chosen*, 33–35; Ashburn, *Peabody of Groton*, 317–22.

20. McLachlan, *American Boarding Schools*, 292–95; Ashburn, *Peabody of Groton*, 250–51.

21. George Biddle, "As I Remember Groton School," *Harper's Magazine* (August 1939): 293–94, 300; Freidel, *Franklin D. Roosevelt*, 42.

22. Biddle, "As I Remember Groton School," 294; McLachlan, *American Boarding Schools*, 276; Karabel, *The Chosen*, 31.

23. Dean Acheson, *Morning and Noon: A Memoir* (Houghton Mifflin Co., 1965), 24; McLachlan, *American Boarding Schools*, 276; Gunther, *Roosevelt in Retrospect*, 172 ("Young FDR didn't like Groton much; and it didn't like him. He was not a success there."); Welles, *Sumner Welles*, 3.

24. Ashburn, *Peabody of Groton*, 117; Biddle, "As I Remember Groton School," 299; McLachlan, *American Boarding Schools*, 277, 279.

25. Ibid., 214–15; Larissa MacFarquhar, "East Side Story: How Louis Auchincloss Came to Terms with His World," *The New Yorker*, February 25, 2008, 61.

26. Peabody et al., *The Education of the Modern Boy*, 108.

27. *The Works of Theodore Roosevelt*, 13:636.

28. Isaacson and Thomas, *The Wise Men*, 60.

29. Ibid., 56–57; Beisner, *Dean Acheson*, 8; Heinrichs, *American Ambassador*, 97–98 (quoting E. Digby Baltzell).

30. Martin Weil, *A Pretty Good Club: The Founding Fathers of the U.S. Foreign Service* (W. W. Norton, 1978), 18.

31. Ibid., 19; McLachlan, *American Boarding Schools*, 295.

32. Robert Bendiner, *The Riddle of the State Department* (Farrar & Rinehart, 1942), 111–12; Weil, *A Pretty Good Club*, 46.

33. Heinrichs, *American Ambassador*, 97–98.

34. Weil, *A Pretty Good Club*, 47; Bendiner, *The Riddle of the State Department*, 120–21.

35. Bendiner, *The Riddle of the State Department*, 122–24. Even then the officer was technically only suspended and his name remained in the Register of the Department of State. The officer, one Ogden Hammond Jr., had been asked to resign because he had engaged in "disloyal dealings" while a vice-consul in Vienna and Leipzig, ridiculed President Roosevelt at a party in Newport, advocated "bullets" for the unemployed, and boasted of his friendship with a leading American fascist. Notwithstanding the charges, Hammond filed an injunctive action against his superiors to prevent his dismissal.

36. Register of the State Department, 1942, 102, 240, 262. The four were Samuel Reber (Groton), Charles E. Bohlen (St. Paul's), James C. H. Bonbright (St. Paul's), and Edward T. Wailes (Lawrenceville).

37. Weil, *A Pretty Good Club*, 47 (interview of I.F. Stone).

38. George Orwell, *The Road to Wigan Pier* (Houghton Brace, 1958), 159 (emphasis in original).

39. Heinrichs, *American Ambassador*, 47; Moffat to Gibson, August 8, 1920, quoted in Weil, *A Pretty Good Club*, 34; ibid., 22.

40. Reverend Edmund A. Walsh, S.J., "An Epistle to the Romans," *The Atlantic Monthly* (February 1938), 242; David S. Wyman, *The Abandonment of the Jews: America and the Holocaust, 1941–45* (The New Press, 2007), 190, 190 n.

41. Weil, *A Pretty Good Club*, 39; Nina Berberova, *Moura: The Dangerous Life of the Baroness Budberg* (New York Review of Books, 2005), 24–25, 319 (describing Chicherin as a scholar and musician of aristocratic birth).

42. Weil, *A Pretty Good Club*, 39–41.

43. Gellman, *Secret Affairs*, 37–38; Robert D. Kaplan, *The Arabists: Romance of an American Elite* (The Free Press, 1995), 88–90; Ted Morgan, *FDR: A Biography* (Simon & Schuster, 1985), 498; Breckinridge Long Diaries, February 6, 1938, quoted in Henry L. Feingold, *The Politics of Rescue: The Roosevelt Administration and the Holocaust 1938–1945* (Rutgers University Press, 1970), 135; Billings, *So Close to Greatness*, 14–15.

44. Fred L. Israel, ed., *The War Diary of Breckinridge Long: Selections from the Years 1939–44* (University of Nebraska Press, 1966), introduction, xviii–xix, 19. Later, Long took a different view.

45. Weil, *A Pretty Good Club*, 103, 125, 184.

46. Edgar Mowrer, "Our State Department and North Africa" (Union for Democratic Action pamphlet, 1943), quoted in Weil, *A Pretty Good Club*, 127.

47. Cannon to Atherton and Dunn, November 12, 1941, SD 871.4016/281. In the end, Cannon recommended that the State Department respond to "the representations on the part of American Jewish leaders, which I have been expecting since the alarming reports from Romania and Hungary have become current" by endorsing the participation of the American minister in discussions with the British and French embassies in Turkey about the rescue plan. Cavendish then reassured his superiors that ultimately the Turkish government was unlikely to be enthusiastic about rescue based on the same considerations in his memorandum. Register of the State Department, 1942, 112–13.

CHAPTER V   THE MAGICAL VILLAGE OF MILIE

1. Gold, *Ruth's Journey*, 49–50. In some columns, those who could stand no more, lay down, stretched out, and waited for a bullet. Others lost their minds,

dancing and singing wild songs; some carried on conversations with a dead family member or spouse. See also Shachan, *Burning Ice*, 173.

2. Gold, *Ruth's Journey*, 4–7.
3. Ibid., 53–54; see also Sheina Medwed, *Live! Remember! Tell the World! The Story of a Hidden Child Survivor of Transnistria* (Mesorah Publications, Ltd., 2005), 61 (describing the cold). This is the story of Leah Kaufman.
4. Gold, *Ruth's Journey*, 56; see also Shachan, *Burning Ice*, 179–80.
5. Gold, *Ruth's Journey*, 57–59.

CHAPTER VI THE CROQUET PLAYER AND THE THIRD FLOOR

1. David F. Schmitz, *Henry L. Stimson: The First Wise Man* (Scholarly Resources, Inc., 2001), 80.
2. Harold B. Hinton, *Cordell Hull: A Biography* (Doubleday, Doran & Co., Inc., 1942), 15.
3. Ibid., 22, 27–28, 32–34. Pickett County, at the time of Hull's birth, was called Overton County. "The Legacy of Cordell Hull," Cordell Hull Museum, available at http://www.cordellhullmuseum.com/history.html.
4. Gellman, *Secret Affairs*, 30; Acheson, *Present at the Creation*, 10.
5. Gellman, *Secret Affairs*, 30–31; Israel, *The War Diary of Breckinridge Long*, 1–2, 209, 258. While away from Washington, Hull did receive a pouch of daily dispatches and telephone briefings by Welles, which only increased his dependence on his undersecretary. Gellman, *Secret Affairs*, 161.
6. Gellman, *Secret Affairs*, 141; Israel, *The War Diary of Breckinridge Long*, xi–xii, 1; Bendiner, *The Riddle of the State Department*, 171–175 (Berle), 182–83 (Shaw).
7. Beisner, *Dean Acheson*, 16; Gellman, *Secret Affairs*, 32.
8. Beatrice Bishop Berle and Travis Beal Jacobs, eds., *Navigating the Rapids 1918–71: From the Papers of Adolf A. Berle* (Harcourt Brace Jovanovich Inc., 1973), 151, 205.
9. Welles, *Sumner Welles*, 188, 195.
10. Israel, *The War Diary of Breckinridge Long*, 116.
11. Ibid., 91.
12. Berle and Jacobs, *Navigating the Rapids*, 415, 431.
13. Acheson, *Present at the Creation*, 9
14. Gellman, *Secret Affairs*, 25–26, 28.
15. Medoff, *Blowing the Whistle on Genocide*, 2–3; Watkins, *Righteous Pilgrim*, 677; Gellman, *Secret Affairs*, 98; see Hinton, *Cordell Hull*, 9–16, author biography; Wyman, *The Abandonment of the Jews*, 190.

16. See Nancy Harvison Hooker, ed., *The Moffat Papers: Selections from the Diplomatic Journals of Jay Pierrepont Moffat* (Harvard University Press, 1956), 221–22. In his entry for November 14, 1938, Moffat, then head of the Division of European Affairs, refers to "the increasing attacks not only on Jews [known as *Kristallnacht*], but on Catholics [that] have aroused opinion here to a point where if something is not done there will be combustion." In a muted gesture of protest, the Roosevelt administration brought the American ambassador to Germany back to Washington for "report and consultation." However, because the ambassador, as Moffat noted, "happened to be planning to come home on leave next week, we therefore had to telegraph him without delay to sail on the next non-German ship. " Moffat ruefully commented that "the papers played it up even more than we anticipated"(ibid., 222).

17. Weil, *A Pretty Good Club*, 126 (I.F. Stone interview).

18. Acheson, *Present at the Creation*, 15–16.

19. Hooker, *The Moffat Papers*, 309; Bendiner, *The Riddle of the State Department*, 193.

20. Charles Higham, *The Duchess of Windsor: The Secret Life* (John Wiley & Sons, Inc., 2005), 274; Heinrichs, *American Ambassador*, 120 (describing one Foreign Service officer who was a contemporary of Atherton).

21. Edgar B. Nixon, ed., *Franklin D. Roosevelt and Foreign Affairs*, vol. 3, *September 1935–January 1937* (The Belknap Press of Harvard University Press, 1969), 234 (letter from Bullitt to Roosevelt, March 4, 1936), 507 (letter from Moore to Roosevelt, November 25, 1936 ["Some time ago you spoke of transferring Mr. Atherton from London. . . ."]); Weil, *A Pretty Good Club*, 116; Bendiner, *The Riddle of the State Department*, 93

22. Weil, *A Pretty Good Club*, 82–83, 116.

23. William E. Leuchtenburg, *Franklin D. Roosevelt and the New Deal 1932–1940* (Harper & Row, 1963), 64, quoting letter from Sherwood Anderson to Burton and Mary Emmett, October 8, 1933 (spelling errors corrected).

24. *From the Diaries of Felix Frankfurter, with a Biographical Essay and Notes by Joseph P. Lash* (W. W. Norton & Co., 1975), 196; Kenneth S. Davis, *FDR: The War President: A History 1940–1943* (Random House, 2000), 664–66; see Weil, *A Pretty Good Club*, 48.

25. "Peyrouton Sets Up Economic Council," *New York Times*, February 10, 1943, 1.

26. Robert O. Paxton, *Vichy France: Old Guard and New Order, 1940–1944* (Alfred A. Knopf, 1972), 92, 142, 181–84, 284; Richard H. Weisberg, *Vichy Law and the Holocaust in France* (New York University Press, 1996), xv (foreword by Michael R. Marrus), 56; Michael R. Marrus and Robert O. Paxton, *Vichy France and the Jews* (Basic Books, 1981), 193, 343.

27. "The Reminiscences of Paul Appleby," Oral History Research Office, Columbia University (1957), 305–13; Weil, *A Pretty Good Club*, 114. Admiral

Leahy had served as United States ambassador to the Vichy government before becoming an aide to Roosevelt and, in effect, the first chairman of the Joint Chiefs of Staff. See Fleet Admiral William D. Leahy, available at http://williamdleahy.com/.

28. "The Reminiscences of Paul Appleby," 315–18; "Speedy Shipments for Africa Urged," *New York Times*, December 31, 1942, 3; Edwin L. James, "Giraud Ruling on Jews Forms Algerian Puzzle," *New York Times*, March 21, 1943, E3; Marrus and Paxton, *Vichy France and the Jews*, 195; Dwight D. Eisenhower, *Crusade in Europe* (Doubleday, 1948), 131. Eisenhower was equivocal in his memoir as to whether he was personally aware that Peyrouton had been a Nazi collaborator before bringing him to North Africa. After protests by Jewish organizations and the arrival of General de Gaulle in Algiers, the Crémieux Law of 1870 was finally reinstated on October 20, 1943. Sara Sussman, "Jews in North Africa After the Allied Landings," *Holocaust Encyclopedia*, United States Holocaust Memorial Museum, available at http://www.ushmm.org/wlc/en/article.php?ModuleId=10007313. In his oral history, Appleby stated that he did not resign solely because of the Peyrouton affair, "although the procedure within the State Department in connection with it was a part of the general situation that caused me to leave" ("The Reminiscences of Paul Appleby," 320).

CHAPTER VII THE RABBI AND THE DIPLOMAT

1. Culbertson to J.W.J., August 13, 1942, SD 862.4016/2233, reprinted in Wyman, *America and the Holocaust*, 1:184.

2. Ibid.; Weil, *A Pretty Good Club*, 120. Culbertson may have been the official whom Paul Appleby, at Ray Atherton's direction, first consulted about Marcel Peyrouton. See "The Reminiscences of Paul Appleby," 310–11.

3. Livia Rothkirchen, *The Jews of Bohemia and Moravia: Facing the Holocaust* (University of Nebraska Press and Yad Vashem, 2005), 250.

4. Durbrow, memorandum, August 13, 1942, SD 862.4016/2235, reprinted in Wyman, *America and the Holocaust*, 1:194; Hull to American Legation (Bern), August 17, 1942 (instructions to legation crossed out), SD 862.4016/2233, reprinted in Wyman, *America and the Holocaust*, 1:188.

5. Riegner, *Never Despair*, 42–43; Wyman, *The Abandonment of the Jews*, 44.

6. Stephen Wise, *Challenging Years: The Autobiography of Stephen Wise* (Putnam, 1949), xi, 3.

7. Ibid., 3–4, 109, 149–51.

8. Ibid., 16–18, 26, 61–62, 110, 117.

9. Ibid., 216–217.

10. Ibid., 217–18. In his autobiography, Wise blames the enmity of Roosevelt adviser Louis Howe for blocking his access to the president. However, in Roosevelt's letter to Wise after the 1932 presidential election, Roosevelt wrote at the end: "If you will let me, I will gladly talk over with you my reasons for feeling

this." Despite this direct invitation to, in effect, pick up the phone, Wise apparently felt that he needed to be expressly invited: "[President Roosevelt] first asked me to come to the White House in late 1935 or early 1936" (ibid.), 218. See Melvin I. Urofsky, *A Voice That Spoke for Justice: The Life and Times of Stephen S. Wise* (State University of New York Press, 1982), 255 (quoting Wise's letter to Roosevelt).

11. Wise, *Challenging Years*, 219. As one example of his unqualified support for Roosevelt, Wise supported Roosevelt's 1937 plan to increase the size of the Supreme Court in order to dilute the power of the justices who had struck down New Deal legislation. The court-packing plan, regarded as one of Roosevelt's greatest mistakes, went down to defeat in the face of condemnation across the political and legal spectrum (ibid., 222–24).

12. Carl Hermann Voss, ed., *Stephen S. Wise: Servant of the People, Selected Letters* (The Jewish Publication Society of America, 1969), 250 (letter to Felix Frankfurter, September 16, 1942).

13. Wise to Welles, September 2, 1942, SD 840.48/Refugees/3080, reprinted in Wyman, *America and the Holocaust*, 1:196; Wise, *Challenging Years*, 275; Welles, *Sumner Welles*, 29, 36, 109; Gellman, *Secret Affairs*, 146 (quoting Harold Ickes).

14. Welles, *Sumner Welles*, 7–9, 18–19.

15. Ibid., 9.

16. Ibid., 11; Gunther, *Roosevelt in Retrospect*, 172.

17. Welles, *Sumner Welles*, 29, 31–33, 35.

18. Ibid., 36.

19. Ibid., 37, 42.

20. Ibid., 58–59.

21. Ibid., 60, 63–64, 83, 85.

22. Ibid., 95, 97, 99, 111.

23. Ibid., 114; "Mrs. P. G. Gerry Weds Diplomat," *New York Times*, June 29, 1925, 17.

24. Acheson, *Present at the Creation*, 12; Welles, *Sumner Welles*, 118–19, 155.

25. Gellman, *Secret Affairs*, 63–64, 213.

26. Welles, *Sumner Welles*, 215–16. On August 12, in a telephone call with Welles, Roosevelt suggested that he return from vacation, but Welles advised him that war was not likely for at least another week (ibid., 215). See Berle and Jacobs, *Navigating the Rapids*, 237.

27. Billings, *So Close to Greatness*, 238; Welles, *Sumner Welles*, 216; Elliott Roosevelt and James Brough, *A Rendezvous with Destiny: The Roosevelts of the White House* (Putnam, 1975), 239.

28. Berle and Jacobs, *Navigating the Rapids*, 250; Welles, *Sumner Welles*, 217.

29. Gellman, *Secret Affairs*, 173–75; Welles, *Sumner Welles*, 245–46.
30. Sumner Welles, *The Time for Decision* (Harper & Brothers, 1944), 77, 112–15, 117.
31. Ibid., 129; Hooker, *The Moffat Papers*, 301–2.
32. Ibid., 306–7. Welles, *The Time for Decision*, 148; Israel, *The War Diary of Breckinridge Long*, 89–91, 102; Berle and Jacobs, *Navigating the Rapids*, 312.
33. Larry Tye, *Rising from the Rails: Pullman Porters and the Making of the Black Middle Class* (Henry Holt, 2004), 33, 44.
34. Welles, *Sumner Welles*, 2–3.
35. Douglas Frantz and Catherine Collins, *Death on the Black Sea: The Untold Story of the* Struma *and World War II's Holocaust at Sea* (HarperCollins, 2003), 147, 230–31, 295–300.
36. Voss, *Stephen S. Wise*, 246–47; Lash, *Eleanor and Franklin*, 743. Lash wrote that Secretary of State Cordell Hull kept Eleanor Roosevelt "at arm's length. Letters that she sent to him were answered in State Department officialese" (ibid., 742).
37. Polier to Eleanor Roosevelt, March 8, 1942, and Eleanor Roosevelt to Welles, March 9, 1942 (Eleanor Roosevelt Papers, FDR Library, Box 853), reprinted in Wyman, *America and the Holocaust*, 5:112–113, see Wyman, *The Abandonment of the Jews*, 158–60; Welles, *Sumner Welles*, 227.
38. Voss, *Stephen S. Wise*, 247 (letter to Eleanor Roosevelt, April 1, 1942). The reference to taking British children refers to the evacuation in 1940 of British children to the United States, discussed in more detail in Chapter XII.
39. Atherton to Welles, September 3, 1942, SD 840.48/Refugees/3080, reprinted in Wyman, *America and the Holocaust*, 1:201; Davis, *FDR: The War President*, 727 (describing how Atherton passed the report from a Polish source, "Poland Under German Occupation," to the head of the intelligence and espionage agency that would become the wartime Office of Strategic Services, the forerunner of the CIA).
40. Wise, *Challenging Years*, 275; Voss, *Stephen S. Wise*, 249. In his autobiography, Wise wrote that he immediately contacted Sumner Welles after receiving the Silverman cable on August 28; however, David Wyman writes in *The Abandonment of the Jews* that Wise waited several days before contacting Welles by letter dated September 2 (376 n. 9).
41. Voss, *Stephen S. Wise*, 251.
42. Urofsky, *A Voice That Spoke for Justice*, 319; Riegner, *Never Despair*, 71.
43. Wyman, *The Abandonment of the Jews*, 45–46; Urofsky, *A Voice That Spoke for Justice*, 321.
44. Voss, *Stephen S. Wise*, 249. According to one historian, Frankfurter did speak to Roosevelt in mid-September, but the president only repeated the slave labor line of the State Department. Whether Frankfurter described the extermination scheme in any detail is unclear. Davis, *FDR*, 729.

45. Riegner, *Never Despair*, 57; Breitman, *Architect of Genocide*, 6–7. The Reich Security Main Office, which reported to Himmler, was the umbrella organization that resulted from the merger of the Gestapo, the SD (security service), and the Kripo (criminal police). Helmut Langerbein, *Hitler's Death Squads: The Logic of Mass Murder* (Texas A & M University Press, 2004), 18–20; see Laqueur and Baumel, *The Holocaust Encyclopedia,* 604, 608.

46. Welles to Taylor, September 23, 1942, SD740.00116/EW597A, reprinted in Wyman, *America and the Holocaust*, 1:211–14; see Wyman, *The Abandonment of the Jews*, 49.

47. Wyman, *The Abandonment of the Jews*, 48–50 (". . . in Lodz thousands of Jewish families are taken away from the ghetto systematically and nobody ever hears from them again. They are poisoned by gas."), quoting the *Jewish Telegraphic Agency*, October 6, 1942, 4. The report from the *Jewish Telegraphic Agency* was published the day after the October 5 Welles–Wise meeting, but the information may have been known to Wise earlier. The *Jewish Morning Journal* had also published an account on September 20, 1942, by a Swedish businessman who had traveled through Poland and learned that half the Jews in ghettos in Warsaw, Lodz, Krakow, and Lvov had been killed. See Wyman, *The Abandonment of the Jews*, 48–50, quoting the *Jewish Morning Journal*, September 20, 1942.

48. Riegner, *Never Despair*, 45.

49. Ibid., 45–49; Squire to Hull, September 28, 1942, enclosing two memoranda and letter to Stephen Wise, September 28, 1942, SD 862.4016/2242, reprinted in Wyman, *America and the Holocaust*, 1:203–10; Mrs. Leland Harrison to Sumner Welles, January 9, 1940; Oliver Quayle to Mrs. Leland Harrison, October 28, 1940 (FDRL, Sumner Welles Papers, Box 60); Mrs. Leland Harrison to Welles, November 29, 1942; Mrs. Leland Harrison to Sumner Welles, May 21, 1942 (FDRL, Sumner Welles Papers, Box 79). Harrison had been informed by the Division of European Affairs that the State Department had not delivered the Riegner telegram to Wise because of its "unsubstantiated" nature. Heinrichs, *American Ambassador*, 38; Arthur D. Morse, *While Six Million Died: A Chronicle of American Apathy* (Random House, 1967), 9; Laqueur and Breitman, *Breaking the Silence*, 136, 156, 159–60.

50. Laquer and Breitman, *Breaking the Silence*, 157–58; Aide Memoir Concerning the Persecution of the Jews of Europe, October 22, 1942 (FDRL, Sumner Welles Papers, Box 79).

51. Ibid.; Riegner, *Never Despair*, 44–51; Laqueur and Breitman, *Breaking the Silence*, 157.

52. Harrison to Welles, November 23, 1942, SD 740.00116/653, reprinted in Wyman, *America and the Holocaust*, 1:219; see Squire to Hull, October 29, 1942, SD 862.4016/10–2942, reprinted in Wyman, *America and the Holocaust*, 1:215–18; Wyman, *The Abandonment of the Jews*, 50–51; Laqueur and Breitman, *Breaking the Silence*, 158–59. The November 23 cable from Harrison to Welles referred to making only Germany "free" of all Jews, but the unquestionable import of the information received by Harrison was that the extermination

order was to be carried out in all German-occupied countries. If Hitler did sign such an order, it has been destroyed or never found.

53. Wise, *Challenging Years*, 275–76; Welles, *Sumner Welles*, 231. Wise earned a doctorate from Columbia University by doing a dissertation on (and translating from Arabic) an eleventh-century treatise on ethics by a Jewish philosopher. Urofsky, *A Voice That Spoke for Justice*, 12.

CHAPTER VIII   A REASON TO LIVE

1. Gold, *Ruth's Journey*, 63–64; Shachan, *Burning Ice*, 195.
2. Gold, *Ruth's Journey*, 14–15, 65–70.
3. Ibid., 72–74.
4. Ibid., 76–78.
5. Ibid., 80–81.

CHAPTER IX   THE CHIEF

1. "40,000 Here View Memorial to Jews," *New York Times*, March 10, 1943, 12; Ben Hecht, *A Child of the Century* (Simon & Schuster, 1954), 558–60; "We Will Never Die Pageant," March 9, 1943, America and the Holocaust, available at http://www.pbs.org/wgbh/amex/holocaust/peopleevents/pandeAMEX104.html.).
2. Wise, *Challenging Years*, 276. It is unclear whether Wise actually received and disclosed the diplomatic cables. Welles may have meant that Wise should provide the information contained in the documents to the press, as opposed to publicly handing out State Department cables.
3. Wise, *Challenging Years*, 276; "Wise Says Hitler Has Ordered 4,000,000 Jews Slain in 1942," *New York Herald-Tribune*, November 25, 1942, 1.
4. Wyman, *The Abandonment of the Jews*, 51–52, 70–71.
5. Voss, *Stephen S. Wise*, 253–54; Wyman, *The Abandonment of the Jews*, 72. Wyman reports that a representative of the Union of Orthodox Rabbis, Rabbi Israel Rosenberg, was present, although the notes of the meeting refer to Rosenberg as present on behalf of the Agudath Israel of America, which was aligned with the Union of Orthodox Rabbis.
6. William Manchester, *The Glory and the Dream: A Narrative History of America 1932–1972* (Little, Brown, 1973), 19, 33, 36–37, 40, 74–77, 80; Adam Cohen, *Nothing to Fear: FDR's Inner Circle and the Hundred Days That Created Modern America* (Penguin Press, 2009), 1 (quoting Edmund Wilson), 14–16; Lawrence W. Levine, *The Unpredictable Past: Explorations in American Cultural History* (Oxford University Press, 1993), 314.
7. Cohen, *Nothing to Fear*, 3; Manchester, *The Glory and the Dream*, 83; William E. Leuchtenberg, "The FDR Years: On Roosevelt and His Legacy" (originally an essay presented as a paper at a Conference on Leadership in the Modern

Presidency at the Woodrow Wilson School of Princeton University, April 3, 1987, available at http://www.washingtonpost.com/wp-srv/style/longterm/books/chap1/fdryears.htm.

8. Manchester, *The Glory and the Dream*, 81, 90, 196.

9. "Franklin D. Roosevelt," *New York Times*, April 13, 1945, 16; Henry Kissinger, *Diplomacy* (Simon & Schuster, 1994), 370.

10. Lash, *Eleanor and Franklin*, 369 (emphasis in the original).

11. Welles, *Sumner Welles*, 123, quoting interview with Sumner Welles by Aluizio Napoleao, second secretary, Brazilian Embassy, June 13, 1947 (Sumner Welles Papers); Hooker, *The Moffat Papers*, 95–96 (entry for May 6, 1933).

12. Biddle, "As I Remember Groton School," 296; Gunther, *Roosevelt in Retrospect*, 18 (paraphrasing Winston Churchill); "Franklin D. Roosevelt," *New York Times*, April 13, 1945, 16.

13. Joseph Goebbels, "Die Juden sind schuld!"(The Jews are guilty!), *Das eherne Herz (The Iron Heart)* (Munich: Zentralverlag der NSDAP, 1943), 85–91 (reprinting the essay dated November 16, 1941), available at http://www.calvin.edu/academic/cas/gpa/goeb1.htm. In fact, New York attorney Samuel Untermyer had died before the Goebbels essay appeared in print. Robert G. L. Waite, *The Psychopathic God: Adolf Hitler* (Basic Books, 1977), 76; see Richard N. Rosen, *Saving the Jews: Franklin D. Roosevelt and the Holocaust* (Thunder Mouth's Press, 2006), 12 (reprinting anti-Semitic cartoon of Roosevelt titled, in part, "Jews Are the Cause of High Taxes, Slavery, Starvation and Death").

14. Morgenthau Presidential Diaries, Part II, 1061–62 (January 27, 1942); Manchester, *The Glory and the Dream*, 82; Arthur M. Schlesinger Jr., *The Coming of the New Deal*, vol. 2, *The Age of Roosevelt* (First Mariner Books, 2003), 539.

15. Compare Wyman, *The Abandonment of the Jews*, 311 ("If he had wanted to, he could have aroused substantial public backing for a vital rescue effort by speaking out on the issue. . . . But he had little to say about the problem and gave no priority at all to rescue."), with Rosen, *Saving the Jews*, xxiv (introduction) ("Roosevelt did not abandon the Jews of Europe. On the contrary, he led the worldwide coalition against Nazism in a war that took fifty million lives. He marshaled American opinion against antisemitism at home and Nazism abroad.").

16. Manchester, *The Glory and the Dream*, 82; Herman Wouk, *The Winds of War* (Little, Brown, 1971), 655.

17. *The Secret Diary of Harold L. Ickes*, vol. II, *The Inside Struggle*, 1936–39 (Simon & Schuster, 1954), 720

18. Richard Breitman, Barbara McDonald Stewart, and Severin Hochberg, eds., *Refugees and Rescue: The Diaries and Papers of James G. McDonald 1935–1945* (Indiana University Press, 2009), 182–83, quoting Bullitt to Hull, September 19, 1939, NA RG 59,740.00/2138 confidential file.

19. Goodwin, *No Ordinary Time*, 103, 322–23; Greg Robinson, *By Order of the*

President: FDR and the Internment of Japanese-Americans (Harvard University Press, 2001), 4, 91–93.

20. Ibid., 169; Goodwin, *No Ordinary Time*, 610.

21. Wyman, *The Abandonment of the Jews*, 124–26; Breitman et al., *Refugees and Rescue*, 3, 122–23, 125–26, 147 (press conference on *Kristallnacht*), 150–51 (press conference on the German and Austrian refugees); Smith, *FDR*, 428.

22. Breitman et al., *Refugees and Rescue*, 205. Patricia Cohen, "In Old Files, Fading Hopes of Anne Frank's Family," *New York Times*, February 15, 2007, 1. In late 1941, Otto Frank did obtain a visa for himself to Cuba, as a start for his family, which was forwarded to him on December 1. "No one knows if it ever arrived; 10 days later, Germany and Italy declared war on the United States, and Havana cancelled the visa" (ibid., B7); Wyman, *The Abandonment of the Jews*, 126.

23. As he told one of his speechwriters, Roosevelt thought it would be "wonderful, poetic justice if we could get a Jew to head the agency which is going to feed and clothe and shelter the millions whom Hitler has robbed and starved and tortured—a member of the group Hitler first selected for extermination. It would be a fine object lesson in tolerance and human brotherhood to have a Jew head up this operation, and I think Herbert would be fine." Samuel I. Rosenman, *Working with Roosevelt* (Harper & Brothers, 1952), 399.

24. Notes of Adolph Held, December 8, 1942, available at www.jewishvirtuallibrary.org/jsource.Holocaust/fdrmeet.html..

25. Wyman, *The Abandonment of the Jews*, 61.

26. Biographic Register of the State Department, 1945, 240. His educational record is murky. Reams's biography states: "DuBois High School, grad.; Allegheny Coll. 1921–23 and George Washington Law Sch." No undergraduate or law school degrees are listed, as is the case for other State Department biographies of college and law school graduates, and no dates of attendance are given for George Washington Law School, contrary to usual practice. Shaw to Welles, December 22, 1942, SD 840.48/R[efugees]/3526.

27. Eddy to Gordon, December 7, 1942, SD 862.4016/2251, reprinted in Wyman, *America and the Holocaust*, 2:102. The memorandum refers to an imminent meeting between Reams and Atherton to discuss having Wise "call off" the publicity. In light of the State Department's subsequent conduct, the meeting likely took place and Atherton authorized Reams to proceed.

28. Voss, *Stephen S. Wise*, 254–55; Wyman, *The Abandonment of the Jews*, 65. Even after the American and British governments issued a statement condemning the extermination plan, the *Christian Century* still insisted that the State Department "did not support Dr. Wise's contention." Deborah E. Lipstadt, *Beyond Belief: The American Press and the Coming of the Holocaust 1939–1945* (The Free Press, 1986), 183, 185.

29. Reams to Hickerson & Atherton, December 10, 1942, SD 740.00116, EW/674, reprinted in Wyman, *America and the Holocaust*, 2:106.

30. Winant to Hull, December 8, 1942, SD 740.0116, EW/664, reprinted in

Wyman, *America and the Holocaust*, 2:110–11; Wyman, *The Abandonment of the Jews*, 73.

31. Reams to Atherton & Hickerson, December 9, 1942, SD 740.00116, EW/1939/694, reprinted in Wyman, *America and the Holocaust*, 2:107.

32. Reams to Atherton & Hickerson, December 10, 1942, SD 740.00116, EW/1939/694, reprinted in Wyman, *America and the Holocaust*, 2:108–9.

33. "German Policy of Extermination of the Jewish Race" (publicly released on December 17, 1943), U.S. Department of State Bulletin, December 19, 1942, 1009, reprinted in Wyman, *America and the Holocaust*, 2:113; Wyman, *The Abandonment of the Jews*, 75.

34. "11 Allies Condemn Nazi War on Jews," *New York Times*, December 18, 1942, 1; Wyman, *The Abandonment of the Jews*, 76; see Rosen, *Saving the Jews*, 246.

35. Telegram, Barou/Easterman to Perlzweig, American Jewish Congress, December 17, 1942, American Jewish Archives, World Jewish Congress Collection, Administrative Departments, 177A/50, reprinted in Wyman, *America and the Holocaust*, 2:100; "Reactions to Revelations Regarding the Extermination of the Jews of Europe," available at http://www.jewishvirtuallibrary.org/jsource/Holocaust/UKShoah.html. Robert Rhodes James, ed., *Chips: The Diary of Sir Henry Channon* (Weidenfeld & Nicolson, 1967), 347.

36. Louis Rapoport, *Shake Heaven and Earth: Peter Bergson and the Struggle to Rescue the Jews of Europe* (Gefen Publishing House, 1999), 13–19.

37. Hecht, *A Child of the Century*, 522, 524; Rapoport, *Shake Heaven and Earth*, vii (foreword by author), 41–43, 53.

38. Israel, *The War Diary of Breckinridge Long*, 336. Playwright Ben Hecht attempted to bring the Wise and Bergson groups together in January 1943 to coordinate their mass publicity campaigns but was unsuccessful. Rapoport, *Shake Heaven and Earth*, 73.

39. Memorandum of the Interim Committee of the American Jewish Conference, December 29, 1943, SD 840.48/Refugees/5025, reprinted in Wyman, *America and the Holocaust*, 6:448; Wyman, *The Abandonment of the Jews*, 14. In this case, the American Jewish Conference was referring to the Emergency Committee to Save the Jewish People of Europe, which Bergson formed in mid-1943 (ibid., 146–47).

40. David S. Wyman and Rafael Medoff, *A Race Against Death: Peter Bergson, America, and the Holocaust* (The New Press, 2002), 107 (interview of Peter Bergson), 168 n.

41. Rapoport, *Shake Heaven and Earth*, 68.

42. Ibid., 57.

43. "My Day," Eleanor Roosevelt, April 14, 1943, reprinted at http://www.gwu.edu/~erpapers/myday/displaydoc.cfm?y=1943&_f=md056470; see Wyman, *The Abandonment of the Jews*, 91–92.

44. Ibid., 85, 92; Rapoport, *Shake Heaven and Earth*, 72; Wyman and Medoff, *A Race Against Death*, 207–10 (appendix: "Report on Attempts to Stage *We Will Never Die*").
45. Jan Karski, *Story of a Secret State* (Houghton Mifflin, 1944), 30–42, 49, 51, 155–67, 190.
46. Ibid., 323–29.
47. Wyman, *The Abandonment of the Jews*, 80.
48. Karski, *Story of a Secret State*, 329–31, 334; E. Thomas Wood and Stanislaw M. Jankowski, *Karski: How One Man Tried to Stop the Holocaust* (John Wiley & Sons, 1994), 122–24.
49. Karski, *Story of a Secret State*, 339–51. Karski's biographers suggest that he was mistaken about the identity of the concentration camp and that, rather than Bełżec, it more likely was a camp in Izbica Lubelska used as a "sorting point" (Wood and Jankowski, *Karski*, 128–29).
50. Karski, *Story of a Secret State*, 383; Wood and Jankowski, *Karski*, 168.
51. Wyman, *The Abandonment of the Jews*, 80.
52. Morgenthau Diaries, Book 688, Part II, 223R–223S (American Legation [in Bern] to Welles, January 21, 1943 [paraphrase of cable 482]).
53. Wyman, *The Abandonment of the Jews*, 80–81; Welles to Wise, February 9, 1943, American Jewish Archives, World Jewish Congress Collection, Lillie Schultz/Stephen Wise Files, Central Files, reprinted in Wyman, *America and the Holocaust*, vol. 2, 150. By one account, when Jewish groups received cable 482 on February 9, 1943, "they decided to call a mass meeting in Madison Square Garden, at which they would try to elicit public support and map out a program." Morgenthau Diaries, Book 688, Part II, 244–45 (December 31, 1943) (11:45 AM) (statement of Josiah DuBois Jr.). It is unclear whether the Division of European Affairs was actually aware that such a rally was imminent, although Jewish groups were communicating, in intercepted cables, about the rally. See, for example, Wise to Barou/Easterman, February 26, 1943, NA548.G1/181. While this cable postdated cable 354 by five days, earlier intercepted cables may have also discussed plans for the rally. But, at the least, the division acted in the general belief that reports from Europe inevitably created pressure for rescue.
54. Wyman, *The Abandonment of the Jews*, 87; Rapoport, *Shake Heaven and Earth*, 73.
55. Wyman, *The Abandonment of the Jews*, 81. This was certainly the view of the Treasury Department lawyers who reviewed the State Department cables. See Morgenthau Diaries, Book 688, Part II, 247 (December 31, 1943, 11:45 AM) ("Now, that February 10 cable [Cable 354] which was designed to stop all the information which had been causing pressure in this country, as you know, was so drafted that Welles might well not have known what was in it when he signed it.") (statement of Josiah DuBois Jr.).
56. Morgenthau Diaries, Book 688, Part II, 223T (Hull to American Legation in

Bern, February 10, 1943 [paraphrase of cable 354]); 223M ("The initialed file copy of the cable indicates that the men responsible were Atherton and Dunn as well as Durbrow and Hickerson") (Memorandum: For Secretary Morgenthau's Information Only).

CHAPTER X   JEWS FOR SALE

1. Stephen Walsh, *Stalingrad 1942–1943: The Infernal Cauldron* (Thomas Dunne Books, 2000), 165–66; C. L. Sulzberger, "Romania Proposes Transfer of Jews," *New York Times*, February 13, 1943, 5. The Bergson advertisement placed the value of 20,000 lei at $50; other historians have used a higher figure, around $130. Wyman, *The Abandonment of the Jews*, 82, 86–87, 380 n. 11.

2. "For Sale To Humanity," *New York Times*, February 16, 1943, 11.

3. Michael S. Sweeney, *Secrets of Victory: The Office of Censorship and the American Press and Radio in World War II* (University of North Carolina Press, 2001), 45, 155; Executive Order 8985; Brandt to Alexander, February 25, 1943, attaching Barou/Easterman to Wise, Perlzweig, Miller, February 22, 1943, Kubwitzki/Miller to Barou/Easterman, March 16, 1943; Merlin to Lubotzky, February 24, 1943; Schwarzbart to World Jewish Congress, March 14, 1943, NA 548. G1/181. "Price Will Share Kellems Inquiry," *New York Times*, April 9, 1944, 24. Brandt's cover note did not identify the attached intercepts; but the proximity of the dates of the note and the Barou/Easterman intercept suggests that the latter was one of the note's attachments.

4. Rapoport, *Shake Heaven and Earth*, 115–16; Wyman, *The Abandonment of the Jews*, 87; Morgenthau Diaries, Book 609, 39 (February 15, 1943, 11:39 AM); Morgenthau Diaries, Book 611, 275–77 (Welles to Morgenthau, February 24, 1943, attaching paraphrase of memorandum from the American Embassy in Ankara). The February 20, 1943, minutes of a meeting of the Zionist Organization of America's Executive Committee record one participant's condemnation of the *New York Times* advertisement as a "very cheap and vulgar attempt to get money for the Jewish Army Committee—$50 a Jew—and we understand from many sources that many Jews have sent in checks." Minutes of the Meeting of the Zionist Organization of America Executive Committee, February 20, 1943, 9; Stephen Wise Papers, Zionist Organization of America Executive Committee (1920–1946), reprinted in Wyman, *America and the Holocaust*, vol. 2, 153.

5. Welles to Wagner, March 10, 1943 (Georgetown University, Robert Wagner Papers, Palestine File, Box 2), and Welles to Davis, March 11, 1943, SD 840.48/Refugees/3608, reprinted in Wyman, *America and the Holocaust*, 2:160–61.

6. Wise to Welles, March 31, 1943, SD 862.4016/2266, reprinted in Wyman, *America and the Holocaust*, 6:1.

7. Welles to Atherton, April 5, 1943, SD 862.4016/2266, and Hull to American Legation, April 10, 1943, SD 862.4016/2266A, reprinted in Wyman, *America and the Holocaust*, 6:2–3.

8. Morgenthau Diaries, Book 688, Part II, 142 (Harrison to Hull, April 20, 1943 [Cable 2460] [Section One]); Wyman, *The Abandonment of the Jews*, 81, 179.

9. Riegner, *Never Despair*, 60.

10. Harrison to Secretary of State, April 20, 1943, SD 862.4016/2269 (Sections One & Two), reprinted in Wyman, *America and the Holocaust*, 6:5–8. A week later, in a cable sent under Hull's and Welles's names, Harrison was advised: "In view of your recommendations you are authorized to transmit messages from R when they contain information of interest to the Department. . . . Your acceptance of messages from R should also be conditioned by a distinct understanding with him that they will be transmitted to his correspondent in this country [Stephen Wise] only in the discretion of the Department" (Hull to Bern Legation, April 27, 1943, SD 862.4016/2268, reprinted in Wyman, *America and the Holocaust*, 6:12).

11. Wise to Welles, May 3, 1943, SD 840.48/Refugees/3821, and Harrison to Hull, June 14, 1943, SD862.4016/2274, reprinted in Wyman, *America and the Holocaust*, 6:13–14, 21; Morgenthau Diaries, Book 646, 68 (July 1, 1943) (J. J. O'Connell and John W. Pehle memorandum to Morgenthau). The proposal contemplated that funds would be spent on both relief (i.e., purchase of food and clothing) and on the evacuation of Romanian Jews. The Treasury Department, while prepared to approve the evacuation arrangement, initially expressed concern about the relief aspect because "special arrangements for Jews would create an embarrassing precedent which would make it difficult to deny similar requests by private American citizens to provide relief for relatives and friends in occupied areas" (Meltzer memorandum to Feis, Reams, Brandt, Welles, July 30, 1943, SD 840.48/Refugees/4211, reprinted in Wyman, *America and the Holocaust*, 6:46–48). Ultimately, the Treasury Department supported using the funds "for relief preparatory to evacuation as well as for evacuation, itself." Morgenthau Diaries, Book 688, Part II, 8 (December 13, 1943, 3:00 PM (meeting between Morgenthau, White, Pehle, Luxford, and DuBois)).

12. The Special Division had responsibility for miscellaneous activities such as "the whereabouts and welfare of Americans abroad" and—pertinent here—"transmission of funds." Register of the Department of State 1942, 42; Morgenthau Diaries, Book 688, Part I, 198–202 (DuBois to files, December 9, 1943).

13. Bendiner, *The Riddle of the State Department*, 188–89; *Time* magazine, November 8, 1943, "U.S. at War: Dr. Feis Gives Notice," available at http://www.time.com/time/magazine/article/0,9171,796235,00.html; Register of the State Department 1942, 142.

14. "Bernard Meltzer: Nuremberg Prosecutor," *The Independent*, February 16, 2007, available at http://www.independent.co.uk/news/obituaries/bernard–meltzer–436541.html; "Legal Scholar, Labor Specialist Bernard D. Meltzer Dies at 92," *University of Chicago Law School News*, January 4, 2007, available at http://webcast–law.uchicago.edu/news/meltzer–obituary.html; Register of the State Department 1942, 26, 203; Wyman, *The Abandonment of the Jews*, 180.

15. Hull to Harrison, May 25, 1943, SD 862.4016/2269, reprinted in Wyman, *America and the Holocaust*, 6:18–20.

16. Harrison to Hull, June 14, 1943 (Sections I–VIII) (paraphrase), and Meltzer to Pehle, June 25, 1943, SD862.4016/2274, reprinted in Wyman, *America and the Holocaust*, 6:21–33; see May 25, 1943, paraphrase of Cable 2461, SD 862.4016.2269, furnished to the Treasury Department (ibid., 34–36).

17. Profiles in Tax History: Randolph E. Paul, October 6, 2004, The Tax History Project, available at http://www.taxhistory.org/thp/readings.nsf/cf7c9c870b600b9585256df80075b9dd/afd2a67073f6b87085256f8600681f74?OpenDocument.

18. Morgenthau Diaries, Book 688, Part I, 198–202 (DuBois to files, December 9, 1943); Wyman, *The Abandonment of the Jews*, 180.

19. Morgenthau Diaries, Book 688, Part I, 15–18, 198–202 (Paul to Morgenthau, August 12, 1943, and DuBois to files, December 9, 1943). By way of explanation for the State Department's position, Paul mentioned a recent article by the columnist Drew Pearson about a State Department initiative to bar "any further discussion of Palestine and the Jews until after the war." He pointed out that the article had even asserted that a high-ranking American government official had "agreed with Ibn Saud, the powerful Arab leader, that the Jews should be driven from all Arab lands, including Palestine." Paul concluded that, "From the opposition with which the instant proposal has been met by some factions within the State Department, it is possible to tie Pearson's article into the State Department attitude on the Romanian refugee proposal." Reams repeated his arguments in an internal State Department meeting four days later, with a few additional objections. See W. J. Hull to Meltzer & Reams, July 19, 1943, SD 840.48/Refugees/4102, reprinted in Wyman, *America and the Holocaust*, 6:44–45.

20. Meltzer to Feis, Reams, Brandt [executive assistant to Breckinridge Long], Welles, July 30, 1943, SD 840.48/Refugees/4211, reprinted in Wyman, *America and the Holocaust*, 6:46–48; W. J. Hull to Meltzer & Reams, July 19, 1943, SD 840.48/Refugees/4102, reprinted in Wyman, *America and the Holocaust*, 6:44–45.

21. Israel, *The War Diary of Breckinridge Long*, 319.

22. Brandt to Feis, August 3, 1943, SD 840.48/Refugees/4212, reprinted in Wyman, *America and the Holocaust*, 6:62; Morgenthau Diaries, Book 688, Part I, 200 (DuBois to files, December 9, 1943).

23. Wise, *Challenging Years*, 277–78. In his autobiography, Wise recalls the proposal as involving both the Romanian and the French rescue, but he also recalls the rescue of Polish Jews and only mentioning the latter in his conversation with Roosevelt. He apparently mis-recalled the conversation with Roosevelt on this point, since all of the discussions in the State and Treasury departments, as well as his letter to Roosevelt the following day, concerned the rescue of the Transnistrian Jews and the French children. Holocaust historians, without

disputing Wise's account, have all but ignored Roosevelt's personal approval of a plan to rescue the Transnistrian Jews even though it was one of the largest rescue efforts of the war. For example, David Wyman and Arthur D. Morse each devoted a single paragraph to the conversation: the former in *The Abandonment of the Jews*, 180; the latter in *While Six Million Died*, 79.

24. Wise to Roosevelt, July 23, 1943 (FDRL, Franklin D. Roosevelt Papers, OF 76–C), reprinted in Wyman, *America and the Holocaust*, 6:49.

25. Morgenthau Diaries, Book 688, Part I, 11 (letter from Morgenthau to Hull, August 5, 1943, and letter from Roosevelt to Wise, August 14, 1943) [FDRL, Franklin D. Roosevelt Papers, OF 76–C]), reprinted in Wyman, *America and the Holocaust*, 6:50–51. A few months later, the Treasury lawyers appeared uncertain whether, in fact, the president had formally approved the rescue plan. One even suggested that the president had "weaseled on us." Morgenthau Diaries, Book 688, Part II, 107–9 (December 19, 1943, 5:30 PM). Nevertheless, the letter from Roosevelt appears to confirm the statement in Wise's letter to Roosevelt thanking him for his approval of the rescue plan.

26. Morgenthau Diaries, Book 688, Part I, 10 (memorandum from Hull to Morgenthau, August 7, 1943). Hull may, in fact, have subsequently read Meltzer's memorandum and its clear assurance that under the rescue proposal no funds would be paid to the Romanian government or any other enemy of the United States. At the very least, for the record, Hull added at the end of the memorandum: "Any view that this would make funds available to the enemy is not correct; the funds would remain blocked in Switzerland until the end of the war."

27. Morgenthau Diaries, Book 688, Part I, 198–99 (DuBois to files, December 9, 1943).

28. Wood and Jankowski, *Karski,* 187–88.

29. Rosen, *Saving the Jews*, 294.

30. Wood and Jankowski, *Karski*, 189–90.

31. Ibid., 197–200; Karski, *Story of a Secret State*, 387; Jan Ciechanowski, *Defeat in Victory* (Doubleday, 1947), 180–90. This meeting, as may have been the case with the Jewish leaders in December 1942, apparently took place on the second floor of the White House in a more accessible presidential study, the "Oval Room—not to be confused with the Oval Office, which is located in another wing of the [White House]" (Wood and Jankowski, *Karski*, 197).

32. Wood and Jankowski, *Karski*, 201–2.

33. Morgenthau Diaries, Book 688, Part I, 88–89 (Harrison to Hull, October 6, 1943 [paraphrase]).

CHAPTER XI   FROM FOSTER PARENTS TO THE ORPHANAGE

1. Gold, *Ruth's Journey*, 80, 82.

2. Shachan, *Burning Ice*, 192–93, 263–64. In the fall of 1941, 25,000 people lived in Bershad (in 337 houses); six months later, only 10,000 were still alive (ibid., 195). In November 1941, 1,200 Jews had been interned in the town of Tibulovka; before the end of January 1942, less than 200 were still alive, "most of these suffering from frozen extremities" (Radu Ioanid, *The Holocaust in Romania: The Destruction of Jews and Gypsies Under the Antonescu Regime, 1940–1944* [Ivan R. Dee, 2000], 205–6).

3. Gold, *Ruth's Journey*, 82–84.

4. Ibid., 84–85.

5. Shachan, *Burning Ice*, 201–2.

6. Gold, *Ruth's Journey*, 85–86.

CHAPTER XII BRECK AND ELEANOR

1. Dan Kurzman, *The Bravest Battle: The Twenty-eight Days of the Warsaw Ghetto Uprising* (G. P. Putnam's Sons, 1976), 23, 91, 94–97.

2. The Consul General at Hamilton (Beck) to Secretary of State, April 8, 1943, SD 548G1/14, reprinted in Foreign Relations of the United States, vol. 1 (1943), 148.

3. Views of the Government of the United States Regarding Topics Included in the Agenda for Discussion with the British Government, March 1943 ("The refugee problem should not be considered as being confined to persons of any particular race or faith. Nazi measures against minorities have caused the flights of persons of various races and faiths, as well as of other persons because of their political beliefs. False charges have been made by the Nazi-Fascist propagandists who have attempted to distort the humanitarian interest of the United Nations into a sole interest in certain minorities. The conferees in their findings should endeavor to avoid any possible implication which might be of assistance to the Nazi-Fascist propagandists."), reprinted at *America and the Holocaust*, available at http://www.pbs.org/wgbh/amex/holocaust/filmmore/reference/primary/bermmemorandum.html.

4. Alexander to Long, May 7, 1943 (Breckinridge Long Papers, Box 203), Refugee Movement and National Groups, reprinted in Wyman, *America and the Holocaust*, 2:265–67 ("It is not difficult—once the facts are known—to see who is really behind the pressure groups. However, we must not permit Hitler to get away with it. We must not permit the emotionalists, who are misled by Hitler, to mislead us."). See Wyman, *The Abandonment of the Jews*, 108–9, 112–13.

5. Feingold, *The Politics of Rescue*, 194, 196.

6. Israel, *The War Diary of Breckinridge Long*, 307–9; Wyman, *The Abandonment of the Jews*, 112.

7. American Minutes of the Bermuda Conference [on the Refugee Problem] Morning Conference, April 20, 1943, available at http://www.jewishvirtual library.org/jsource/Holocaust/bermudadiscuss.html and reprinted in Wyman, *America and the Holocaust*, 3:78–81; see Wyman, *The Abandonment of the Jews*, 114–15, 122; Feingold, *The Politics of Rescue*, 198–99; "Mass Refugee Shift Rejected at Parley," *New York Times*, April 22, 1943, 10. After the conference, Bloom was bitterly attacked by Jewish leaders, including Congressman Emanuel Celler of Brooklyn. In a memorandum to State Department Political Advisor James Dunn, Borden Reams noted that "Congressman Celler and others have attacked Congressman Bloom for his part in the Bermuda Conference. Mr. Bloom is extremely upset about it . . ." (Reams to Dunn, July 15, 1943, FW 740.00116 /EW 1939/1008). Bloom alternated between defiance—"No one can criticize what we did in Bermuda without knowing what we did. But I as a Jew am perfectly satisfied with the results"—and unsubtle threats that might have been made by Breckinridge Long—"The security of winning the war is our first step. We as Jews must keep this in mind" (Wyman, *The Abandonment of the Jews*, 121; see Minutes of Meeting of the American Delegation, April 25, 1943, reprinted in Wyman, *America and the Holocaust*, 3:218–29 [discussion of Romanian Jews in Transnistria]).

8. "The Day in Washington," *New York Times*, June 25, 1943, 9; Welles to Atherton, August 22, 1943 (FDRL, Sumner Welles Papers, Box 91) (congratulating Atherton on his recent appointment).

9. Israel, *The War Diary of Breckinridge Long*, xi–xix (introduction by Israel); Acheson, *Present at the Creation*, 12.

10. Israel, *The War Diary of Breckinridge Long*, xviii–xxii (introduction by Israel); Gunther, *Roosevelt in Retrospect*, 263; Nixon, *Franklin D. Roosevelt and Foreign Affairs*, 3:28 (Howe to Roosevelt, October 18, 1935).

11. Israel, *The War Diary of Breckinridge Long*, xxiii–xxiv (introduction by Israel); Acheson, *Present at the Creation*, 12.

12. Israel, *The War Diary of Breckinridge Long*, 181 (describing a Jewish lawyer sent by Roosevelt on a mission to Great Britain as an able "representative of his racial group and philosophy"), 243; Acheson, *Present at the Creation*, 87. David Wyman suggests that whether, in addition to having nativist attitudes, "Long was also anti-Semitic is not clear" (Wyman, *The Abandonment of the Jews*, 191 n). Wyman's expression of ambivalence on this point, in the face of Long's fulminations in his diary and his record in the State Department on Jewish issues, requires an exceedingly narrow (or outdated) definition of anti-Semitism. It is difficult to imagine in our times a State Department official, who had made these and the other statements quoted in this book, convincing anyone that he was not anti-Semitic. Indeed, *A Race Against Death*, which Wyman later coauthored, states unequivocally that Long was "anti-Semitic"(ibid., 6). No explanation is offered to account for this inconsistency.

13. Israel, *The War Diary of Breckinridge Long*, 151–52, 156, 196. One of the major landowners in the Virgin Islands sent Roosevelt an "angry letter of opposition"

(Watkins, *Righteous Pilgrim*, 673). Ickes's continued advocacy of the proposal to use the Virgin Islands as a refugee haven, and Roosevelt's unwillingness to close the door on the plan, may have prompted Long in April 1941 to seek the assistance of the United States Navy. Ultimately, in the spring of 1941, Ickes gave up (ibid.). The quotes from Ickes's diary are from *The Secret Diary of Harold L. Ickes,* vol. 3: *The Lowering Clouds 1939–41* (Simon & Schuster, 1955), 398–99. In his diary entry of May 19, 1943, Long referred to the German effort to "use uranium powder in connection with split atoms in a compound explosive of alleged incredible violence," and then added, "It seems we have some plans of our own and want to perfect ours first" (Israel, *The War Diary of Breckinridge Long*, 312–13).

14. Wyman, *The Abandonment of the Jews*, 131; Israel, *The War Diary of Breckinridge Long*, 95.

15. Long to Berle and Dunn, June 26, 1940, *America and the Holocaust*, available at http://www.pbs.org/wgbh/amex/holocaust/filmmore/reference/primary/barmemo.html; Feingold, *The Politics of Rescue*, 142; Israel, *The War Diary of Breckinridge Long*, 134; Wyman, *The Abandonment of the Jews*, 125. The meeting between Roosevelt and Long took place on October 3, 1940. The members of the PACPR included Rabbi Stephen Wise and representatives of non-Jewish religious organizations (Feingold, *The Politics of Rescue*, 25–26). See Minutes of Meeting of American Delegation to the Bermuda Conference on the Refugee Problem, April 25, 1943 ("In order for a [refugee in Spain] to have the slightest chance of getting in he must have a sponsor in the United States. That sponsor is investigated by the FBI. His record is entirely gone over." [remarks of George Backer]), reprinted in Wyman, *America and the Holocaust*, 3:193.

16. Morse, *While Six Million Died*, 303–4 (quoting letter from Einstein to Eleanor Roosevelt dated July 26, 1941).

17. The United States Committee for the Care of European Children, Eleanor Roosevelt National Historic Site, New Hyde Park, New York, available at http://www.nps.gov/archive/elro/glossary/uscom.htm. Eight hundred children were evacuated before the evacuation efforts were suspended in the fall of 1940.

18. Israel, *The War Diary of Breckinridge Long*, 118–19; Goodwin, *No Ordinary Time*, 101.

19. Gunther, *Roosevelt in Retrospect*, 33; Lash, *Eleanor and Franklin*, 98; Carol Felsenthal, *Alice Roosevelt Longworth* (Putnam, 1988), 138; Peter Collier, with David Horowitz, *The Roosevelts: An American Saga* (Simon & Schuster, 1994), 81.

20. *The Autobiography of Eleanor Roosevelt*, 20–22.

21. Ibid., 22; Lash, *Eleanor and Franklin*, 118.

22. Eleanor and Franklin, 125, 170–72.

23. Doug Wead, *The Raising of a President: The Mothers and Fathers of Our Nation's Leaders* (Atria Books 2005), 148; Freidel, Franklin D. Roosevelt, 35.

24. Lash, *Eleanor and Franklin*, 302, 309–11. Five of the six children of Franklin and Eleanor Roosevelt survived infancy. See Joseph E. Persico, *Franklin and Lucy: President Roosevelt, Mrs. Rutherfurd and the Other Remarkable Women in His Life* (Random House, 2008), 11.

25. Lash, *Eleanor and Franklin*, 363, 371; James MacGregor Burns, *Roosevelt: The Lion and the Fox, 1882–1940* (Houghton Mifflin Harcourt, 2002), 88; Gunther, *Roosevelt in Retrospect*, 228.

26. Manchester, *The Glory and the Dream*, 92.

27. Israel, *The War Diary of Breckinridge Long*, 109, 134.

28. Feingold, *The Politics of Rescue*, 143; Israel, *The War Diary of Breckinridge Long*, 130; see Cara Buckley, "Fleeing Hitler and Finding Miss Liberty," *New York Times*, July 8, 2007, 20.

29. Israel, *The War Diary of Breckinridge Long*, 130.

30. Frank Overton Brown Jr., "Jacob L. Morewitz, Eleanor Roosevelt and the Steamship *Quanza*" (Senior Lawyers Conference), reprinted at http://www.vsb.org/docs/valawyermagazine/vl0408_quanza.pdf; Feingold, *The Politics of Rescue*, 144; Breitman et al., *Refugees and Rescue*, 210; Goodwin, *No Ordinary Time*, 174. Some of the accounts suggest that 83 passengers got off.

31. Israel, *The War Diary of Breckinridge Long*, 131, 134; Feingold, *The Politics of Rescue*, 143–44.

32. Goodwin, *No Ordinary Time*, 175–76; Breitman et al., *Refugees and Rescue*, 299; Wyman, *The Abandonment of the Jews*, 315; Manchester, *The Glory and the Dream*, 93 (quoting former Democratic Presidential candidate Adlai Stevenson); Israel, *The War Diary of Breckinridge Long*, 282 (emphasis in original).

33. Israel, *The War Diary of Breckinridge Long*, 196, 216–17.

34. Wyman, *The Abandonment of the Jews*, 123; "Warsaw Ghetto Uprising," *Holocaust Encyclopedia*, United States Holocaust Memorial Museum, available at http://www.ushmm.org/wlc/en/article.php?ModuleId=10005188; Tikva Fatal Kna'ani, "Zivia Lubetkin," Jewish Women's Archive, available at http://jwa.org/encyclopedia/article/lubetkin–zivia.; Kurzman, *The Bravest Battle*, 309, 334.

35. Wyman, *The Abandonment of the Jews*, 119, 121–23; Borden Reams to James Dunn, July 15, 1943, FW 740.00116/ EW1939/1008 (attaching draft of letter from Cordell Hull to Max Lerner of the Emergency Conference to Save the Jewish People of Europe [later Emergency Committee]).

36. Wise and others to Welles, June 1, 1943, NA548.G1/198, also found in the American Jewish Committee Archives, Joint Emergency Committee on European Affairs, reprinted in Wyman, *America and the Holocaust*, 5:130; Welles to Long and Hackworth, June 7, 1943, NA548. G1/198; Brandt to Long, June 22, 1943, NA 548.GI /198, also reprinted in Wyman, *America and the Holocaust*, 3:303; Israel, *The War Diary of Breckinridge Long*, 316 (June 23, 1943); Welles to Wise, June 24, 1943, NA 548.GI/198, also found in American Jewish Archives, World Jewish Congress, reprinted in Wyman, *America and the Holocaust*, 5:134.

The intercepted Perlzweig correspondence could not be found either in the National Archives file containing the Brandt memorandum or in the extensive Perlzweig correspondence file in the American Jewish Archives. (November 16, 2010, e-mail to author from Dorothy Smith, coordinator of Archival Activities & Technology, The Jacob Rader Marcus Center of the American Jewish Archives.) In his memorandum to Long, Brandt identified the British correspondent in the intercepted communications as "Barou Easterman"; in doing so, Brandt conflated the names of Noah Barou and Alex Easterman, members of the British section of the World Jewish Congress. See, generally, Pamela Shatzkes, *Holocaust and Rescue: Impotent or Indifferent? Anglo–Jewry 1938–1945* (Palgrave, 2002), 11. According to Long, the recommendations of the Bermuda Conference had not been implemented because "the British have had a little different idea of the program than we have had" (Israel, *The War Diary of Breckinridge Long*, 316).

37. Curt Gentry, *J. Edgar Hoover: The Man and the Secrets* (W. W. Norton, 1991), 308–9.

38. Welles, *Sumner Welles*, 342–43.

39. Orville H. Bullitt, ed., *For the President, Personal and Secret: Correspondence Between Franklin D. Roosevelt and William C. Bullitt* (Houghton Mifflin, 1972), xv–xvi (George F. Kennan's introduction).

40. Billings, *So Close to Greatness*, xi (foreword by the authors), 20, 96–99. Secretary of State Robert Lansing later explained that "Mr. Bullitt, by repeating only a part of my words and by omitting the context, entirely changed the meaning of what was said. My attitude was, and I intended to show it at the time, that the Treaty should be signed and ratified . . . because the restoration of peace was paramount." Lansing resigned several months after Bullitt's testimony (ibid.); Janet Flanner, "Mr. Ambassador," *The New Yorker*, December 17, 1938 (Part II), 23.

41. Billings, *So Close to Greatness*, 110–11, 113–16, 121–22, 202.

42. Flanner, "Mr. Ambassador" (Part II), 26.

43. Billings, *So Close to Greatness*, 202–3; Gellman, *Secret Affairs*, 140; Flanner, "Mr. Ambassador," *The New Yorker*, December 10, 1938 (Part I), 30, 32.

44. Gellman, *Secret Affairs*, 175, 238; Welles, *Sumner Welles*, 245–46.

45. Bullitt, *For the President*, xi–xiii, 512–14.

46. Israel, *The War Diary of Breckinridge Long*, 281.

47. Welles, *Sumner Welles*, 342–43.

48. Ibid., 343–44.

49. Ibid., 342–45; Teague, *Mrs. L.*, 199; Carol Felsenthal, *Princess Alice: The Life and Times of Alice Roosevelt Longworth* (St. Martin's Press, 1988), 194; Lawrence L. Knutson, *Alice Roosevelt Longworth, Wild Thing* (Salon.com, July 7, 1999), available at http://www.salon.com/people/feature/1999/06/07/longworth/.

50. Welles, *Sumner Welles*, 345, quoting Carmel Offie confidential memorandum to Orville H. Bullitt, Benjamin Welles Papers. While Benjamin Welles writes that Bullitt dictated a contemporaneous memorandum of this conversation, the footnote to this assertion in *Sumner Welles* states: "Offie confidential memo to Orville H. Bullitt, Philadelphia, 1970," which appears to describe a memorandum dictated by Bullitt's aide to Bullitt's brother many years after the event. William Bullitt made a contemporaneous record of a similar conversation about Cissy Patterson in early May with Stephen Early, the White House press secretary. Billings, *So Close to Greatness*, 296 (citing memorandum dictated by William Bullitt on May 5, 1943).

51. Letter from Sumner Welles to Mathilde Welles, August 12, 1943, and Sumner Welles to FDR, August 16, 1943, both quoted in Welles, *Sumner Welles*, 347–50; Billings, *So Close to Greatness*, 297.

52. Berle, *Navigating the Rapids,* 829 (recalling the St. Peter conversation in a 1967 diary entry); Welles, *Sumner Welles*, 279, 345 (based on an interview of Adolph Berle in 1970); Billings, *So Close to Greatness*, 297. It's unclear whether Roosevelt actually made the St. Peter remarks to Bullitt. Berle, for example, does not explain why he waited until Bullitt's death in 1967 to mention the conversation with Roosevelt in his diary.

53. Billings, *So Close to Greatness*, 297, 301 (interview with Clare Boothe Luce).

54. The letters to Welles from Jewish leaders are quoted in Gellman, *Secret Affairs*, 330.

CHAPTER XIII   THE FARMER

1. Henry Morgenthau III, *Mostly Morgenthaus: A Family History* (Ticknor & Fields, 1991), 213–17. The boarding school was Phillips Exeter Academy.

2. Morgenthau, *Mostly Morgenthaus*, 174, 179, 213.

3. Ibid., 217–18, 239, 244–45.

4. Ibid., 245–46; Roosevelt to Howe, August 12, 1918, quoted in Morgenthau, *Mostly Morgenthaus*, 246.

5. Morgenthau, *Mostly Morgenthaus*, 220–27; John Morton Blum, *From the Morgenthau Diaries: Years of Crisis, 1928–1938* (Houghton Mifflin, 1959), 7–9.

6. Morgenthau, *Mostly Morgenthaus*, 245–49.

7. John W. Jeffries, General Introduction, Henry Morgenthau Jr. and The Morgenthau Diaries (Microfilm Project of University Publications of America, 2000), x, available at http://www.lexisnexis.com/documents/academic/upa_cis/9691_MorgDiariesDepression.pdf; Morgenthau, *Mostly Morgenthaus*, 250.

8. Ibid., 250.

9. Ibid., 257, 301; John Morton Blum, *From the Morgenthau Diaries: Years of Urgency, 1938–1941* (Houghton Mifflin, 1965), 3.

10. Morgenthau, *Mostly Morgenthaus*, 256–57, 262–63, 267–68, 272–73. In the first

Roosevelt gubernatorial term, Henry Jr. also was appointed to a seat (vacated by Roosevelt) on the Taconic State Parkway Commission.

11. Blum, *Years of Urgency*, 49; Kissinger, *Diplomacy*, 379, 381; Smith, *FDR*, 424–25, 428; Stuart, *The Department of State*, 337–38; David Faber, *Munich, 1938: Appeasement and World War II* (Simon & Schuster, 2008), 7, 399.

12. Blum, *Years of Urgency*, 98, 200; Kissinger, *Diplomacy*, 378, 385–87 ("No contemporary president could resort to Roosevelt's methods and remain in office."); Smith, *FDR*, 482.

13. Blum, *Years of Urgency*, 149–55; Smith, *FDR*, 447–48.

14. Blum, *Years of Urgency*, 205–6; Manchester, *The Glory and the Dream*, 229; Joseph E. Persico, *Roosevelt's Secret War: FDR and World War II Espionage* (Random House, 2001), 66.

15. Manchester, *The Glory and the Dream*, 229–30; Kissinger, *Diplomacy*, 370; Goodwin, *No Ordinary Time*, 193–95; Smith, *FDR*, 483–87 (describing how, when the State Department crossed off the phrase "many of them in high places" in a draft of the speech, Roosevelt insisted it stay in, telling his speechwriter, "In fact, I'm very much tempted to say, 'many of them in high places, especially in the State Department'"); Blum, *Years of Urgency*, 208–9, 211.

16. Blum, *Years of Urgency*, 234.

17. Morgenthau Diaries, Book 694, 108–9 (January 15, 1944, 9:30 AM).

18. Jeffries, General Introduction, x–xi (quoting from Morgenthau's *New York Times* obituary).

19. Morgenthau Presidential Diaries, Part II, 1200 (December 3, 1942). Due to space considerations, the transcripts quoted in this book have been edited.

20. Morgenthau Presidential Diaries, Part II, 1020–21 (November 26, 1941). See Theodore S. Hamerow, *Why We Watched: Europe, America, and the Holocaust* (W. W. Norton, 2008), 268 (describing how Roosevelt told his cabinet in the fall of 1941 that he had received a letter from a friend in Portland, Oregon, "who complained about some Jews on the Bonneville [Dam] staff without mentioning them." Roosevelt commented that he was not surprised by the complaint because Portland was a "transplanted Maine city where Jews were not popular" [citing *The Secret Diary of Harold L. Ickes*, 3:644]). Roosevelt also stated that he had discussed his concerns with Morgenthau's father, who agreed that the matter should be taken up with the Harvard Board of Overseers; *Morgenthau Presidential Diaries*, Part II, 1020–21, (November 26, 1941). Roosevelt was apparently referring to Harvard University's successful policy in the 1920s to reduce the number of Jewish students from 25 percent of the student body to 15 percent. See Karabel, *The Chosen*, 105–7, 109 (describing how a Yale dean learned that "they [Harvard] are also going to reduce their 25% Hebrew total to 15% or less by simply rejecting without detailed explanation. They are giving no details to any candidate any longer.").

21. Morgenthau, *Mostly Morgenthaus*, 306–7.

22. Morgenthau Presidential Diaries, Part II, 1242–44, 1255–60 (note dated July 30, 1943); "The Cabinet: Friendly Words," *Time* magazine (November 22, 1937).
23. Morgenthau Presidential Diaries, Part II, 1039–39A (December 7, 1941) (6:40 PM).
24. Acheson, *Present at the Creation*, 22; Bernard Bernstein Oral History Interview, Truman Library, July 23, 1975, 4–5, available at http://www.trumanlibrary.org/oralhist/bernsten.htm.
25. Medoff, *Blowing the Whistle on Genocide*, 16; Morse, *While Six Million Died*, 92; Morgenthau, *Mostly Morgenthaus*, 323.
26. Morgenthau Diaries, Book 688, Part I, 85–86 (memorandum from Paul to Morgenthau, November 2, 1943); Reams to Long & Matthews, October 25, 1943, SD862.4016/2292, reprinted in Wyman, *America and the Holocaust*, 6:70; see Long memorandum of conversation with John Pehle, October 28, 1943, VD862.4016/2292, reprinted in Wyman, *America and the Holocaust*, 6:69.
27. Morgenthau Diaries, Book 688, Part I, 85–86 (memorandum from Paul to Morgenthau, November 2, 1943); Morse, *While Six Million Died*, 82.
28. Stettinius to American Legation (Bern), October 26, 1943, SD 862.4016/2292, reprinted in Wyman, *America and the Holocaust*, 6:72.
29. Two months later, Treasury Department officials recognized that Harrison had hedged his bets in the bureaucratic battle. They discussed demonstrating to Harrison their success in pressuring the State Department to stop blocking the rescue efforts. "I was thinking that he can get the feel[ing] that the tide is changing," said Ansel Luxford of Harrison. Morgenthau Diaries, Book 693, 84 (meeting of January 12, 1944, 10:45 AM).
30. Morgenthau Diaries, Book 688, Part I, 109–10 (British Embassy to John Pehle, dated November 13, 1943, and Bern Legation to Secretary of State, November 14, 1943 [paraphrase]).
31. Morgenthau Diaries, Book 685, 111–18 (November 23, 1943, 2:45 PM).
32. Morgenthau Diaries, Book 688, Part I, 134–36 (Morgenthau to Hull, November 24, 1943).
33. Morgenthau Diaries, Book 685, 84–87 (Hull to Morgenthau, December 6, 1943).
34. Morgenthau Diaries, Book 688, Part I, 174–75 (draft letter from Morgenthau to Hull), 179–89 (telephone call between Paul and Morgenthau) (December 6, 1943, 9:33 AM).
35. Morgenthau Diaries, Book 688, Part II, 99–100 (DuBois to files, December 18, 1943, 1); Medoff, *Blowing the Whistle on Genocide*, 13–14, 21–22, 37 n. 25.
36. Morgenthau Diaries, Book 688, Part II, 66–75 (Paul to Morgenthau, December 17, 1943). Both DuBois's and Luxford's initials appear at the end of the draft memorandum.

37. Morgenthau Diaries, Book 688, Part I, 198–202 (DuBois to files, December 9, 1943).
38. Morgenthau Diaries, Book 688, Part II, 1–19 (December 13, 1943, 3:00 PM).
39. Morgenthau Diaries, Book 688, Part II, 47–A (G. F. Thorold to Pehle, December 13, 1943).
40. Morgenthau Diaries, Book 688, Part II, 50–62 (December 17, 1943, 10:30 AM).

CHAPTER XIV   THE ORPHANS OF TRANSNISTRIA

1. Shachan, *Burning Ice*, 255; see I. C. Butnaru, *The Silent Holocaust: Romania and Its Jews* (Greenwood Press, 1992), 144 ("Living a vagabond existence, naked, hungry, sick and uncared for, these children presented a living image accusing a criminal regime of unforgivable deeds.").
2. Shachan, *Burning Ice*, 255–57; Ioanid, *The Holocaust in Romania*, 220.
3. Medwed, *Live! Remember! Tell the World!* 83.
4. Gold, *Ruth's Journey*, 87–88.
5. Ibid.
6. Shachan, *Burning Ice*, 261 (describing the conditions and the volunteers at the Bershad orphanage).
7. Gold, *Ruth's Journey*, 89–90.
8. Ibid.

CHAPTER XV   CABLE 354

1. Morgenthau Diaries, Book 688, Part II, 48–49 (Ambassador Winant to the Secretary of State, December 15, 1943) (transmitting contents of letter from the Ministry of Economic Warfare that described the Foreign Office position on the Romanian rescue plan).
2. Morgenthau Diaries, Book 688, Part II, 82–94 (December 18, 1943, 12:00 PM).
3. Morgenthau Diaries, Book 688, Part II, 99–100 (DuBois memorandum to files, December 18, 1943), 223M ("The initialed file copy of the cable indicates that the men responsible were Atherton and Dunn as well as Durbrow and Hickerson.") (Memorandum: For Secretary Morgenthau's Information Only).

CHAPTER XVI   "THIS MOVEMENT TO LET THE JEWS BE KILLED"

1. Morgenthau Diaries, Book 688, Part II, 103–32 (December 19, 1943, 5:30 PM; and draft "Memorandum for Secretary Hull"). One of the participants in this meeting, Oscar Cox, assistant solicitor general of the United States, observed that the House Foreign Affairs Committee was considering a resolution to create a "special commission" to handle the refugee problem. For several months,

Cox had been pressing for such a "War Refugee Rescue Committee" to handle refugee issues and bypass the State Department. See Cox to Stettinius, October 13, 1943, SD 840.48/Refugees/5129, reprinted in Wyman, *America and the Holocaust*, vol. 6, 128–35. A proposal was even drafted by Milton Handler, a special counsel at the Foreign Economic Administration. Medoff, *Blowing the Whistle on Genocide*, 25.

2. Morgenthau Diaries, Book 688, Part II, 134–41 (December 20, 1943, 9:00 AM).
3. Morgenthau Diaries, Book 688, Part II, 133–42 (December 20, 1943, 9:00 AM, and cable dated April 20, 1943, from Harrison to Hull).
4. The license was ultimately conveyed to Gerhart Riegner, who sent a message to the U.S. legation to convey to a Jewish leader in the United States. "I have received from the American Legation the license and your authorization to act in accordance therewith, together with the Swiss franc equivalent of $25,000. I highly appreciate your prompt action and the attitude of the American authorities." Morgenthau Diaries, Book 692, 222 (paraphrase of January 8, 1944 cable from the American Legation to Hull). The reference by Riegner to his "appreciation" for the "the attitude" of the American authorities has a ring of veiled irony. See Henry Morgenthau Jr., "The Morgenthau Diaries VI—The Refugee Run-Around," *Collier's* (November 1, 1947), 62.
5. Morgenthau Diaries, Book 688, Part II, 148–71 (December 20, 1943, 10:30 AM).
6. Morgenthau Diaries, Book 688, Part II, 172–85 (December 20, 1943, 2:25 PM).
7. Morgenthau Diaries, Book 688, Part II, 186–88 (memorandum for the files, December 20, 1943) and 201–5 (2:30 PM); see ibid., 223J–223O (Memorandum: For Secretary Morgenthau's Information Only, December 23, 1943).
8. Morgenthau Diaries, Book 688, Part II, 205–18 (December 21, 1943, 2:30 PM).

Chapter XVII THE CEMETERY OF BERSHAD

1. Gold, *Ruth's Journey*, 91–93, 103–4.
2. Ibid., 93–94.
3. Ibid., 95–98, 103–04.

CHAPTER XVIII MARCH OF THE RABBIS

1. The Holocaust History Project, The Complete Text of the Poznan Speech, available at http://www.holocaust-history.org/himmler-poznan/speech-text.shtml; Breitman, *The Architect of Genocide*, 242–43.
2. Eric Jabotinsky, Emergency Committee, to Leib Altman, October 12, 1943 (Yale University Library, Palestine Statehood Committee Papers, Box 1), reprinted in Wyman, *America and the Holocaust*, 5:82–83; Rafael Medoff, "The Day the Rabbis Marched," the David Wyman Institute for Holocaust Studies,

3. Wyman, *The Abandonment of the Jews*, 193–94.
4. Hearings Before the Committee on Foreign Affairs, Rescue of the Jewish and Other Peoples in Nazi-occupied Territory, House of Representatives, H. Res. 350 and H. Res. 352 (78th Cong.), November 26, 1943, 15 (Testimony of Breckinridge Long).
5. Ibid., 31–33. See Wyman, *The Abandonment of the Jews*, 196 (Long "greatly exaggerated the little that had been attempted since Hitler's rise to power . . .").
6. Hearings Before the Committee on Foreign Affairs, 23, 32–35, 41.
7. Wyman, *The Abandonment of the Jews*, 196–201.
8. Ibid., 196–97, 201.
9. Morgenthau Diaries, Book 693, 212–29 (Report To The Secretary On The Acquiescence Of This Government In The Murder Of The Jews, dated January 13, 1944); Frederick R. Barkley, "580,000 Refugees Admitted to United States in Decade," *New York Times*, December 11, 1943, 1; Wyman, *The Abandonment of the Jews*, 197–98.
10. Israel, *The War Diary of Breckinridge Long*, 334–35.
11. Morgenthau Diaries, Book 688, Part II, 172 (December 20, 1943, 2:25 PM).
12. Fireside Chat of December 24, 1943, reprinted at Fireside Chats of Franklin D. Roosevelt, available at http://www.mhric.org/fdr/chat27.html; Rosenman, *Working with Roosevelt*, 92–93; Frances Perkins, *The Roosevelt I Knew* (Viking Press, 1946), 72; Russell D. Buhite and David W. Levy, eds., *FDR's Fireside Chats* (University of Oklahoma Press, 1992), 272–80.
13. Morgenthau Diaries, Book 688, Part II, 223–223I (December 23, 1943, 3:00 PM); see ibid., 223J–223O (Memorandum: For Secretary Morgenthau's Information Only, December 23, 1943).

CHAPTER XIX THE ACQUIESCENCE OF THIS GOVERNMENT IN THE MURDER OF THE JEWS

1. R. Bruce Craig, *Treasonable Doubt: The Harry Dexter White Spy Case* (University Press of Kansas, 2004), 28–30, 135–37, 146, 212; Harry Dexter White Papers, Princeton University Library, Mudd Manuscript Library, available at http://diglib.princeton.edu/ead/getEad?eadid=MC140&kw=Economic%20history.
2. Morgenthau Diaries, Book 692, 287–91 (January 10, 1944, 3:00 PM). On December 31, 1943, the four aides had reviewed with Morgenthau the history of the State Department's "obviously deliberate acts to prevent action," including the Bermuda Conference. Luxford then told Morgenthau, "I might say there is more indication that Hull isn't the right man to go to on this." Morgenthau

replied, "Well, you still will have to follow my tactics on the thing until he turns me down." Morgenthau Diaries, Book 688, Part II, 249 (December 31, 1943, 11:45 AM).

3. Morgenthau Diaries, Book 693, 212–29 ("Report To The Secretary On The Acquiescence Of This Government On The Murder Of The Jews").

4. Morgenthau Diaries, Book 693, 254 (January 13, 1944, letter to the secretary of war).

5. Morgenthau Diaries, Book 693, 187–211 (January 13, 1944, 11:00 AM).

6. *Time* magazine, "The Presidency: The Roosevelt Week," July 19, 1937, available at http://www.time.com/time/magazine/article/0,9171,882733,00.html; Morgenthau Diaries, Book 693, 205–11 (January 13, 1944, 11:33 AM).

7. William Lasser, *Benjamin V. Cohen: Architect of the New Deal* (The Century Foundation, 2002), x (foreword by Richard C. Leone), xi–xii (preface by Arthur Schlesinger Jr.), 3, 23, 210, 259; Manchester, *The Glory and the Dream*, 105.

8. Morgenthau Diaries, Book 694, 111–18, 194–202 ("Personal Report To The President").

9. Morgenthau Diaries, Book 694, 59–110 (January 15, 1944, 9:30 AM).

10. Morgenthau Diaries, Book 694, 148–51 (January 15, 1944, 12:49 PM).

11. Morgenthau, *Mostly Morgenthaus*, 327 n.; Medoff, *Blowing the Whistle on Genocide*, 53. (DuBois was referring to "Report To The Secretary On The Acquiescence Of This Government On The Murder Of The Jews.")

12. Gunther, *Roosevelt in Retrospect*, 117.

13. Morgenthau Diaries, Book 694, 190–93 (memorandum from John Pehle for the Treasury Secretary's files (January 16, 1941).

14. Record of a Conversation Between Nahum Goldmann, World Jewish Congress, and Isaiah Berlin, British Embassy, November 11, 1943, British Government, Public Record Office FO 371/35041 XC/AO47702, reprinted in Wyman, *America and the Holocaust*, 5:104.

15. White House Press Release, January 22, 1944, Jewish Virtual Library, available at http://www.jewishvirtuallibrary.org/jsource/Holocaust/wrb1.html.

CHAPTER XX WHY DIDN'T YOU COME SOONER?

1. Ira Hirschmann, *Caution to the Winds* (David McKay, 1962), 155; Jan Whitaker, *Service and Style: How the American Department Store Fashioned the Middle Class* (St. Martin's Press, 2006), 309 (describing how in 1941 Bloomingdale's Vice President Ira Hirschmann organized a furniture design contest with the Museum of Modern Art).

2. Hirschmann, *Caution to the Winds*, 9, 14, 132–34.

3. Wyman, *The Abandonment of the Jews*, 210.

4. Mann, WRB, London, to Pehle, Director, WRB, September 19, 1944 (FDRL, War Refugee Board, Box 70), reprinted in Wyman, *America and the Holocaust*, 9:33; Rapoport, *Shake Heaven and Earth*, 153.
5. Hirschmann, *Caution to the Winds*, 134–40, 152–59.
6. Gold, *Ruth's Journey*, 116 (Ruth Glasberg's translation). According to Radu Ioanid, the repatriation of 1,846 orphans to Romania took place on March 6, 1944, which may have preceded Hirschmann's meeting with Cretzianu. However, the fact that soon five ships were carrying thousands of orphans to Palestine was due to Hirschmann's deal with Cretzianu. Another important factor was the efforts of Wilhelm Filderman, a Romanian Jew who had once been a classmate of Mihai Antonescu, a distant relative of Marshal Ion Antonescu and the vice president of the Council of Ministers. Filderman tirelessly lobbied the Romanian government to repatriate the Transnistrian Jews. Ioanid, *The Holocaust in Romania*, 32–33, 252–53, 256–57 ("Cretzianu brought an answer from Ion and Mihai Antonescu and soon five ships were carrying about three thousand Jewish orphans to Palestine. . . . Officials repatriated 10,744 Romanian Jews from Transnistria at this time, including 1,846 orphaned children, approximately one-fifth surviving as of fall 1943.").
7. Gold, *Ruth's Journey*, 107, 112–17.
8. Hirschmann, *Caution to the Winds*, 159.

AFTERWORD

1. "The War Refugee Board," The United States Holocaust Memorial Museum, available at http://www.ushmm.org/wlc/article.php?lang=en&ModuleId=10007409; Hirschmann, *Caution to the Winds*, 131–32; Wyman, *The Abandonment of the Jews*, 211, 213–14, 241, 287; John Morton Blum, *From the Morgenthau Diaries: Years of War 1941–1945* (Houghton Mifflin, 1967), 223; Medoff, *Blowing the Whistle on Genocide*, 101 (McCloy to Pehle, July 4, 1944), 104 (McCloy to Kubowitzki, August 14, 1944); "US Leaders From Both Parties Agree: America Should Have Bombed Auschwitz," the David S. Wyman Institute for Holocaust Studies, available at http://www.wymaninstitute.org/bombedauschwitz.php; see "Bush—U.S. Should Have Acted on Auschwitz," MSNBC.com, January 11, 2008, available at http://www.msnbc.msn.com/id/22616187/page/2/.
2. Manvell and Fraenkel, *Heinrich Himmler*, 240–48, Albert Speer, *Inside the Third Reich: Memoirs by Albert Speer* (Simon & Schuster, 1970), 512; Gilbert, *The Holocaust*, 18, 824.
3. Riegner, *Never Despair*, 434; Glare Nullis, "Gerhart Riegner, warned of Holocaust," *Miami Herald*, December 5, 2001.
4. Ashburn, *Peabody of Groton*, 387; Gunther, *Roosevelt in Retrospect*, 175; The Groton School website: http://www.groton.org/home/content.asp?id=1.
5. Gellman, *Secret Affairs*, 361, 383–84; Presentation Speech by Gunner Jahn,

Chairman of the Nobel Committee, December 10, 1945, available at http://nobelprize.org/nobel_prizes/peace/laureates/1945/press.html; see Michael Dobbs, *Madeleine Albright: A Twentieth-Century Odyssey* (Henry Holt, 2000), 6.

6. Welles, *Sumner Welles*, 219, 373, 379–80.
7. Billings, *So Close to Greatness*, 306–32 (also quoting George T. Boswell, who wrote a doctoral dissertation on Bullitt).
8. Israel, *The War Diary of Breckinridge Long*, xxiv (introduction by Israel), 336–37, 391.
9. *University of Chicago Law School News*, "Professor Emeritus Bernard D. Meltzer Dies At Age 92," available at http://www–news.uchicago.edu/releases/07/070104.meltzer.shtml; The Pulitzer Prizes, 1961 Winners, available at http://www.pulitzer.org/awards/1961.
10. Elmer Plischke, *U.S. Department of State: A Reference History* (Greenwood Press, 1999), 303; John D. Hickerson Oral History, Truman Library, November 10, 1972, January 26 and June 5, 1973; Wolfgang Saxon, "Elbridge Durbrow, U.S. Diplomat, Dies at 93," *New York Times*, May 23, 1997, A25; Hirschmann, *Caution to the Winds*, 213, 216, 286, 287–88; Morse, *While Six Million Died*, 32. The comment regarding Reams's standing in the State Department came from Ira Hirschmann, who apparently was not aware of Reams's wartime role in blocking the rescue of Jews.
11. Wood and Jankowski, *Karski*, 193, 216, 236, 238, 246–47, 259; Michael T. Kaufman, "Jan Karski Dies at 86: Warned West About Holocaust," *New York Times*, July 15, 2000, C15.
12. Voss, *Stephen S. Wise*, 282, 296–97 (letter from Albert Einstein to James Waterman Wise and Justine Wise Polier, April 25, 1949).
13. Rapoport, *Shake Heaven and Earth*, 199, 206–9; see Stephanie Flanders, "Peter Bergson, Who Helped European Jews, Dies at 86," *New York Times*, August 20, 2001, B6.
14. Gold, *Ruth's Journey*, 286.
15. Brandon and Lower, *The Shoah in Ukraine*, 157.
16. Ioanid, *The Holocaust in Romania*, 3–4; Wyman, *The Abandonment of the Jews*, 220 n.
17. Acheson, *Present at the Creation*, 103; Buhite and Levy, *FDR's Fireside Chats*, xx (introduction); Gunther, *Roosevelt in Retrospect*, 131 (quoting columnist Samuel Grafton); Gilbert, *The Holocaust*, 18.
18. Morgenthau, *Mostly Morgenthaus*, 402–4, 411.
19. Lash, *Eleanor and Franklin*, 929; Manchester, *The Glory and the Dream*, 93.
20. "John W. Pehle," *The Washington Post*, March 27, 1999, 35. Profiles in Tax History: Randolph E. Paul, October 6, 2004, The Tax History Project, available at http://www.taxhistory.org/thp/readings.nsf/cf7c9c870b600b9585256df80075b9dd/afd2a67073f6b87085256f8600681f74?OpenDocument; Medoff,

Blowing the Whistle on Genocide, 131–35; Ansel F. Luxford Papers (Administrative/Biographical History), Bretton Woods Conference Collection, IMF Archives, available at http://www.imf.org/external/np/arc/eng/fa/bwc/s2.htm; Congress Passes Rep. Woolsey Bill Honoring Government Officials Who Rescued Countless Number From the Holocaust, http://woolsey.house.gov/index.cfm?sectionid=18&parentid=6&sectiontree=6,18&itemid=255.

INDEX

A

Acheson, Dean, 55–57, 59, 62, 75, 77, 79, 94, 171, 202, 277
"The Acquiescence Of This Government" report, 252–54, 256, 261
Alexander, Robert C., 167
Algeria, 82–84
American Jewish community. *See also* Bergson, Peter H.; Wise, Stephen
    Bermuda Conference and, 167
    censorship of, 144–45
    letters to State Department, 181–82
    meeting with FDR, 116, 126–28
    public awareness campaigns, 114–16, 127–29, 132–36, 143–44, 146, 240–42
    rabbis march on Washington, DC, 240–42
    refugee support by, 268, 271
    on U.S. rescue resolution, 244, 245
    on Warsaw ghetto murders, 102–3
    on Welles resignation, 190–91
American Jewish Conference, 134, 244
American Jewish Congress, 43, 136
    anti-Semitism
    in America, 60–61, 77–78
    in Europe, 44, 82
    Riegner's story, 18
    at State Department, 3, 4, 65–68, 121, 170, 215, 231, 257
Antonescu, Ion, 34–35, 277
Appleby, Paul, 80–84, 151

aristocracy in America. *See also* Groton School
    anti-Semitism, 3, 60–61, 77–78
    Christianity and, 3, 5, 52–54, 56, 57, 60–62, 88, 206, 211
    diplomatic corps and, 50–53, 62–68
    disdain for lower classes, 60–61, 64–65
    State Department personnel, 3, 5, 62, 64, 67
Atherton, Ray. *See also* Division of European Affairs
    background, 79–80
    Bermuda Conference, 167
    blocking rescue efforts, 85–86, 101, 128–31, 148, 214
    cable 354 and, 141, 225, 235
    as minister to Canada, 169, 274
    Peyrouton affair, 81–83
Auschwitz concentration camp, 27–29, 158

B

Barou, Noah, 144, 145
Ben-Gurion, David, 266
Bergson, Peter H., 132–36, 141, 143, 146, 241–42, 244, 276
Berle, Adolf A., 75–77, 79, 95–98, 157–58, 172, 189–90
Bermuda Conference, 166–69, 181
Biddle, Francis, 183
Biddle, George, 60–61, 120
Bloom, Sol, 166, 168
Bracht, Fritz, 27, 30–31

Brandt, George, 144–45, 153–54, 214
Britain
Bermuda Conference, 166–69, 181
    children's evacuation from, 173–74, 177
    Czechoslovakia and, 197–98
    FDR's war aid to, 198–202
    license approval delays, 207–9, 214–18, 226–29, 231, 233
    London bombings, 201
    reply to rescue plan, 222–24
    Struma incident, 99–100
    war crimes statement, 131–32
Bullitt, William C., 66–67, 95, 96, 122, 183–90, 274

C
cable 2460, 148–49, 212, 227, 229
cables 354 and 482
    authors, 141–42, 147, 157, 235
    Harrison's frustration, 148–49, 212
    Hiss and, 212–15
    as incriminating evidence, 225, 242, 257–58, 260–61, 262
    text of, 14–16, 142, 225
    Treasury's discovery, 9, 13–16, 212–13, 222–25, 227, 229–30, 232–36, 247
Cannon, Cavendish W., 68
Carr, Wilbur, 66
Celler, Emanuel, 245
censorship, 46, 144–45, 258
Chamberlain, Neville, 44, 97, 197
Churchill, Winston, 26, 42–43, 47, 187, 197, 199, 246
Ciechanowski, Jan, 157, 158, 159
Clinton, Bill, 271
Cohen, Ben, 256, 257–59, 260
concentration camps, 4, 18, 27–29, 139, 158–59, 275
Coolidge, Calvin, 94
Cretzianu, Alexandre, 267–70, 277
Culbertson, Paul, 85–86

Czechoslovakia, 44, 122–23, 197–98

D
Division of European Affairs. *See also* Atherton, Ray
    blocking rescue efforts, 128–30
    cables 354 and 482, 141–42, 225, 235
    culture, 64–65, 67, 78–79
    Long's influence, 169, 190
    Riegner telegram conspiracy, 85–86, 90, 148
    Romanian rescue proposal, 147, 152, 207–8
Doris (Schulte's mistress), 39, 272
DuBois, Josiah E., Jr.
    cable 354 discovery, 212–13, 224–25, 227
    character, 206, 211–12
    honors, 278
    Meltzer and, 156, 213–14
    postwar and death, 278
    on State Department obstruction, 211–18, 222–25, 230, 232, 234–36, 247–49, 251–54, 258, 260, 261
    on War Refugee Board, 266, 271
Dunn, James, 141, 172, 235, 274–75
Durbrow, Elbridge, 86, 141, 157, 275

E
Easterman, Alex, 144, 145
Eden, Anthony, 132, 139–40, 229
education, 63, 65, 175–76. *See also* Groton School
Eichmann, Adolf, 27, 28, 268
Einstein, Albert, 173, 276
Eisenhower, Dwight D., 81–84
Elting, Howard, Jr., 46–47

F
FDR. *See* Roosevelt, Franklin Delano

Feis, Herbert, 150–51, 154, 156, 213, 230–32, 274
Fish, Hamilton, 130, 217
"For Sale to Humanity" ad, 143–44, 146
"For Secretary Morgenthau's Information Only" memo, 247–52, 256, 261
France, 82, 84, 149, 150, 151, 153, 179, 197, 206, 271
Frank, Anne family, 125–26
Frankfurter, Felix, 90, 102, 103, 157, 266

G
Georgetown School of Foreign Service, 63, 65
Germany and Nazi Party. *See also* Hitler, Adolf
  expansionism by, 19, 23, 44, 95, 97–98, 122–23, 197
  leadership, 24–25
  London bombings by, 201
  Munich Conference, 44, 123, 197–98
  Schulte's dislike of Nazis, 21–23
  U.S. aid to Britain against, 198–202
Gerry, Mathilde Townsend, 93–94
Gerson, Walter, 19
Giesche, 20–24, 27, 30, 41
Glasberg, Ruth, 4, 36–37, 69–71, 110–13, 161–64, 219–21, 237–39, 268–69, 276
Goebbels, Joseph, 24, 25, 120, 122, 201, 272
Goodwin, Doris Kearns, 13, 124, 201
Göring, Hermann, 21–22, 24, 25, 30, 96–97, 119, 272
Great Britain. *See* Britain
Great Depression, 116–19, 120
Grew, Joseph, 50–51, 62, 63, 65, 66
Groton School. *See also* Peabody, Endicott
  Allenswood compared with, 175–76
  alumni careers, 57, 62–63, 64–65, 75
  Anglo-Saxon superiority views, 56, 60–61, 121, 175

life at, 53–56, 58–59
present day, 273

H
Harrison, Leland
  cable 354 and, 148–49, 212, 225
  cable 2460, 227
  Riegner meeting with, 106–9
  Riegner's telegram and, 47, 90, 105
  Romanian rescue proposal, 147–51, 154, 160, 207–10, 212, 215
Hickerson, John D., 141, 275
Himmler, Heinrich, 24–31, 104, 240–41, 272
Hirschmann, Ira, 265–70, 277
Hiss, Donald, 212–15, 224–25, 235, 236
Hitler, Adolf. *See also* Germany and Nazi Party
  death, 272
  extermination of Jews, 19, 26–27, 39, 44–46, 106–9, 115, 131, 158
  on FDR, 120
  Schulte on, 21–22
Holocaust. *See also* Glasberg, Ruth; refugees; Romanian rescue proposal
  America's response, 1–6, 78, 79, 116, 121–22, 129, 271, 277–79
  concentration camps, 4, 18, 27–29, 139, 158–59, 275
  deaths, 272, 276
  FDR's failings, 1, 5, 116, 121–22, 277
  Himmler's speech, 240–41
  Hitler's plan, 19, 26–27, 39, 44–46, 106–9, 115, 131, 158
  Karski's story, 136–40, 157–59
  Kristallnacht, 44, 124
  public awareness campaigns, 114–16, 127–29, 132–36, 146, 240–42
  recent parallels, 5–6, 278–79
  State Department response, 2–6, 16, 128–32, 140–42, 232–33

Hoover, Herbert, 87, 135
Hoover, J. Edgar, 183, 187
Höss, Rudolf, 26–32, 44–45, 107, 272
Hull, Cordell
    blaming Riegner for delay, 210, 211–18
    character, 72–75, 77
    FDR and, 5, 76
    Jewish issues avoidance, 77–78
    on Karski's visit with FDR, 159
    Morgenthau's meeting with, 226–30
    Peyrouton affair, 80–84
    postwar and death, 263, 273
    rivalry with Welles, 3–4, 75–78, 94, 96, 185–86
    Romanian rescue proposal, 153–56, 210–16, 223–24, 258–59
    as Secretary of State, 75–77, 78, 95, 229
    Welles demise and, 183–84, 186–90
Hull, Frances, 77–78, 224

I
Ickes, Harold, 78, 171–72
immigration policy. *See under* State Department
Israel, 266, 275, 276

J
Japanese-Americans, 123–24
Jewish Agency for Palestine, 43, 106, 147
Jewish people. *See* American Jewish community; anti-Semitism; Glasberg, Ruth; Holocaust; Romanian rescue proposal
Joint Emergency Committee for European Jewish Affairs, 181–82

K
Karski (Kozielewski), Jan, 136–40, 157–59, 275
Katz, Moishe, 36
Kersten, Felix, 25, 30

Kissinger, Henry, 119, 198
Kook, Hillel. *See* Bergson, Peter H.
Koppelmann, Isidor, 38–42, 45, 47

L
Laqueur, Walter, 22, 281
Lash, Joseph, 119, 174–76
Latvia, 105, 107
League of Nations, 19, 184
Lehman, Herbert, 126–27, 196
Lend-Lease program, 200–202
Levi, Primo, 25, 28–29
Lichtheim, Richard, 106–7, 140
Long, Breckinridge
    attitude toward Jews, 134, 170–71, 231
    background, 75, 169–70
    Bermuda Conference, 166–69
    cables 354 and 482 cover-up, 229, 232–35, 242, 257
    Congressional testimony, 243–46
    diary usage, 79, 170–71, 177, 180, 233, 245–46, 274
    on FDR, 180
    FDR on, 262
    on Hull, 74
    license issuance by, 229, 230
    Morgenthau meeting with, 229–31
    on *Quanza* incident, 177–79
    on refugee immigration, 67, 170–74, 177–82
    Romanian rescue proposal, 78, 145, 150–51, 153–54, 156, 207, 214, 229, 233, 263
    on War Refugee Board, 274
    on Welles, 186–87
Longworth, Alice Roosevelt, 49, 188
Lubetkin, Zivia, 165–66, 180
Luxford, Ansel F.
    character, 206
    postwar and death, 278

on State Department obstruction, 214, 216, 218, 223–25, 228, 230–36, 254–55, 258

M

Meltzer, Bernard, 151–54, 156, 213, 230–32, 274

Mercer, Lucy, 176, 278

Moffat, Jay Pierrepont, 65, 66, 79, 80, 97

Morgenthau, Elinor, 194–95, 196, 226

Morgenthau, Henry, Jr.
  "The Acquiescence of this Government" report, 252–54, 256, 261
  background, 192–93
  British war aid, 199–202
  cables 354 and 482, 232–36
  diaries, 204–6
  FDR and, 5, 193–97, 277–78
  "For Secretary Morgenthau's Information Only" memo, 247–52, 256, 261
  honors, 278
  Jewish issues sensitivity, 217–18, 231
  job insecurity beliefs, 121, 196, 202–3, 205
  meeting with FDR, 261–63
  meeting with Hull, 226–30
  meeting with Long, 230–31
  "Personal Report To The President," 256–64
  on Riegner's telegram, 103–4
  Romanian rescue proposal, 146, 155–56, 209–11, 215–18, 222–24
  as Treasury Secretary, 7, 197, 204–6
  War Refugee Board, 266

Morgenthau, Henry, Sr., 192–93, 194, 195, 197, 289

Morgenthau, Henry III, 195–96, 197, 204, 278

Murphy, Robert, 81, 84

N

Nazi Party. *See* Germany and Nazi Party; Hitler, Adolf

the Netherlands, 97, 107

New York Times, 49, 119, 120, 132, 245

North Africa, 81–84, 101, 167, 211, 214

Nuremberg Tribunal, 272, 274, 278

O

orphanages, 219–21, 237–39, 268–69

P

Paul, Randolph E.
  character, 152–53, 206
  meeting with FDR, 261
  postwar and death, 278
  on State Department obstruction, 211, 216, 218, 222–23, 228, 230, 232–33, 236, 248, 252, 253–55, 257, 260

Peabody, Endicott
  character, 53–54, 88
  death, 273
  on diplomatic service, 52–53, 56–57
  on FDR, 56, 273
  FDR wedding and, 49
  as Groton headmaster, 54–61
  personal moral views, 57–58, 60–61
  Souvestre contrasted with, 175–76

Pehle, John
  character, 206
  honors, 278
  meeting with FDR, 261–62
  postwar and death, 278
  Riegner's license approval, 207–9
  on State Department obstruction, 215–18, 222–23, 227–28, 230, 232–33, 235–36, 248, 251, 256, 257, 259
  Treasury Department role, 151
  on War Refugee Board, 266

"Personal Report To The President" (Morgenthau), 256–64

Peyrouton, Marcel, 81–84
Phillips, William, 62, 66, 92
Poland
    deportations and murders, 101, 102–3, 104, 105, 107, 137–39, 145
    invasion of, 19, 23, 95
    Karski's story, 136–40, 157–59, 275
    refugees, 65
    Warsaw ghetto, 4, 102–3, 159, 165–66, 180
President's Advisory Committee on Political Refugees, 173, 178–79, 245
Price, Byron, 145

Q
Quanza incident, 177–79

R
Reams, R. Borden, 128–32, 141, 152, 167, 169, 181, 208, 214, 243, 275
refugees. *See also* Romanian rescue proposal
    Bermuda Conference, 166–69, 181
    censorship of cables about, 144–45
    independent rescue plan, 223, 241–42, 254–55
    Quanza incident, 177–79
    Struma incident, 100–101
    U.S. Congress debates, 242–46
    Virgin Islands plan, 171–72
"Report To The Secretary On The Acquiescence Of This Government In The Murder Of The Jews," 252–54, 256, 261
Riegner, Gerhart. *See also* Riegner telegram of August 1942
    background, 18
    Hull's blame of, for delay, 210, 211–18
    license for funds transfer, 150–54, 156, 160, 206–10, 213–17, 229, 232
    meeting with Harrison, 106–7
    meeting with Koppelmann, 45
    meeting with Sagalowitz, 17–18, 43–44

    postwar and death, 272–73
    reports from Europe by, 105–7, 147–49
    on Wise, 102
Riegner telegram of August 1942. *See also* cables 354 and 482
    confirmation of, 108–9, 115, 127–31, 132, 142
    State Department handling of, 46–47, 85–87, 90, 101–9, 141, 149–50
    text of, 45
Romania. *See also* Glasberg, Ruth
    Bershad, 110–13, 220, 237–39, 268–69
    communist government, 277
    Czernowitz, 36–37, 111, 163, 220, 237, 269
    deaths, 107, 140, 276
    Dniester River march, 34–37, 69–71, 86
    gypsies, 28, 70
    orphans, 219–21, 237–39, 268–69
Romanian rescue proposal. *See also* Riegner, Gerhart; Treasury-State Department confrontation
    FDR's approval, 154–56, 159–60
    "For Sale to Humanity" ad, 143–44, 146
    Hirschmann's plan, 267–69
    State's blockage of, 2, 6, 68, 140–42, 146–50, 152–56, 160, 167, 225
Roosevelt, Alice, 49, 188
Roosevelt, Eleanor
    battles with Long, 177–79
    death, 278
    FDR contrasted with, 174–77
    on FDR's death, 278
    Hitler on, 120
    on Japanese relocation, 123
    Jewish refugee support, 100, 135–36, 173, 179
    Morgenthaus and, 194–95
    Quanza incident and, 178–79
    wedding, 48–50
    Welles' friendship with, 3, 92

Roosevelt, Franklin Delano (FDR) and administration
Anglo-Saxon superiority views, 121
British war aid by, 198–202
Bullitt and, 185–86
character, 120–22, 176
childhood, 176
death, 120, 261, 277
Eleanor contrasted with, 174–77
fear of fifth columnists, 122–24, 201
Great Depression and, 116–19, 120
Groton and, 55, 56, 59
health issues, 119–20, 176–77, 261
Hitler on, 120
Holocaust failings, 1, 5, 116, 121–22, 277
immigration policy, 124–26, 159, 171, 173
inauguration, 116–18
Jewish appointments by, 120–21
Jewish delegation meeting with, 116, 126–28
on Jewish issues, 203–4
Karski meeting with, 157, 158–59
Lend-Lease program, 200–202
Morgenthau and, 5, 193–97, 277–78
Morgenthau's report to, 252, 254–55, 261–63
on Munich Conference, 197–98
political career, 57, 88–89
Quanza incident and, 178
refusal to meet with rabbis, 242
Romanian Jews rescue proposal, 154–56, 159–60, 242
State Department appointments, 74, 75, 80, 170
on State Department neutrality, 67
Virgin Islands refugee plan, 171–72
war preparations, 198, 246–47, 249
wedding, 48–50
Welles and, 5, 75, 76, 92, 94, 96, 99

Welles demise and, 183, 186–90
Wise and, 43, 88–90, 242
Roosevelt, Hall, 92
Roosevelt, Mr. and Mrs. Elliott, 49
Roosevelt, Sara Delano, 176–77, 194–95
Roosevelt, Theodore, 48–52, 56, 61
Roosevelt, Theodore, Jr., 59
Rosenman, Samuel, 255–56, 260, 261, 262–63
Rutherfurd, Lucy Mercer, 176, 278

S
Sagalowitz, Benjamin, 17–18, 40–42, 43–44, 47, 107
Sattinger family, 112–13, 161–64, 220
Schulte, Eduard Reinhold Karl, 20–24, 31–33, 38–42, 47, 107, 108, 119, 272
Silverman, Samuel Sidney, 86, 90
Slater, Esther, 92–93, 94
Soviet Union, 13, 23–24, 28–29, 34, 66, 111, 202, 206, 268, 277
Squire, Paul, 46, 47, 106
Stalin, Joseph, 23, 95, 246
State Department. *See also* cables 354 and 482; Division of European Affairs; Hull, Cordell; Long, Breckinridge; Romanian rescue proposal; Treasury-State Department confrontation
anti-Semitism in, 3, 4, 65–68, 121, 170, 215, 231, 257
Bermuda Conference, 166–69, 181
cable intercepts by, 145–46, 182, 190–91
cover-up of mass murders, 16, 128–32, 140–42, 232–33
culture, 50–53, 62–68, 75
on DuBois, 266
dysfunction of, 3–4, 76–84, 153
education of officials of, 3, 52–53, 57, 62–64, 75
immigration policy, 67, 124–26, 159, 167–68, 170–74, 181, 262

Jewish employees, 151
meeting with Treasury Department, 151–52
message transmission by, 46–47
Peyrouton affair, 80–84
Riegner telegram confirmation, 108–9, 115, 127–31, 132, 142
Riegner telegram handling by, 46–47, 85–87, 90, 101–9, 141, 149–50
Romanian rescue proposal, 128–32, 140–42, 146–50, 152–56, 160, 206–18
secretaries of state, 273
subordinate powers within, 83, 142, 156
Treasury Department comparisons with, 10–12
on War Crimes Commission, 266
war crimes statement, 131–32
Stettinius, Edward, 262–63
Stimson, Henry L., 72, 253
Stone, John, 98–99
Struma affair, 99–101
Switzerland. *See also* Harrison, Leland
  Bern legation, 46–47, 85, 86, 108–9, 141, 148, 151, 156, 160, 208–9, 215, 227
  as espionage center, 32

T

Transnistria, 34–35. *See also* Glasberg, Ruth; Romania; Romanian rescue proposal
Treasury Department. *See also* Morgenthau, Henry, Jr.
  Lend-Lease program, 200–202
  State Department comparisons with, 10–11
Treasury-State Department confrontation. *See also* Morgenthau, Henry, Jr.
  British delays on license, 226–29, 231, 233
  cables discovery and cover-up, 9, 13–16, 222–25, 227, 229–30, 232–36, 247–49
  Hull's explanation for delay, 210, 211–18
  introduction, 1–7, 9–16
  legal team, 1, 2, 5, 9–10, 206, 211, 217
  legal team preparations for, 250–61
  Long's excuses, 229, 230–31
  Long's testimony, 243–46
  Morgenthau's meeting with FDR, 261–63
  Morgenthau's meeting with Hull, 226–30
  Romanian rescue proposal, 150–54, 206–18
Truman, Harry (and administration), 135, 188, 274, 275, 278
Tunisia, 211, 214

U

Ukraine, 16, 34–35, 40, 133
United Nations, 266, 278
United States. *See* Roosevelt, Franklin Delano (and administration); State Department; Treasury Department
U.S. Congress, 118, 134, 174, 198, 200, 242–46, 254–55, 259
U.S. Virgin Islands, 171–72

W

Wallenberg, Raoul, 271
Walsh, Edmund A., 65
War Refugee Board, 257, 262–64, 265–70, 271, 274
Welles, Benjamin, 92, 93, 94, 99, 187, 273–74
Welles, Esther, 92–93
Welles, Mathilde, 93–94
Welles, Sumner
  on Bermuda Conference, 167

on British war aid, 199
cable 354 and, 141–42, 225, 235, 258
character, 91–95, 98–99
demise of, 183–90
diplomatic missions, 95–97, 185–86
FDR's relationship with, 5, 76, 92, 94, 96, 99, 119, 183
Jewish refugee support, 84, 90, 100, 101, 108–9, 115, 190–91, 248
postwar and death, 273–74
rivalry with Hull, 3–4, 75–78, 94, 96, 185–86
Romanian rescue proposal, 146–47, 148, 150, 151
sex scandal, 91–93, 98–99, 183
Struma incident, 100–101
as trainbearer at FDR wedding, 49, 50, 92
as undersecretary of State, 76–79, 95, 106
Wise asking for help from, 90–91, 100–105, 108–9, 115, 167, 181–82
We Will Never Die (pageant), 114–15, 135–36, 141
White, Harry Dexter, 250–51, 253, 254, 256, 258, 277
Whitney, Rosetta "Rose" Frances Witz, 77–78, 224
Wiesel, Elie, 102
Wilson, Woodrow, 184
Wise, James, 103–4, 108–9

Wise, Stephen
on Bermuda Conference, 167
character, 87–88
FDR and, 43, 88–90, 242
postwar and death, 275–76
public awareness campaigns, 115–16, 127–28, 129, 132–35
Riegner's telegram to, 44–47, 85–87, 140–41
Riegner telegram confirmation, 108–9
rivalry with Bergson, 133–35, 244
Romanian rescue proposal, 146, 147–48, 150, 154–56, 159–60
on U.S. rescue resolution, 244
Welles' help sought by, 90–91, 101–5, 108–9, 115, 181–82
on Welles resignation, 190
Zionist cause and, 100–101
Witz, Frances, 77–78, 224
World Jewish Congress, 14, 19, 43, 144, 182, 210, 271, 272
World War II. *See also* Germany and Nazi Party; Holocaust; Roosevelt, Franklin Delano (and administration); State Department
American views on, 5–6, 12–13, 174, 198–99
corporate profits during, 13
Wyman, David, 2, 65, 131–32, 180, 244